Bernard Malamud
and the Critics

Bernard Malamud
and the Critics

edited with an introduction by
Leslie A. Field
and
Joyce W. Field

New York   New York University Press

1970

Reprinted 1971

For

      Jeffrey and Linda

and

      our parents

Acknowledgments

It is with great pleasure that we acknowledge the authors and publishers who have granted us permission to reprint their copyright works in this volume. And a special word of thanks must go to those who assisted us in unravelling some of the bibliographical problems inherent in the assembling of a collection of essays. Finally, to EL AL, for help of another sort.

Please note that page references for each entry below refer to pages of original publication.

"The Jewish Literary Tradition," by Earl H. Rovit. Originally published as "Bernard Malamud and the Jewish Literary Tradition" in *Critique*, 3:2 (Winter-Spring 1960), 3–10. Copyright © 1960 by *Critique*. Reprinted by permission of the author and the publisher.

"Women, Children, and Idiots First: Transformation Psychology," by Samuel Irving Bellman. Originally published as "Women, Children, and Idiots First: The Transformation Psychology of Bernard Malamud" in *Critique*, 7:2 (Winter 1964–65), 123–138. Copyright © by The Bolingbroke Society. Reprinted by permission of the author and the publisher.

"Jewishness as Metaphor," by Robert Alter. Originally published as "Bernard Malamud: Jewishness as Metaphor," pp. 116–130. From the book *After the Tradition* by Robert Alter. Copy-

"The New Romanticism," by Charles Alva Hoyt. Originally published as "Bernard Malamud and the New Romanticism," pp. 65–79. A selection from *Contemporary American Novelists* by Harry T. Moore. Copyright © 1964 by Southern Illinois University Press. Reprinted by permission of Southern Illinois University Press and the author.

"Mythic Proletarians," by Max F. Schulz. Originally published as "Bernard Malamud's Mythic Proletarians," pp. 56–68. Reprinted from *Radical Sophistication* by Max F. Schulz, Copyright © 1969 by Max F. Schulz with permission of the Ohio University Press, Athens, Ohio. Permission granted also by the author.

"The Qualified Encounter," by Ihab Hassan. Originally published as "The Qualified Encounter: Three Novels by Buechner, Malamud, and Ellison." From *Radical Innocence: Studies in the Contemporary Novel,* by Ihab Hassan (Copyright © 1961 by Princeton University Press), pp. 161–168. Reprinted by permission of Princeton University Press and the author.

"Culture Conflict," by Walter Shear. Originally published as "Culture Conflict in *The Assistant*" in *The Midwest Quarterly,* 7:4 (July 1966), 367–380. Copyright © 1966 by *The Midwest Quarterly.* Reprinted by permission of the author and the publisher.

"The Complex Pattern of Redemption," by Peter L. Hays. Originally published as "The Complex Pattern of Redemption in *The Assistant*" in *The Centennial Review,* 13:2 (Spring 1969), 200–214. Copyright © 1969 by Centennial Review. Reprinted by permission of the author and the publisher.

"The Old Life and the New," by Theodore Solotaroff. Originally published as "Bernard Malamud's Fiction: The Old Life and the New" in *Commentary,* 33:3 (March 1962), 197–204. Reprinted from *Commentary* by permission; Copyright © 1962 by The American Jewish Committee. Also reprinted by permission of the author.

"The Sadness of Goodness," by Marcus Klein. Originally published as "Bernard Malamud: The Sadness of Goodness," pp. 280–293. Reprinted by permission of The World Publishing Company from *After Alienation* by Marcus Klein. Copyright

Contents

Part I In the Jewish Tradition?

Part II Myth, Ritual, Folklore

Part III *Varied Approaches*

Part IV *Specific Novels and Stories*

The Assistant

A New Life

The Fixer

Introduction

Reading all the scholarship on Bernard Malamud, one is impressed by the sensitive and serious attention which was given to this author in the 1960s when critical recognition began to appear more frequently. In the 1950s, one usually finds only a mention of Malamud's work in passing or brief, ephemeral reviews appearing shortly after the publication of each of his books. But in that decade three men do stand out because of their early understanding of Malamud's fiction—Norman Podhoretz, Alfred Kazin, and Leslie A. Fiedler. Still, by and large, the most valuable and lasting scholarship was written in the 1960s, and from this period the articles in this collection have been chosen.

It may seem audacious to collect material about an author who is still relatively young, who is still writing and whose popularity was born only twelve or thirteen years ago. Malamud began to be recognized with the publication of *The Assistant* in 1957. His popularity soared with *The Magic Barrel* in 1958 and the subsequent National Book Award for this work. It tapered off with *A New Life* in 1961 and rose slightly with *Idiot's First* in 1963. It soared to its greatest heights with *The Fixer* in 1966, which also won a National Book Award as well as the Pulitzer Prize. But *Pictures of Fidelman* in 1969 created hardly a ripple since three of the six stories were already well-known and had been generally praised upon their first appearance.

This collection does not intend to entomb Malamud with a coda. The consensus of the critics represented here is that Malamud has an enduring place in American fiction. But these evaluations are certainly not absolute and immutable. They do, though, illuminate the depth and virtuosity of this writer as seen by critics of the 1960s. Regrettably there is no separate section on Malamud's style simply because we found very little criticism solely on this topic. However, in the course of discussing theme, or myth, or ritual, or Malamud's place in a tradition, numerous critics commented—incidentally or extensively—on Malamud's use of symbolism, Jewish folk idiom, and his means of telling a tale. Nevertheless, we decided that there was insufficient weight given to style itself to justify isolating this topic—especially since our policy was not to use excerpts from single articles.

In the early planning stages of this book we had hoped to include some contemporary reviews of each Malamud work to indicate first reactions to it. However, we reconsidered because too often these reviews were more remarkable for what they ignored than for what they noted, and thus they were of limited value except for the literary historian. It must be admitted, though, that a few reviewers did perceive the direction of Malamud's thoughts as early as *The Assistant*. By the time of *The Fixer*, when critics should have known what Malamud was doing, some —unfortunately too many—still did not, and Malamud was often praised for the wrong reasons, even in the National Book Award citation for *The Fixer*. Therefore, we have bypassed some rather substantial reviews of *The Fixer* which appeared in weekly book-review supplements and bi-weekly literary reviews because initial critical reactions curiously categorized it solely as an historical novel on the Jewish persecution theme with overtones of universal inhumanity to man. Although many of these early reviewers sensed, within limits, the novel's significance, not until later did more judicious assessments appear which delved into the complex and subtle intimations of theme and characterization and suggested the novel's relevance to Malamud's preceding work.

After *The Fixer*, critics began re-examining the earlier fiction, especially *The Natural*. These reappraisals of Malamud *in toto* were not always successful. Because Malamud alters the mode, tone, and locale in each subsequent work, some readers and some critics are confounded. But although Malamud may change the scene and the names of the protagonists, he is nevertheless reworking the same idea with increasing skill and dynamism. Therefore, many critics are looking with fresh insights into the first three novels, insights gained from a close reading of *The Fixer*. In 1967 and 1968 alone six full-scale articles appeared doing just that. The consensus is that *The Fixer* is to be viewed as a progression in Malamud's constant reworking of a constant theme, which was announced in *The Natural*. One important consequence is the overdue reassessment of *The Natural* and *A New Life*, which is establishing their importance in the Malamud canon. Many of the articles in this collection examine this relationship.

As we said before, we do not wish to bury Malamud prematurely with a festschrift. But we do want to put him in perspective by reprinting as many of the best articles on his work as space permits and to organize these interpretations into a few unforced categories which reveal the major concerns of the critics. Where groupings would have been unnatural we simply placed the articles under the heading of Varied Approaches. The collection is divided into four sections and within each section the articles are arranged chronologically because many of the authors drew on previous scholarship. The first three parts are devoted to "themes" or variety of interpretations, and the fourth to essays which, for the most part, focus on one individual work. Naturally, there is some unavoidable overlapping.

II

The first section briefly treats the question "Is Malamud in the Jewish Tradition?" By no means, however, does it give the final answer which first would have to define the illusive nature of this tradition. What this section modestly offers are three individual grapplings with this question.

Earl H. Rovit's essay, much quoted in later articles, introduces us to Malamud's place in this tradition. The Jewish-

American writer, says Rovit, usually has not used Yiddish folklore. But Malamud's ironic vision is in "the tradition of the Yiddish teller of tales," even though his means of telling tales is not. Rovit explores Malamud's uses of esthetic form to resolve "unresolvable dramatic conflicts" and demonstrates that Malamud's vision is both part of and apart from the Jewish tradition. He finally criticizes Malamud for retreating into " 'Jewish irony.' "

In a provocative essay Samuel I. Bellman castigates those critics who have a one-theme reading of Malamud—his "Judaization of society." Bellman would not, it seems, place Malamud in a Jewish tradition. He sees three basic and *equally* important themes running through Malamud's work: conversion (universalizing the Jewish problem), a decaying and rotting world, and a new life. He then says that not all of Malamud's material is derived from Yiddish sources. His varied sources include Jesse Weston, James Joyce, Henry James, and Edgar Allen Poe. And to Bellman there are apparently "chunks of poorly-digested derived material."

A totally different approach is taken by Robert Alter, who states that although Malamud's protagonists are Jewish, he doesn't write *about* Jews and doesn't "represent a Jewish milieu." To Malamud Jewishness is "an ethical symbol," a moral stance. Alter sees in Malamud's writing qualities deriving from Jewish folklore, most notably the juxtaposition of reality and fantasy and the folk figure of the *schlemiel-schlimazel,* used by Malamud as the symbol of the Jew, a person who is involved in the world and becomes its victim. Alter traces what he considers Malamud's "central metaphor of Jewishness," the prison, which, he argues, is the perfect emblem for both the human and the Jewish condition. Alter also presents a detailed analysis of *The Fixer,* commending it as Malamud's best and most unified work, in which "central metaphor and literal fact," represented by the prison, are one.

The second section deals with myth, ritual, folklore—topics on which so much has been written recently that hard decisions on which articles to print had to be made. This theme has been isolated from articles analyzing individual works because we wished to emphasize the scholarship on mythic-ritualistic-folk-loristic elements by devoting an entire section to this topic. Therefore, *The Natural* is discussed exhaustively in Section II rather than in Section IV.

There was little doubt about which should be the lead-off article in this section. Earl R. Wasserman's essay was the first full-scale analysis of myth in *The Natural* which showed that the mythic element was *integral* and not a superficial appendage. There is no intention here of deemphasizing the importance of either Norman Podhoretz's bravura review of *The Natural* (1953) or Jonathan Baumbach's two excellent essays on Malamud (1963, 1965). Mr. Podhoretz's no-nonsense discussion of some heroic elements in *The Natural* is still lively reading; however, he did not thoroughly analyze all the mythic elements in *The Natural* even though he concluded that the novel was "over-loaded" with them. Mr. Baumbach offered some titillating hints (which others later picked up) about the mythic elements, but he concluded that "the mythic superstructure of Malamud's first novel is unobtrusive, . . . somewhat gratuitous, a semiprivate literary joke between author and academic reader." Therefore, we judged Wasserman's essay to be the first full-scale treatment which conclusively underscored that myth was integral. Evidence seems to indicate that subsequent mythological interpretations of Malamud's work derive (even when the debt is not overtly acknowledged) from Wasserman's inspiration.

In "World Ceres," a seminal essay in Malamud scholarship, Wasserman painstakingly traced the rich mythic and ritual symbolism in *The Natural*. According to Wasserman, Malamud sees baseball history as "the distillation of American life." Malamud used real events to avoid contrivance and to reveal baseball as the ritual for expressing American life and its predicament. Other layers, Arthurian legend and Jungian mythic psychology, which are used to interpret the ritual, make baseball into a symbol of "man's psychological and moral situation."

James M. Mellard extends Wasserman's essay by analyzing myths in all of Malamud's novels. Mellard argues that although Malamud is considered by some critics to be a failure in realism, he is a success in pastoral because this mode "has given him an

archetypal narrative structure of great flexibility, a durable convention of characterization, a consistent pattern of imagery and
symbols, and a style and rhetorical strategy of lucidity and
power."

Mellard traces vegetation myths and rituals, seasonal and
pastoral rhythms and imagery, symbolism of vegetation myths
and Grail quests in the four novels. Furthermore, he shows the
progression of Malamud's central concerns in each successive
novel and judges *The Fixer* to be "Malamud's finest expression
of pastoral."

Edwin M. Eigner openly acknowledges his debt to Wasserman. His direction, he states, derives from Wasserman's last sentence, ". . . *The Natural* is the necessary reference text for a
reading of . . . [Malamud's] subsequent fiction." Eigner then
uses *The Natural* as well as Wasserman's essay for his reference
points. And he extends Mellard's analysis by examining the
short stories as well as the novels. Eigner identifies the characters
of the Percival myth and the recurring thematic patterns in
Malamud's work, focusing especially on the Loathly Lady. In
his detailed analyses of the novels, he shows that "the pattern of
thematically significant action is basically the same throughout
Malamud's major fiction."

Frederick W. Turner, III, accuses some of the myth-hunting
critics of failing to show *why* Malamud uses myths. Turner's aim
is to show the kinship of *The Natural* and *The Fixer* by revealing
how the latter is the latest step in Malamud's sequential reworking of his major theme, "the conflict between myths and the
outer world," which appeared first in *The Natural*. Malamud's
heroes, says Turner, have had "to see beyond myths without at
the same time losing sight of them." *The Natural's* "myth of the
baseball hero is an amalgam of the heroic myth and its democratic
offspring, the Horatio Alger story." Roy Hobbs is a failed hero
because he cannot "act within a mythology" while simultaneously
seeing beyond it in order "to defend it."

In the third section we have tried to include a representative
sampling of the many different critical approaches to Malamud.
Because of space limitations (the perennial excuse), many worthy

essays unfortunately could not be printed. Hopefully, though, the four which finally were chosen are a valid cross-section of viewpoints reflecting the wide diversity of interpretations of Malamud's fiction.

Ben Siegel examines Malamud's first three novels and *The Magic Barrel,* seeing each work as "a moral critique," an exploration of "the melancholic state of the human condition." Siegel approaches the works through Malamud's own point of view, "the dark prison of the self." Malamud's characters are, as the title of Siegel's essay indicates, "sad and bitter clowns." But they are not merely the victims of forces; they also contain within themselves the seeds of their own destruction.

Through an anlysis of the short stories, Sam Bluefarb argues that Malamud's characters are often caricatures, but caricatures with allegorical significance. He traces certain types—the Repenant Reprobate, the Poor Young Writer, the Poor Tailor as Suffering Servant, for example. Bluefarb agrees with Siegel that Malamud is a moralist, but one who objectifies "his characters into an experience lifted out of allegory."

Mark Goldman denies Rovit's criticism that Malamud retreats at times from his tragic vision into " 'Jewish irony.' " Goldman asserts that Malamud's fiction has "really two basic attitudes . . . tragic and comic (combined in some of his best work)" and that it is unreasonable to insist that Malamud follow a critic's demand for "poetic consistency." Malamud's two separate attitudes "focus on the same material, serve the same thematic ends" albeit by different means. Malamud's comic vein "is a rich, complex mixture of irony and satire, fantasy and moral fervor." Goldman analyzes this comic vision by relating it to the characters' search for identity.

Malamud's most revealing characteristic, says Charles A. Hoyt, is his romanticism. After cataloging the varieties of current romantic attitudes, Hoyt concludes that Malamud is the "philosopher, or deepest thinker, perhaps" of this "ill-assorted group." According to Hoyt, romanticism is "Romantic Rejection of Objectivity." "Suffering is Malamud's theme," claims Hoyt, and he discusses how Malamud the Romantic translates suffering "into action" by using the *schlemiel,* "football of the Gods," to dramatize his theme.

Max F. Schulz sees two patterns in Malamud's work. *The Assistant* and *The Fixer* are "mutations of the proletarian impulse of the Jewish intellectual of the 1930's," while *The Natural* and *A New Life* reveal the "mythic pattern of vegetation ritual and Grail quest." Thus Malamud unites Marx and myth and "the Malamud novel conceptualizes this duality of theme and structure in the appropriately disparate language of realism and symbolism." In a well-documented analysis, Schulz concludes that the Malamud hero is both "mythic savior and . . . social scapegoat," "the proletarian hero winning justice for society, with the mythic hero renewing life for the community."

The last section has four subsections, each dealing with a different work. There is, however, no separate section for *The Natural* since this novel was covered so copiously in Part II. Neither are there separate sections for *Idiot's First* and *Pictures of Fidelman* because many of the stories in these collections were analyzed previously in a number of essays (for example, Bluefarb's and Hoyt's essays). Some readers might wonder why the articles by Alter, Mellard, and Turner are not in *Part IV* with essays on *The Fixer,* as they well might be. We wished to emphasize Alter's assessment of Malamud in the Jewish tradition by placing his essay in Part I, and we wished to emphasize Mellard's and Turner's mythic interpretations by placing their essays in Part II.

The Assistant is represented by three viewpoints. Ihab Hassan judges irony to be "the key to Malamud's attitude toward man, to his estimate of him." Although the Bobers are "victims of circumstance," they still possess "spiritual freedom." Hassan considers the theme of the book to be "the regeneration of Frank," his conversion. His assessment of the two main characters, Morris and Frank, is that they are "heroes of irony," not tragic heroes.

Walter Shear sees Malamud's work as novels of culture rather than as novels of manners. Contrasting the two types, he discerns that the former "examines more minutely the ambiguities in the relationship between the individual and his values—and thus is both closer to its characters and at the same time attentive to an area beyond them." *The Assistant* constructs two cultures, "the Jewish tradition and the American heritage," and exemplifies the collision between old-world wisdom and new-world practicality with its ethos of success. The characters "exist in an ironic relationship" to both worlds.

Peter L. Hays traces "the complex pattern of redemption" in *The Assistant,* emphasizing first the meaning of Frank Alpine's circumcision and conversion at Passover time. He then unravels the symbolism of Helen's name as well as the numerous bird and flower images. He also compares the similarity of the beliefs of Martin Buber and those expressed in *The Assistant.* His final judgment of the novel is that it is "a story of redemption which expresses realities of psychological and philosophical truth."

A New Life is also represented by three different viewpoints which supplement those expressed in essays in previous sections. To Theodore Solotaroff, "Malamud's Jewishness is a type of metaphor—for anyone's life." *A New Life* is "mainly a study of the difficulties of undoing the hold of a deprived and wasted past," and emerging into "freedom and control." Solotaroff shows the similarities in themes between Malamud's third novel and his previous two. Finally, Solotaroff criticizes Malamud's handling of the theme in *A New Life.* "The real point of the novel—all but buried under the moral theme—is the collision . . . of the post-ghetto sensibility and the culture of the hinterlands."

Marcus Klein investigates Malamud's statement that *A New Life* is patterned after Stendhal. He finds that "the spirit is Stendhal's but neither the problem nor the manner nor the voice could be." Part of the book is social satire, but more akin to Sinclair Lewis than Stendhal. Another element is a love story. Stendhal and love story unite "in an intention toward engagement."

Ruth B. Mandel sees both *The Assistant* and *A New Life* as "novels of ironic affirmation. . . . for the possibility of human salvation and identity through a consciously constructed personal ethic." Each moral act offers two good results—one, for the world; another, for the individual. But the redemption is ironic since grace is "accompanied by continual suffering" and need for continual reaffirmation of "spiritual freedom and integrity." Furthermore, the moral law "makes one an isolated victim of the world."

In the next section two quite different views of *The Fixer* are given. In his review-article of *The Fixer*, Maurice Friedberg looks at Malamud's fourth novel along with *Blood Accusation* by Maurice Samuel, a detailed history of the Beiliss case, which, coincidentally, was published at the same time as *The Fixer*. With the dual perspective of these two versions of the Beiliss case, Friedberg traces Malamud's "distillation of history into a product of artistic imagination" and shows how Malamud changed "actual events . . . to fit the inner logic of the narrative."

Alan Warren Friedman argues that *The Fixer*, Malamud's "finest" novel to date, "contains the essential Malamudian note: simultaneous passivity and seemingly senseless action, intimations of bitterness and defeat, a vague but certain sense of impending doom." Although Malamud's is "an essentially absurd universe" as viewed through an anti-hero, Malamud's work exhibits not only "existential anguish" but also a quality which comes from "Jewish teachings and spirit embodied in the Torah . . . and the Talmud."

The Magic Barrel is thoroughly discussed by Sidney Richman. He mentions the sources of influence, but concludes that "for Malamud, borrowed technique seems only the means of shoring up and extending a vision that is essentially his own." He begins his analysis with the novels because, he claims, the tales "recapitulate the central themes of the novels" and, furthermore, the best stories are most similar to "the techniques and the vision of *The Assistant*." He groups the stories into four illuminating categories: tales of New York Jews, New York tales without Jews, Italian stories, and finally "The Last Mohican" with "The Magic Barrel."

III

It is worth noting that although Malamud has been examined through a number of critical perspectives, no significant evaluation of his place in the hierarchy of contemporary American fiction has yet appeared. Perhaps an assessment of this scope is premature.

A common critical parlor game weighs and juggles the half-dozen or so of the foremost "Jewish-American" writers of today. Now Bellow is in the ascendancy, with Malamud running a close second. At another time Philip Roth edged out both Bellow and Malamud. As for Isaac Bashevis Singer, who lives in America, writes in Yiddish, and is published in English, no one knows just where to place him. Every now and then a serious attempt is made, with a greater or lesser degree of success, to fit one or another of these writers into a Jewish literary tradition. Of those who can be classified as Jewish-American, Bellow, it appears, has fared the best in studies which attempt to see an author in the very large context of American and world literature.

Insofar as Malamud is concerned, that story is yet to be told. Is it that Malamud has not yet attracted a universal readership and a broad spectrum of critical commentators? Do students in universities read Malamud as part of their course-work? Has he ever had the extra-curricular campus popularity of, say, a Salinger? Is it mere coincidence that ninety percent or more of those critics writing for publication on Malamud are American Jews?

Malamud, by many tests, is a great American writer. On reading through all his stories and novels, one is struck by the fact that he is not simply another Jewish-American writer attempting to capture Jewish themes and commonplaces in his fiction. On one hand, he seems to have grasped and powerfully rendered the idiom of the old world Jew in a new world context much as Faulkner was able to do with the Snopeses, the Sartorises, and the South against the macrocosm of the United States and the world. On the other hand, one can say of Malamud what has often been said of Hawthorne. Both have been concerned with man and the deepest forces that have moved him, whether they be religion, myth, folklore, or ritual. And just as Hawthorne was never interested in merely portraying his characters in a Puritan society in order to dissect Puritanism, so Malamud has never been overly concerned with depicting American Jewish types in order to discuss Judaism. Both, apparently, are acutely conscious of the significant influence of religion on man—either the home-grown or the imported variety. But that's just the point. Neither one is interested in wrestling with the force itself. Malamud is saying, in effect, as Hawthorne did before him: Powerful forces are at work to mold man. Now what does man do and how does he act when confronted with these forces—whether they be American, European, or some other? In short, Malamud, like all great writers before him, is concerned with man, the human animal evolving *his* world within a world he never made. And how man chooses *his own* world and what happens to man in the process of that choice constitute the significant world of Bernard Malamud's fiction.

Leslie A. Field
Joyce W. Field
Ramat-Chen, Ramat-Gan
Israel

Bernard Malamud
and the Critics

Part I
In the Jewish Tradition?

false arrest are even more important to him as an extreme paradigm for the condition of impotence in a mad world that all
people today share, whether they live under absolutist regimes or
in the mass societies of that part of the world which ritualistically
calls itself free. The credo of Bibikov, the one sympathetic government investigator, confided to Yakov Bok in his cell, is substantially the implicit credo of Malamud's earlier fiction, where
the settings are contemporary, but it is an affirmation spoken
from the heart of a tensely dramatic situation that gives a new
kind of stark and bold concreteness to its moral abstractions:

> One often feels helpless in the face of the confusion of these
> times, such a mass of apparently uncontrollable events and
> experiences to live through, attempt to understand, and if at
> all possible, give order to; but one must not withdraw from
> the task if he has some small thing to offer—he does so at
> the risk of diminishing his humanity.

The Fixer is clearly Malamud's most powerful novel—and,
it seems to me, his first wholly successful one. An important reason
for its tight artistic unity is the identity in it between central
metaphor and literal fact: the Malamudian prison is here not
merely an analogy, a moral and metaphysical state, but has real,
clammy, stone walls, excretory stenches, heavy-fisted jailers, dank
unheated cells, lice. Similarly, Malamud's symbolic Jew is much
more believable here than in his last two novels because the
character's symbolic implications flow naturally from the literal
fact of his Jewishness which is, after all, the real reason for his
arrest. Though to be a Jew in this novel does imply a general
moral stance, it also means being involved in the fate of a particular people, actively identifying with its history—in contrast,
for example, to Morris Bober, for whom the meaning of Jewishness is exhausted in "to do what is right, to be honest, to be
good."
    In this connection, one difference between Yakov Bok and
Mendel Beiliss is revealing. The brickworks in which Beiliss was
employed were in a section of Kiev forbidden for Jewish resi-

dence, except to certain classes of Jews who could obtain special permits. Mendel Beiliss had such a permit and lived at the brickworks openly, with his wife and children, on terms of respect and cordiality with his fellow workers. Yakov Bok has no residence permit: he lives alone at the brickworks, under a Gentile name, suspected as a Jew by his fellow workers and thoroughly hated by them. His masquerading as a Russian is the beginning of his troubles when he is arrested, and it is the one crime he freely confesses: "He had stupidly pretended to be somebody he wasn't, hoping it would create 'opportunities,' had learned otherwise—the wrong opportunities—and was paying for learning." (Malamud once before touched on this idea, in a somewhat lighter mood, in "The Lady of the Lake," where Henry Levin-Freeman loses the girl of his dreams by pretending to be a Gentile and thus dissociating himself from the Jewish fate in which she has been tragically involved and to which she is committed.)

Circumstances force Yakov Bok, who sought to escape from the *shtetl* to a new world of possibilities in the big city, into being a Jew despite himself. And he becomes, of course, a Jew in Malamud's special sense, a prisoner placed in progressively restricting confinement—from communal cell to solitary confinement to being shackled to the wall hand and foot—who is mangled physically and mentally by his imprisonment but never lets himself surrender his integrity because of it. Emblems of membership in the traditional community of Jews are thrust on him by his jailers, and he accepts them, with a kind of ironic gratitude, because he has no choice. He is thrown a prayer shawl and phylacteries—the phylacteries he puts aside, the prayer shawl he wraps about him because it gives him warmth. A fistful of bloodstained pages from a Hebrew Bible is flung into his cell—he pieces them together and reads them over and over, fitting the verses to his own fate and hopes, though the God that speaks through the ancient words, in Whom he does not believe, alternately angers him and stirs his pity. Forced in this and related ways to summon up all his inner resources of survival in order to stay sane and alive in solitary confinement, Bok in his cell recapitulates the darkest, most heroic aspects of Jewish existence in the diaspora.

The quality of his character, moreover, makes him admirably suited to the task of survival and to his larger symbolic role in the novel. Though the vividly comic aspects of the type are naturally muted, Bok is another of Malamud's plain, earthy Jews, the first of these figures, so happily used in the short stories, to work effectively as a major character in a novel. There is a touch of the knowing *shlemiel* in him—"If there's a mistake to make," he thinks, "I'll make it"—which leads him to expect calamity and ruefully resolve to hold up under it. Meagerly self-taught, he is not a subtle man but is shrewd and straight-thinking. His speech and reflections are laced with the salt of wry Yiddish irony, and his skepticism is tough-minded and unpretentious: "Take my word for it," he tells his pious father-in-law, who tries to convince him that faith in God can sustain him in his sufferings, "it's not easy to be a freethinker, especially in this terrible cell." Perhaps Mendel Beiliss was not so different from this: he laughed out loud just once at his trial, Maurice Samuel reports, when the prosecution solemnly averred that he had the reputation among his fellow workers of being a *tzaddik,* a Hasidic wonder-rabbi.

There is, furthermore, a special thematic appropriateness in the fact that the hero of *The Fixer* is a simple man. Yakov Bok has no desire to become involved in history; at the beginning of the novel, we see him as someone who has led a deprived, unhappy life and who merely wants to find a better existence for himself, in that vague and rather pathetic way in which so many of Malamud's protagonists long for "something more worthwhile." But history seizes him by the collar, and at first all he can do is wonder, stunned, why it should all be happening to him —again, Malamud's previous protagonists repeatedly ask themselves much the same question about their misfortunes—"What was a poor harmless fixer doing in prison?" The obvious answer is that he is in prison because he is a Jew. Bok soon arrives at the generalization that "being born a Jew meant being vulnerable to history, including its worst errors." This has largely been true of Jews collectively during two thousand years of exile, and Bok now finds it to bear just as directly and heavily on his own life. Confronted with such awful vulnerability, a man may want to rebel or opt out, seeking to escape the inescapable, but the only alternative for Yakov Bok that will allow him to retain his self-respect is to accept the entanglement in the worst of history together with the responsibility for those who are similarly entangled, making a "covenant with himself," since he can't make one with God, that he will not betray his fellow Jews, that if necessary he will die rather than assent, even through the most oblique compromise, to the lie that would deny their humanity.

The lesson that Bok learns, in short, is Malamud's familiar lesson of the necessity for moral involvement, with all its painful, awkward, humiliating consequences, though the idea emerges from Bok's anguish with greater force than anywhere in the earlier fiction. At the very end of his two-year ordeal of incarceration, as he is carried through the streets of Kiev to the courthouse, surrounded by a mob of faces, some curious or hostile, some even compassionate, he summarizes what he has gradually made clear to himself: "One thing I've learned . . . there's no such thing as an unpolitical man, especially a Jew."

This last sentence nicely states the relationship between particular and universal in this novel and in Malamud's work as a whole. The speaker is undeniably a Jew in all the distinctive qualities of his mental and physical being, his wasted flesh and aching bones. The Jew, however, is conceived by the writer not as a creature *sui generis* but as an extreme and therefore pellucid instance of all men's inevitable exposure to the caprice of circumstance and the insidious snarl of history: all people are in this way "chosen," Jews only more transparently than others. The Jew as Everyman is a kind of literary symbol that is likely to wear thin very quickly; it is a tribute to Malamud's resourcefulness as a writer that he has been able to make the symbolic equation succeed to the extent he has in his stories and novels. In his most recent book, he gives new imaginative weight to his conception of Jewishness by adding to it the crucially important dimension of history, and in so doing he manages to transform his recurrent symbol into the stuff of an urgent, tautly controlled novel that firmly engages the emotions and the intellect as well.

presentation—Finkle with the bouquet, Salzman reciting the prayer, and Stella dressed in white with red shoes, smoking under a lamp post. Each point on the triangle enlists the reader's sympathy, but each is also treated with a basic irony. The aesthetic form of the story rounds upon itself and the "meaning" of the story—the precise evaluation of forces—is left to the reader. It is in this sense—a sense in which aesthetic form resolves unresolvable dramatic conflicts—that Malamud departs drastically from the tradition of the Yiddish tale and confronts the demands of modern fictional form.

In the best of his stories in *The Magic Barrel,* the same pattern of ultimate poetic resolution by metaphor is evident. In "The Mourners," Kessler, the dispossessed egg-candler, and Mr. Gruber, the dispossessing landlord, are locked together in the mute companionship of unutterable grief, reciting the Kaddish with bed-sheets for prayer-shawls in the stark poverty of Kessler's one-room flat. In "Take Pity," Eva Kalish stands desperate and beseeching outside the window of Rosen, her benefactor. In "The Last Mohican," Fidelman chases the be-knickered Susskind through the streets of Rome, vainly trying to catch up with the flying green coat-tails that are beyond his grasp. In each of these stories, as in "The Magic Barrel," Malamud successfully develops his dramatic conflicts and then freezes them into a final image which can be dissolved only by the reader. In his less successful stories ("Angel Levine," "Behold the Key," "The Lady of the Lake"), the final climactic images seem to be too obvious or too heavily mechanical to hold the meanings in a tense equilibrium. In other words, Malamud differs from the Yiddish tale-teller in his poetic sensitivity to the implications which he brings to his stories, rather than in the ironic delight in grotesque characterization and anecdotal episode which seem to me to be at the heart of the Yiddish tale. He does use both the irony and the grotesque evocation of Yiddish background, but he goes beyond them to incarnate his own vision.

It is this accomplished mastery of short story technique which makes Malamud, I think, a fresh and exciting figure in Jewish-American letters. His thematic range, even when it deals with characters of non-Jewish backgrounds, is unmistakably Hebraic. His people are drawn from the intensely unassimilated lives of New

York City first- and second-generation American Jews. They are presented in the cramped prisons of themselves—in dark and tiny "variety" stores where drab monotony stocks the counters; in overfurnished and underlighted tenement apartments; within the strict unyielding barriers of their own uneasy identities. Hedged in and thwarted by the fatal limitations of human existence, and imprisoned even beyond that by a pervasive sense of being "alien" in a Gentile world, his Morris Bobers (*The Assistant*) gradually dry up externally until they make a small disturbance in the relentless routine of life with their deaths. As we see in the following excerpt from "Take Pity," death is a small thing and an inevitable thing which is perhaps the crowning and ironic achievement of a buried life:

> "How did he die?" Davidov spoke impatiently. "Say in one word."
> "From what he died?—he died, that's all."
> "Answer, please, this question."
> "Broke in him something. That's how."
> "Broke what?"
> "Broke what breaks. He was talking to me how bitter was his life, and he touched me on the sleeve to say something else, but the next minute his face got small and he fell down dead. . . ."

In Malamud's stories, over and over we find echoed the agonized strain of Job's unanswered question: "Why is light given to a man whose way is hid, and whom God hath hedged in?" Thus the succession of dark cramped places in which Malamud's characters live takes on symbolic resonance. Caught in a ghetto-isolation without either the liberating fellowship of a ghetto sense of community, or as sustaining spiritual security derived from directed religious commitment, his characters are defined in burdensome images of loneliness—weighed down by poverty, commercial greed, and natural calamity. But yet, like Job's man, unto them a "light" is given; upon them is visited a glimpse of infinity, of freedom, of existence without barriers. Whether it is, as with Morris Bober, a felt-sense of The Law, or, as with Leo Finkle, a

romantic illusion of love, they all have enough light in their darkness to know that their ways are "hid," and to be able to imagine
a life of light without necessarily believing in the possibilities of
attaining such a life. This glimpse gives them a contagious
strength as characters, which can be seen in the effect that Morris
Bober's inner security has on Frank Alpine—an effect which somewhat unconvincingly leads to Alpine's conversion to Judaism.
This also invests the characters with a capacity for evoking pathos,
as with Kessler the egg-candler, whose glimpse of light awakens in
him an acute sensitivity to the wretchedness with which he has
lived his life.

For Malamud seems to insist that there *is* a way of escaping
the fatal limitations of the human condition. Man need not remain buried in the isolation of himself. He must accept the fatal-
ity of his own identity—be it Jew or Gentile, success or failure—
and working within that identity, transcend himself and burst his
prison. In the following quotation from "The Bill," this faith is
most explicitly stated, but it is an implicit undercurrent in all his
stories:

> He said that everything was run on credit, business and
> everything else, because after all what was credit but the
> fact that people were human beings, and if you were really
> a human being you gave credit to somebody else and he
> gave credit to you.

To fail to give "credit" to another human being—even when
you know that the credit is undeserved and may even be repaid
in hatred—is to deny the humanity in yourself, to extinguish
within your own being the light which has been given you. It is
this denial which dries up the humanness in Julius Karp (*The
Assistant*), transforming him from a man into the proprietor of
a liquor store. It results in the punishment of Henry Freeman
("The Lady of the Lake") whose refusal to credit himself with
his own identity causes him—too melodramatically—to lose his
chance for love. The most memorable characters in Malamud's
fictions either possess already, or learn that they must strive to

possess, this capacity for giving unlimited credit to any human demand made upon them.

And yet there is one rather grave limitation in Malamud's fictions which seems to me to forestall what could be an even fuller exploitation of his considerable talents; and this limitation, like his powers, may also find its roots in the tradition of the Yiddish tale. Malamud has demonstrated his mastery, so to speak, over a piece of the tragic vision. He has given eloquent and ironic voice to Job's anguished, rebellious cry from the ash-heap; he has presented man as that most pathetic of victims who is fully aware of his complete envelopment by a whimsical fate. He has succeeded in his best stories in evoking a controlled pathos and sympathy which is surely an artistic achievement of high merit. But at the crucial point of his dramas, when his characters are most acutely aware of their impotence before the inevitable, *and are aware of themselves being aware,* his tragic vision fails him and he retreats into his "Jewish irony"—a defensive humor which deflates the portentous momentum of his art. He forgets, as I think the Yiddish tale-teller has always forgotten, that Job also says later in his ordeal: "Though he slay me, yet will I trust in him; but I will maintain mine own ways before him."

Job rebels and accepts simultaneously, and even keeps a firm grip on his precious individuality while doing so. Malamud's characters cry out, defy, and accept, but fail to maintain their own ways before him *with dignity.* They become grotesque or slightly ridiculous—in the ways that Kessler, Gruber, Finkle, Salzman, and Rosen are grotesque and ridiculous—before the mercilessly cynical eye of the Yiddish humorist whose irony turns now on himself as a protective shield. And although this deflating common-sense approach may be the healthiest way to deal with practical affairs, it falls short of the requirements of the grandest level of art, which demands not common, but *un*common sense, not sanity, but poetry. Malamud has amply shown that he can employ the fertile resources of the Yiddish tale as a functional element in the form of the modern short story. If he can continue to refine and develop his vision, and learn somehow to leap beyond his irony when it no longer serves his art, he may succeed in producing work of the very highest order of imaginative achievement.

Samuel Irving Bellman

2.

Women, Children, and Idiots First:
Transformation Psychology

"'A wonderful thing, Fanny,'" Bernard Malamud's poor
little tailor Manischevitz tells his wife, who has just been resurrected by a Negro angel (at the end of the story "Angel Levine").
"'Believe me, there are Jews everywhere.'"[1] "Cronin," Malamud
tells us at the begining of "A Choice of Profession" (a recent
story which is included in *Idiots First*), "after discovering that his
wife, Marge, had been two-timing him with a friend, suffered
months of crisis."[2] These two tachistoscopic flashes provide important clues to the Great Malamud Mystery that has been be-
guiling readers for over a decade. Stated simply, the mystery is
this: what is Malamud really getting at, in his weird hopespun
stories of suffering storekeepers and a host of other insulted and
injured types? His last books have been enormously successful with
the critics and the upper middlebrow readers: *The Assistant*
(1957) is one of the most talked-about novels of the postwar period,
the story collection *The Magic Barrel* (1958) won the National
Book Award, and his academic novel *A New Life* (1961) has also
come in for a great deal of respectful praise. If it is too much to
ask why Malamud should be singled out above such consistent

prize-winners as Flannery O'Connor, George P. Elliott, and J. F. Powers (to name only three), since his books do not seem markedly superior to theirs, what then is the secret of Malamud's charisma or literary power?

Style, surely, it cannot be, for Malamud's diction is not seldom gratingly inappropriate. Contents then? At first reading, Malamud's stories generally leave the reader little to wonder about. The central figure is a drab, down-and-out little nobody who invites our instant pity (and sometimes contempt) because of his hard luck—Sobel the shoemaker's helper, Fidelman the expatriate art student, Morris Bober the unsuccessful grocer, Seymour Levin the novice college instructor, Marcus the weak-hearted tailor, Etta the Roman widow who is twice betrayed. Always, it seems, the central character is poverty-stricken—no money in hand and the wolf at the door. If money is not the problem, it will be a matter of another kind of poverty: judgment, perhaps, or resiliency, or even just plain luck. Harmonizing with the drabness of the agonist and many of the other characters is the dull and cheerless setting: skies are gray, buildings are ancient and decrepit, the entire prospect is at best depressing.

Malamud seems, on the surface at least, to be giving us the "natural history of man": man is born, man suffers, and then man dies. If Malamud sometimes stops short of this last step, he will substitute the perversion of hope: wanhope (despair), misguided hope, or miserable resignation. Even when the supernatural is invoked, as happens occasionally when Malamud resorts to allegory to dramatize the plight of his marginal folk, life is a pretty sorry affair. Once in a long while there is an almost unbelievable happy ending (as in "Angel Levine"), but the effect is that of a momentary respite on the part of Malamud's forces of doom: before long, we fear, things will be back to normal.

We used the term "at first reading." Malamud has a tendency to seed his tales and novels with all sorts of suggestive passages that prey on the mind and cause the reader to reread and rethink Malamud's experiments in misery. In his first novel, *The Natural* (1952), a weird and somewhat carelessly written story about a venal baseball player lost in the Grail Quest world of Jesse Weston's *From Ritual to Romance,* the charmed ball player, Roy

Hobbs, tells an inquisitive girl that his ultimate hope is to be known as " 'the best there ever was in the game.' " But she is troubled: " 'Isn't there something over and above earthly things —some more glamorous meaning to one's life and activities?' " And later in the story, another girl tells this clay-footed hero why she hates to see a hero fail. Not only are there so few of them, but . . . " 'Without heroes we're all plain people and don't know how far we can go.' " [3]

In "The Last Mohican" (included in *The Magic Barrel*) there is the shameless parasite and *Jewish Refugee from Israel*, Shimon Susskind, with his strange way of standing motionless, "like a cigar store Indian about to burst into flight." In *A New Life* there is the daimon of Seymour Levin, a bumbling Jewish intellectual from New York self-exiled to a state college in Oregon: "Although thoughts of 'making things better' continued to arrive by inspiration, at Cascadia College he restrained them." [4] At the end of "Naked Nude" (included in *Idiots First*) the reckless art student Fidelman outwits his sadistic captors and steals his own painting. "In the pitch black, on the lake's choppy waters, he saw she was indeed his, and by the light of numerous matches adored his handiwork." [5]

In other words, there is something special about the coordinates Malamud chooses to graph man's progress along the road of life, and this particular quality—or series of graphic locations—contrasts sharply with the all-too-familiar story line of Malamud's fictions. Yes, the curve runs predictably from birth to suffering to death, or to false hope (or wanhope) but there are strange divagations in the curve, and it is a mistake to describe it only in terms of its origin, midpoint, and endpoint, as many have been tempted to do. Malamud, for all the apparent simplicity of his plots, for all the obviousness of his subject matter, is actually a very complicated writer, complicated enough it seems to have snared his reviewers into falling for easy answers to profound questions or meeting the Malamudian ambiguity of meaning by merely describing it, in oblique or fragmentary terms.

Malamud has been read as an allegorist, a fabulist, a romancer asserting the need of the modern American artist to transcend the stultifying realism or naturalism which has so restricted fictional

art.[6] He has been excessively patronized for his quaint Jewish themes, and stereotyped with baffled admiration. Thus Ihab Hassan in *Radical Innocence: The Contemporary American Novel* (Princeton University Press, 1961, pp. 161-162): *

> Malamud's vision is preeminently moral, yet his form is sly. It owes something to the wile of Yiddish folklore, the ambiguous irony of the Jewish joke. Pain twisted into humor twists humor back into pain. The starkness of suffering, the leaden weight of ignorance or poverty, the alienation of the Jew in a land of jostling Gentiles—all these become transmuted, in luminous metaphors and strange rhythms, into forms a little quaint or ludicrous, a bittersweet irony of life, into something, finally, elusive.

Understandably, it has become good form to take particular notice of the search-for-love aspect of Malamud's fictions, a feature that mid-twentieth-century writers (Graham Greene, J. D. Salinger, William Styron, George P. Elliott, etc.), following Erich Fromm and other public-relations-minded psychoanalysts, have made *de rigueur* in their studies of fragmented modern man in a pluralistic society. Thus Ben Siegel, in "Victims in Motion: Bernard Malamud's Sad and Bitter Clowns" (*Northwest Review*, Spring, 1962),† speaks of "Malamud's reluctance to give up on anyone. Each being is unique, responsible, imperfect, and redeemable. No one is beyond redemption, and in most instances love is the surest means of attaining it." [7] And Jonathan Baumbach, in "The Economy of Love: The Novels of Bernard Malamud" (*The Kenyon Review*, Summer, 1963), points out that "Bernard Malamud, in his fables of defeated love and failed ambition, has extended the tradition of the American romance-novel, has made the form into something uniquely and significantly his own. . . . Malamud's fiction delineates the broken dreams and private griefs of the spirit, the needs of the heart, the pain of loss, the economy of love. . . . The amount

* See Chapter 13 in this collection.
† See Chapter 8 in this collection.

of love a man is able and willing to commit to life is, in Malamud's universe, the measure of his grace." [8]

With the appearance of Malamud's new collection of short stories, *Idiots First* (which contains material published between 1950 and 1963), it is possible to come to a clearer understanding of just what Malamud is getting at in his fictions, and of just what significance some of his less obvious or subliminal ideas have, set against the background of his gray, forbidding, Thomas Hardyan world. To begin with, Malamud appears to confront the reader with a reconstructionist view of society and man's position in it. Life victimizes poor Jews, does it? We'll make the best of it—*and* the worst of it—and let their tribe increase. But up to now Jews have been a vanishing breed? The same solution for both problems: safety in numbers, and spread the misery around. "Believe me, there are Jews everywhere." So in *The Assistant* Frank Alpine, the Italian delinquent, atones for all his wrongs to Morris Bober's family and then converts to Judaism, suffering the pain of circumcision ("The pain enraged and inspired him."). In "Angel Levine" we are reminded that there are black Jews too, and they are also capable of being hurt. And in the stories in *Idiots First* we are introduced to entire new categories of Jews— if they don't suffer themselves, they help others suffer: the butler and the Angel of Death in "Idiots First"; the father confessor, complete with cassock and biretta, in "Still Life"; the bird family in "The Jewbird." There is even another gratuitous conversion to Judaism, the German wife of a refugee critic in "The German Refugee" (after her conversion she is martyred by the Nazis).

Malamud's partial Judaization of society is a daring literary expedient at best. One of its most interesting features, the spontaneous conversion, is apt to cause resentment in otherwise sympathetic readers. Thus Ihab Hassan in *Radical Innocence* (p. 168), comments ironically on Frank Alpine's conversion: "The act is one of self-purification, of initiation too, in Frank's case, but it is also an act of self-repudiation, if not, as some may be tempted to say, of symbolic castration." But there is a certain poetic justice in reversing the basic idea of Karl Marx's destructive *World Without Jews* or the "friendly" story by Philip Wylie some years ago

in which all Jews suddenly vanish at the stroke of midnight, to the eventual shame and discomfort of their enemies. And there is the psychological element too (as indicated above), what Kenneth Burke calls the "socialization of losses"—a rhetorical device which minimizes an adverse circumstance by projecting it onto others. Still, the "conversion" theme by its very nature demands an embarrassing sentimental credulity from the reader. Thus Philip Roth's tale, "The Conversion of the Jews" (which appeared in *The Paris Review* after Malamud's *The Assistant* was published), in reversing Malamud's Judaization tendency reads like a hallucinatory tour de force.

Two special matters relating to Malamud's partial Judaization of society must be examined here. One is touched on in Milton R. Stern's review of *Idiots First*, "All Men Are Jews," in *The Nation*, October 19, 1963. Quoting Malamud to the effect that " 'All men are Jews . . . although few men know it' " (p. 243), Stern develops a reductivist view which encompasses *all* of society, not merely special categories such as converts, birds, and a number of other particular types. Malamud, Stern implies (p. 243), brings all men down to a specified—i.e., Jewish—condition. "Malamud's compelling force as one of our major talents comes from his ability to evoke the sense of helplessness, anonymity and dislocation that besets the modern psyche. It is precisely in this sense that he identifies his Jews as modern everyman."

There is a charming academicism in equating Malamud's submerged Jewish *misérables* with the majority of humanity, which is more fortunate because it is less vulnerable to the besetting horrors of oppression, poverty, and privation. Jews and non-Jews both, it appears, can observe their common humanity in Malamud's fictions; since there is such a heavy Jewish cast in the various novels and stories, we move outward from the "Jewish problem" to the universal human problem, which is not very different after all. But such a reading of Malamud is precisely what was meant earlier by the suggestion that Malamud has snared his reviewers into falling for easy answers to profound questions or into evading the Malamudian ambiguity of meaning by partially paraphrasing it.

For example, one of Malamud's finest and most representative stories, "The Magic Barrel" (in the story collection of that

name), deals with a rabbinical student, Leo Finkle, who seeks a
wife but is unable to love. He tries a marriage broker, Salzman,
and rejects all the proffered candidates. Finally, he discovers a
picture of Salzman's daughter and insists on making a match with
her—even though she has become a prostitute and her father will
not hear of a meeting. So a match is made. "He . . . concluded to
convert her to goodness, himself to God," Malamud says of Finkle
before he nags Salzman into arranging a rendezvous. And when
Finkle sees her, "her eyes—clearly her father's—were filled with
desperate innocence. He pictured, in her, his own redemption." [9]
Familiar enough, in the experience of Western Man, from the allegory of Jerusalem the faithless wife and God's forgiveness (Eze-
kiel *16*), the story of Mary Magdalene, and the traditional saintly-
prostitute motif in Russian literature (Dostoevsky, etc.), to say
nothing of modern American writers like Steinbeck? A surface
familiarity, no more. Even recalling cases we have known in which
men married prostitutes and there was mutual regeneration, this
tale does *not* make kinsmen of us all, and is not translatable into
universal terms.

Consider. Finkle, before he discovers the prostitute's picture,
is acutely miserable because of the emptiness of his life—"unloved
and loveless." "Out of this, however, he drew the consolation that
he was a Jew and that a Jew suffered." [10] Salzman is a weird, almost supernatural figure, half devil, half cupid or pan, who constantly shadows Finkle (like the unshakable Angel of Death in
"Idiots First") and in fact seems to have planned the match . . .
even though he says his daughter has died to him, and, when Finkle meets her (under a lamp post), Salzman waits around the
corner, chanting prayers for the dead. Such characters in so deliberately ambiguous a story are certainly not emblematic of the
modern psyche. Nor are very many characters in *Idiots First:* a
poor Jewish father contending against the Jewish Angel of Death
(who goes by the name of Ginzburg); a Jewish storekeeper in
Harlem seeking marriage with a Negro woman; a Jewish art student in Italy beset by adversities; a Jewish blackbird (who has
other Jewbird relatives) victimized by "anti-Semeets" and later
killed by another Jew, whose son he has helped greatly; another
Jewish storekeeper who goes broke; a Jewish clothier who dies of

a heart attack caused by a fight between his two employees, a Pole and a Sicilian.

In other words, Malamud's partial Judaization of society is so limited a process, involving as it does only special categories of individuals, that it should not be confused with a generalized process covering the entire population. But related to Stern's view in "All Men Are Jews" is the idea developed by Leslie Fiedler that American culture itself is becoming quite Jewish and that Americans *as* Americans are the Jews of the present age. Ever the class-conscious ex-Marxist ferreting out conflicts and social upheavals, pinning labels, and descrying portents of the coming societal revolution, Fiedler rises to extravagant new heights as he thunders home this view in article after article and even in his recent novel, *The Second Stone.*

Where Stern's reductivist view refers to the human condition, Fiedler's view relates to culture and politics. But Fiedler has simply come to see everything, including American literature, in Jewish terms. All of his cultural experience is recast so that it comes out Jewish, and even when he is dealing with a specifically Jewish work (i.e., Malamud's *The Assistant*) he must re-Judaize his material: "This is a book which ends with a conversion and circumcision of its central character to Judaism. What *The Assistant* really suggests is that, after all, Jews are the best Christians and that a good Christian might as well get circumcised and face up to this fact." [11] Here Fiedler's point in re-Judaizing Malamud is that Malamud, like other contemporary Jewish-American writers, is de-Judaizing his material.

True, Stern's and Fiedler's extremist positions show what might be made of the plausible argument that Malamud extends his Jewish materials somewhat beyond their natural bounds. But Stern is quite unwarranted in attributing a *reductively Jewish* literary effect to Malamud just as Fiedler is unwarranted in crediting him with a de-Judaizing strategy: the cause of Christianity, after all, is hardly advanced when Alpine converts to Judaism. Yet there is a modest measure of usefulness in the generalizing views advanced by Stern and Fiedler, the usefulness of a discountable (i.e., partially salvageable) claim. To a degree, as Stern argues, Malamud's tales of Jewish suffering illustrate the miseries of all

humanity (although Malamud's suffering Italians should not be left out of account), and to a degree, as Fiedler insists, Jewish writers, comedians, and toy and wine producers remind Americans of the Jewish cultural tradition, and the hostility Americans encounter abroad is reminiscent of the geo-political hostility long familiar to Jews. The usefulness of such arguments is reflected in the limited suggestive quality of the generalizations, not in their literal applicability.

But Fiedler is even more usefully suggestive in regard to Malamud when he pursues his class-dislocation scheme to a shocking conclusion: "At the moment that young Europeans everywhere (even, at last, in England) become Imaginary Americans, the American is becoming an Imaginary Jew. But this is only one half of the total irony we confront; for at the same moment, the Jew whom his Gentile fellow-citizen emulates may himself be in the process of becoming an Imaginary Negro." [12]

This tendency, if that is the right word, seems to go back to a European work of fiction, Kafka's novel *Amerika* (published after his death in 1924), in which the crypto-Jewish protagonist Karl Rossmann, an incurable victim of persecution, bureaucracy, and mischance, applies for a job and after being ignominiously downgraded is asked his name. "So as no other name occurred to him at the moment, he gave the nickname he had had in his last post: 'Negro.' " [13] One thinks of the Jewish jazz musician who undertook to live as a Negro in Harlem some decades ago, and of Norman Mailer's essay "The White Negro" (in *Dissent,* 1957). But even more significant here are two of Malamud's stories in *Idiots First:* "Black Is My Favorite Color" and "Naked Nude." In the first, a Jewish liquor store operator in Harlem repeatedly tries to assimilate with Negroes, only to be spurned and beaten for his pains. In the second, Fidelman the *schlimihl* art student in Milan, steals a Texan's wallet, is pursued by the carabinieri, and seeks refuge in a brothel where the debased brothel operators enslave him. In his spare time Fidelman draws. "Scarpio pointed to a street scene. In front of American Express here's this starving white Negro pursued by a hooting mob of cowboys on horses. Embarrassed by the recent past Fidelman blushed." [14]

Is there a special point to Malamud's reconstructionist view

of society, whereby non-Jews turn into Jews and some Jews begin turning into Negroes ("Angel Levine," "Black Is My Favorite Color," etc.), much to their discomfort? Yes, Malamud suggests. The world is losing its oxygen and becoming unfit to live in; people grow desperate in their plight (like fish out of water), turn black perhaps, sicken unto death, and make a pitiful spectacle as they fight a losing battle. Not all are affected . . . at least at the beginning. We see rich, pompous Jews ("Idiots First," "The Cost of Living") and even some very ordinary types (Professor Krantz in "The Maid's Shoes," Feuer in the dramatic sketch "Suppose A Wedding") who appear relatively untouched by the lethal conditions in the atmosphere. This situation of decay and death, of selective, encroaching evil and its fey victims is not at all what we have called the "natural history of man," suggested to the reader by a first reading of Malamud. There is an actual poison in the air, and some unfortunates succumb to it early in the game.

"The Jewbird" is a striking illustration of the baneful world that Malamud projects. "The window was open so the skinny bird flew in. Flappity-flap with its frazzled black wings. That's how it goes. It's open, you're in. Closed, you're out and that's your fate." [15] Like a refugee from some nameless destruction Schwartz the Jewish blackbird seeks shelter in the apartment of salesman Harry Cohen, near the lower East River. Triply reduced as an earnest of what is to befall him, the winged Negro Jew (an inverted Angel Levine, doomed to ignominious destruction) cannot explain to the puzzled Cohens how he came to be what he is. Is he an old Jew changed into a bird by somebody? " 'Who knows?' answered Schwartz. 'Does God tell us everything?' " From the outset Cohen hates him and tries to drive him away. Ironically, Schwartz came in the window because he was escaping from "anti-Semeets." Although he takes a liking to Cohen's dull-witted son and helps him out with his schoolwork, Schwartz is treated no more kindly by Cohen. Finally, after a campaign of terror Cohen severely torments the bird and then murders him. Afraid to leave Cohen's dwelling because the "anti-Semeets" would get him, Schwartz dies at the hands of a Jewish "anti-Semeet." Note: once doomed to blackbird-hood, the unfortunate but unsavory Schwartz has no basis for survival; one of his innumerable "natural enemies" will be sure

to get him. It is his utter inability to change his appearance or his habits (he insists on remaining a smelly, unkempt moocher) that infuriates Cohen and drives him to murder . . . a murder without remorse, because to Cohen Schwartz is only an imposter and a *schnorrer*.

In Malamud's poisoned world the precipitating factor bringing on painful destruction is very often an utterly human event: the death or defection of a spouse. Once the family is no longer cemented together, the oxygen in the atmosphere thins out progressively and the surviving spouse finds it harder and harder to exist. If he (or she) does not actually die, life becomes a source of misery and emptiness and the individual is literally left gasping for breath. In "Black Is My Favorite Color" Nathan the Harlem liquor store operator courts Ornita, who rejects him not only because she is Negro but because of her husband: dead, he is still alive in her memory. " 'Nat,' she answered me, 'I like you but I'd be afraid. My husband woulda killed me.' " [16] And Nat's fruitless courtship brings her only suffering. The two Italian widows, in "Life Is Better Than Death" and "The Maid's Shoes," are *twice* displaced and rendered wretched—after their husbands' deaths they take lovers who use them and leave them in a state of limbo. In "A Choice of Profession" a man with a well-paying job, "Cronin, after discovering that his wife, Marge, had been two-timing him with a friend, suffered months of crisis." [17] He deteriorates and in the process harms a girl who comes to him for help.

In "The German Refugee" Oskar Gassner, fleeing the Nazis, leaves his Gentile wife behind and considers himself well parted from her. Then, discovering that she has converted to Judaism and been killed by the Nazis, he commits suicide. In "Idiots First" Mendel, with the hand of death upon him, begs tearfully for an instant's time to get his idiot son on the train, and sums up for the implacable Angel of Death his doomed life: " 'All my life . . . what did I have? I was poor. I suffered from my health. When I worked I worked too hard. When I didn't work was worse. My wife died a young woman. . . .' " [18] The same pattern is seen in Malamud's poor-little-storekeeper tales. He seems to treat the little grocery store as a man's vital center, almost like his spouse. When the store goes, the man goes too, or is permanently injured by the

loss. *The Assistant* and some of the stories in *The Magic Barrel* illustrate this, and in *Idiots First* the idea is repeated in "The Cost of Living." "Sam and Sura closed the store and moved away. So long as he lived he would not return to the old neighborhood, afraid his store was standing empty, and he dreaded to look through the window." [19]

But Malamud's reconstructionist view of society and 'poisoned world' prospect do not tell the whole story. The gray despair, the pogrom-colored chronicles of defeat are abated somewhat by another motif, generally presented in a deceptively oblique manner so that it seems almost to reinforce the destruction it is apparently designed to mitigate. This is the "new life" theme, representing the transformation psychology Malamud makes use of to give his down-and-outers a second chance, another "go." Even though the "new life" sometimes overlaps and seals the earlier, doomed life ("The Jewbird"), it is in this (occasionally muted) sanction of hope that Malamud's compassion, his almost undetectable optimism are to be found. And perhaps what has made Malamud's work stand out at a time when such alchemists of grace and love as Flannery O'Connor and George P. Elliott have written at length on the redemption of the lost is that Malamud's transformations generally demand less credulity on the reader's part, less acceptance of a specific religious dogma to account for the changes. Although Malamud does occasionally invoke the supernatural, his new lives have an inner consistency that does not embarrass the reader who is unwilling to accept suddenly an alien body of religious tradition (Frank Alpine's circumcision may possibly be an exception). If Malamud's ghetto tales of suffering and turning over a new leaf do not make kinsmen of us all, do not exactly represent emblems of the modern psyche, at least they strike a very sympathetic chord, and this is a sufficient achievement in its own right.

On the opening page of *Idiots First* Malamud has placed a quotation: "Women and children first. *Old Saying.*" Taking this in conjunction with the book title and the title story, it appears that Malamud is suggesting "new life" transformation possibilities for the traditional helpless ones: women, children, idiots. In "Idiots First" the moribund father Mendel engages in what seems

like mortal combat with the Angel of Death, who is unwilling to extend Mendel's deadline; suddenly there is Divine intervention, and Mendel is at last able to assure his idiot boy a new life, in California. "Mendel found Isaac a coach seat and hastily embraced him. 'Help Uncle Leo, Isaakil. Also remember your father and mother.' " [20] There is a slight touch of Faulkner in all this. Aside from Faulkner's penchant for idiots, *The Hamlet* contains a scene in which Flem Snopes has the upper hand over the devil. And there is a touch of Malamud's own *A New Life,* in which another New York misfit will be reborn on the Pacific coast. In "Still Life" a new life is killed at the outset because the attitude of reverence that actuates Mendel is not felt by the parent. Fidelman's prostitute-landlady, as she confesses to him, took her uncle as her lover, became pregnant, and when the baby was born, threw it into the river. " 'I was afraid it was an idiot.' "

Occasionally the "new life" brings disappointment and death, or a new kind of misery, as in "The German Refugee," "The Maid's Shoes," and "Life Is Better Than Death." In the first, Mrs. Gassner is reborn as a Jew, and immediately killed by the Nazis; her husband, realizing the failure of his "new life" in America without her, at once takes his own life. The last two stories concern hopeless, drab Italian women who take lovers— thereby transforming their empty widowed existences—but remain in a limbo state of squalor and alienation. Ironically, it is the "new life" in "Life Is Better Than Death" that proves the female agonist's undoing: learning from the lonely widow whom he has seduced that she is now carrying his child, Cesare flees, depriving her of the one satisfaction that made her early life supportable, fidelity to her faithless husband. In the dramatic sketch, "Suppose A Wedding," a young engaged woman is on the threshold of forsaking her store-owner fiancé for a poor writer who seems capable of opening up a new world to her. To be sure, women, children, and idiots may be first, but all of Malamud's agonists are *theoretically* eligible for "new life" salvation. In "Black Is My Favorite Color" the liquor store owner is desperately trying to achieve it—through union with Negroes—but he cannot break through. The two antagonistic clothier's assistants in "The Death of Me" stubbornly refuse the new life (of amity and peace-

ful coexistence) that their employer urges upon them, and through their refusal cause his death. In the two Fidelman stories, "Still Life" and "Naked Nude," the art student in Italy finally achieves a temporary love-union with the prostitute of his dreams, and realizes at last his long-dormant artistic powers, at the same time outwitting the brothel-keepers who have enslaved him and forced him to copy a masterpiece. But "new life" salvation in Malamud is generally a strictly academic affair.

Where does Malamud obtain the material for his fictions? The "Jewish mystique" theory by means of which reviewers have pampered, imprisoned, and dematurated Malamud (what might be considered a literary analogue of Betty Friedan's "feminine mystique" process which men have employed to keep women from achieving adulthood) would have it that he is bringing the riches of classic Yiddish literature, modernized somewhat, to our present-day "lonely crowd" society in which Jews are indistinguishable from Gentiles. Alfred Kazin, for example, in his 1958 review of *The Magic Barrel*, says that reading certain passages in Malamud, "I get something of the same deep satisfaction that I do from the great realistic masters of Yiddish literature." [21]

Malamud, apparently, derives certain of his story lines from a great variety of sources other than the classic Yiddish writers. As most commentators are aware, his first novel, *The Natural*, is quite unlike his later work and derives quite obviously from Jesse Weston's recension of the Arthurian legend, *From Ritual to Romance*. *A New Life* recasts Joyce's Leopold Bloom as Seymour Levin. Malamud's Italian stories appear to owe much to Henry James. "Naked Nude" is a clever retelling of the basic idea he conveyed in "The Real Thing": the spurious becomes more genuine than the original. "Life Is Better Than Death" is a humanized treatment of James's ridiculously unreal graveyard lovers in "The Altar of the Dead." "Still Life" with its striking sketch (executed by Fidelman) of the Italian woman and her long-dead child, is a reconstruction, in part, of James's "The Madonna of the Future." "The Maid's Shoes," with its familiar Malamudian theme of incommunicability ("Only two souls in the whole apartment, you would think they would want to talk to each other once in a while." [22]), reads like a rewrite of James by Alberto Moravia. "The

Jewbird" seems to hark back to Poe's "The Raven." "Idiots First" with its Angel of Death and midnight-deadline, is based on an ancient folktale; many years ago the essential idea was adapted by Al Capp for a "L'il Abner" strip. The "poor little grocery store" theme of "The Cost of Living" is a fragment of *The Assistant*, as are three of the stories in *The Magic Barrel* ("The Bill," "The Prison," "Take Pity"). Malamud has borrowed from himself also in "A Choice of Profession," which is simply a de-Judaized version of a portion of *A New Life*.

The question of literary origins in Malamud is well worth raising, because his work—hypnotically compelling on different levels though it may be—is not without its chunks of poorly-digested derived material. To cite one more example . . . One of his most striking images, the beggar Susskind in "The Last Mohican" ("like a cigar store Indian about to burst into flight"), seems very much like a literary changeling. Susskind, in this tale which appeared in *Partisan Review* in the Spring, 1958 issue, may be considered the last honest man, honest to art and to conscience, that is. His Jewishness—and he is a refugee *from Israel in Italy*—heightens his uniqueness: Hitler has just killed six million Jews, and the survivors are fast losing their Jewish identity. An impressive picture. But in the Spring, 1955 issue of *Antioch Review* Samuel Yellen's story, "Reginald Pomfret Skelton," which deals with a lonely, fearful Jewish refugee professor at a midwestern university, describes the exile figure in this manner: "He himself, however, belonged to the Lost Tribe, those scholars cut off, alien, adrift, growing fewer month by month, a vanishing race like the early American Indian." [23]

But Malamud's talent is enormous, and if his underlying symbolizations of a reconstructed society, a poisoned world, and a new life are not immediately clear to the general or the critical reader, there is still enough left in his haunting stories to cause the reader to brood for a long time after the stories have been read and reread. Who is strong in this life, Malamud asks, the unchallengeable Angel of Death whose "no" means "*no*," or a weak, dying Job with a human millstone around his neck? Who knows his rightful place, a wiseguy salesman kicking out a smelly old *schnorrer* of a Jewbird, or the intruder himself, who (like the

"loathsome hag" in Chaucer or the frog prince) may be all the more worthy because he is so hard to put up with? The real question, Malamud makes clear, is who will give a little? " 'Don't you understand what it means human?' " shouts Mendel, choking the Angel of Death, in a Malamudian gesture protesting a blighted universe. " 'Don't you know what it means peace, acceptance, humanity?' " shout Malamud's characters mutely as they feel the corrosive rejection of their fellows. Love maybe is a lot to ask, but at least attachment or respect? Adele in "Suppose A Wedding" enters the room and discovers her parents in each other's arms. " 'Ah, you've been fighting again,' " she says sadly. And before that they have betrayed each other, again and again, just as Malamud's other story characters have repeatedly betrayed or been betrayed. But, Malamud shouts out to us, Mendel won *his* battle!

It would be well, though, if Malamud changed his pace and his style somewhat, perhaps even his subject matter. Not in the direction of his early baseball novel, *The Natural,* however; ever since that work he has managed a fairly tight control over his materials, except in the long academic novel, *A New Life.* It is just that his imagination of disaster is becoming a commonplace with the reader as it has already become a commonplace with the critics. " 'If a chain store grocery comes in you're finished,' " Kaufman tells Sam ("The Cost of Living," p. 149). " 'Get out of here before the birds pick the meat out of your bones.' " We can imagine what will happen here. And the disaster stories for which we can't write our own Malamudian ending after we've read the first few pages ("The Jewbird" perhaps, or "Naked Nude") are all too few. Perhaps the forthcoming Fidelman tales which Malamud has promised us will give him the new scope he needs to utilize his fragile storytelling gifts. More than any other Malamudian character Fidelman is constantly growing, realizing himself, transforming his unsatisfactory old life into a more satisfactory new one. As for what Malamud must guard against, as he splices rhythms and catchphrases from any number of dialects to develop his future materials, he has already sounded the warning himself. The narrator in "The German Refugee," in observing the European exiles and their peculiar problem with English, remarks: "To many of these people, articulate as they were, the

great loss was the loss of language—that they could not say what was in them to say. You have some subtle thought and it comes out like a piece of broken bottle. They could, of course, manage to communicate but just to communicate was frustrating." [24]

Notes

1. Bernard Malamud, *The Magic Barrel* (New York: Farrar, Straus & Cudahy, 1958), p. 56.
2. *Idiots First*, p. 69.
3. Bernard Malamud, *The Natural* (New York: Noonday Press edition, 1961), pp. 33, 154.
4. Bernard Malamud, *A New Life* (New York: Farrar, Strauss & Cudahy, 1961), p. 229.
5. *Idiots First*, p. 139.
6. John Gross, in his review of *Idiots First* (*The New York Review of Books,* October 17, 1963), p. 14, remarks: "The American-Jewish novelist has been emancipated; Bernard Malamud's generation finally struck off the fetters of uncompromising naturalism. . . . It has been Bernard Malamud's particular triumph in his short stories to have succeeded not in abandoning naturalism but in crossing it with fantasy."
7. Reprinted in Joseph J. Waldmeir, ed., *Recent American Fiction: Some Critical Views* (Boston: Houghton Miffin Company, 1963), p. 211. (See Chapter 8 in this collection.)
8. Pp. 439, 457. Jack Ludwig, in his pamphlet, *Recent American Novelists* (Minneapolis: University of Minnesota Press, 1962), p. 41, points out that "Love, or the lack of it, is the dominant theme of this generation's fiction. Disaffected man contemplates the lack of love—of self, of man, of calling, of the world, of God. Affirmation, when it occurs, is, at best, the tentative, whispered 'aye' of Malamud's *A New Life,* or the consciously equivocal 'yes' and 'no' of *Invisible Man."*
9. *The Magic Barrel,* pp. 213, 214.
10. *Ibid.,* p. 205.
11. Leslie A. Fiedler, "Address" at the Second Dialogue in Israel, *Congress bi-Weekly,* September 16, 1963, p. 56. Fiedler's views, mentioned above, are presented throughout this issue, which is devoted entirely to the Second Dialogue in Israel, June 17-20, 1963. See also Leslie A. Fiedler, "The Jew As Mythic American," *Ramparts,* Autumn, 1963, pp. 32-48.
12. "The Jew As Mythic American," p. 43.
13. Franz Kafka, *Amerika* (Garden City, N.Y.: Doubleday Anchor Books, n.d.), p. 287.
14. *Idiots First*, p. 116.
15. Too much need not be made of the "locked door" symbol in Malamud, stressed by Herbert Leibowitz in his review of *Idiots First,* "Malamud and the Anthropomorphic Business," *The New Republic,* December

21, 1963, pp. 21-23. The dying Mendel in "Idiots First" (p. 8) tells the hard-hearted Fishbein, who refuses to help him, " 'Where is open the door there we go in the house.' " In both stories, entry turns out to be an undesirable thing. A hint of the strange anthropomorphizing of birds on which "The Jewbird" is predicated is to be found in *A New Life* (p. 196). Levin sees a flock of robins overhead "from Canada, he had been told, while the Cscadian species was vactioning in California; you were dealing with strangers who looked like friends . . ."

16. *Idiots First,* p. 26.
17. *Ibid.,* p. 69.
18. *Ibid.,* p. 14.
19. *Ibid.,* p. 152.
20. *Ibid.,* p. 15. The last request is painfully ironic, since the idiot Isaac is hardly in a position to say the Kaddish prayer for his departed parents.
21. Alfred Kazin, "Bernard Malamud: The Magic and the Dread," reprinted in Alfred Kazin, *Contemporaries* (Boston: Atlantic-Little, Brown and Company, 1962), p. 204.
22. *Idiots First,* p. 158.
23. Samuel Yellen, "Regional Pomfret Skelton," *Antioch Review,* Spring 1955, p. 88.
24. *Idiots First,* p. 200.

Robert Alter

3.

Jewishness as Metaphor

From his earliest stories in the fifties, the relationship between Bernard Malamud's literary imagination and his Jewish background has been a peculiar one. For the most part, it has proved to be a remarkably creative relationship, though there are a few points in his work where the wedding of Jewish materials and fictional invention seems largely a shotgun affair, performed to legitimize imaginative offspring that ought to have validated themselves without benefit of skull-capped clergy. Now, American Jewish novelists, from Abraham Cahan and Ludwig Lewisohn to Philip Roth, have, quite understandably, often written about Jews, as the kind of people they have known best; and since the novel as a rule tries to reconstruct the social matrices of individual character, this has generally meant writing about Jewish milieux, first in the ghetto, more recently in suburbia. The concentration on Jewish social environments has not, however, led to anything like a distinctively Jewish mode of imaginative writing. Henry Roth's *Call It Sleep,* for example, still probably the most fully achieved work of fiction by an American writer of Jewish descent, is a novel of immigrant experience, using Joycean methods for the lyric rendering of consciousness; the principal characters happen to be Jews, but I see nothing in the conception or execution of this ex-

traordinary book that could not be readily transferred to a novel about a family from some other immigrant group.

In Malamud's work, on the other hand, the immigrant experience is at once more peripheral and more central than in writers of comparable background. Although most of his protagonists are avowedly Jewish, he has never really written *about* Jews, in the manner of other American Jewish novelists. Especially revealing in this connection is the fact that nowhere does he attempt to represent a Jewish milieu, that a Jewish community never enters into his books, except as the shadow of a vestige of a specter. What literary sense, then, does Malamud make of the emphatic, vividly elaborated ethnic identity of his characters— those whitefish-eating, Yiddish-accented isolates in a bleak, generalized world of harsh necessity? He clearly means Jewishness to function as an ethical symbol; it is, as Theodore Solotaroff has written, "a type of metaphor . . . both for the tragic dimension of anyone's life and for a code of personal morality." * I have had occasion to observe elsewhere that such symbolism (as in the relationship between Morris Bober and Frank Alpine in Malamud's *The Assistant*) can become uncomfortable; when a writer assigns a set of abstract moral values to the representatives of a particular group, the connection thus insisted on may strike a reader as arbitrary, an artistic confusion of actualities and ideals. The symbolic use Malamud makes of Jewishness deserves more detailed attention, but before we consider that, it is worth noting another, more organic, way in which Jewish experience enters into his writing.

Malamud is, to the best of my knowledge, the first important American writer to shape out of his early experiences in the immigrant milieu a whole distinctive style of imagination and, to a lesser degree, a distinctive technique of fiction as well. He is by no means a "folk" artist, but his ear for the rhythms of speech and the tonalities of implication, his eye for the shadings of attitude and feeling, of Jewish folk culture, have helped make the fictional world he has created uniquely his own. Though such influences are hard to prove, I suspect that the piquant juxtaposition in his fiction of tough, ground-gripping realism and high-flying

* See Chapter 16 in this collection.

fantasy ultimately derives from the paradoxical conjoining of those same qualities that has often characterized Jewish folklore.

To put this another way, it would seem as though the home-spun Jewishness of Malamud's characters affords him a means of anchoring his brilliant fantasies in reality, for the dreariness of daily privation and frustration familiar to him through the ghetto are his indicators of what the real world is like, reminding him of the gritty, harsh-grained texture of ordinary human experience. It is significant that the only book he has written in which there are no identifiable Jews, his first novel, *The Natural,* is also the only one in which the underpinnings of reality are finally pulled away by the powerful tug of fantasy. *The Natural* is a spectacular performance, a sort of *Parzival* on the ball field that combines serious moral fable with pointed comedy, superbly sustained suspense, and sheer wishfulfillment, zestfully imagined; but in the end the novel entertains more than it convinces because too much of the world as we know it has been rearranged in the service of imaginative play.

The Jewish folk figure on which Malamud has modeled most of his protagonists is, of course, the *shlemiel,* the well-meaning bungler, compounded with the *shlimazel,* the hapless soul who is invariably at the wrong end of the bungling. The way he handles this doubly ill-starred figure illuminates his whole artistic relation-ship to his Jewishness. The *shlemiel* is, we hardly need to be re-minded, often an engaging kind of character, and Malamud treats him—most memorably, in the Fidelman stories—with a very spe-cial quality of amused sympathy modified by satiric awareness. The spirit of wry folk humor that Malamud has caught in his personages is nicely expressed in the Yiddish joke about the man who comes to a doctor to complain that he talks to himself all the time: when the doctor answers that he, too, talks to himself and that it is really nothing to worry about, the man objects, "But, Doctor, you have no idea what a *nudnik* I am!" Malamud's pro-tagonists are frequently just this: *shlemiels* who talk to themselves, who repeatedly engage in self-confrontation, shrewdly but futilely aware of their own limitations, like Fidelman, "self-confessed failures" caught in the trap of themselves and rankling over their predicament, though just a little amused by it, too.

The *shlemiel-shlimazel*, however, is not merely a source of colorfulness in Malamud's fiction, the stock comic property that the type has become in so much American Jewish fiction. To be a *shlemiel*—which, for Malamud, is almost interchangeable with the idea of being a Jew—means to assume a moral stance, virtually the only possible moral stance in his fictional world. For if circumstances are at best indifferent to this individual, if human beings are so complicated, varied, and confused that to be truly open to another person means to get mixed up with and by him, even hurt by him, the very act of wholehearted commitment to the world of men means being a blunderer and a victim. The only clearly visible alternative to the stance of the *shlemiel* in Malamud's fiction (and this is, of course, a boldly foreshortened version of reality, one good reason why it works better in the short stories than in the novels) is the stance of the manipulator. Gus the Gambler and the sinister club-owner, the Judge, in *The Natural;* Karp, the "lucky" liquor-store neighbor of inveterately luckless Morris Bober in *The Assistant;* Gerald Gilley, the Cascadia professor scheming for the departmental chairmanship in *A New Life* —all these are characters who in varying degrees take a sharply instrumental view of humanity, who manage to stay on top of circumstances and people by being detached from them so that they can merely use them. Gerald Gilley's physical sterility is emblematic of the general condition of moral withdrawal shared by all the manipulators: he can "enjoy" his wife sexually, but, in her expression, "he has no seeds," he cannot give of himself what is ultimately a man's to give a woman in the most intimate of shared experiences. By contrast, S. Levin, the novel's hero, can and does give all to Pauline Gilley, even when he scarcely intends it, so that his openness to the world and his commitment to accept the consequences of his own acts brings him, inevitably, to a *shlemiel's* fate—ousted from the profession of his choice, burdened with a family he didn't bargain for, and a woman he loves only as a matter of principle, rolling westward in his overheating jalopy toward a horizon full of pitfalls.

The *shlemiel*, it should be said, lends himself much more readily to revelation in a short story than to development in a novel, perhaps because his comic victimhood invites the suddenness

and externality of slapstick; when that technique is merely multi-plied in being transferred to a novel—where we expect more subtlety and innerness, a more discursive and analytic treatment of character—the comedy becomes a little tedious. Thus, in the first hundred pages or so of *A New Life*, S. Levin has a casserole spilled in his lap, is pissed on by a three-year-old, steps into a cow pie, walks in to teach his first class with (of course) his fly open, slips in front of his school building with an armful of books, is interrupted on two separate occasions at the point of sexual entry. Even when he tries to scale a stone across a pond on a walk with a girl, it sinks! All this is funny up to a point, but after so much repetition it begins to look like sheer reflex on the writer's part, and it is not particularly helpful in establishing the inner life of an anguished intellectual struggling against both his own weak-ness and the resistance of the world around him to make himself a new man. The accumulated calamities, however, of S. Levin—whose Jewish identity is mentioned only once in the novel, at the very end—suggest why Malamud's symbolic Jews must be *shle-miels*, for, as we shall see, Malamud's central metaphor for Jewish-ness is imprisonment, and even when no actual enclosing walls are present, his Jews remain manacled and hobbled to their own scapegrace ineptitude.

The central development of the idea of Jewishness as im-prisonment occurs in *The Assistant*. That novel is suffused with images of claustrophobic containment, and Morris Bober's grocery, which is the symbolic locus of being a Jew with all the hard responsibilities entailed thereby, is frequently referred to as a prison. "What kind of man did you have to be," wonders Frank Alpine, "to be born to shut yourself in an overgrown coffin? . . . You had to be a Jew. They were born prisoners." Later, Frank reads some Jewish history, and his understanding of it (Mala-mud's, too, it would appear) is much of a piece with his vision of Bober in the store: "He . . . read about the ghettos, where the half-starved, bearded prisoners spent their lives trying to figure it out why they were the Chosen People." Frank himself is from the outset an ideal proselyte in being a kind of Italianate *shlemiel* on his own way into a tight prison: "With me one wrong thing leads to another and it ends in a trap." The real sym-

bol of his conversion to Judaism is his clumsy act of toppling onto
Morris Bober's coffin as it is being lowered into the grave; the
subsequent circumcision merely pays obeisance to the institu-
tional forms. In this respect, the curve of Frank's experience is
paralleled by that of Arthur Fidelman—from the frustrations of
a bungler ("The Last Mohican") through the captivity of sexual
bewitchment ("Still Life") to the iron jaws of imprisonment
("Naked Nude," where Fidelman is held prisoner by gangsters
in a whorehouse, at one point chained hand and foot to his bed).

Claustrophobic images of Jewish experience are hardly Malamud's invention—they recur frequently, for example, in Hebrew
writers of the late nineteenth and early twentieth century who
rebelled against all that was stifling in the life of the *shtetl*. But
the way such images function in Malamud's work is quite new.
Since his Jews are, after all, more metaphoric than literal, the
imagery of imprisonment turns out to be the symbolic representation of an already symbolic state. This is made explicit in the
case of S. Levin, where the prison motif is invoked for the first
time in the end of the novel, to elucidate the denouement. Levin,
we learn, was originally accepted for the teaching profession that
led to his comic-disastrous entanglement with the Gilleys because
Pauline Gilley happened to spot his picture in a stack of applications and was attracted by his Jewish face—thus capricious fate
selects its victims, hardly intending them as victims, and we see
how the Jew-as-*shlemiel* is, in the most ironic sense, "chosen"
for his destiny. After hearing this story, Levin ponders his future
with Pauline Gilley:

> His doubts were the bricks of a windowless prison he was
> in. . . . The prison was really himself, flawed edifice of
> failures, each locking up tight the one before. . . . Unless
> the true prison was to stick it out chained to her ribs. He
> would look like a free man but whoever peered into his eyes
> would see the lines of a brick wall.

Imprisonment, like the condition of being a Jew with which
it is elsewhere identified, is seen here as a general image for the

moral life with all its imponderable obstacles to spontaneous self-fulfillment: it is living in concern for the state of one's soul, which means knowing with an awful lucidity how circumscribed the will is in its ability to effect significant change, how recalcitrant and cowardly it can be, and shouldering the terrible onus of responsibility for one's acts, especially as they are implicated in the lives of others. The prison, like the *shlemiel* who is usually its chief inmate, is Malamud's way of suggesting that to be fully a man is to accept the most painful limitations; those who escape these limitations achieve only an illusory self-negating kind of freedom, for they become less than responsible human beings. One does not have to be a Jew to be thus enmeshed in the endless untidiness of moral experience—witness the protagonist of "The Prison," an Italian in a candy store instead of a Jew in a grocery—but, as the saying goes, it helps, for the Jew, at least as Malamud sees him, has undergone the kind of history that made it difficult for him to delude himself about his defeats and humiliations, that forced him to accept the worst conditions because he had no alternative while trying to preserve his essential human dignity. Malamud sees, moreover, in the collective Jewish experience of the past a model not only of suffering and confinement but also of a very limited yet precious possibility of triumph in defeat, freedom in imprisonment. His reading of Jewish history is clearly undertaken from a rather special angle, and with perhaps less than adequate information—European Jewry, even in the ghettos, often was, and felt itself to be, much more than a trapped group of "half-starved, bearded prisoners." Historical accuracy, however, is beside the point, for what is relevant to Malamud's literary achievement is that an aspect of Jewish experience, isolated and magnified, has afforded him the means of focusing in an image his own vision of the human condition.

Against this whole background, Malamud's new novel, *The Fixer,* emerges as a far less radical departure from his earlier fiction than one might initially conclude. The surface differences, to be sure, between this book and his previous work are abundant and striking. Malamud has always written about spheres of experience with which he was personally familiar; here he sets his

novel in Kiev, toward the end of the Czarist regime. Except in a few of his comic fantasies, he has always written about everyday people in a world whose most basic quality is uneventfulness; here his subject is a lurid murder case and an incredible conspiracy against justice. Suffering in his novels and stories has generally been a matter of humiliated egos or the gnawing fears of poverty; in *The Fixer* the central action is a process of suffering through violence, torture by inches, complete with the obscene inventions of a jailer's sadism, an attempted poisoning, a suicide, even Dostoevskian hallucinations, including one where a frantic-eyed horse is beaten over the head with a log. Malamud has always known the art of counterpointing a flat, understated style with flights of whimsy and poetic invention, but never before has he written such taut, vigorous prose—as, for example, in this prisoner's nightmare, with its staccato parade of short declarative sentences and sharply-etched physical images that give fantasy the weight and tactile hardness of palpable fact:

> The wind wailed mutely in the prison yard. His heart was like a rusted chain, his muscles taut, as though each had been bound with wire. Even in the cold he sweated. Amid the darkly luminous prisoners he saw spies waiting to kill him. One was the grayhaired warden with a gleaming two-headed ax. He tried to hide his crossed eye behind his hand but it shone like a jewel through his fingers. The Deputy Warden, his fly open, held a black bullwhip behind his back. And though the Tsar wore a white mask over his face and another on the back of his head, Yakov recognized him standing in the far corner of the cell, dropping green drops into a glass of hot milk.

Perhaps the greatest external difference between *The Fixer* and Malamud's earlier work is the relationship in it between fiction and actual events. The novel is very closely based on the Beiliss Case, the last conspicuous occasion after the Middle Ages when a Jew was actually brought to trial on the charge of ritual murder. By an odd but happy coincidence, Malamud's novel

appears in print almost simultaneously with Maurice Samuel's *Blood Accusation,* an elaborate, painstaking, yet eminently readable account of the complicated details of the Beiliss Case. Many readers of Malamud's novel will want to consult Samuel's book, out of simple historical curiosity, which the novel rouses but of course cannot satisfy, and because of the readily available opportunity to see, through a comparison with the facts, how a novelist has transmuted history into art. On the whole, Malamud has altered very few of the basic facts of the case. His protagonist, Yakov Bok, is, like Mendel Beiliss, the overseer in a Kiev brick factory, a simple man, not much of an observant Jew, who one early spring day in 1911 finds himself to his utter amazement arrested for the murder of a Christian boy whose body has been found in a cave near the brickyard, stabbed many times with a sharp instrument, in a manner, say the accusers, which indicates that the blood was slowly drained to be collected for use in *matzos.* Bok, like Beiliss, is incarcerated for more than two years while the investigating magistrates, in collusion with the most fanatical forces of reaction, trump up a case against him for a murder they more or less know has been committed by a stunningly brazen Russian woman (in the novel, the boy's mother, in fact, the mother of a friend) together with a gang of her habitual partners in theft and orgy.

Malamud's novel follows the train of events from the discovery of the body to the point at which the accused is brought out of prison to be tried. The actual trial ended on an appropriate note of muddled ambiguity, the jury at once acquitting Mendel Beiliss and concluding that the murder had occurred in the brickworks, not in the apartment of the Cheberyak woman where the clearest evidence placed it, and that the child's blood had been methodically drained for unspecified purposes. Malamud rearranges some details of the Beiliss affair in the interests of necessary simplification or even credibility—the Czarist government's case against Beiliss, for instance, was based on such a shabby patchwork of anti-Semitic fantasies that Malamud, in order not to violate novelistic probability, had to invent some shreds of circumstantial evidence for his prosecution to grasp at.

Other changes in the actual circumstances are made in order to emphasize themes; to a few of these we shall have occasion to return.

Why should the Beiliss Case attract a serious contemporary novelist and why in particular should Malamud find it a congenial subject? The first half of this question is answered in part by Maurice Samuel in the suggestive, though regrettably brief, Epilogue to his account of the case. The significance of these events, Samuel argues, extends far beyond the historical question of anti-Semitism. The case was really "a crude preview of the possibilities of the twentieth century," one of the early instances of the use by a government of the big lie, through which a powerful bureaucracy totally subverts the moral sense of its individual members and, as Samuel aptly puts it, "makes its assertions with brazen disregard for what is known . . . , seeks, by immense clamor, by vast rhythmic repetition, to make thinking impossible." To translate Samuel's observation from politics to the viewpoint of individual experience, the Beiliss Case is one of the first striking public occasions in this century when Kafka's fiction of arbitrary arraignment, of a reality which is governed by an insane, inscrutably perverse logic, became historical fact.

One often feels in *The Fixer* that for Malamud 1911 is 1943 in small compass and sharp focus, and 1966 writ large. The Beiliss Case gives him, to begin with, a way of approaching the European Holocaust on a scale that is imaginable, susceptible of fictional representation. For the Beiliss Case transparently holds within it the core of the cultural sickness around which the Nazi madness grew, representing as it does a symptomatic junction of the medieval demonological conception of the Jew as satanic enemy to Christ and mankind, and the modern phobic vision of an international Jewish conspiracy, manipulated through commerce and politics and underworld activity by the sinister Elders of Zion. (Murky hints of genocide actually crept into some of the verbal attacks on the Jews during the Beiliss affair, as when they were characterized in the reactionary Russian press, quoted by Samuel, as "an exclusively criminal class which brings death to any wholesome society.") Malamud seems quite conscious of this aspect of his subject, but I would assume that the blood libel and

Earl H. Rovit

1.

The Jewish Literary Tradition

The problem of a "tradition," or "a usable past," has long been recognized as one of the salient difficulties confronting the serious American writer. It was a problem which forced Hawthorne into "romances," and Henry James into an eventual British citizenship; and it is a problem which to a certain extent yet sustains the strengths and weaknesses of the best of twentieth century American fiction. For the writer of fiction is automatically committed to at least a minimal surface realism in the depiction of his characters and his milieu, and, speaking generally, his degree of success in presenting a convincing "slice" of simulated life will determine the cogency of his symbols. This is not to suggest that American life has suffered from a deficiency in reality; it merely restates what we have been gradually realizing in recent years: namely, that the writer of fiction needs some institutionalized framework of social stresses and harmonies, automatically recognizable to his audience, within which he can cast his own visions of truth. And American society has—at least up to yesterday—been unable to supply such a cohesive and generally acceptable image.

For this reason the great American writers have tended to ignore the approaches to realistic fiction which were perfected by the nineteenth-century European masters, electing to work instead within frameworks of their own creation—frameworks made usually out of the experience and folklore that were most immediate to them. Hence the best of American fiction has been essentially more subjective than objective, more symbolic than realistic.

But if this problem is enormous for the American writer under the best circumstances, it is many times intensified for the minority-group writer—for the American Negro, the Catholic, and the Jewish writer. Somehow each writer must come to terms with the problem of setting down his own particular milieu and of discovering his own technique for communicating his vision effectively. In practice the Jewish writer of fiction has tended to follow one of three alternate ways. He can, like Herman Wouk or Jerome Weidman, exploit the Jewish background, concentrating on catching the broken accents and mores of the Jewish immigrant in America. In doing this he runs the almost inevitable danger of sentimentalizing his milieu, sacrificing the integrity and ambiguity of his transcendent vision (if he has one) for the manipulation of his somewhat exotic stage-setting. If he is dexterous in his craft, he will also—as a casual byproduct—have a good chance of commercial success.

A second choice is to ignore almost entirely the Jewish background, choosing rather to work within an individualized or abstracted framework. The results will naturally vary in proportion to the talent and intensity of vision which the writer can bring to bear on his material. In the fiction of Nathanael West and J. D. Salinger, the results are often undeniably effective, gaining as much in emotional cogency as they lose perhaps in their excessively subjective bases. This is certainly a valid and honest approach to fiction, even though surface realism is sacrificed to the fixing of a poetic metaphor.

The third choice is the attempt to utilize the Jewish-American background as a fictional frame without adopting the stance of the local-colorist. This choice attempts to fuse the world of Yiddish folklore and Jewish life in America with the rigorous demands of modern fictional form. In our own time I think this alternate approach has been followed with varying success by

Saul Bellow, Paul Goodman, Philip Roth, and Bernard Malamud, but I will concentrate on the latter's work in trying to analyze the process of this fusion.

The use of elements of folklore in fiction is, of course, the rule rather than the exception. Indeed, storeytelling is probably the oldest and still the lustiest vehicle for folklore itself. And heterogeneous America, with its many regional differences and its polyglot ancestry, has characteristically drawn into its literature the national legends of its peoples, as well as their differing dialects and styles. But the Yiddish "tale" has seemed to remain relatively impervious to literary assimilation. Whether because its psychology and situation is too organically East European, or whether because it depends too intimately on the absorbed nuance of dialect, it has generally been true that the Jewish-American writer has been unable to exploit the vast mine of Yiddish folklore in a way comparable to Mark Twain's or Faulkner's use of Southern folklore. And when he has tried to, he has usually succeeded only in adding a pale Americanized imitation of Sholom Aleichem's inexhaustible repertory.

Bernard Malamud, the winner of the 1958 National Book Award for his short story collection, *The Magic Barrel,* is quite obviously within the tradition of the Yiddish teller of tales—tales narrated with a discernible echo of the eternal chant, tales of misery, frustration, insensate violence, greed, man's inhumanity to man, and nature's inexorable victory over both the proud and humble flesh. And yet, faithful to the strange luminous quality of this tradition, his stories are bittersweet rather than bitter. As he says in "The Loan," the dough which is moistened by tears makes a sweeter bread than the unwept-on cake. Malamud is expert at invoking the saving grace of "Jewish humor"—that indefinable quality of humanity which doggedly persists in twisting a smile even under the grip of total adversity; the egotistical triumph of a mock humility which testifies unwaveringly to the essential dignity of being human in an inhuman universe. That more often than not the smile is self-ridiculing, or ultimately ambiguous as to the target of its ridicule, may be one of the dominant characteristics of Jewish humor. The affectionate insult and the wry self-deprecation are parts of the same ironic vision which values one's self and mankind as both less and more than they seem to be worth, at one and the same time.

But although Malamud captures the elusive tones and shadows of the traditional Yiddish tale, he is not at all a teller of tales in the traditional manner. He is an extremely self-conscious short story writer, keenly sensitive to the formal demands of the short story, and unwilling to let a character vignette or Aleichem-like evocation of atmosphere embody his vision. His manner is frequently that of the teller of tales, but his technique of structure is poetic and symbolic. He seems, as it were, to construct his stories backwards—beginning with his final climactic image and then manipulating his characters into the appropriate dramatic poses which will contribute to the total significance of that image. These final images usually resemble tableaux, as in the old children's game of "Statues." The dramatic action of the story attempts to lead the characters into a situation of conflict which is "resolved" by being fixed poetically in the final ambiguity of conflicting forces frozen and united in their very opposition.

Thus, for example, "The Magic Barrel" establishes the pervasive conflict between the orthodox and the "new" values of Jewish behavior in modern American life. The oddity of the rabbinical student, Leo Finkle, calling in a matchmaker, Pinye Salzman (who smells always of whitefish), immediately brings into focus the ambiguous stresses of attempting to live correctly in a cultural situation where values are in flux. The grotesqueness of Pinye Salzman—his gluttonish mannerisms, his used-car salesman's approach to marital arrangements, his commercial rapacity —is balanced by his final dignified behavior when he intones the Kaddish (the Prayer for the Dead) around the corner from the rendezvous between Finkle and Salzman's dishonored daughter, Stella. Conversely, Finkle's austere dignity, which is dramatically established by his honesty, his ruthless introspection, his querying himself about the exact extent of his faith, is counterbalanced by his final appearance at the rendezvous with a bouquet of flowers awkwardly and eagerly thrust out in front of him. The resultant tableau is tense and richly ambiguous. The conflicting forces are held in poetic suspension—each receiving its full measure of re-

Earl R. Wasserman

4.

The Natural: *World Ceres*

The Doges of Venice dropped a ring into the Adriatic to renew annually its marriage to their city and to assure that the sea be propitious. The British monarch ceremonially opens the annual session of Parliament that it may undertake its care of the kingdom. In the United States the President annually sanctifies baseball by throwing the first ball of the season into the field; and, having received its presidential commission, baseball proceeds to its yearly task of working the welfare of the national spirit. The wonder is that we do not have a whole library of significant baseball fiction since so much of the American spirit has been seriously poured into the game and its codes until it has a life of its own that affects the national temperament. Just as a personal indiscretion can topple an English government, the White Sox scandal strained the collective American conscience, and Babe Ruth's bellyache was a crisis that depressed the national spirit nearly as much as the bombing of Pearl Harbor infuriated it. Like any national engagement, baseball, especially in that form that Ring Lardner called the "World Serious," has had not only its heroic victories and tragedies but also its eccentricities that express aspects of the American character and have become part of our folklore: Vance, Fewster, and Herman, all piled up on

third base; Hilda (the Bell) Chester, the Dodger fan; Rabbit Maranville's penchant for crawling on window ledges, especially in the rain; Wilbert Robinson's attempt to catch a grapefruit dropped from a plane; Chuck Hostetler's historic fall between third and home when he could have won the sixth game of the '45 Series.

These are not merely like the materials of Malamud's *The Natural;* the items mentioned are among its actual stuff. For what Malamud has written is a novel that coherently organizes the rites of baseball and many of its memorable historic episodes into the epic inherent in baseball as a measure of man, as it once was inherent in Homeric battles or chivalric tournaments or the Arthurian quest for the Grail. Coming, like Babe Ruth, from an orphanage, Roy Hobbs, unknown pitcher of nineteen on his way to a try-out with the Cubs, strikes out the aging winner of the Most Valuable Player award and then, like Eddie Waitkus in 1949, is shot without apparent motive by a mad girl in her Chicago hotel room. The try-out never takes place, and the years that follow are degrading failures at everything. But at thirty-four, having switched—as Ruth did—from pitcher to fielder and prodigious batter, Roy joins a New York team and, with his miraculous bat, lifts it from the cellar into contention for the league championship. Like Ruth, too, his homerun cheers a sick boy into recovery, and a monumental bellyache sends him to a hospital, as it did Ruth in 1925, and endangers the battle for the pennant. Like the White Sox of 1919, Roy and another player sell out to Gus, an Arnold Rothstein gambler, to throw the crucial game for the pennant, and the novel ends with a heartbroken boy pleading, as legend claims one did to Shoeless Joe Jackson of the traitorous White Sox, "Say it ain't true, Roy." In fact, nearly all the baseball story derives from real events, and to this extent the novel is a distillation of baseball history as itself the distillation of American life: its opportunities for heroism, the elevating or dispiriting influence of the hero on his community, the moral obligations thrust on him by this fact, and the corruption available to him. By drawing on memorable real events, Malamud has avoided the risk of contrived allegory that lurks in inventing a fiction in order to carry a meaning. Instead, he has rendered the

lived events of the American game so as to compel it to reveal what it essentially is, the ritual whereby we express the psychological nature of American life and its moral predicament. Pageant history is alchemized into revelatory myth.

I

But the clean surface of this baseball story, as a number of critics have noticed, repeatedly shows beneath its translucency another myth of another culture's heroic ritual by which man once measured the moral power of his humanness—another and yet the same, so that Roy's baseball career may slip the bonds of time and place and unfold as the everlastingly crucial story of man. Harriet, mad maimer of champions, conceives of Roy's strike-out of the Whammer as a "tourney"; Roy's obscure, remote origin and clumsy ignorance have their archetypal form in the youth of Sir Perceval; the New York team he ultimately joins is the "Knights"; and one opponent, sick at the thought of pitching to him, sees him "in full armor, mounted on a black charger . . . coming at him with a long lance." Of the mountain of gifts Roy receives on his Day at the ballpark one is a white Mercedes-Benz, which he drives triumphantly around the field and stops before the box of Memo, coldly disdainful lady of courtly love, to ask for a date. By subsuming the chivalric tourney and the Arthurian quest, baseball expands beyond time, and Roy's baseball career becomes, not merely representative, but symbolic of man's psychological and moral situation. Because of the *trompe-l'oeil*, Roy at bat is every quester who has had to shape his own character to fulfill his goal, whether it be the Grail or the league pennant. By drawing his material from actual baseball and yet fusing it with the Arthurian legend, Malamud sets and sustains his novel in a region that is both real and mythic, particular and universal, ludicrous melodrama and spiritual probing—Ring Lardner and Jung.

Sir James Frazer, Jessie Weston, and T. S. Eliot have transformed the significance of the Arthurian myth for the modern mind, and their anthropological and psychological interpretation now almost necessarily invests the legend. To the twentieth century the Grail story is the archetypal fertility myth embodying, in Miss Weston's words, "an ancient Ritual, having for its ultimate object the initiation into the secret of the sources of Life, physical and spiritual." Malamud's syncretism of baseball and the Arthurian legend therefore invites a further consideration of the novel in these terms: the psychological, moral, and communal needs of the baseball champion—the American hero—to gain access to the "sources of Life." Roy long since had made his own bat out of a tree, a sort of Ygdresel, and named it "Wonderboy," and a miraculous bat it is, with an energy of its own. Derived from nature's life and shaped by Roy for the game in which he is determined to be the hero, it flashes in the sun, blinds his opponents with its golden splendor, and crashes the ball with thunder and lightning. It is, in other words, the modern Excalibur and Arthurian lance, which Weston and others have identified as talismans of male potency and reproductive energy. The phallic instrument is the raw vitality and fertility he has drawn from the universal "sources of Life." After Roy's fruit-full night with Memo, Bump says to him, "I hear you had a swell time, wonderboy," and during Roy's slump Wonderboy sags like a baloney.

With Wonderboy, Roy joins the dispirited last-place Knights in a remarkably dry season, and the manager, Pop Fisher, who laments, "I shoulda been a farmer" and whose heart "feels as dry as dirt," suffers, as his form of the Fisher King's affliction, athlete's foot on his hands. Even the water fountain is broken, yielding only rusty water. But when Wonderboy crashes the ball, its thunder cracks the sky, the rains leave the players ankle-deep, the brown field turns green, and Pop Fisher's affliction vanishes. When Roy first appeared and merely entered the batting cage, the flagging Knights suddenly "came to life." The Quester has brought his virility to the Waste Land, and, like Jung's mana-personality, he restores the dying father-king. Roy, the questing Knight, by access to the sources of life, has restored virility to his community and the vegetative process to nature. In the radical sense of the word, he is the "natural."

The Grail vegetation myth has been precisely translated into its modern American mode and is carefully sustained in this baseball story. The "Pre-Game" section, in which young Roy is shot, takes places in early spring, prior to the baseball season. When the story is resumed years later, Roy joins the Knights in summer, a third of the baseball season having passed; and with Roy's failure in the last crucial game the novel ends in a wintry autumn to complete the fertility cycle inherent in both the Grail Quest and the schedule of the baseball season. The traditional Arthurian dwarf who taunts the hero and beats him with a scourge takes his place in the bleachers as the dwarf Otto Zipp, who reviles Roy, honks a Harpo Marx horn at him, contributes razor blades on Roy's Day with the advice, "Here, cut your throat." This stunted growth, who also embodies a good deal of Homer's Thersites, is that portion of the community envious of and antagonistic to the hero's regenerative potency that spreads to the entire team, although Zipp had worshipped Roy's predecessor Bump, whose sterile triumphs were wholly his own while the team slumped; and Zipp exults over Roy's downfall with the empty gesture of hitting a phantom ball for a visionary homerun. Merlin the Magician and Morgan le Fay have evolved into the league of Gus the "Supreme Bookie," who plays the percentages, and Memo, Morganatic in every sense, the temptress for whom Roy sells out. Because of the complementary parts played in King Arthur's life by Morgan, who works for evil and slays knights, and the Lady of the Lake, who works for good and beneficently aids them, Arthurian scholars have claimed they were originally one. Correspondingly, of Roy's two women, red haired Memo is customarily clad in black, and black-haired Iris, complementarily, in red; and it is Iris who knows Lake Michigan intimately and whose presence restores the power of Wonderboy, his Excalibur. Like the Grail fertility hero, Roy displaces the current hero whose power has waned. In the "Pre-Game" section, like Perceval slaying the Red Knight, he succeeds to the hero's office by striking out the thirty-three-year-old Whammer, thrice chosen the Most Valuable Player, who now knows he is, "in the truest sense of it, out" and trots off, an "old man." In the main narrative Roy gains his life-giving position with the Knights by inducing the death of Bump, who, although the leading league hitter, has transmitted no potency to his team. (Le Roi est mort, vive le Roy.) And at the novel's end thirty-four-year-old Roy's spiritual death is his being struck out by the young pitcher whose yearning, like Pop Fisher's, is to be a farmer, just as years before Roy had struck out the aging Whammer. Yet at one point Roy confuses the Whammer with Bump, at another sees Bump when he looks in his own mirror, and later dresses exactly like the Whammer; and when Roy succeeds the dead Bump the newspapers marvel at the identity of the two in body and manners. For in fact they are all the same fertility hero, displacing each other with each new seasonal resurgence and decline of potency. In nature, quite independently of moral failures, life and strength are forever renewed.

Besides the hero's charismatic power to restore the maimed Fisher King and bring the fertile waters to the Waste Land, Arthurians have added that the characteristics of the seasonal Grail hero are possession of a talisman, like Excalibur or Wonderboy, representing "the lightning and fecundity of the earth," and "marriage to the vegetation goddess." In every respect, then, Roy seems to fulfill his role as fecundity hero, except for the marriage, despite his yearning for Memo and his passing affair with Iris. His tragic failure therefore is linked with this omission; and the search for the reason takes us to the core of the novel, where we must seek the psychic and moral flaw within the fertility theme—which is embodied in the Arthurian Grail myth—which has been assimilated to the baseball story—which is purified out of actual events.

II

Superficially, Roy's moral failure is his lust for Memo, who induces him to throw the final game for a bribe, supposedly that he may marry her. He is further tempted by knowledge that his athlete's heart will allow no more baseball seasons; the season god is fading, and he would harvest for himself alone. But this hardly touches on the grounds of his inner corruption. The very opening of the novel establishes a condition that will repeatedly symbolize the central psychic theme: nineteen-year-old Roy, awakening from sleep, kneels in a Pullman berth and strikes a match to see his reflection in the window as the train passes through a tunnel. Crouched in this fetal position, in his berth, during passage through the uterine tunnel he then feels "a splurge of freedom" on seeing the world of pre-dawn early spring while lulled by the mothering train. Throughout this prelude the subtly muted intimations of Roy's infantilism persist in what appears mere naiveté like that of the young Perceval. The porter treats Roy as a child who must be led by the hand to the men's room and humored with mock misunderstanding and exaggeration.

> "I'm going to Chicago, where the Cubs are."
> "Lions and tigers in the zoo?"
> "No, the ballplayers."
> "Oh, the ball—" Eddie clapped a hand to his mouth. "Are you one of them?"
> "I hope to be."
> The porter bowed low. "My hero. Let me kiss your hand."

Without solicitous, fatherly Sam, the scout who has discovered him and is taking him for a try-out with (appropriately) the Cubs, Roy is completely infantile: clumsy, embarrassed, spilling water on the tablecloth as though he were wetting his diapers. The region in which his spirit is anchored becomes clear when, instead of writing down his order in the dining car, he absently prints his name and date of birth. The train taking him from his origin on the Pacific Coast to Chicago is obviously something more than motion through space: travelling "over long years," it is the time of Roy's life translated into space, and, having carried him to his youthful wound and failure in the Midwest, it will later take him to his heroic tragedy with the Knights in New York. The completion of transcontinental space will be identical with the fulfillment of the season cycle of fecundity and with the transformation of Roy the pitcher who strikes out the aging Whammer into Roy the aging batter struck out by youthful Youngberry. When, therefore, in "Pre-Game" the train is halted by a doctor who has a mysterious telegram about a sick passenger and does not know it is that failing fertility hero the Whammer, it is appropriate that the train stop beside a carnival with its "kiddie rides" and "try-your-skill booths" and that in this childish setting

with the Ferris wheel looking "like a stopped clock," Roy strike
out the Whammer, slay the aging hero, "bury" him, as Roy thinks
of it.

We shall come closer to the meaning of this infantilism when
we recognize that in striking out the Whammer, Roy also slays
Sam, his fatherly scout who, serving as catcher in this track-side
"tournament," is mortally shaken by the pitch that puts the
Whammer out. During alcoholic Sam's three years in baseball
long ago, he had slumped badly at bat but, as catcher, had never
made an error. No hero, he is the flawless receiver and support
for that conqueror, the pitcher. On him Roy leans like an infant,
and Sam has accepted his role as substitute father. The young
hero's symbolic slaying of the waning baseball god and thus his
accession to his own potency role is simultaneously the slaying of
the father image to which he had been a servile appendage. The
severance from the father image is not traumatic. Despite Roy's
"No, oh no, Sam, not without you," self-effacing Sam accepts his
own disappearance into death, orders Roy on alone to Chicago,
gives him his wallet and thereby his name. The mother image is
another matter.

Aboard the train had come Harriet Bird guarding a hat box as
jealously as Roy guards Wonderboy's case. The two objects—bat
and hat—correspond to the Arthurian symbols, sword and chalice,
which Jessie Weston and others have identified as talismans of
male and female potency. Each has selfishly made the talisman for
himself and will not relinquish it to others. Yet, through Harriet Roy feels "a great longing in his life" and a tenderness towards her "as if she might be his mother (That bird)." Repressing
his incestuous attachment to his real mother as hate (later he will
call her a whore), Roy has unconsciously substituted Harriet for
her. But the quality of Harriet as mother image must be determined by Roy's psychic state. Having struck out the old hero and
mortally wounded the father substitute, Roy seems to have free
possession of his life-energy, or, in psychoanalytic terms, his libido:
"I'll break every record in the book for throwing and hitting,"
he tells Harriet; "I'll be the best there ever was in the game."
But Harriet submits him to the hero's "test": "Is that all?" And

Roy flunks, unable to understand the question or the implication that such self-centered triumph leaves one alone and is purposeless, just as the Grail Knight fails by neglecting to ask whom his talisman is meant to serve. For Roy admits that Wonderboy is something he made "for myself." With Roy's blindness to the communal and reproductive purpose of his vitality, Harriet becomes what Jung has called the "terrible mother," *mater saeva cupidinum,* and not ("snappy goddess" though she seems to Roy) the Mother Goddess of fertility, not the World Ceres. Consequently, when the train again enters a tunnel Roy slips his hand on Harriet's breast and, compelled by the infantile regression to the tunnel, tweaks the nipple. With a scream she contorts head and arms. "Look," she says, "I'm a twisted tree"—a distortion of the tree of life from which Roy had drawn his talismanic bat.

It is the infantilism of the American hero that Malamud is concerned with, the psychic and therefore moral regression of the gifted "natural" who could vitalize society and reveal to it the capacities of human strength; the selfish attachment to the "terrible mother" that introverts and blocks the psychic energy that could flow outwardly from the mature hero and restore the Waste Land. "When wil you grow up, Roy?" Iris, that Lady of the Lake, will later ask. Alone in Chicago and regressively "sick for home," Roy is summoned to Harriet's hotel room. Wonderboy in hand, he reaffirms his determination to be "the best there ever was in the game," and the nude terrible mother reaches into her hat box, fits the talismanic hat on her head and pumps a spirit-shattering silver bullet into his guts, into his vital force. Harriet is the psychic mother from whose dual nature Roy has evoked the destructive, for when she dances about the stricken hero she makes noises of both triumph and despair. Eddie Waitkus would have been startled to learn what really hit him at the Edgewater Beach Hotel in 1949.

III

The main narrative now evolves out of the brief prologue of infantilism in the same manner that from the childish stuff of its opening pages Joyce evolves his *Portrait of the Artist,* that other novel about growing up and releasing creative power by cutting free from inherited bonds.

The moral world Malamud postulates—the one Roy, like all of us, enters—is Satan's by more than half. The land no longer belongs to the Fisher King, for the manager, Pop Fisher, whose only concern is the human team and the game they play, has been forced by need to sell sixty percent of the Knights' stock to the Judge, a scripture-quoting Mammon whose favorite element is darkness, whose profits increase in proportion as he weakens the team and debases the game, and who is trying to squeeze out the Fisher-father entirely. The Judge is the futility of all codes artificially imposed from without—religion, the law, codified morality, golden maxims; and he is an illustration of how they can be hypocritically applied for selfish material ends. But if the satanic Judge —who, like Wagner's Klingsor, lives in a dark, crooked tower above the field and who has something of both Charlie Comiskey and Branch Rickey in him—has gained major control over the material world, Fisher, frustrated father-god of human strength, has sold only with the understanding that he control all player deals "as long as he lives." Human values are in his hands so long as psychic vitality is a possibility. "Keep us alive," he begs Roy at the moment of last hope in the final game. But the contest is hardly an equal one, for the something over Setebos, the power behind the Judge, is Gus, the Supreme Bookie, who knows that the long-range odds of chance are on his side and that the threat of a vitality-hero like Roy can probably be removed by a bribe. Into this world Roy enters to make his psychic choice: his accession to heroic life-force, an *élan vital* that will give itself to his team and win Pop Fisher the pennant, or infantile, self-centered security that will betray his fellows and human values. For although Roy is the "natural" athlete, possessing the same energy that lives in nature, he must make a decision. Miraculous though Wonderboy is, Roy also hits at bad pitches, at "lemons": "I mistrust a bad ball hitter," says Pop. "They sometimes make some harmful mistakes." But moral discrimination is not presented as a conscious act of the reason; it is a psychic condition and has something to do with the will to be mature.

The libido, in Jung's formulation, naturally yearns to retreat from harsh reality into the fantasy indolence of maternal protection; but because this incest tendency is checked by society's prohibition, the consequent repression drives the psychic energy backwards into infancy and locks it inertly in the mother image. The mother so defined is the "terrible" mother of death, the destroyer who drowns man in his own source. This retrogressive mother must be renounced; yet, creative strength must derive from the mother, and hence, paradoxically, renunciation of Mater Saeva is access to Mater Magna, the life-giving mother. Through this other mother one is mature, and the libido is freed to flow unselfishly into the world of reality, rather than backwards into the subjective fantasy world. In Jung's words, "as long as the libido is satisfied merely with fantasies, it moves . . . in its own depths, in the mother. When the longing . . . rises . . . to escape the magic circle of the incestuous and, therefore, pernicious, object, and it does not succeed in finding reality, then the object is and remains irrevocably the mother. Only the overcoming of the obstacles of reality brings the deliverance from the mother, who is the continuous and inexhaustible source of life for the creator, but death for the cowardly, timid and sluggish."

The relation of Jung's two mother images is that of Lilith to Eve, Morgan le Fay to the Lady of the Lake, red-haired, black-clad Memo to black-haired, red-clad Iris; and Roy's maturity and hero-role will hang on his choice. Occasionally Roy reflected of Memo: ". . . what if the red were black and ditto the other way? Here, for example, was this black-haired dame in red and what about it? He could take her or leave her . . . but with Memo, flaming above and dark below, there was no choice." And in a delirium he thinks of Iris and Memo exchanging heads and bodies. Memo is mistress to Bump, leading hitter of the league, self-centered practical joker in this life-game, who, though "full of life," transmits none of his energy to his team and wants to be released from it. Identical in body and batting style with Roy, he contrives that Roy occupy his bed so that unsuspecting Memo sleep with unexpecting Roy. Their sexual possession therefore is a kind of unwilled incest, and the episode symbolically repeats his encounter years before with Harriet. Before Memo's entrance into the bedroom, he had been dreaming of the horrifying, aimless train of time roaring out of his origin into the world, "a place where he did not want to go," then of Harriet, who had cut him down in his youth, and then of a fantasy love affair in an indolent rural scene. The psychic scene having been set, Memo now enters his bed and slashes his hot body with her icy hands and feet, just as that terrible mother had once slashed it with a silver ghost-killing bullet. The oedipal pattern is then completed by Roy's driving Bump into competition with his flawless fielding so that Bump kills himself in a Pete Reiser crash against the wall. Roy now replaces his mirror-image on the team, wonders whether he had willed his death, and hungers for his predecessor's mistress, who detests him for their night together and violently mourns for Bump as women once violently mourned the broken season gods Tammuz, Adonis, and Osiris. Roy half recognizes that his yearning is regressive: "It was a confusing proposition to want a girl you'd already had and couldn't get because you had; a situation common in his life, of having first and then wanting what he had had, as if he hadn't had it." The significance of Memo's name should now be clear, but we can call on Jung to annotate it more richly: "the libido sinks into its 'own depths' . . . and finds there below, in the shadows of the unconscious, the substitute for the upper world, which it had abandoned: the world of memories . . . , the strongest and most influential of which are the early infantile memory pictures. It is the world of the child, this paradise-like state of earliest childhood, from which we are separated by a hard law." Being the destructive and infantile, not the nourishing life-mother, Memo pretends to Roy that her breast is "sick," and Pop warns, she "will weaken your strength."

On Roy's day of tribute at the ballpark, Memo relents for the first time and agrees to a drive, longing to see the ocean. In view of the presence of the Waste Land theme, we do not need Jung to connect water with the maternally derived life-energy in the unconscious; but Jung does make much of the "maternal significance" of water, of the fact that the libido wishes "the black water of death might be the water of life," and that the black water of death "represents the devouring mother." In Harriet's presence infantile Roy could not manage the water, spilling it on the table; and the description, "the pitcher thumped the pitcher down" can be read either way. Sam, the fading father figure, sneaks a shower in the train crew's compartment because the life-water is not the privilege of coach-travellers; and Sam deliriously foresees his death in terms of being thrown off the train of time and being carried off by a foaming river. Harriet had seen Roy defeating the Whammer as Sir Perceval slaying Sir Maldemer—the water-sick, failing hero. Before his infantile assault on Harriet, Roy had seen through the train window the "black water" and "tormented trees"; and beyond her fatal hotel room he saw "the endless dark lake." The Judge confesses his childhood nightmare was drowning and, unaware he is admitting repression and consequent fixation in the terrible mother, boasts that through discipline—that extremely imposed restraint—"water is my favorite beverage." On the drive with Memo, then, Roy, who naturally "liked the water," does not care if they never reach it; Memo intends only to wade in some pond; and when they reach a stream, the sign reads, "Danger. Polluted Water. No Swimming." Memo of the poisoned water is not the Great Mother because she herself is regressive. Father-abandoned (just as Roy had been mother-abandoned), introverted, and yearning for protection from reality, she is allied, like the Judge, with Gus the Bookie, whom she considers a "daddy" and over whose battered body she at length makes "mothering noises."

IV

Before continuing with Roy's drive with Memo it is necessary to consider a few other symbols. Roy has a recurrent subconscious image of himself as a boy sheltered within a silent, moonlit forest filled with bird cries. Moon and bird, not unexpectedly, are among Jung's major symbols of the mother, as the forest is of psychic energy. Murderous Harriet's name is Bird, and Roy had seen in her a resemblance to his own mother, adding, "That bird." Memo, corrupting Roy by playing on his sympathy, looked "like a little lost bird." To the fading Whammer the ball Roy pitched to him recalled a boyhood image of a "bird-form"; when Roy is at the height of his power the ball he hits plummets "like a dead bird," the terrible mother having been defeated for the moment; and, in his perfect fielding, he instinctively catches a flying object that turns out to be a bird he has crushed into a bloody mess. The vision of the boy, moreover, is associated in his mind with going back home and withdrawing from the hardships of reality; and, in its inwardness, it is juxtaposed to the train, symbolic of the inexorable movement of time in the world and of Roy's worldly ambitions. The boy in the woods is symbolic of his entirely private, mother-protected self that, because of the womb-like security, he refuses to mature. When, then, beside the polluted water he makes advances, Memo, crosseyed with fear, takes the wheel of the car, and, like a bacchante, this demon mother drives insanely in the total dark. Understandably, the vision of going home returns to Roy, and with it the boy in the moonlit woods. In the horror of this hallucinatory experience Roy convinces himself the boy is real and that, the maternal moon suddenly vanishing, Memo has struck the boy down with the car as he emerges from the guardian maternal woods. "I heard somebody groan." "That was yourself," Memo says. It was indeed, for Roy's incestuous yearning for the mother of the "world of memories" has released the wild terrible mother to shatter his treasured infantile image of his private self. In the dark, Memo crashes the car into a tree, that psychic living strength from which Roy had fashioned Wonderboy. Back in his hotel, the vision of moon, woods, and smashed boy returns to him as a reality, and when his own shadow falls over this vision of "his lost youth" and replaces him, Roy feels "a burning pain in his guts." Like Harriet earlier, Memo has shattered the spirit, drained his psychic energy. A day later his slump begins, as years before Harriet's silver bullet, cutting across a vision of water, had caused his years of failure.

For her own security from reality, Memo has allied herself with Gus the Bookie, and for his benefit she sets out to corrupt Roy. Meanwhile, Roy's regression has moved his sexual libido back to the related but even more infantile "hunger libido," and Babe Ruth's big bellyache has begun. In Jung's terms, the libido has regressed to the "presexual stage." Unlike his incestuous desire for Memo, which was a regressive wanting of what he had had, hunger is the ultimate regression, food, like breast-feeding, giving him "a feeling of both having something and wanting it the same minute he was having it." Through this monumental hunger, Memo, carrying in her name the memory of the infant's nursing, plans to corrupt Roy and wreck the Knights' quest for the pennant. "Food," she says like a Jungian, "is a woman's work" and, with Gus's money, prepares a Circean feast for Roy and the team the night before the crucial game. Even after the gluttonous feast, Roy goes out for hamburgers that look and taste like "dead birds," the symbol of the destructive mother. To complete this destruction, Memo has at last agreed to sleep with him that night, combining Circe's unmanning seductions of bed and board; but when he enters, the great bellyache, like a shaft of lightning, hits "the shattered gut," to repeat the recurrent pattern of the psychic wound. Here the story reaches through the baseball narrative, beyond the Arthurian legend, to an earlier culture-hero myth, for Memo has played Circe to Roy's corrupt anti-Ulysses, Roy refusing to leave the feast or tell the Knights to leave, although they would have listened to their leader. As he sinks in delirious pain, he has a vision of Memo as a "singing green-eyed siren" and then of being sucked down in a whirlpool of dirty water—the polluted water of maternal death—in a nearby toilet. Roy has succumbed to the temptresses—Circe, Siren, and Charybdis—whom Ulysses overcame in order to return to his responsibilities as king and father. In Roy the baseball champion, Arthurian knight, and Homeric hero have betrayed their fellows because of selfish infantilism of spirit. It is the wonderful irony of fate (and Malamud) that rushes stricken Roy to a maternity hospital and allows him to escape under the disguise of a visiting father.

V

Iris Lemon is obviously Memo's reverse, the extrovert's mother image, the other half of what Jung has called "the dual mother role"; and Roy does not want her even though she willingly gives herself. As her name tells, she is a kind of Flora or Ceres, but her mythic origins are manifold. Seduced at sixteen by something between a rape and a yielding to a man's hunger, she has devoted herself to her fatherless daughter. Self-sacrificing acceptance of this burden of the present has freed her of fear of looking at her past and earned her the mature self-possession that opens up the future; and yet she now repeats with Roy her girlhood act. Not only a mother, she is now a grandmother at thirty-three; and the fact sticks in Roy's throat, terrifying him and spoiling "the appetizing part of her." For the grandmother, mother of the mother, is the Great Mother, mother but not wife, both young and old, and, as Roy observes of Iris, a girl above the hips and a woman below. Unlike Memo and Roy's own mother—the terrible seductive mothers whom Roy identifies as whores—the Great Mother is the matrix of psychic powers; and through her, to use Jung's terms, the libido is redirected from its inward, ennervating prison to flow outwardly to the real world, exactly as Iris has gained posession of her self by giving it up to her daughter. Roy's failure is his self-centered inability to turn to her and sacrifice the Memo too vividly recorded on his spirit. What horrifies him is that marriage to Iris would make him a grandfather, which is to say the responsible hero-father who completely possesses his miraculous psychic strength and unselfishly directs it to his human community. "Man leaves the mother, the source of libido," Jung wrote, "and is driven by the eternal thirst to find her again, and to drink renewal from her; thus he completes his cycle and returns to the mother's womb. Every obstacle which obstructs his life's path, and threatens his ascent, wears the shadowy feature of the 'terrible mother,' who paralyzes his energy with the consuming poison of the stealthy, retrospective longing. In each conquest he wins again the smiling love and life-giving mother." For acceptance of Iris would not be selfish Circean delight; fruity though her name is, she is a "Lemon."

Iris makes her first appearance at the depths of Roy's slump, his strength robbed by Memo. The episode is founded on a famous event in Babe Ruth's career and transforms it into a mythic version of the true hero-father's role, the "grandfather" role Roy might have filled. A grievously injured boy, his psychic energy having flagged, is not exerting his will to live, and because he is a fan of Roy's his father lies to him, claiming Roy has promised to hit a homerun for him. Now the father pleads with the weakened Roy to fulfill the promise. Afraid of the "responsibility,"

Roy promises only that he will do the best he can. "A father's blessing on you," the truckdriver calls after him. Pop Fisher, convinced Roy's slump is due to Wonderboy, has benched him for refusing another bat. At this point, wearing the white rose that throughout symbolizes the glory granted by the Great Mother to the hero who accepts the burden of reality, Iris assumes her Great Mother role as Aphrodite and unaccountably rises from a "sea" of faces in the stands, with electric results. A subrational murmur spreads among the fans; a stranger next to her, as though her atmosphere were aphrodisiac, feels "a strong sexual urge"; and the air is filled with "unbelievable fragrance." Her purpose in remaining standing is to show Roy her confidence in him, to transmit it to him; and, she later admits, the price she paid was giving up her own privacy, the same infantile and self-absorptive privacy to which Roy repeatedly flees and refuses to abandon or (psychoanalytically the same thing) make public. Yet for a moment he does. Motivated consciously by the sight of the suffering father and unconsciously by the risen Aphrodite-Iris, he offers to give up Wonderboy, and Pop does an immediate about-face and lets him bat with it: it is his to use because he is willing to give it up. When he then hits the homerun, he is for the moment the Great Father and hero through the agency of the Great Mother. Just as Iris' self-sacrifice becomes Roy's strength, so his life-energy flows into another; and "everybody knew it was Roy alone who had saved the boy's life."

The night before her first meeting with Roy, Iris had enacted the ritual of her role. The summer rain that the fertility hero evokes with his talismanic bat has been falling. But life-energy is not purely benign, for ambivalent Wonderboy, made of a lightning-struck tree, also flashes with lightning, and of the lightning Iris has special dread, afraid prophetically "she would be hurt by it." After the rain, Aphrodite-like she had walked barefoot through the flowers in the park. But on meeting Roy next day she assumes another but related form of the Great Mother. Having once driven with Memo to the polluted water, Roy now drives Iris to Lake Michigan, and this Arthurian Lady of the Lake, no dabbler in pools, knows well and is expert in this maternal water of life in the unconscious. Her own life is summed up in her advising Roy that the lake water is cold, "but you get used to it soon." Like Harriet, Iris also subjects the hero to a "test," and Roy still knows only that he wants to be "the best," to break every record. Still selfishly infantile and fearing death, he wants to set records because in that way "you sorta never die," not learning from Iris' life that one gains his self by giving it to others and that one is immortal in the life-energy he gives. Baffled by the "test," Roy again thinks he hears the train of time, going nowhere in particular; and he freezes in dread. "There are no trains here," Iris says; not, that is, at the water of life. "It must have been a bird cry," she adds.

In the water Roy makes as infantile a gesture as he once had with Harriet and asks for a kiss. When Iris is repelled, he dives down into the lake. This plunge into the waters of the unconscious is not a new experience to Roy. When he first joined the ailing Knights, they were under the care of a hypnotist, whose progenitor is the medicine man of the Arthurian fertility myth and who was as unsuccessful as his Arthurian predecessor, for his efforts through autosuggestion to rouse a winning spirit merely pacified the team. This outside help produced merely euphoria by reconciling the men to their unconscious, instead of releasing from it their life-energy, for that must result from an internal striving. Hypnosis opened to Roy the golden waters of the unconscious that became black as he dived deeper, vainly seeking a mermaid, the water-mother. But, lost in the black depths, he could not find his way back and violently broke off the vision: "no medicine man is going to hypnotize me." Tied to the terrible mother, he could not find his way back from the regression to reality. Roy at least knows the psychic truth: "I want to go through on my own steam." He is both right and wrong, for in fact he wants entirely to avoid facing his unconscious because of all the ugly past he has repressed into it like a dirty closet. Not only does Roy conceal his private self from the sports writer who considers a private life a personal insult and wants to display it simply for the display; he also hides it from himself. Talk about "his inner self was always like plowing up a graveyard."

In Iris' lake, however, Roy dives down to the liquid mud bottom to find his mind crammed with old repressed memories that disgust him, and after he fights his way up through the iron bars of the current, surprised by how far down the maternal moonlight filters, he sees the golden mermaid Iris seeking him. For Roy has taken what Jung called the "night sea journey": the plunge represents withdrawal from the outer world and adaptation to the inner, and the emergence symbolizes recommencement of progression. "What the regression brings to the surface," Jung adds, "certainly seems . . . to be slime from the depths;' but . . . it will be found that this 'slime' contains not merely incompatible and rejected remnants of everyday life . . . but also germs of new life and vital possibilities of the future." Or, as Iris redefines it, we have two lives: one of suffering, to learn with, another to live with in happiness after that. The first existentially constitutes the personal unconscious with all its slime; the second enters that unconscious to release a new life—to use the title of Malamud's latest novel. Or so it should be. But Roy protests, "I am sick of all I have suffered." "All it taught me is to stay away from it." His plunge was a childish withdrawal and a self-concerned determination to make another record, not a wresting of psychic energy from the selfishness in which it inheres.

All the symbolism of the novel now comes powerfully to bear upon the crucial game, which Roy has agreed to throw for the Judge's bribe. As though three strikes were the three times one sinks before drowning, between his second and third drowning strikes two recollections flash into Roy's mind. His sudden childhood memory of his mother's drowning a tom cat is affiliated, of course, with Memo and the polluted water, for Roy is bound to the terrible mother and the death-water in which she drowns the life-energy. His other vision is of his rejection of the Great Mother, who is available to the maturely unselfish, for Roy recalls that after he had had Iris beside the lake, she "wanted him to comfort her but he wouldn't. 'When will you grow up, Roy?' she said." And Roy, in the grip of the mother-bird, then intentionally misses Vogelman's next pitch. Once again at bat, still intending to throw the game, Roy is taunted by Zipp, the dwarf, and, still regressive, lashes out at that hostile, stunted public world by trying to chop the ball at the dwarf. When he succeeds in this rejection of the world, the ball is deflected from Zipp's skull and strikes Iris, wounds the Great Mother who directs the hero's energy out of himself to altruistic good. Injured Iris, pregnant with Roy's child, persuades him to win "for us" and to "protect me," and Roy returns to Wonderboy lying, appropriately, in the mud near the water fountain, determined now to "save the game, the most important thing he ever had to do in his life." But clearly Roy has learned too late, and with the next ball talismanic Wonderboy splits in half. The psycho-moral decision has come only with the death of the psychic energy. Without Wonderboy, Roy fails to lift the bat, and he is out again.

One last chance remains, and Roy now goes to bat fully determined to save the game of existence, to help Fisher and his team, not to betray them. It is now that Vogelman, that bird-man whose nemesis Roy had been at the height of his strength, sees Roy as the Arthurian hero charging him with a lance. "Take me outa here," Vogelman moans, and after pitching three balls keels over in a faint. But it is too late for Roy to be the father-hero. Twenty-year-old Youngberry, wishing to be a farmer and seeing visions of fields of golden wheat, takes the mound, and with the score at three and two, Roy strikes out. At a "bad" ball. Nature's season cycle has fulfilled itself: the new hero slays his fading predecessor, and Roy joins the ranks of Whammer and Bump.

In the night of defeat Roy performs the ritual of psychic mourning. In the now parched earth he digs a grave for his split bat, his shattered vital power, and, wishing it could take root and become a living tree again, he hesitates over the thought of wetting the earth with water from the fountain. But he knows the futility—it would only leak through his fingers. Because Roy's failure to be the hero is his failure to accept the mature father role, it is properly a boy who ends the novel, begging hopefully in disillusionment, "Say it ain't true, Roy." More was lost by Shoeless Joe Jackson than merely the honor of the White Sox or even the honor of the national game. For in the boy is each new American generation hopefully pleading that those on whom it depends will grow mature through the difficult love that renders the life of the human community the self-sacrificing and yet self-gaining purpose of their vital resources; that they not, selfishly seeking the womb-like security of disengagement, evade the slime that human existence must deposit within, but willingly and heroically plunge into it, with all its horror, to release for others its life-giving power.

With the insight sometimes granted the tourist, Virginia Woolf once wrote that baseball solved for Ring Lardner "one of the most difficult problems of the American writer; it has given him a clue, a centre, a meeting place for the divers activities of people whom a vast continent isolates, whom no tradition controls. Games give him what society gives his English brother." Baseball has given Malamud a ritualistic system that cuts across all our regional and social differences. The assimilation of the Arthurian myth defines the historical perspective, translating baseball into the ritual man has always been compelled to perform in one shape or another; and the Jungian psychology with which Malamud interprets the ritual locates the central human problem precisely where it must always be, in one's human use of one's human spirit. *The Natural* is the broad formulation of Malamud's world of meaning, for in it he evolved the structure of symbols and the design of thematic patterns and relationships on which he has drawn in *The Assistant* and *A New Life.* In addition to its own artistic integrity, *The Natural* is the necessary reference text for a reading of his subsequent fiction.

uffy foreshadows Levin's role, but he does not add to it; simi-
ly, as Levin replaces Gilley with Pauline, so Gilley replaces the
department chairman, Fairchild, but the changes seem only
academic musical chairs and there are no important themes
arly visible.

In this respect, therefore, *The Fixer* is comparable to *The*
istant, for its variations of the central pattern add many levels
the novel's theme. Early in the novel, the important "father-
" pair is Yakov Bok and Shmuel, Yakov's father-in-law. Soon,
wever, this is replaced by the obviously untenable relationship
he anti-Semitic Lebedev to Yakov, who has allowed himself to
romanced by Lebedev's daughter, Zinaida. After this episode,
he end of which Yakov is imprisoned for alleged child-murder,
ov finds a parental surrogate in the kindly Assistant Prosecutor
ikov, who seeks to defend Yakov as well as to instruct him.
, finally, after his two-and-a-half-years' imprisonment, Yakov
gnizes his last paternal figure in the Tsar, Nicholas II, "Little
er." [5] In addition to these variations, Malamud also increases
novel's thematic range by offering variations in other ways.
example, he implicitly contrasts Shmuel's relationship to Ya-
with Marfa Golov's murder of her son, Zhenia. Along with
there are extensions of the pastoral scapegoat ritual in many
: Yakov is sacrificed for the Golov child, who supposedly was
lly murdered by the Jews; Bibikov is sacrificed for Yakov,
also becomes a "martyr" to the Russian Jews; and the prison
Kogin dies for Yakov's freedom. Finally, juxtaposed to all
, is the figure of Christ, who serves throughout as a powerful
type for the scapegoat figure. All these variations, as they
d, serve to embroider the central theme by thrusting it into
t every aspect of man's life: Shmuel and Raisl, Yakov's wife,
duce themes of justice and law on the family and religious
(Raisl, an anagram for Israel, is clearly identified with Juda-
self); Lebedev and Zinaida and Kogin and his son Trofim
he interests to personal and economic relationships; Bibikov
he central ideas to a philosophic and theoretical plane;
nally, Nicholas the Second shifts the center of interests to
cal politics, the concern that seems most vital to Yakov,
Malamud, by the novel's conclusion.

James M. Mellard

5.

Four Versions of Pastoral

Bernard Malamud has achieved a notable variety in his four
novels to date, for having begun with a baseball novel in *The
Natural* and a city novel in *The Assistant*, he has since produced
an academic novel in a *A New Life* and a historical novel in *The
Fixer*. But Malamud has also achieved a steady development in
the handling of his own special fictional mode in the novels, and
the latest work, *The Fixer*, represents the most powerful demonstration of its range and effectiveness. Nothing more than a modernization of the pastoral, a putting of the complex into the simple so that "something fundamentally true about everybody" [1]
may be expressed, this method has been contemned by critics like
Marcus Klein and novelists like Philip Roth because it lacks realistic specificity.[2] * But the truth is that the failure of the realism
is the success of the pastoral. For Malamud, the pastoral mode is
his greatest strength as a writer of fiction, because it has given him
an archetypal narrative structure of great flexibility, a durable convention of characterization, a consistent pattern of imagery and
symbols, and a style and rhetorical strategy of lucidity and power.
Although Malamud employs different versions of pastoral in each

* See Chapter 17 in this collection.

novel, *The Fixer* not only does all that the others do in developing his major themes but also pushes the mode into areas never quite reached in *The Natural, The Assistant,* or *A New Life.*

The very flexible structural archetype the pastoral offers Malamud is the pattern of vegetation rituals and myths. Based upon the seasonal cycle of change, this pattern gives Malamud a central controlling form in the pastoral fertility myths of dying and reviving gods, of youthful heroes replacing the aged, of the son replacing the father, the primary expression of which is found in vegetation life rituals, myths of the Fisher King, and its historical successor, the Grail quest.[3] The form that this archetype takes in each of Malamud's novels is that of the son finding and replacing the father or of the young hero or leader replacing the old. In *The Natural*, though there are other mythic associations, the central myth is the pastoral, bringing together vegetation rites, the Fisher King motif, suggestions of Grail quest, and, perhaps most importantly, the relationship of youthful son and aged father. The Fisher King reigning over a desolate wasteland is, of course, Pop Fisher, the veteran manager of the New York Knights baseball team, and the heroic "youth" who revives the team (and the outfield grass) is Roy Hobbs, the thirty-four-year-old rookie who leads the Knights to the verge of a pennant and then sells out to the forces of corruption. In *The Assistant,* the "wasteland" is the Lower East Side of New York City, the weakened and dessicated "king" is the old Jewish storekeeper, Morris Bober, while the youth who replaces him and brings new life to the female Bobers is Frank Alpine, the indigent westerner who does penance to Bober and eventually takes over the store after Bober's death. The Fisher King of *A New Life* is Gerald Gilley, the chairman of freshman composition at Cascadia College, which serves as spiritual and intellectual wasteland, and the new king who takes Gilley's place as husband of the previously barren Pauline is the English instructor from New York, S. Levin, who both finds and creates a new life. Although discovered only very late in the novel, the ineffectual king who reigns over desolation, "a valley of bones," in *The Fixer* is Tsar Nicholas II, who is symbolically confronted by the new hero, the Jewish repairman Yakov Bok, in the hero's vision at the end of the novel.

Adapting this archetype in each of his n— vises two important strategies that both concea— plicity and expand its significance: one, the us— dependent upon the basic archetypal relation— assimilation of the significant nodes of the na— rhythm. Used partially to "displace" the featu— the multiplying of father-son relationships i— primarily to reinforce and to extend its meani— for example, Malamud sets up the central *tra*— fuzzy-cheeked nineteen-year-old Roy Hobbs st— year-old "Whammer" Whambold, the Amer— hitter, in the novel's opening section, "Pre— central relationship, between Pop Fisher a— owed, moreover, in the same section, wher— covers Roy, Sam Simpson, becomes like a fat— dies after the contest between Roy and Wh— Roy's fast balls hits the old man in the che— gives the novel a tragic form, if not a tragi— by a variation of the central pattern, for— older than "Whammer" in the novel's cer— not have replaced Bump, the carefree youn— the near-fatal wound inflicted by Harriet F— giving way to the younger hero.[4] What hap— Roy's pursuit of greatness forces him to tr— not now actually suited, his flaw being s— season slump and the climactic splitting of— derboy," a symbolic sword, lance, and phal— in *The Natural* is only structural, prepa— Roy's "fall," but in *The Assistant* it o— quite effectively to increase the novel's— well. The "father-son" relationships betv— Karp and Louis Karp, Pearl and Nat F— Ward Minogue involve many areas of— society, the letter and the spirit of the l— idealism and materialism, love and dut— cause of *The Assistant's* superiority over— it also uses the device of multiplication,— numbers but not necessarily the signifi—

Whereas the multiplying of the basic patterns is a device for variety and extension, the device by which Malamud gives his simple narratives a sense of unity and movement is the seasonal rhythm and variations of it. The baseball season of *The Natural*, for example, offers Malamud a handy seasonal rhythm and he uses it pretty carefully, the first section, "Pre-Game," taking place in spring and coinciding with spring-training, and the major portion, "Batter-Up," taking place mostly in summer (late spring is the period of the Knights' terrific slump) and early autumn. It is almost as if Roy Hobbs were only a sun god whose fate is decreed by the seasonal movement, for he bursts into stardom on June 21 (the last day of spring) and suffers his tragic fall *after* the official beginning of autumn on September 23, the day on which the Knights clinch a tie for the pennant, have their victory celebration, and Roy gorges himself until he becomes dreadfully ill, leaving himself vulnerable to Judge Banner's bribery. Consequently, it appears that Malamud has used the seasonal cycle for structuring a tragic narrative,[6] but, unfortunately, the tone of the novel is rather comic and one feels a lessening, rather than a heightening, of man's dignity because of Roy Hobbs's fall. Here, again, *The Assistant* seems to use the pastoral conventions more effectively, for, though the seasonal rhythm also controls the narrative, it does not obtrude or seem contrived as in *The Natural*. *The Assistant* opens on a windy day in early November and closes after April and Passover, showing along the way the moral and religious rebirth of Frank Alpine, the physical deterioration and death of Morris Bober (as the result of shoveling an unexpected April snow), and the spiritual death and revival of Helen Bober, Bober's daughter and, ultimately, Frank's lover. But here, instead of forcing all the changes into one short half-year, Malamud shows Frank replacing Bober in the first cycle from November to April and then allows Frank another year, from Morris' death to another April, to win back the affections of the daughter. Like *The Natural*, *A New Life* uses a single unit but the time allotted is slightly longer, for it follows the pattern of the academic year. It is divided into four major parts to coincide with the seasonal cycle as well as to the important aspects of the death and rebirth pastoral motif. The first section, summer, shows Levin arriving at Cascadia College (located in a truly pastoral setting), getting settled, and finally being told by Laverne, the moonlighting waitress, that he "ain't a man." The second section, fall, begins with the first day of the fall quarter and ends with Levin's recognition that Gerald Gilley (the "Fisher King") is his enemy; subsequently, in the third section, corresponding to winter, Levin begins, consummates, and ends (he thinks) his affair with Pauline Gilley; in the fourth section, opening with "May sunbursts" and corresponding to spring, Levin takes up his departmental causes, replaces Leo Duffy as the "political" liberal, gives Gilley a losing fight for the position of department head, but wins Pauline away, and leaves Cascadia with her, her two adopted children, and a child soon to be born, having found both a new life and a new identity.

Although Malamud pays careful attention to the rhythm of the seasons in *The Fixer,* he also uses it more freely and successfully assimilates it to a broader, though still pastoral, cycle. Because the central event of *The Fixer* lands Yakov Bok in prison, there is inevitably less *action* than in the other novels, the narrative interest focusing on Yakov's ability to withstand pain and torment and to maintain his innocence. But for this reason the sense of narrative *movement* depends even more on the fixer's noting the seasonal changes. Consequently, Malamud gives us frequent details to suggest seasonal change and he notes months and seasons carefully, Yakov's tale beginning in November when he leaves the Pale for Kiev, and going through the arrest and imprisonment in April, followed by a detailed account of the first year and foreshortened accounts of the second and third years, ending in autumn about the same time of year it had begun. More important than the seasonal rhythms, however, is the pattern of Biblical myth that the novel incorporates: the story coincides rather carefully with the period of Christ's ministry, since Yakov leaves his family and community at the age of thirty, "ministers" to his people for three years, and goes to his trial and possible death at the age of thirty-three. Obviously there is a great deal of irony in such a use of a "Christ-figure" by a Jewish novelist, but Malamud's point in using it is to insist upon the universality of the pattern, an implication admirably accounted for by the *pastoral*, rather than the simply Christian, aspects. Broadly pastoral or narrowly Christian, *The Fixer* insists as strongly as *The Assistant* upon the cyclicality of life, the necessity for endurance and hope, and the value of suffering as well as its needlessness. Yakov Bok's ministry, the heart of his teaching, is in fact the two and a half years in prison he maintained his innocence and became a hero and a "potential savior" of his people, a people including not only the Jews but all men who suffer without cause. Thus one feels strongly that Yakov will die, like Zhenia Golov, Bibikov, Kogin, and Christ, but one feels as well that his death will presage a better life for man.[7]

Because of the pastoral conventions in Malamud's novels, the vegetation cycles to which the human lives are attached, the most important source of imagery and symbolism for Malamud is the world of nature, its benevolent elements of fields and streams, groves and parks, birds and fish and flowers contrasted to its demonic wastes, sinisters forests, torturous mountains, and tomblike caves. Inescapably related to the cycles of the narratives, the kinds of imagery normally revolve from one pole to another in the novels, the final form being determined by the structure of the work. At least a parody of tragedy, *The Natural,* for example, opens in spring, in the American West, among virgin forests, then shifts to the probably too obvious "wasteland" of the Knights' ballpark. After Roy Hobbs's emergence as "hero," rain comes, the diamond regains its greenery, and the climate becomes more temperate. By the novel's end, however, there are many hints not only of autumn, which actually arrives, but also "thoughts of the barren winds of winter" (p. 176). Illustrating the same principle, but reversing the movement, *The Assistant* and *A New Life* have a comedic structure and thus their patterns of imagery conclude with details of spring and summer. In *The Assistant,* for example, Malamud finds an objective correlative for the attitudes of his characters in the mutations of weather, Morris Bober feeling buffeted by life as November's winds blow upon him, Helen feeling "tormented" by winter, but thinking of Frank Alpine when the rains come, and both Helen and Frank feeling life within them awakening when flowers begin to bloom and trees to bud in the spring. Similarly, in *A New Life* Levin's personal preoccupation with the world of nature in the West takes on an appropriate academic cast in his careful study of *Western Birds, Trees and Flowers,* a book perused in summer, laid away "all winter" (p. 195), and taken up again at a hint of spring. Pursuing the tragic implications of *The Natural,* as well as its interests in the "hero," *The Fixer* both opens and closes in a wasteland, wintry setting. And during Yakov's imprisonment, in order to show its importance to human life, nature imagery is brought in through Yakov's memory of and desire for it. We are told, for example, that Yakov "felt the change of weather in his head" (p. 229) and, later, that he imagined the "scent of spring" (p. 235).

Related to these patterns of natural imagery are the ways Malamud depicts characters and character relationships. The most satisfying sexual relationships are almost invariably at least begun in natural settings; Roy Hobbs, for example, makes love to Iris Lemon, who becomes pregnant, beside a grove on the beach of Lake Michigan, Frank Alpine first has Helen Bober in a city park, Levin makes love to Pauline the first time in the woods, and Yakov Bok, who goes often to the woods with Raisl, tells her, "You got me in the woods" (p. 285). As one might guess, principles of life and fertility in Malamud's novels are associated with women and, more specifically, with their mammalian traits; consequently, in them the female breast has unusual significance. Women associated with infertility and death, therefore, have "sick breasts," like Memo Paris (*The Natural*) and Avis Fliss (*A New Life*), or very small ones, like Helen, Pauline, and Raisl before they are revitalized by their lovers. Full breasted women like Iris Lemon and Zinaida Lebedev seem always to offer the promises of life.

For Malamud, the arcadian, as opposed to the naturalistic, aspects of nature represent a kind of ideal of beauty and peace and fulfillment. Consequently, all of his protagonists long for them when they are not present in their lives, often remembering pleasant natural scenes in their pasts or dreaming of them in their futures. In the midst of a hot pennant fight, Roy Hobbs yearns for a family life and "going fishing in a way that made it satisfying to fish" and "with this in mind he fished the stream in peace . . ." (p. 179). Frank Alpine and Helen Bober both dream of spring time in the midst of winter, and when they are together they often feel that the edge has been taken off the cold winds. Levin finds

James M. Mellard

5.

Four Versions of Pastoral

Bernard Malamud has achieved a notable variety in his four novels to date, for having begun with a baseball novel in *The Natural* and a city novel in *The Assistant,* he has since produced an academic novel in a *A New Life* and a historical novel in *The Fixer.* But Malamud has also achieved a steady development in the handling of his own special fictional mode in the novels, and the latest work, *The Fixer,* represents the most powerful demonstration of its range and effectiveness. Nothing more than a modernization of the pastoral, a putting of the complex into the simple so that "something fundamentally true about everybody" [1] may be expressed, this method has been contemned by critics like Marcus Klein and novelists like Philip Roth because it lacks realistic specificity. [2] * But the truth is that the failure of the realism is the success of the pastoral. For Malamud, the pastoral mode is his greatest strength as a writer of fiction, because it has given him an archetypal narrative structure of great flexibility, a durable convention of characterization, a consistent pattern of imagery and symbols, and a style and rhetorical strategy of lucidity and power. Although Malamud employs different versions of pastoral in each

* See Chapter 17 in this collection.

novel, *The Fixer* not only does all that the others do in developing his major themes but also pushes the mode into areas never quite reached in *The Natural, The Assistant,* or *A New Life.*

The very flexible structural archetype the pastoral offers Malamud is the pattern of vegetation rituals and myths. Based upon the seasonal cycle of change, this pattern gives Malamud a central controlling form in the pastoral fertility myths of dying and reviving gods, of youthful heroes replacing the aged, of the son replacing the father, the primary expression of which is found in vegetation life rituals, myths of the Fisher King, and its historical successor, the Grail quest.[3] The form that this archetype takes in each of Malamud's novels is that of the son finding and replacing the father or of the young hero or leader replacing the old. In *The Natural,* though there are other mythic associations, the central myth is the pastoral, bringing together vegetation rites, the Fisher King motif, suggestions of Grail quest, and, perhaps most importantly, the relationship of youthful son and aged father. The Fisher King reigning over a desolate wasteland is, of course, Pop Fisher, the veteran manager of the New York Knights baseball team, and the heroic "youth" who revives the team (and the outfield grass) is Roy Hobbs, the thirty-four-year-old rookie who leads the Knights to the verge of a pennant and then sells out to the forces of corruption. In *The Assistant,* the "wasteland" is the Lower East Side of New York City, the weakened and dessicated "king" is the old Jewish storekeeper, Morris Bober, while the youth who replaces him and brings new life to the female Bobers is Frank Alpine, the indigent westerner who does penance to Bober and eventually takes over the store after Bober's death. The Fisher King of *A New Life* is Gerald Gilley, the chairman of freshman composition at Cascadia College, which serves as spiritual and intellectual wasteland, and the new king who takes Gilley's place as husband of the previously barren Pauline is the English instructor from New York, S. Levin, who both finds and creates a new life. Although discovered only very late in the novel, the ineffectual king who reigns over desolation, "a valley of bones," in *The Fixer* is Tsar Nicholas II, who is symbolically confronted by the new hero, the Jewish repairman Yakov Bok, in the hero's vision at the end of the novel.

Adapting this archetype in each of his novels, Malamud devises two important strategies that both conceal the pattern's simplicity and expand its significance: one, the use of multiple levels dependent upon the basic archetypal relationship, and, two, the assimilation of the significant nodes of the narrative to a *seasonal* rhythm. Used partially to "displace" the features of the archetype, the multiplying of father-son relationships in each novel serves primarily to reinforce and to extend its meanings. In *The Natural*, for example, Malamud sets up the central *tragic* plot by having a fuzzy-cheeked nineteen-year-old Roy Hobbs strike out thirty-three-year-old "Whammer" Whambold, the American league's leading hitter, in the novel's opening section, "Pre-Game." The novel's central relationship, between Pop Fisher and Roy, is foreshadowed, moreover, in the same section, where the scout who discovers Roy, Sam Simpson, becomes like a father to the youth, but dies after the contest between Roy and Whammer when one of Roy's fast balls hits the old man in the chest. The situation that gives the novel a tragic form, if not a tragic tone, is also created by a variation of the central pattern, for actually Roy Hobbs, older than "Whammer" in the novel's central narrative, should not have replaced Bump, the carefree young slugger, but, barring the near-fatal wound inflicted by Harriet Bird, he should now be giving way to the younger hero.[4] What happens, of course, is that Roy's pursuit of greatness forces him to try things for which he is not now actually suited, his flaw being symbolized by the mid-season slump and the climactic splitting of the mighty bat, "Wonderboy," a symbolic sword, lance, and phallus. This multiplication in *The Natural* is only structural, preparing for and explaining Roy's "fall," but in *The Assistant* it operates structurally and quite effectively to increase the novel's thematic implications as well. The "father-son" relationships between Morris and Frank, Karp and Louis Karp, Pearl and Nat Pearl, and Minogue and Ward Minogue involve many areas of man's life—family and society, the letter and the spirit of the law, morality and justice, idealism and materialism, love and duty. Here is probably the cause of *The Assistant's* superiority over *A New Life*, for, although it also uses the device of multiplication, *A New Life* increases the numbers but not necessarily the significances. For example, Leo

Duffy foreshadows Levin's role, but he does not add to it; similarly, as Levin replaces Gilley with Pauline, so Gilley replaces the old department chairman, Fairchild, but the changes seem only an academic musical chairs and there are no important themes clearly visible.

In this respect, therefore, *The Fixer* is comparable to *The Assistant*, for its variations of the central pattern add many levels to the novel's theme. Early in the novel, the important "father-son" pair is Yakov Bok and Shmuel, Yakov's father-in-law. Soon, however, this is replaced by the obviously untenable relationship of the anti-Semitic Lebedev to Yakov, who has allowed himself to be romanced by Lebedev's daughter, Zinaida. After this episode, at the end of which Yakov is imprisoned for alleged child-murder, Yakov finds a parental surrogate in the kindly Assistant Prosecutor Bibikov, who seeks to defend Yakov as well as to instruct him. And, finally, after his two-and-a-half-years' imprisonment, Yakov recognizes his last paternal figure in the Tsar, Nicholas II, "Little Father." [5] In addition to these variations, Malamud also increases the novel's thematic range by offering variations in other ways. For example, he implicitly contrasts Shmuel's relationship to Yakov with Marfa Golov's murder of her son, Zhenia. Along with this, there are extensions of the pastoral scapegoat ritual in many ways: Yakov is sacrificed for the Golov child, who supposedly was ritually murdered by the Jews; Bibikov is sacrificed for Yakov, who also becomes a "martyr" to the Russian Jews; and the prison guard Kogin dies for Yakov's freedom. Finally, juxtaposed to all these, is the figure of Christ, who serves throughout as a powerful archetype for the scapegoat figure. All these variations, as they should, serve to embroider the central theme by thrusting it into almost every aspect of man's life: Shmuel and Raisl, Yakov's wife, introduce themes of justice and law on the family and religious levels (Raisl, an anagram for Israel, is clearly identified with Judaism itself); Lebedev and Zinaida and Kogin and his son Trofim shift the interests to personal and economic relationships; Bibikov raises the central ideas to a philosophic and theoretical plane; and, finally, Nicholas the Second shifts the center of interests to practical politics, the concern that seems most vital to Yakov, and to Malamud, by the novel's conclusion.

Whereas the multiplying of the basic patterns is a device for variety and extension, the device by which Malamud gives his simple narratives a sense of unity and movement is the seasonal rhythm and variations of it. The baseball season of *The Natural*, for example, offers Malamud a handy seasonal rhythm and he uses it pretty carefully, the first section, "Pre-Game," taking place in spring and coinciding with spring-training, and the major portion, "Batter-Up," taking place mostly in summer (late spring is the period of the Knights' terrific slump) and early autumn. It is almost as if Roy Hobbs were only a sun god whose fate is decreed by the seasonal movement, for he bursts into stardom on June 21 (the last day of spring) and suffers his tragic fall *after* the official beginning of autumn on September 23, the day on which the Knights clinch a tie for the pennant, have their victory celebration, and Roy gorges himself until he becomes dreadfully ill, leaving himself vulnerable to Judge Banner's bribery. Consequently, it appears that Malamud has used the seasonal cycle for structuring a tragic narrative, [6] but, unfortunately, the tone of the novel is rather comic and one feels a lessening, rather than a heightening, of man's dignity because of Roy Hobbs's fall. Here, again, *The Assistant* seems to use the pastoral conventions more effectively, for, though the seasonal rhythm also controls the narrative, it does not obtrude or seem contrived as in *The Natural*. *The Assistant* opens on a windy day in early November and closes after April and Passover, showing along the way the moral and religious rebirth of Frank Alpine, the physical deterioration and death of Morris Bober (as the result of shoveling an unexpected April snow), and the spiritual death and revival of Helen Bober, Bober's daughter and, ultimately, Frank's lover. But here, instead of forcing all the changes into one short half-year, Malamud shows Frank replacing Bober in the first cycle from November to April and then allows Frank another year, from Morris' death to another April, to win back the affections of the daughter. Like *The Natural*, *A New Life* uses a single unit but the time allotted is slightly longer, for it follows the pattern of the academic year. It is divided into four major parts to coincide with the seasonal cycle as well as to the important aspects of the death and rebirth pastoral motif. The first section, summer, shows Levin arriving at Cascadia College (located in a truly pastoral setting), getting settled, and finally being told by Laverne, the moonlighting waitress, that he "ain't a man." The second section, fall, begins with the first day of the fall quarter and ends with Levin's recognition that Gerald Gilley (the "Fisher King") is his enemy; subsequently, in the third section, corresponding to winter, Levin begins, consummates, and ends (he thinks) his affair with Pauline Gilley; in the fourth section, opening with "May sunbursts" and corresponding to spring, Levin takes up his departmental causes, replaces Leo Duffy as the "political" liberal, gives Gilley a losing fight for the position of department head, but wins Pauline away, and leaves Cascadia with her, her two adopted children, and a child soon to be born, having found both a new life and a new identity.

Although Malamud pays careful attention to the rhythm of the seasons in *The Fixer,* he also uses it more freely and successfully assimilates it to a broader, though still pastoral, cycle. Because the central event of *The Fixer* lands Yakov Bok in prison, there is inevitably less *action* than in the other novels, the narrative interest focusing on Yakov's ability to withstand pain and torment and to maintain his innocence. But for this reason the sense of narrative *movement* depends even more on the fixer's noting the seasonal changes. Consequently, Malamud gives us frequent details to suggest seasonal change and he notes months and seasons carefully, Yakov's tale beginning in November when he leaves the Pale for Kiev, and going through the arrest and imprisonment in April, followed by a detailed account of the first year and foreshortened accounts of the second and third years, ending in autumn about the same time of year it had begun. More important than the seasonal rhythms, however, is the pattern of Biblical myth that the novel incorporates: the story coincides rather carefully with the period of Christ's ministry, since Yakov leaves his family and community at the age of thirty, "ministers" to his people for three years, and goes to his trial and possible death at the age of thirty-three. Obviously there is a great deal of irony in such a use of a "Christ-figure" by a Jewish novelist, but Malamud's point in using it is to insist upon the universality of the pattern, an implication admirably accounted for by the *pastoral,* rather than the simply Christian, aspects. Broadly pastoral or narrowly Christian, *The Fixer* insists as strongly as *The Assistant* upon the cyclicality of life, the necessity for endurance and hope, and the value of suffering as well as its needlessness. Yakov Bok's ministry, the heart of his teaching, is in fact the two and a half years in prison he maintained his innocence and became a hero and a "potential savior" of his people, a people including not only the Jews but all men who suffer without cause. Thus one feels strongly that Yakov will die, like Zhenia Golov, Bibikov, Kogin, and Christ, but one feels as well that his death will presage a better life for man.[7]

Because of the pastoral conventions in Malamud's novels, the vegetation cycles to which the human lives are attached, the most important source of imagery and symbolism for Malamud is the world of nature, its benevolent elements of fields and streams, groves and parks, birds and fish and flowers contrasted to its demonic wastes, sinisters forests, torturous mountains, and tomblike caves. Inescapably related to the cycles of the narratives, the kinds of imagery normally revolve from one pole to another in the novels, the final form being determined by the structure of the work. At least a parody of tragedy, *The Natural*, for example, opens in spring, in the American West, among virgin forests, then shifts to the probably too obvious "wasteland" of the Knights' ballpark. After Roy Hobbs's emergence as "hero," rain comes, the diamond regains its greenery, and the climate becomes more temperate. By the novel's end, however, there are many hints not only of autumn, which actually arrives, but also "thoughts of the barren winds of winter" (p. 176). Illustrating the same principle, but reversing the movement, *The Assistant* and *A New Life* have a comedic structure and thus their patterns of imagery conclude with details of spring and summer. In *The Assistant*, for example, Malamud finds an objective correlative for the attitudes of his characters in the mutations of weather, Morris Bober feeling buffeted by life as November's winds blow upon him, Helen feeling "tormented" by winter, but thinking of Frank Alpine when the rains come, and both Helen and Frank feeling life within them awakening when flowers begin to bloom and trees to bud in the spring. Similarly, in *A New Life* Levin's personal preoccupation with the world of nature in the West takes on an appropriate academic cast in his careful study of *Western Birds, Trees and Flowers,* a book perused in summer, laid away "all winter" (p. 195), and taken up again at a hint of spring. Pursuing the tragic implications of *The Natural,* as well as its interests in the "hero," *The Fixer* both opens and closes in a wasteland, wintry setting. And during Yakov's imprisonment, in order to show its importance to human life, nature imagery is brought in through Yakov's memory of and desire for it. We are told, for example, that Yakov "felt the change of weather in his head" (p. 229) and, later, that he imagined the "scent of spring" (p. 235).

Related to these patterns of natural imagery are the ways Malamud depicts characters and character relationships. The most satisfying sexual relationships are almost invariably at least begun in natural settings; Roy Hobbs, for example, makes love to Iris Lemon, who becomes pregnant, beside a grove on the beach of Lake Michigan, Frank Alpine first has Helen Bober in a city park, Levin makes love to Pauline the first time in the woods, and Yakov Bok, who goes often to the woods with Raisl, tells her, "You got me in the woods" (p. 285). As one might guess, principles of life and fertility in Malamud's novels are associated with women and, more specifically, with their mammalian traits; consequently, in them the female breast has unusual significance. Women associated with infertility and death, therefore, have "sick breasts," like Memo Paris (*The Natural*) and Avis Fliss (*A New Life*), or very small ones, like Helen, Pauline, and Raisl before they are revitalized by their lovers. Full breasted women like Iris Lemon and Zinaida Lebedev seem always to offer the promises of life.

For Malamud, the arcadian, as opposed to the naturalistic, aspects of nature represent a kind of ideal of beauty and peace and fulfillment. Consequently, all of his protagonists long for them when they are not present in their lives, often remembering pleasant natural scenes in their pasts or dreaming of them in their futures. In the midst of a hot pennant fight, Roy Hobbs yearns for a family life and "going fishing in a way that made it satisfying to fish" and "with this in mind he fished the stream in peace . . ." (p. 179). Frank Alpine and Helen Bober both dream of spring time in the midst of winter, and when they are together they often feel that the edge has been taken off the cold winds. Levin finds his real love in the idyll with Pauline in the woods, looks back to it, and forward to a similar state in the future. For Yakov Bok, bound in solitary confinement, a beam of sunlight showing momentarily on his cell wall is enough to recall to him thoughts of a better life; a brief trip from the cell to an interview with Grubeshov, the Prosecuting Attorney, and the sight of imitation flowers on a woman's hat reaffirm for him the existence of a less malevolent nature. He too dreams of his mating with his woman in the woods, and he prays to a sky that he seldom sees for deliverance.

Because of his idealization of benevolent nature, Malamud finds his dominant symbols in natural objects, the major symbols in the novels being unusually consistent with the symbolism of vegetation myths and Grail quests. For example, three symbols consistently used are birds, fish, and flowers. As in vegetation rituals, fish in the novels are associated with principles of fertility and life, so when Roy Hobbs dreams of fishing and eating the fish he reveals a concern that he has not devoted his life to the right pursuits, a failure to achieve all life has to offer that is symbolized later in his mad orgy of gluttony. In *The Assistant*, incorporating the symbolism of the emblematic names of *The Natural*, a devotion to life is represented by birds, rather than fish, Frank Alpine being associated with St. Francis and the innocent mating of pigeons with the love of Frank and Helen. More complex as symbols than in *The Natural*, birds are also linked, in *The Assistant*, to the flower symbolism: at the end of the novel, St. Francis, "with scrawny birds flying around over his head," plucked out of a garbage can a wooden rose that Frank had carved, "tossed it into the air and it turned into a real flower" that he caught and gave to Helen, suggesting, of course, that Frank's sterile lust has now become life-giving love. With more nature *imagery*, but fewer fully developed symbols, *A New Life* brings in the fish symbolism through Gilley, the avid fisherman, a dream Levin has of struggling with a fish and pulling its tail off, and Pauline's dropping tuna fish in Levin's lap. Bird symbolism, although rather negatively, also comes through name associations, the plagiarist, Albert O. Bird*less*, being an unusually uninspired, unidealistic student (apparently the bird as symbol also represents the ideal, for that

seems to be what Harriet Bird, of *The Natural,* represents). More
suggestions of such symbolism are Levin's being a bird watcher
and his carefully noting their return in spring. The bird symbolism of *The Fixer,* in keeping with the novel's dominant interests,
is associated with the double-headed eagle of the anti-Semitic
Black Hundreds and thus brings together in ironic juxtaposition
a symbol of fertility and socio-political revolution: "A black bird
flew out of the sky. Crow? Hawk? Or the black egg of a black eagle
falling towards the carriage?" (p. 326). Having seen and wondered
thus on his way through Black Hundreds mobs, Yakov shudders
in terror a few moments later when he sees a bomb like a "black
bird" seem to fly out of a "white hand clawing the air" (p. 329).
But it is also unironically associated with life and freedom: for
example, when finally freed to begin his trial, "through a window
[he] saw a bird in the sky and watched with emotion until he
could no longer see it" (p. 327). Although one must recognize that
Malamud's symbols in the novels are essentially pastoral, one must
also recognize that the novels' power comes not so much from the
sometimes obvious symbolism but from the total complex of pastoral conventions.

In some ways more important than the myth, the imagery, or
the symbolism is the convention of characterization that the pastoral affords Malamud. Empson has said, "the essential trick of the
old pastoral . . . was to make simple people express strong feelings
. . . in learned and fashionable language . . ." (p. 11). Rather
pedantically denigrated at times for being unrealistic, Malamud's
simple characters are germane to the pastoral's major strategy.
Thus in each novel Malamud has chosen as central characters people who are less worldly, more innocent, inexperienced, or naive
than most human beings. Roy Hobbs, for example, is tremendously unfamiliar with the sophistications of modern life, and
Malamud creates some cheap comedy at his expense in the novel's
opening section. Similarly, Frank Alpine, though he has seen the
world, gets into trouble because he is so naive about crime and
people, getting involved with Ward Minogue because he does not
recognize evil when he sees it and with Morris Bober because he
has such a simple idea of penance. Even Levin, the New York
M.A., is considered naive and by people who in New York City

would be only country bumpkins. And Yakov Bok, the simple "fixer," always insists that he is ignorant, uneducated, cowardly, a stranger "from the provinces," a "country boy." But these rustics, whether ballplayer, indigent, academic, or peasant, implement the pastoral's strategic contrast of simple and complex characters, of the *eironic* pastoralite and the *alazonic* cosmopolite. Thus Malamud, through this convention, achieves a great deal of irony, both comic and tragic. It is comic, for example, that the antagonists in *The Natural* take Roy Hobbs at face value, assuming that he is nothing more than "hayseed," only to discover that he is an adept "magician" who can play tricks on the gambler, Gus Sands, and an accomplished actor who can dupe the sportswriter, Max Mercy, with his portrayal of a dish-dropping waiter. And it is quite tragic that Yakov Bok should assume that one like Lebedev who quotes from the Sermon on the Mount should practice its principles or that he should believe he will be freed simply because his accusors can look into his face and see that he is not a child-murderer. But comic or tragic, irony is a major result of the contrast between the apparently naive protagonists and the obviously misguided antagonists, for there is always some kind of disparity between principle and action underlined by the protagonists' innocent assumptions.

In many ways, the most important result of the pastoral's convention of simple characters is the consequent simplification of style in the handling of rather complex materials. An aspect of pastoralism since Theocritus and Virgil, a simple style has immeasurable advantages to a novelist because it frees him to do other things, particularly to develop themes that could be handled only obtrusively in a complex, highly reflexive style, like, say, Faulkner's at times. In Malamud, style is primarily a function of character, and not only in dialogue, because the author's point of view almost always is assimilated into that of the characters. Because of the simplicity of the characters the style necessarily is relatively elemental in syntax, diction, imagery, and symbol, and yet Malamud's language *is* fashionable and learned—an astonishing feat, perhaps, but still his most distinctive stylistic achievement. He can do this in the novels because the general concerns of pastoral art happen to be the concerns of modern literature and

criticism. In *The Natural*, for example, he treats the same materials as Eliot in *The Waste Land*, but he does it in the combined idioms of baseball journalism and the Grail romance. The
idea of "the hero" is a major theme here and in *The Fixer*, but
Malamud could have found no less complex way of underlining
it than to have Iris Lemon tell Roy, "I hate to see a hero fail.
There are so few of them. . . . Without heroes we're all plain people and don't know how far we can go." Roy paraphrases even
more simply: "You mean the big guys set the records and the
little buggers try and bust them?" and Iris answers, "Yes, it's
their function to be the best and for the rest of us to understand
what they represent and guide ourselves accordingly" (p. 154).
Established on a sports pages level—"There are so many young
boys you influence."—the theme, as witnessed in John F. Ken-
nedy, has undeniable connection to modern intellectual and emotional concerns. *The Assistant*, like so many modern novels,
probes the question of identity, but so much more directly, Frank
Alpine saying to Bober, "I don't understand myself" (p. 33). It is
also concerned with death and rebirth, and, though at the time
she has little direct evidence, Helen Bober can say, "Life renews
itself" (p. 81), stating unaffectedly the basic truth of the novel's
pastoral vegetation archetype. It is concerned, moreover, with the
problem of "the Law," ostensibly only Jewish Law, though it has
manifold implications, and Morris Bober distills a people's infinite
wisdom to, "I suffer for you. . . . you suffer for me" (pp. 99-100).
And the *theme* of suffering, which may be compared to treat-
ments by Faulkner or Hemingway, is summarized in Bober's
funeral eulogy by Malamud's simple rabbi: "He suffered, he
endu-red, but with hope" (p. 180). In *A New Life*, that most un-
academic of academic novels, even Levin, a New York University
Master of Arts, comes to express rather graphically the reason for
the most important decision of his life, to marry Pauline and
father her children. Answering the sterile Gerald Gilley, he says
only, "because I can, you son of a bitch" (p. 360).

Employing devices used occasionally in the other novels, *The
Fixer* exploits the pastoral's stylistic simplicity in many ways.
Seen through Yakov's consciousness, the story, except for the flash-
back after the opening chapter, is straightforwardly narrated, the

dialogue is uncomplex, and the language is concrete, and in *The Fixer*, as in *The Assistant*, the contrast between the manifest content and the symbolic content is enormous. Himself also an *alazon* like his oppressors, though Malamud uses him as an *eiron*, Yakov continually brings our attention to the ironies of man's existence by uttering a few simple words:

> I am in history, . . . yet not in it. In a way of speaking I'm far out, it passes me by. Is this good, or something lacking in my character? What a question! Of course lacking but what can I do about it? And besides is this really such a great worry? Best to stay where one is, unless he has something to give to history, like for instance Spinoza . . . (p. 60).

But, of course, we see, as he himself finally does, that Yakov did not stay where he was and thus discovered that what he has to give to history—himself—we all have to give. Through his attempt to understand Spinoza, moreover, Yakov Bok encounters another problem that "fashionable and learned" journals (*Life* and *Time*, et al) take up, though probably not even *Time* solves it so succinctly: "If there was a God, after reading Spinoza he had closed up his shop and become an idea" (p. 60). Also through Spinoza, Yakov Bok is forced to grapple with what finally becomes the novel's major theme, the relationship of politics to freedom. Implied in Yakov's continual protests that he is "not a political man," this theme is expressed most simply in Bibikov's question, "cannot one be free without being politically free?" (p. 77), the answer to which is given by Yakov himself near the novel's end: "One thing I've learned, he thought, there's no such thing as an unpolitical man, especially a Jew. . . . Afterwards he thought, where there's no fight for it there's no freedom. What is it Spinoza says? If the state acts in ways that are abhorrent to human nature it's the lesser evil to destroy it. Death to the anti-Semites! Long live revolutions! Long live liberty!" (p. 335).

Imbedded in the phrase, "Death to the anti-Semites!" is the real heart of Malamud's versions of pastoral. Departing from Leslie Fiedler, who sees "Zion as Mainstreet" and "The Jew as

Mythical American," Malamud envisions the Jew as mythical man, having said "All men are Jews" and using the Jew, at least in the last three novels, as the pastoral "swain," emblem of a realizable humanity. In Malamud, therefore, to be anti-Semitic is to be against the human being. And we are consequently forced to see that the people and the settings of Malamud's novels stand to the "real" world in the same way as those of all pastoral writers from, say, Virgil to Robert Frost. Each novel, in an important way, treats a microcosmic view of the macrocosm, and each theme may then be extrapolated to a universal level. Concretely embodied in the relationship of son to father, the universal theme for Malamud is man's relationship to the "Law," and the treatment of the theme of the Law gains in breadth and depth and sophistication from the first novels to the last one. In *The Natural*, the Law is primitive, is simply chance and fate, symbolized by Gus Sands, the "Supreme Bookie"; in *The Assistant* it is Old Testament Jewish Law, or the "spirit" of it represented by Morris Bober; and in *A New Life* it is liberal and humanistic, and is represented by Levin's "Laws": "Levin's Law II: One becomes his victim's victim. III. Stand for something and somebody around will feel persecuted" (p. 308). But in *The Fixer*, it is all these and many more, for the Law is Christian, " 'But it is easier for heaven and earth to pass away, than for one dot of the law to become void' " (p. 234). It is judaic, "Don't look for God in the wrong place, look in the Torah, the law" (p. 258), Shmuel tells Yakov. It is legalistic, "As for the law it was invented by man," Yakov replies to Shmuel. And it is humanistic, "The law lives in the minds of men," Ostrovsky, Yakov's lawyer says; "If a judge is honest the law is protected" (p. 311). But most of all, as Shmuel tells Yakov, the Law is God, and even if God has been reduced to an idea, in the Idea, God exists and therefore embraces every facet of existence, whether personal, social, religious or historical.[8]

In *The Fixer*, the universality of Yakov's role and the effectiveness of his suffering is shown in the influence he has on other men—and these are willing to die for him: Bibikov, a socialist, Kogin, a Catholic, and Shmuel, a Jew. And it is for these, "and for a lot more that I won't even mention" (p. 334), that Yakov is himself prepared to die by novel's end. More tragic in vision than any of the first three novels, *The Fixer* is also more affirmative and more convincing in its affirmation, for there is a sense at the novel's conclusion that at last someone has come who may revitalize the law and lead a demoralized people out of a political wilderness. Consequently, *The Fixer*, though much more, is Malamud's finest expression of pastoral, and one suspects the fact that Yakov (Jacob) is named both *Bok* (German *Bock*—goat) and *Shepsovitch* (apparently intended to mean "son of sheep") is more than accidentally appropriate to the novel's major strategy.

Notes

1. William Empson, *Some Versions of Pastoral* (Norfolk, Conn.: New Directions, n.d.), p. 11. For my assumptions and remarks about the pastoral mode, I have also drawn upon Jessie Weston, *From Ritual to Romance* (Garden City, N.Y.: Doubleday, 1957), Northrop Frye, *Anatomy of Criticism* (Princeton, N. J., 1957), Joseph Campbell, *The Hero with a Thousand Faces* (New York: Meridian Books, 1956), and Leo Marx, *The Machine in the Garden* (New York: Galaxy Books, 1967). Note one to chapter one of Marx's book gives an excellent selective bibliography on pastoralism.

2. Marcus Klein, *After Alienation: American Novels in Mid-Century* (Cleveland, Ohio: Meridian Books, 1965), pp. 247-93, esp. 261; Philip Roth, "Writing American Fiction," *Commentary*, XXIII (March, 1961), 228-29. (For Klein's essay see Chapter 17 in this collection.)

3. See *From Ritual to Romance* for a discussion of these materials. For discussions of the mythic elements in *The Natural*, see Norman Podhoretz, "Achilles in Left Field," *Commentary*, XV (March, 1953), 321-26; Jonathan Baumbach, *The Landscape of Nightmare: Studies in the Contemporary American Novel* (New York, 1965); and Sidney Richman, *Bernard Malamud* (New Haven, Conn., 1966). Earl Wasserman, in *"The Natural*: Malamud's World Ceres," *Centennial Review of Arts and Science*, IX (Fall, 1965), 438-60, also makes clear connections between the mythic and the pastoral archetypes in Malamud's first novel: ". . . what Malamud has written is a novel that coherently organizes the rites of baseball and many of its memorable historic episodes into the epic inherent in baseball as a measure of man, as it once was inherent in Homeric battles or chivalric tournaments or the Arthurian quest for the Grail . . . . Malamud's syncretism of baseball and the Arthurian legend therefore invites a further consideration of the novel in these terms: the psychological, moral, and communal needs of the baseball

champion—the American hero—to gain access to the 'sources of Life.'
. . . It is the infantilism of the American hero that Malamud is concerned with, the psychic and therefore moral regression of the gifted
'natural' who would vitalize society and reveal to it the capacities of
human strength; the selfish attachment to the 'terrible mother' that
introverts and blocks the psychic energy that could flow outwardly from
the mature hero and restore the Waste Land" (439, 441, 446). (See
Chapter 4 in this collection.)

4. Through the device of the nearly mortal wound, Malamud achieves a
    considerable foreshortening of the novel's action, for it allows him both
    to strengthen Roy's desire for greatness and to eliminate what would
    have been about fifteen years of the "king's" reign, but it does this
    without eliminating the *height* of that reign, the height necessary for
    simulating a tragic fall, of course.

5. *The Fixer* (New York: Farrar, Straus, and Giroux, 1966), p. 333. Further
    citations from this novel) as well as the other three, will be given
    parenthetically in the body of the article. Texts of the remaining novels
    are: *The Natural* (New York: Noonday, 1966), *The Assistant* (New
    York: Signet, n.d.), and *A New Life* (New York: Farrar, Straus and
    Cudahy, 1961).

6. See *Anatomy of Criticism* for a discussion of "The Mythos of Autumn:
    Tragedy," pp. 206-23.

7. Malamud pretty obviously hopes his readers will see Yakov's story within
    the context of the impending Bolshevik revolution, but he also hopes
    that we will place it within the context of other historical events, having
    said of Yakov: "To his trials in prison I added something of Dreyfus'
    and Vanzetti's, shaping the whole to suggest the quality of the afflictions
    of the Jews under Hitler." The plot itself is broadly based upon the
    case of Mendel Beiliss, treated exhaustively in Maurice Samuel's *Blood
    Accusation: The Strange History of the Beiliss Case* (New York:
    Knopf, 1966). The "facts" of Malamud's plot are rather close to those of
    the Beiliss case, but details of characterization are mostly Malamud's.
    Of the parallel, Malamud says: "Beiliss, when arrested for killing a boy
    and hiding his body in a cave, was a man of thirty-nine. For almost
    two and a half years he was kept in prison without an indictment. He
    suffered greatly but was finally brought to trial and acquitted. In *The
    Fixer* I use some of his experiences, though not, basically, the man, partly
    because his life came to less than he had paid for by his suffering and
    endurance, and because I had to have room to invent." Beiliss was
    actually acquitted of the crimes, though it was ruled by the jury, upon
    instruction from the bench, that a ritual murder had been committed,
    but Malamud does not specify what Yakov Bok's fate is to be. The main
    difference one might find between the historical and the imaginative
    treatments is the sense of incredibility, found in Samuel's book, that
    such a conspiracy against a man and a people could be attempted and
    the sense of man's innate heroism and dignity found in Malamud's.
    Of Bok, Malamud says: "Yakov had a lot to learn and maybe he learned
    it. His experiences in prison lead to a change in him that is the drama
    of the book."

8. I am assuming, of course, that Malamud shares with Yakov his admiration for Spinoza's rather idealistic pantheism, while, at the same time, neither author nor character seems to care for its impersonality. Yakov's remark, "A force is not a father" (p. 257), thus suggests the need for a law more personal than mere "Necessity," the consequent identification of the law with God, and the further identification of the search for a father with the search for both law and God.

Edwin M. Eigner

6.

The Loathly Ladies

In a penetrating article on *The Natural*,[1] Earl Wasserman has documented the profundity and complexity of Malamud's use of mythic theme and subject matter. Elements of medieval romance in Malamud's first novel had, of course, long been noted; what Wasserman shows is that such material is not, as an earlier critic had concluded, "somewhat gratuitous, a semi-private literary joke between author and academic reader," merely "a witty idea."[2] Rather he explains how it is related to a central concern over "the infantilism of the American hero . . . the psychic and therefore moral regression of the gifted 'natural' who could [but does not] vitalize society and reveal to it the capacities of human strength" (p. 446). Wasserman's arguments are compelling, and while I cannot follow him through each of the Jungian implications he suggests, I should like to explore and finally to support his concluding statement that *"The Natural* is the broad formulation of Malamud's world of meaning . . . the necessary reference text for a reading of his subsequent fiction" (p. 460). *

On a simple level the claim may be substantiated at once; for

---

* See Chapter 4 in this collection.

the cast of characters from the Percival myth are identifiable throughout Malamud's works. After Iris Lemon's nude swim in *The Natural,* Ladies of the Lake appear everywhere. In *A New Life,* Pauline Gilley bathes naked, and a coed writes a personal experience paper about lake-swimming in the nude. In "A Choice of Profession," another coed undresses and swims before the impure eyes of her English instructor. Where a metropolitan setting makes open-air nudity unlikely, the women take shower baths while the heroes peer through the keyhole ("Naked Nude") or through the bathroom window (*The Assistant*). In *The Fixer,* Yakov Bok watches a naked woman as she sponges herself from a bowl. Turning to another archetypal figure, Pop Fisher, the drought-cursed Fisher-King of *The Natural,* is repeated in Morris Bober of *The Assistant,* Salzman of "The Magic Barrel," Shmuel of *The Fixer,* and in Fairchild, the son-seeking Department Chairman of *A New Life.* And as for the central characters, all are drawn after the model of Roy Hobbs, rainmaking outfielder of the New York Knights; and each hero has the potential to redeem himself, the maiden, the king, and, of course, the society. Indeed, one of the heroes, Levin of *A New Life,* sees himself as a knight errant "in his trusty Hudson, his lance at his side, driving through a series of amorous and philanthropic adventures." [3] Just as Hobbs dreams of ending the drought by bringing a pennant to New York, so Levin dedicates himself to restoring a cultural life in Cascadia, to making Eastchester "flower" (p. 315).

Moreover, the pattern of thematically significant action is basically the same throughout Malamud's major fiction. Each of the four novels concerns a not-quite young man, an "aged rookie" like Hobbs, deeply ashamed of his orphaned youth and of his first humiliating failure in life. To escape shame, the man sets out on a long journey, usually across the American continent, carrying with him a plan for a new life of freedom. Hobbs revives the baseball dream; he "will be the champ and have what goes with it" (p. 121). Frank Alpine of *The Assistant* and S. Levin of *A New Life,* two derelicts, awaken in somebody's filthy cellar, each with an inspiration. Frank's "terrific idea" is "that he was meant for crime," that "at crime he would change his

luck, make adventure, live like a prince" (pp. 91-92). Therefore
he buys a gun and heads east from San Francisco to New York.
Levin has a vision which leads him to become "a man of principle." He feels "a new identity" and discovers "that the source
of freedom is the human spirit" (pp. 201-202). Therefore he
picks up a Master's at New York University, lands an instructor-
ship at a college in the Pacific northwest, and sets out across the
country with a newly-grown academic beard. Yakov Bok, a ghetto
Jew, after the shame of six years in a childless, impoverished
marriage, culminated by the humiliating desertion of his unfaithful wife, cuts off his Jewish beard and begins a journey which is
symbolically even longer than those of the other heroes. Bok
means to satisfy wants "that can't sleep and keep me awake for
company":

> a full stomach now and then. A job that pays rubles,
> not noodles. Even some education if I can get it . . . .
> What I want to know is what's going on in the world . . . .
> All I've had in this miserable town is a beggarly existence.
> Now I'll try Kiev. If I can live there decently that's
> what I'll do. If not, I'll make sacrifices, save up, and
> head for Amsterdam for a boat to America. To sum it
> up, I have little but I have plans. (pp. 12-13)

Thus the starting points of the four novels are almost identical.
The subsequent action is also remarkably similar, for as each of
the questers is forced to come to terms with a Lady of the Lake,
his new plan for freedom must be abandoned.

In the first two novels it is easy to see why the plans have to
fail: Hobbs' desire to be the champ and Alpine's dream of becoming a crime lord are unworthy schemes, clearly indicative of
what Wasserman called the heroes' "infantilism." The way in
which the heroine exposes this shallowness is perhaps best demonstrated in an early story, appropriately entitled "The Lady of
the Lake." Here is the tale of an American Jew, once more with
the name Levin,[4] who crosses the Atlantic to find a new life. "For
no reason he was sure of, except that he was tired of the past—
tired of the limitations it had imposed on him . . . [he has taken]

to calling himself Henry R. Freeman" (*The Magic Barrel,* p. 105). In Italy, on a lake-island, he falls in love with beautiful Isabella del Dongo,[5] whom he mistakes for an aristocrat, a fit woman to share his scarcely defined new life of freedom. Therefore, he hides his shameful Jewish identity from her.

Throughout the story, Levin childishly angles for a view of Isabella's breasts. He misses one opportunity when she swims naked in the lake. But later, when she finally undresses for him, it is only to display a bluish line of distorted numbers which the Nazis had tattooed on her chest when she was a Jewish prisoner at Buchenwald. "I can't marry you," Isabella tells the astonished Levin. "My past is meaningful to me. I treasure what I suffered for" (p. 132). And even now, while Isabella disappears from him, as though magically into the lake, Levin stutters and is unable to claim his future or his past.

The interest which Levin takes in Isabella's breasts is typical of Malamud's heroes, who always characterize their women by the size, shape, quality, even by the health of their breasts. From *The Natural* through *The Fixer,* Malamud's power of invention in this particular is remarkable: besides breasts that are described as sick, well stacked, hard, neat, little, and full, there are also breasts that pierce and breasts that beat like hearts; some are like flowers or like small birds; there are even green breasts. Moreover, when at the conclusion of *A New Life* the heroine changes her role in relation to the hero, the nature of her breasts begins also to change.

But this emphasis does more than characterize the woman; it is also in keeping with her identity as Lady of the Lake, who besides being a teacher of knights, is a protector and nurse of orphans. As we have noted, all of Malamud's questing heroes are motherless. Of course we have also seen in "The Lady of the Lake" that breasts can be ambiguous symbols. In spite of his infantilism (like the infantilism Wasserman notes in Roy Hobbs) Levin is not only interested in Isabella's breasts as emblems of her potential motherhood to him. He thinks of them as belonging to the life of sensual beauty and erotic freedom which, with his new identity as Freeman, he is seeking in Italy. And, despite the message for Levin which the Nazis have written on them, Isa-

[handwritten margin note:] It is obvious that if the world of values, it is nevertheless saturated with pain, flooded with contradictions. 9 — The Assistant

"high-arched" (p. 112) in the

has attempted to guide her
have led him to accept and
she and her breasts are also
/in, Isabella has taken a false
/e that she owns the Palazzo
:etaker. Moreover, she tempts
dy. In fact, she presents two
n two lives; and in the end,
, she judges him.
: sources of this material in
iote that the gentle and help-
of the forms assumed by the
:r of her identities is that of
'ivian.[6] In the first aspect the
and heals him when he is
:ms bent on luring him to his
i the seductress is not cruel,
i simply a test which he must
ito her ardently desired lover.
All her actions, in both forms, are attempts to prepare him for
her love and for his manhood.[7]

Still another variant of the same supernatural woman—the
one which Malamud finds most meaningful—is the Loathly Lady
of Chaucer, Gower, and many anonymous writers from Iceland,
Scotland, and Ireland. The Loathly Lady appears sometimes as
a lovely, young, well-born girl, and at other times as an ugly,
impoverished old hag, *negatively* tempting the knight, who must
love her apparent ugliness to win her real beauty and, as in the
Irish tale of the five sons of Eochaid, to become the king.

Isabella del Dongo (or whatever her real name is) tests shallow
Levin-Freeman with the sight of her desecrated breasts, and,
stuttering, he fails. Similarly, Roy Hobbs of *The Natural* cannot accept the apparent loathliness of his nature goddess, Iris
Lemon, whose very name suggests her identities. Before meeting
Iris, Roy had encountered two seductresses and had "flunked"
the "test" (p. 34), both by his sexual responses and by the inade-

quate answers he gave to their significant questions about what he hoped to accomplish (p. 33) and where he meant to get (p. 121). Each woman tried to kill him. With Iris, however, Roy has a better chance. She is a kinder Lady of the Lake with a greater faith in her hero, and she tries to instruct him not by sphinx-like questions but by carefully explained maxims. Moreover, he has twice dreamed of Iris, and when he sees her naked body from under the lake water, a "pair of golden arms searching, and a golden head . . . golden breasts . . . the hair between her legs was golden too" (p. 161)—he recognizes his dream, a hopeful sign.

But when Iris administers the test of the Loathly Lady, Roy fails as badly as he had with the two questioning seductresses. For though she gives herself sexually to Roy instead of attempting his life, and while her breasts, besides being golden, are hard, shapely, and neat, whereas the other women had both been sick-breasted, Iris has had a shameful past. She has given birth to an illegitimate child, a daughter; and the child, now grown and married, has recently herself become a mother. "What for the love of mud," he reflects, "had made her take him for a sucker who would be interested in a grandmother?" (p. 165). He retreats into the shallow baseball dream, deciding that grandmothers do not go with being the champ, and the rest of his progress is all downhill. Now he takes a bribe to throw the playoff game, breaks his magical bat, strikes out, and departs from the novel an unshaven bum. A woman remarks, "He coulda been a king" (p. 237).

"When her kid's kid came to mind, despite grandma's age of only thirty-three, that was asking too much and spoiled the appetizing part of her" (p. 165). Thus Roy Hobbs rationalizes his rejection of Iris, and the word "appetizing" provides part of the key to his failure. Appetite, as a reflection of Roy's too earthly goals in life, characterizes all the sex relations in the novel. Roy's first desire for a woman had ended in a bullet wound, a terrible pain in the stomach. Later when he flees Iris, he turns to literal gourmandizing and to a neurotic temptress, who, "like all the food he had lately been eating . . . left him, after the having of it, unsatisfied, sometimes even with a greater hunger than before" (p. 166). Instead of love, she serves him a gigantic banquet, and he very nearly dies of the resulting stomach ache. Iris's first lover had "pounced like a tiger" (p. 150), and so, in effect, does Roy, using Iris to feed his lust, leaving her beaten and once again pregnant, leaving himself unredeemed.

Love as appetite figures again in Malamud's second novel, *The Assistant,* where Helen Bober, a grocer's daughter, is an attractive morsel for a number of sex-hungry men. Frank Alpine first hears of her from his accomplice in crime, Ward Minogue, a man with a stomach condition, who tells him that "those Jew girls make nice ripe lays" (p. 74). Frank is quick to adopt this gustatory view of Helen. As he watches her naked through the bathroom window, "he felt greedy as he gazed, all eyes at a banquet, hungry so long as he must look" (p. 75).

Here again the metaphor is a comment on the shallow new life which the hero has chosen for himself, for Frank's life in crime and his sexual pursuit of Helen are always seen together. In the last section of the novel, which narrates Frank's ultimate reformation, a single paragraph tells us that he gave up short-changing his customers and stopped climbing up the air shaft to peek at Helen. But before this reformation can take place Frank's criminal career and his hunger for the aptly named Helen culminate as we might have expected—he makes a "starved leap" and rapes her (p. 239). Afterwards he realizes that he cannot find freedom with the new life he had planned, that he cannot get away from the "garbage," the spoiled food, which he smells in his bed. "He couldn't because he was it—the stink in his own broken nose. What you did," he concludes, "was how bad you smelled" (p. 174).

In keeping with her role as Fairy Queen, Helen Bober unknowingly helps Frank to this crucial insight. She judges him immediately after the rape, calling him "Dog—uncircumcised dog!" (p. 168), an epithet of increasing significance in Malamud's more recent novels. But the reader does not need Helen's judgment, for as we began by saying, it is easy to see why the unworthy, immature dreams of Roy and Frank must fail. With *A New Life* and *The Fixer,* however, the case is more difficult to make out. Malamud seems to share S. Levin's new found commitment to democracy, liberalism, and human spirit. So, one would guess, do

a majority of his readers. Yakov Bok's dream of "good fortune, accomplishment, affluence . . . a comfortable home, good business—
maybe a small factory of some kind—a faithful wife, dark-haired,
pretty, and three healthy children, God bless them" (p. 24) is, after
all, the dream of our immigrant forebears, from 1607 on. Moreover, Bok's interest in Spinoza gives his plan solid philosophical
credentials. Yet the appealing programs of S. Levin and Yakov
Bok, like the infantile schemes of the earlier heroes, do not succeed, for they are doomed again by the interference of a Loathly
Lady.

Malamud's two most recent novels are seriously political—
The Fixer, of course, profoundly so—but though the credos of
S. Levin are self-consciously undercut by his habit of pronouncing
them with his fly open (once before a class and again before a
urinal), there is little question of their basic seriousness. The
novel insists that democracy is in danger because it is defended
only "by cripples who crippled it" (p. 229), the impotent Gerald
Gilley, the sex-frightened C.D. Fabricant, and their superior,
President Marion Labhart, who believes "that Plato, Shelley, and
Emerson have done more harm than good to society" (p. 288).
When Levin claims that "democracy is a moral philosophy and
can't be defended by lopping off its head," i.e. the humanities, his
words carry conviction. Moreover, his modest belief that "it takes
only one good man to make the world a little better" (p. 275) is
easy enough to accept. Surely, though some administrators may
demur, the English Department at Cascadia College and democracy in America would be in a more hopeful state if Levin were
chairman instead of Gilley, or Gilley's predecessor, Fairchild, who
says that "the first duty of a good leader is to carry out orders"
(p. 53). There is, therefore, reason to mourn when Levin's plan
of a new life must be abandoned.

The terms of the freedom which S. Levin seeks in the liberal
arts are given explicitly: he wants "order, value, accomplishment,
love" (p. 189). At Cascadia College he finds plenty of order, what
with all the regulations, the eight o'clock classes, the departmental
objective examinations, and the mandatory syllabus for freshman
composition. Value and accomplishment, however, are much
harder to come by, or rather, to keep, for though he has brought

plenty of ideals with him, at Cascadia he is almost ashamed to own them. And his sense of accomplishment is blunted when he sometimes feels that he is "engaged in a great irrelevancy, teaching composition, not teaching how to keep civilization from destroying itself" (p. 115). Love, which he has significantly placed last on his list, offers itself continually, but, though, like the other heroes, he always *hungers* after sex, he spends most of the novel running away from it.

Levin's humanism derives from Greece, and it is well mixed with pastoral poetry of nymphs and shepherds and of exhilarating sexual license. Yet Levin rejects a number of bucolic sexual experiences: once with the waitress Laverne in her brother-in-law's barn—her breasts smell like hay—twice with his colleague Avis Fliss, who spreads a football blanket for him. At length the appetite becomes so demanding that in a cabin overlooking the Pacific he succumbs to one of his students—"her gloriously young body shed light as he hungrily embraced it" (p. 151)—but he quickly ends the affair. But these refusals are not tokens of moral maturity. In each case, Levin refuses the woman simply because he is afraid of losing his job. He does not perceive, as Frank Alpine had, that sex as mere appetite is unworthy of a man of principle; he abstains because love, like everything else pertaining to the human spirit, has been forbidden in Cascadia.

As a culmination to this nature-sex motif, Pauline Gilley makes a free gift of herself to Levin, no strings attached, in a Cascadian pine forest. "He was throughout conscious of the marvel of it—in the open forest, nothing less, what triumph!" (p. 199). Aftewards "he silently celebrated his performance in the open—his first married woman, sex uncomplicated in a bed of leaves, short hours, good pay" (p. 204). Moreover, when Pauline has heard his plans for a new life, she approves, vowing never to interfere with them.

As things turn out, Pauline cannot keep her promise, and the results of the affair which develops are more serious than even the always apprehensive Levin had imagined; he not only loses his job as Cascadia, he must swear never to teach at any college. "Goodbye to your sweet dreams" (p. 360), Pauline's husband calls after him derisively. Instead of the dreams, he gets the love—the ideal he had least regarded—of a woman who promises him none of the other virtues he had sought. He wanted value, but Pauline is more lost than he is. He hoped for accomplishment, but he seems little likely to find it with a wife who is periodically discontented because she realizes, with her advancing age, that she has done nothing with her own life. He had found order, but can he keep it with Pauline, who is irregular in her housekeeping, her health, her sexual desires, even in her bowels?

Levin says that love goes with freedom in his book, but obviously not in Malamud's. Why this should be the case is not easy to answer. Frank Kermode believes that the point of the novel is the fact of life Malamud hates most, "that Nature [Pauline Gilley] does betray the heart that loves her." [8] Most readers disagree, sensing a triumph for Levin in the last pages, albeit "a success," as Theodore Solotaroff * writes, "that is qualified to the bone." [9] Solotaroff, however, offers us no solution; he finds the novel "finally inscrutable." [10] It used to be possible to argue that Pauline redeems Levin from his unsavory practices in departmental politics (he invades the privacy of his opponents, photostats a personal letter, even uses blackmail, all in the cause of the human spirit), but *The Fixer* seems to contradict such an interpretation. There, in a dream vision, Bok murders the Tsar in spite of a wild "no, no, no, no" from the ghost of Bibikov, the passionate, due-process magistrate, perhaps the most sympathetic character in the novel. And the hero's comment on his imagined assassination—"Better him than us"—would seem to indicate that Malamud is not trapped in his liberalism, that for him ends do sometimes justify means. No, both of Levin's choices are of tremendous value, his love for Pauline *and* his plans for a new life of freedom; and we are still left with the task of explaining why Malamud should have presented them as mutually exclusive.

For a possible answer, let us return again to the earlier novels, this time not to note how Levin's plans differ from Roy's and Frank's, but to restate what they have in common, the fact that all the questers are trying to escape from the shame of their pasts. Perhaps Malamud is saying that a man ought not to seek such free-

* See Chapter 16 in this collection.

dom, and that what is really wrong with the new lives is not their objective unworthiness, as we have been supposing heretofore, but simply their irrelevancy.

Once again *The Natural* is our "necessary reference text," for this is precisely the point of the lesson which Iris Lemon tries to teach Roy Hobbs. "Experience makes good people better," she tells Roy, "through their suffering . . . . We have two lives, Roy, the life we learn with and the life we live with after that. Suffering is what brings us towards happiness" (p. 158). But Roy feels he has had enough of shameful suffering, and what really renders Iris loathly to him is that she, an unwed mother who has been associated with suffering, does not wish to bury her past but insists on bringing the memory of her shame into her present life and into Roy's. Thus when she asks him questions about his own past, he refuses to answer. And thus at the end of the novel, Roy is left struggling with "overwhelming self-hatred. In each stinking wave of it he remembered some disgusting happening of his life. He thought, I never did learn anything out of my past life, now I have to suffer again" (p. 236).

Frank Alpine, when we last spoke of him, was in a situation similar to Roy's final predicament; he too was caught in an overpowering smell from the refuse of the life in crime he had intended to live. But Frank had come East bearing the seeds of another, more mature inspiration, a concept of a new life born not in reaction to the shameful orphanage of his youth but actually fostered there by an old priest who told him stories of St. Francis. It is particularly interesting that Malamud should have perceived in this saint's legend an analogue to the Loathly Lady myth. Frank admires St. Francis because "he took a fresh view of things," he "said poverty was a queen and he loved her like she was a beautiful woman" (p. 31). Frank comes from San Francisco, and when he reads about his patron, he has to fight to keep from crying.

In the action of *The Assistant*, this fresh view is translated into the second and superficially less attractive aspect of Helen Bober, in which she appears as St. Francis's Lady Poverty. Previously we saw her as a ripe morsel, designed to satisfy an appetite, but in her other guise there is "something starved about

her, a hunger in her eyes" (p. 61). Frank's first perception of
Helen's naked body, before he is overwhelmed by greed, is presented in terms of Franciscan symbols, "the breasts like small
birds in flight, her ass like a flower" (p. 75). She is "in her way a
lone bird" (p. 63), and after the rape she looks to him "like last
year's flower" (p. 179).

As Mistress Poverty, Helen is haughty and bitter. When she
plays this role, Malamud phrases her speech in the rhythms of
her mother, a discontented, bigoted, and unforgiving woman.
Moreover, her own attitude towards her father's poverty makes
it clear that she will never respect Frank once he has completed
his new project of taking the saintlike Morris Bober's place. "Who
can admire a man passing his life in such a store?" she says of her
dead father. "He buried himself in it; he didn't have the imagination to know what he was missing. He made himself a victim. He
could, with a little more courage, have been more than he was"
(p. 230). Earlier, when Frank demonstrated imagination and courage to her, she had condemned him as an "uncircumcised dog";
she had also taught Frank to prefer Dostoevsky's Prince Myshkin
over Napoleon; but now, as Frank tries to imitate the selfless love
and suffering of Myshkin, St. Francis, and her father, she tells
him contemptuously, "you remind me of everything I want to
forget" (p. 234).

This feeling, of course, is more than mutual, for Frank, we
recall, had come East precisely to forget suffering and poverty.
Nevertheless, he cannot withhold his "tender pity," a pity "mixed
with shame for having made her pitiable" (p. 184); and to get the
stink of garbage out of his broken nose, he carves presents for her,
Franciscan birds and flowers, which she significantly throws into
the garbage pail.

Earlier in the novel Frank had asked, "Who could be a hero
in a grocery store?" (p. 93). Two answers are suggested. Frank
began his life in crime by robbing a grocery, and while *The
Assistant* has rejected this kind of heroism, it has surely maintained that Morris Bober, the suffering Jewish grocer, is a more
legitimate hero. Frank, if he keeps St. Francis in mind, can become a hero of the same kind. Moreover, as Frank's final vision of
St. Francis indicates, the saint was a lover as well:

He saw St. Francis come dancing out of the woods in his brown rags, a couple of scrawny birds flying around his head. St. F. stopped in front of the grocery, and reaching into the garbage can, plucked the wooden rose out of it. He tossed it into the air and it turned into a real flower that he caught in his hand. With a bow he gave it to Helen . . . . "Little sister, here is your little sister the rose." From him she took it, although it was with the love and best wishes of Frank Alpine. (pp. 245-246)

In the next paragraph, which is the last of the novel, Frank has himself circumcised, receiving the stigmata,[11] and he becomes a Jew, thus wedding himself irrevocably to suffering, which has been seen throughout as the sole if not the exclusive property of Bober. He hopes, moreover, to marry discontented, suffering Helen, and it is right that he should. For though he comes from the opposite end of the country and is originally of a different religion, poor Helen is not only Frank's most valuable heritage, she is his most legitimate.

In a grocery store world, it appears, one can choose to be a dog or a saint, a "holdupnic" and a rapist, or a holy fool. Malamud, by his use of the Loathly Lady *motif* has effectively removed the middle possibilities. In the world of *A New Life,* the same discontented and hard-to-live-with lady has put the hero on a similar spot: he can either be an English professor or a father. And the choice, as in the earlier novels, is not so much a question of objective value but of relevancy to the hero's past suffering.

S. Levin writes in his notebook, "The new life hangs on an old soul" (p. 58). And when he arrives at Cascadia College a new academic beard hangs from and hides his suffering face. He grew the beard, as he admits, "in a time of doubt . . . when I couldn't look myself in the face" (p. 188). Each of the three women who precede Pauline urges him to remove the beard. Reluctantly he trims off half-an-inch for one of them. For Pauline, to guard her reputation by making himself less conspicuous, he finally cuts it off altogether; and though Pauline mourns the beard as the symbol of his sacrificed new life, she remembers that she chose Levin for the job at Cascadia College because she saw from his application photograph, taken before the beard, that he needed a friend. This is an old *motif* with Malamud. Leo Finkle of "The Magic Barrel," who wanted to make a respectable marriage so that he could win a "good" congregation, picked the prostitute Stella Salzman because of the suffering he saw in her pictured face. And Iris Lemon chose Roy Hobbs because she saw his suffering in a newspaper photograph. Similarly with Levin: Pauline "marked him x in a distant port and summoned him across the continent" (p. 362), and whether she realized it or not, it was to lead a new life with her, not a life comfortably or even idealistically divorced from their unhappy pasts, but one based directly on the suffering they had each endured.

Levin resents this choice bitterly. "Who was a man," he asks, "if he surrendered freedom in a prior time?" (p. 363). His instinct is to hide when she first appears at the back door of his room, "questioning . . . his existence" (p. 206). He develops a psychosomatic ailment to make sex with Pauline physically painful. And when she comes at last to claim him, he literally flees her over backyard fences. Levin has managed even to fall out of love before he makes *his* final choice.

It is the greatest irony of the novel that Levin comes to his difficult determination to give up his new life in the liberal arts by means of the primary tool of that discipline, the reason.

> Levin, the machinery of his existence creaking, in a private place in the mind put things together thus: . . . What I had from the first to last frustration was worth having—I respect what it was. If I could have it again, I would. I have no cause now not to love her, granted I loved; I grant. I loved her; we loved. She loves me still, I have never been so loved. *That was the premise, and the premise you chose was the one you must live with;* if you chose the wrong one you were done to begin with, your whole life in jail. You cheated yourself of the short freedom you had in the world, the little of life to be alive in . . . . He would hold on when he wanted terribly to let go. Love had led him, he would now lead love. Having reasoned thus he cursed reason. (pp. 338-339, italics mine)

Moreover, the premise which has trapped Levin is older even than any of the action of the novel, for he has long realized that "before meeting her he had loved the idea of Pauline Gilley" (p. 218). It is for this old idea, not even for the woman herself, that Levin sacrifices his new life.

With this sacrifice made, S. Levin has satisfied Malamud's difficult requirements for heroism and, as his first initial would indicate, even for canonization. He has done what two previous knights had failed to do. Leo Duffy, with whom Levin is constantly compared, was Pauline's earlier lover, but Duffy left Cascadia without her. At the last moment he broke down, begging the chairman for another chance. Later, weakly blaming the times for his failure, Duffy killed himself. Levin, who says, "The times are bad but I've decided I'll have no other" (p. 18), is made of more heroic stuff. Levin is familiar in advance with Santayana's aphorism that "if you don't remember the past you were condemned to relive it" (p. 291), but it is the past of his predecessor, Duffy, which he is most fearful of and in the greatest danger of repeating. Levin chooses Pauline, moreover, while her impotent husband, Gerald Gilley, a "dry fly" fisherman, chooses the chairmanship instead. And when Gilley, honestly perplexed, asks Levin why he wants to take such a load on himself, Levin responds with the most heroic line of the novel: "Because I can, you son of a bitch" (p. 360).

But what is the idea of Pauline Gilley which Levin finally chooses? Malamud wrote his M.A. thesis on Hardy, and when Pauline can't sleep, she "wants something by Hardy around" (p. 132). As we might expect, Pauline has read and reread *The Return of the Native,* and as nature goddess she tries *Under the Greenwood Tree* and *The Woodlanders.* She does not mention *Jude the Obscure,* but surely, as a woman in a university novel, she is modeled in large part after Sue Bridehead. One remark of Sue's seems particularly relevant to her. "I fancy we have had enough of Jerusalem," Sue said, "considering we are not descended from the Jews." Before the ends of their novels, Sue Bridehead and S. Levin must learn that this is a wildly inaccurate statement; and perhaps what Malamud and Pauline are teaching is that, glorious as it no doubt was, we may have had a bit much of Athens, considering we are not descended from the Greeks, that, Jew or Christian, our heritage is suffering and not freedom, neither amatory nor academic. After all the choices have been made, Pauline makes two final revelations. She tells Levin that her maiden name was Josephson. "Think of me as Pauline Josephson. Joseph was my father's name and he wanted a son but I was his best-beloved daughter" (p. 361). Joseph, in Jacob's blessing, means "a fruitful bough," and here Levin, erstwhile bachelor instructor of the humanities, finds his rightful heritage. And so does the previously barren Pauline, for her second revelation is that she is pregnant now with Levin's child.

As a political man, Levin has not failed altogether. His idea for a great books course is being pursued and appears to have given some life to the sex-frightened old bachelor, C. D. Fabrikant, the departmental scholar. At last sight Fabrikant is growing the beard which Levin had sacrificed. But of neither S. Levin nor of his predecessor Frank Alpine can it be said that they "vitalize society" as Wasserman would have the hero do. Theirs are saints' legends, and earthly society is perhaps not the saint's primary concern. The more social conception of the hero is better realized in the one novel published after Wasserman's article, *The Fixer*, where the hero ends as the spiritual judge and executioner of the Tsar and as the champion of the Jewish people.

In apparent contrast to Levin, Yakov Bok, we have noted, begins his quest by cutting off his beard. For him freedom means a break from old ways, escaping what he constantly refers to as his fate or his luck, from the shame of his youth, the shame of the Jewish past. Without the beard, Bok does not look Jewish, but this is not the real issue. "Cut off your beard," he is warned, "and you no longer resemble your creator" (p. 9). But Yakov Bok has changed his conception of God along with his own appearance. Taking Spinoza for his guide to a new life of freedom, this humble odd-jobs man becomes "a different Yakov" (p. 212), a modern, liberated thinker, who concludes that "if there was a God, after reading Spinoza he had closed up his shop and become an idea" (p. 60).

Spinoza's philosophy is an elaborate program for freedom,

and Bok, naturally disinclined to politics, relieved of family responsibility by grace of his wife's desertion, goes outside the *shtetl* in search of enough economic security to follow his new master's example. As Bok understands him, Spinoza "was out to make a free man out of himself . . . by thinking things through and connecting everything up" (p. 76). Bok's plan of escape is thus more mature than Roy Hobbs', more moral than Frank Alpine's, and philosophically more respectable, more reasoned than S. Levin's. But even so sophisticated a freedom is not available to Malamud's hero, who ends up, in stark contrast to his master, a family man and a political activist.

The Fixer is structured on a series of stunning ironies, the most obvious of which is that Bok, the apostate Jew, who rejects all enslaving superstitions, is apprehended on a charge of ritual murder and tried, as he fully realizes, "for the crucifixion" (p. 297). Once in prison, another avenue of escape is opened for him. "If you are ashamed of your people," a Russian magistrate suggests to him, "why don't you leave the faith officially?" (p. 87). And another official promises him a full pardon if he will blame the Jews for the murder. The logic of this choice is appealing to the freedom seeker. "The Jews mean very little to you," Bok is reminded. "I size you up as a man who is out for himself. . . . Come, here is an opportunity to free yourself from the confines of the net you have fallen into" (p. 142). Yet Bok cannot take this way. On the contrary, as the prison closes more tightly around him, Bok becomes more, rather than less, Jewish, and he goes forth at last proclaiming "Death to the anti-Semites" (p. 335).

Here we are reminded of another of the novel's ironies, for Bok, who had set out to escape the prison of the *shtetl*, is quickly translated into a literal jail, and before his education is completed, he realizes that all Russia is a prison (pp. 175-176), where men are punished for "the historical evil," for Spinoza's "inexorable Necessity." He had sought the open so that he might educate himself to freedom, but his lessons come in bondage, and though they appear at first to lead him nowhere, to the useless knowledge "that the ocean is salty as you are drowning" (pp. 314-316), they finally give him a direction he had neither expected nor desired. When he becomes a revolutionary, he can scrape up a text from the

Political Treatise to justify his course,[12] but the Spinozan blue-print has quite clearly been abandoned, and so has the enabling immigrant's dream of domestic and economic freedom.

V. S. Prichett has written that "Malamud's hero learns the lesson that the philosophy he has been trying to work out with the aid of Spinoza . . . is really self-regarding." [13] But neither Malamud nor Bok seems so ready to condemn Spinoza. Once again it is not a question of the objective value of the rejected philosophy but of its relevance. "Who am I to compare myself?" Bok asks (p. 207). Spinoza found his way to an understanding of his place in the universe through a process of rigorous thought which Bok lacks the mind, the training, or the conditions to pursue. Whether he wants to or not, Bok must learn through his suffering: it is all he has. His schoolroom is not the study, but the dungeon; and his way to truth is not in geometric reasoning, but by dream visions.

Here again Bok reminds us of Roy Hobbs, Frank Alpine, and S. Levin, all three of them visionaries, but Bok, in dark solitary confinement, living constantly with dreams and hallucinations, is by necessity much farther advanced as a mystic. He is the ideal hero for the kind of mythic romance which Malamud has been all along attempting, for in *The Fixer* the significant characters of Malamud's vision appear more frequently as figures in the hero's dreams than as personages of the novel's "realistic" action. Two figures return again and again to the fevered prison cell. One is Tsar Nicholas II, who corresponds to all the would-be lovers or failed knights of the previous books—the father of Iris's child in *The Natural,* Ward Minogue and Nat Pearl of *The Assistant,* Leo Duffy and Gerald Gilley of *A New Life*—the sons of bitches, those who could not accept the burdens which the legitimate heroes were willing finally to assume. The Tsar appears only in Bok's dreams and visions. The other recurring figure is Raisl, Bok's discontented, unfaithful, and apparently barren wife, who is, of course, the Loathly Lady once again.

Raisl, like the heroines of the previous books, is in one aspect a graphic symbol for the shameful past which the questing hero wishes to escape. "The past was a wound in the head. He thought of Raisl and felt depressed" (p. 14). The early chapters are filled with his curses of her, and when he goes to prison, she, returning to the *shtetl* with her illegitimate child, becomes a pariah among the Jews, who hold her responsible for her husband's "fate" (p. 289). With at least a part of his mind Bok continues to blame her—"You stinking whore, what did you do to me?" (p. 285)—but he really knows better than to blame her, for in his prison dreams he has seen her as a symbol of the Jews, not as an oppressor but as a fellow victim, persecuted by fate and by Russian history. "At night he had terrible dreams, visions of mass slaughter that left him sleepless, moaning. When he dozed again people were being cut down by Cossacks with sabers. Yakov was shot running into the woods. Yakov, hiding under a table in his hut, was dragged forth and beheaded. Yakov, fleeing along a rutted road, had lost an arm, an eye, his bloody balls; Raisl, lying on the sanded floor, had been raped beyond caring, her fruitless guts were eviscerated" (pp. 198–199). Moreover, he has dreamed of her as his own victim "running from him in terror as though he had threatened her with a meat cleaver" (p. 187).

Both visions are justified. Russia is indeed to blame for Raisl's poverty, just as her barrenness was a matter of fate. "With conception," as she says, "you need luck" (p. 289). But Yakov is himself the author of her ultimate loathliness, her unfaithfulness. The women of the earlier books were, in another of their aspects, accurate reflections of the new lives of freedom which the men sought to lead. In *The Fixer* the woman is more than this; she is the creation, the Frankenstein's Monster, of that new life. Turning from his shame, Bok had read his Spinoza night after night instead of going to bed with Raisl. Moreover, he had unknowingly schooled her to the conclusion that to desert him would be her way of leading the new life which he so valued. He had begun this education by killing her beliefs. When she asked why God had cursed her with barrenness, he mocked, "What God?" (p. 212). When she was tormented by sexual guilt, he told her, "Don't be superstitious. . . . If you want to be free, first be free in your mind" (p. 210). An apter pupil than he had imagined, Raisl explains the logic of her adultery: "I slept with no one but you until you stopped sleeping with me. At twenty-eight I was too young for the grave. So, as you advised, I stopped being superstitious and at last took a chance. Otherwise I would soon have been dead. . . . So I decided to leave. . . . I left in desperation to change my life" (p. 286).

Again like the women of the other books, Raisl is also the knight's potential redeemer. At the moment of his greatest fear, Bok cries out "Raisl . . . save me!" (p. 183), and she has been attempting his salvation from the very beginning, trying to force him to assume his responsibilities towards her. Since Raisl stands for the Jews, such a course would have meant embracing his shameful past, and so Bok had chosen Spinoza, had avoided her bed. "I was afraid of you," he confesses. "I never met anybody so dissatisfied. I am a limited man. What could I promise you?" (p. 285). Even her desertion of him was partially intended, as she explains, to make him move (p. 286) and though she had meant movement towards responsibility rather than freedom, he did indeed stir as a result of her action.

Another of the ironies on which *The Fixer* is built concerns Bok's education in charity. "Charity you were always short of," Bok's father-in-law tells him (p. 6), and Bok displays this poverty throughout the early chapters in his unforgiving posture towards Raisl, in his repeated refusals to give alms, in his sexual rejection of crippled Zina Lebedev—"I'm a lonely woman . . . have mercy a little" (p. 53)—and even in his treatment of his old Jewish-looking horse, which he sells for a ruble to pay his ferry passage into the Christian city of Kiev. Later, the nag appears in one of Bok's prison dreams. "Murderer!" the horse neighed. "Horsekiller! Childkiller! You deserve what you get" (p. 249).

The first irony connected with this motif occurs when we realize that Bok got into trouble with the law because he performed two seemingly out-of-character acts of charity, one for an anti-Semite, whom he found drunk in the snow, and the other for an old Jew, who had been beaten by children. In prison Bok asks mercy for himself, and there he learns to forgive his wife, to accept her illegitimate child as his own, to weep for the Jews. When he dreams that Raisl's father is dead, he sighs, "Live. Let me die for you. . . . If I must suffer let it be for something" (pp. 272-273).

The final irony of the novel occurs in the final dream vision when Bok denies his education by refusing charity to the Tsar, whom he is about to execute. "After all," Nicholas pleads, "it isn't as though you yourself are unaware of what suffering is. Surely it has taught you the meaning of mercy." Bok answers, "What suffering has taught me is the uselessness of suffering" (p. 333). But this is far from the whole truth: suffering has taught him to "fear less" (p. 319); it has also taught him to love Raisl, whom he had hated, and to hate the Tsar, whose "loyal subject" (p. 75) he had been.

Nicholas II first enters *The Fixer* as a godlike figure, represented by a pair of portraits, one in the home of the anti-Semite Lebedev, accompanied by a genealogy which traces the descent of the sovereign from Adam, and the other in the office of the law-worshipping magistrate, Bibikov. "Mercy is for God," Bibokov says. "I depend on the law" (p. 80). This second picture seems to stare critically at Bok during his interrogation, adding to his discomfort (p. 81). Later, when Bok is informed that the Tsar is convinced of his guilt and that his persecution is being conducted with the Tsar's "full knowledge and approval," Bok is deeply shaken. "Why should the Tsar believe what isn't true?" (p. 221). In prison, Nicholas appears as the bearded representative of the bearded God which Bok had rejected after reading Spinoza. "The rod of God's anger against the fixer is Nicholas II, the Russian Tsar. He punishes the suffering servant for being godless" (pp. 240-241). He also appears in a dream as Jacob's God, wrestling in the dark with Bok, "beard to beard" [14] (p. 227).

A picture of this same Tsar figures also in Joyce's *A Portrait of the Artist as a Young Man,* another work about a freedom seeker, and although many have been struck by the Tsar's Christ-like portraits, it may be that this is where Malamud found his conception of Nicholas as God. The influence of Joyce on Malamud has already been suggested by Norman Leer, who points out similarities between *The Assistant* and *Ulysses*.[15] In Joyce's earlier novel, MacCann, under a photograph of Nicholas II, urges Stephen Dedalus to sign a testimonial for world peace, "the new gospel of life." Stephen comments that the Tsar "has the face of a besotted Christ," and he refuses to enlist, saying "Keep your icon. If you must have a Jesus, let us have a legitimate Jesus." [16]

In Malamud's novel Nicholas is a strange conception of the God of both Testaments. He is a perversion of Abraham's God, one who tells Bok, the emerging Jewish Patriarch, that the trouble with the Jews is they are too fruitful, they multiply too fast. "The simple fact is there are too many Jews—my how you procreate!" (p. 251). He is, moreover, a travesty on the Christian God, who fears the Jews because he believes they lust after the blood of his haemophiliac son (p. 332). Finally, he is a god who must be rejected without mercy because "in spite of certain sentimental feelings" he himself lacks "the sort of insight, you might call it, that creates in a man charity, respect for the most miserable. You say you are kind and prove it with pogroms" (p. 334).

The implications are clear that Bok has rejected the anthropomorphic God much more soundly than Spinoza had done, but he has not rejected the notion of such a God. In his mind Bok has killed Yahweh, and since he is himself a being now of greater charity and responsibility, he has taken Yahweh's place. Malamud has dramatized this substitution by discovering (with a possible assist from Joyce again) another stunning analogue to the Loathly Lady tale, this time in the Biblical story of the prophet Hosea (p. 242), who marries a prostitute in order to symbolize God's ideal relationship to the Jews. Hosea's God is stern to chastise the wicked, but he is the most manlike of Gods, with a human need to forgive, love, and protect the repentant. He is a cuckold God who suffers torment at His people's betrayal and who begs them almost pathetically to put away their harlotry so that he will not have to punish them.

This is the attitude which Bok has been able to adopt towards Raisl and towards the Jews, whom Raisl symbolizes. But it is not a possible attitude for Spinoza's "eternal infinite" God. "This one says nothing; either he can't talk or has no need to. If you're an idea what can you say?" Nor is such a relationship possible for the august God of the covenant, because "human experience baffles" this God. "What does he know about such things? . . . Has he ever suffered? How much, after all, has he experienced?" (p. 240). Bok, on the other hand, has experienced and suffered much. As a result he pities the Jews "their fate in history . . . He is against those who are against them. He will protect them to the extent that he can. This is his covenant with himself. If God's not a man, he [Bok] has to be" (p. 274). The Tsar, God or God's representative, has failed in his responsibilities to the Jews, failed to love and care for Raisl, failed the test of the Loathly Lady; and since Bok, like S. Levin in *A NEW LIFE,* has discovered now that he *can* love her, he presumes to judge the dog-like ruler, even the doglike God. Not content at calling Nicholas a son of a bitch, Bok presumes even to kill him.

Thus Yakov Bok, like the previous heroes, loses his beautiful though irrelevant dream for freedom. In four novels Malamud has come a long way in the sophistication of his escapes—from baseball stardom to Spinoza—and each way out must be rejected with a greater pang. But so has Malamud's conception of man's possibilities grown, his belief in what Wasserman called "the capacities of human strength." If he had been able to live with the Loathly Lady, emblematic of his suffering, Roy Hobbs "coulda been a king." Frank Alpine and S. Levin, because they were able to accept their shameful pasts, became lover-saints. And Yakov Bok could assume responsibilities which had proved too much even for God. "It's a rich life," Bok reasons. "Maybe he [God] would like to be human, it's possible, nobody knows" (p. 240).

Notes

1. *"The Natural:* Malamud's World Ceres," *Centennial Review,* IX (1965), 438-460. (See Chapter 4 in this collection.)
2. Jonathan Baumbach, "The Economy of Love," *Kenyon Review,* XXV (1963), 448.
3. *A New Life,* p. 136. Subsequent citations to Malamud's works will be made in the text and will refer to the original New York editions, the publication dates of which are *The Natural,* 1952; *The Assistant,* 1957; *The Magic Barrel,* 1958; *A New Life,* 1961; *Idiots First,* 1963, and *The Fixer,* 1966.
4. Levin is a favorite name with Malamud. Another story in *The Magic Barrel* is entitled "Angel Levine," and in *The Assistant* Frank Alpine, reading *Anna Karenina,* is impressed by Levin's conversion in the woods.

5. Isabella's last name is taken from another famous figure of nineteenth-century literature who finds *a new life*, the hero of Stendahl's *The Charterhouse of Parma*.

6. Campbell, Rhys, and Loomis all hold to this theory. Paton denies it, but she notes, nevertheless, that Niniane and the *Dame du lac* are occasionally represented as one person.

7. See Lucy Allen Paton, *Studies in the Fairy Mythology of Arthurian Romance*, 2nd ed. (New York, 1960), pp. 193-194.

8. "Bernard Malamud," *New Statesman*, LXIII (30 March 1962) , 452.

9. "Bernard Malamud's Fiction: The New Life and the Old," *Commentary*, XXXIII (1962), 202. (See Chapter 16 in this collection.)

10. *Ibid.*, p. 204.

11. See Milton's *Upon The Circumcision*.

12. "What is it Spinoza says? If the state acts in ways that are abhorrent to human nature it's the lesser evil to destroy it" (*The Fixer*, p. 335).

13. "Pariah," *New York Review of Books*, VII (22 November 1966), 8.

14. Yakov's beard has been allowed to grow back to be used as evidence against him at his trial.

15. "Three American Novels in Contemporary Society," *Wisconsin Studies in Contemporary Literature*, III (Fall, 1962), 68-86.

16. *Portrait of the Artist as a Young Man* (New York, 1928), pp. 227-231.

Frederick W. Turner, III

7.

Myth Inside and Out: The Natural

Critical comment on Bernard Malamud's most recent novel, *The Fixer,* has been strikingly uniform in its conviction that this work is one toward which all the writer's previous fiction has been pointing. V. S. Pritchett, writing in *The New York Review of Books,* notes that the "hero as sufferer and martyr is a characteristic Jewish theme, comic and tragic, and a continuing one in Malamud's novels." [1] George P. Elliott in *The New York Times Book Review* begins, "For quite a few years it has been clear that Bernard Malamud would be able to tell his story when he found it." [2] And Elliott goes on to guess, *ex post facto,* what that story might be like, hypothesizing from the basis of Malamud's earlier works. So too with Granville Hicks whose review of *The Fixer* in *Saturday Review* makes it clear that this is the kind of novel that Malamud's previous fiction had led us to expect he might write. [3]

It is interesting then to note that none of the above-mentioned reviews seems able to make much of *The Natural* (1952) which was Malamud's first novel. Hicks' passing reference to this work is not atypical of the treatment accorded it, not merely on this recent occasion, but in much of the critical comment which has appeared since Malamud emerged as an American writer of some importance:

Although he began his literary career with a novel based on myth, *The Natural,* and has often introduced elements of fantasy in his short stories, *The Fixer* is realistic in the most precise sense of that term.[4]

The position of *The Natural* as an "although" work in the Malamud canon is indeed strange, especially now that we are in a position to see that the real subject of *The Fixer* is a continuation and extension of that begun in *The Natural.*

The key to both works is supplied by the writer himself. Speaking of *The Fixer,* Malamud notes that he book "has a mythological quality. It has to be treated as a myth, an endless story. . . ." [5] Specifically, Malamud is speaking here of the endless story of injustice, but more to the point of both the first and latest works is the clash between myths and objective reality. Myths are "endless stories" for Malamud, and the "endless story" of his novels has been the conflict between myths and the outer world. It is this theme that has occupied Malamud from the outset of his novelistic career, and it has been the task of the heroes of his novels to see beyond myths without at the same time losing sight of them.

In *The Fixer* it is the terrible and agonizing task of Yakov Bok to finally see beyond, outside the myth of Jewishness, of Jewish suffering; his task is to see himself not *only* as a Jew, sustained in his ordeal by his sense of the role of the Jewish people in an alien world, but to see himself as a man, acting in the stream of events that is history. At the end of his interminable incarceration Bok is brought to this insight as he thinks,

> Once you leave you're out in the open; it rains and snows. It snows history, which means what happens to somebody starts in a web of events outside the personal. It starts of course before he gets there. We're all in history, that's sure, but some are more than others, Jews more than some.[6]

Bok has left the *shtetl* to come to Kiev, and in so doing he has prepared himself to see beyond the myth of Jewishness, to take up the burden of history that falls on all men who become aware of their membership in the human community. But it is important to notice here that in taking up this burden Bok does not give up the myth of Jewishness and Jewish suffering: his final words deal with anti-Semitism; but now he sees the myth in a wider context and because of this he can be a hero in the fullest sense.

Looking at Malamud's novels as a whole it is clear that Bok's realization is the point toward which the author has been steadily moving his fictional heroes. It is the task of these heroes to see and act beyond myths without at the same time destroying the validity of the myths themselves. The stance toward which Malamud moves his heroes from Roy Hobbs to Yakov Bok is that of a man aware of and sustained by a mythology, yet capable, indeed willing, to confront reality in such a fashion as to continually justify and defend the myth on the changing grounds imposed by ever-changing conditions. The only one of Malamud's novels which does not centrally concern itself with this theme is *A New Life,* but even in this failed novel it is apparent that Malamud was originally concerned with the myth-reality conflict. He begins by constructing his familiar situation of a hero immersed in a myth—that of a new life in the virgin land of the American West —and he wishes to demonstrate that this myth may indeed have validity if the hero defends it in a real world filled with unpleasant and agonizing complications. Unfortunately, Malamud allows himself and his hero to become diverted from this central concern into a lengthy and altogether trite consideration of the ins and outs of academia.

It would seem then desirable to go back to *The Natural* to note the writer's early treatment of this clash between myth and reality. In doing so we can more accurately assess Malamud's achievements as a novelist and, at the same time, give this neglected work its due.

The Natural is a curiosity on two counts: first because it is one of the very few "non-Jewish" works of the author; and second because it makes use of a supposedly unadaptable subject for serious fiction—baseball. It is perhaps this latter factor which has contributed most substantially to the novel's wary critical reception. Baseball has resisted the best efforts of American writers to elevate it to a sufficient height to sustain a serious work, though several writers, notably Ring Lardner, Charles Einstein, and Mark Harris, have correctly seen it as a microcosm of American life. The uniqueness of Malamud's treatment derives from the fact that he has been able to invest this boy's game with tragi-comic qualities as opposed, say, to Lardner or Harris, who treat it in largely comic fashion.

Malamud's successful use of baseball in this novel has been commonly attributed to his use of myth, particularly the myth of the hero, and almost every critic who has troubled himself with *The Natural* has dutifully and sometimes painstakingly pointed out the various mythic parallels.[7] Malamud, they observe, has equated the baseball hero of his novel with mythic heroes of the past so that the actions of Roy Hobbs, left fielder for the New York Knights, take on a significance far larger than that guaranteed even the most glorious of sweaty demi-gods.

Despite the ease with which critics have exposed the mythic underpinnings of *The Natural* (or perhaps because of it), there has persisted a sense of uneasiness about the book, as if Malamud were somehow cheating by using myths in such a fashion. So Norman Podhoretz:

> All this amounts to a commendable effort to say that baseball is much more important than it seems to be. Using Homer, however, is not only too easy a way to do it, but also a misconception of what intelligence and seriousness of purpose demand from a writer.[8]

Then too, the mythic parallels themselves seem to lead nowhere, and it has seemed almost as if the use of myth was an end in itself as indeed the critics themselves have made it: to assert the presence of myth in a literary work is not necessarily to explain *why* it is there, and this has unhappily been too often the case with recent criticism; it is as though finding buried traces of myths were but a refinement of the symbol archeology carried on in the journals for the past thirty-five years. Podhoretz and Marcus

Klein can tell us what myths are being used where, but they fail to tell us to what effect. Podhoretz can even suggest that baseball has its own mythology:

> Mr. Malamud is truer to the inherent purpose of his book when he finds the elements of myth, not in ancient Greece, but in the real history of baseball.[9]

Yet he fails to follow up this potentially valuable suggestion as have all other critics who have dealt with *The Natural*. To heed it is to be taken straight to the heart of this novel, and perhaps in some measure to the heart of Malamud's fiction as a whole.

All modern heroic myths are but redactions of the ur-myth of the hero as this has been dissected and outlined by Otto Rank, Lord Raglan, and Joseph Campbell. That myth is too well known to require reproduction here, but anyone can see, for example, that the Horatio Alger story is a form of the heroic myth and that, existing as it does in a democratic and predominantly Protestant society, the story has taken on the characteristics of that society while dropping those features of the old heroic myths which are culturally uncongenial: its aristocratic and sexual overtones. Similarly, it can be seen that the myth of the baseball hero is an amalgam of the heroic myth and its democratic offspring, the Horatio Alger story:

1) the hero is from undistinguished parentage and has a rural background;
2) the hero's father teaches him to play baseball, perhaps thereby fulfilling his own unrealized boyhood ambitions;
3) the hero is discovered in his rural haunts by a hardworking scout;
4) the hero is transported to the city where he finds life frightening and bewildering; he encounters difficulty in convincing the team "brass" that he has the necessary talent;
5) the hero finally gets his chance and displays prodigious talents (fastest fastball, longest home run);

6) the hero rises to stardom, has a "day" at the stadium and inarticulately expresses his humble thanks;
7) everything after the hero's day savors somewhat of anti-climax, his talents gradually decay, and he eventually retires.[10]

Roy Hobbs, Malamud's hero, is one who lives and finds his meaning only within this mythology and this is his tragic weakness. He is obsessed with a sense of mission which is nothing less than to fill out the heroic proportions which the pattern casts for those who would follow it. Roy's lack of any values outside the mythology is one of the major sources of the tragicomic quality which Malamud has been able to impart to the novel: Roy's refusal to think in any terms other than those of baseball is, to begin with, comic, and he becomes the prototypical goon athlete immortalized in our literature by Lardner and James Thurber. So this passage in which Harriet Bird sizes Roy up as a future victim of her sexually-tinged desire to murder famous athletes:

Had he ever read Homer?
Try as he would he could only think of four bases and not a book. His head spun at her allusions. He found her lingo strange with all the college stuff and hoped she would stop it because he wanted to talk about baseball.[11]

And:

"What will you hope to accomplish, Roy?"
He had already told her but after a minute remarked, "Sometimes when I walk down the street I bet people will say there goes Roy Hobbs, the best there ever was in the game."
She gazed at him with touched and troubled eyes. "Is that all?"
He tried to penetrate her question. Twice he had answered it and still she was unsatisfied. He couldn't be sure what she expected him to say. "Is that all?" he repeated. "What more is there?"

"Don't you know?" . . . .

"Isn't there something over and above earthly things—
some more glorious meaning to one's life and activities?"

"In baseball?" (p. 33)

Fifteen years and worlds of agonies later Roy is still held in
the grip of the mythology, still refusing to think or act outside of
it. Now, however, Roy's refusal to see outside the myth is not
comic, but rather tragic. It is so because we are here witness to
the spectacle of a man who has given his life for that myth, and
because myth cannot be defended entirely from within; it must
be defended by a hero who sees *both* inside and outside it. Still,
there is another chance for Roy to save the myth through an acceptance of the love of Iris Lemon. Such an acceptance would
prepare him to confront the world of objective reality while at
the same time remaining true to baseball's mythology: Iris is in
the real world but she still believes in heroes. Here Roy's refusal
of Iris' love guarantees his inevitable (Natural) failure. This time
when Roy reveals in conversation with a woman (Iris) his tragic
limitation it is no longer a laughing matter; his vision has taken
on a kind of Oedipal blindness:

"I wanted everything." His voice boomed out of the
silence.

She waited.

"I had a lot to give to this game."

"Life?"

"Baseball. If I had started out fifteen years ago like I
tried to, I'da been king of them all by now."

"The king of what?"

"The best in the game," he said impatiently.

She sighed deeply. "You're so good now."

"I'da been better. I'da broke most every record there
was."

"Does that mean so much to you?"

"Sure," he answered. . . .

"But I don't understand why you should make so much
of that. Are your values so—!" (p. 156)

Roy's values are "so—" for this is what distinguishes the hero from ordinary people like Iris. A hero is someone who acts within and for a mythology—national, regional, occupational—even when to do so is to jeopardize his very existence. Malamud's ironic vision is that such an insulated hero cannot possibly win out.

What continually threatens the existence of the hero and of the mythology which he serves is what Wallace Stevens called the "pressure of reality." It is always clear that mythologies are in some ways divorced from the real world, though what they contain may be directives for solving the world's problems. Here the fading, sagging ball park where the Knights play their home games functions as metaphor for the other-worldly quality of mythology in the same fashion as the *shtetl* objectifies the gap between the myth of Jewishness and the outer world in *The Fixer*. Inside the park gates one is transported to another world filled with grotesque devotees, magic bats, and super-sized demigods. The drama of the hero's story comes out of the conflict between the mythology within which the hero acts and the pressures of reality which work always to force the hero into a betrayal of his mythology.

In *The Natural* the pressure of reality is represented by the unholy alliance of Judge Goodwill Banner, the Knights' owner; Gus Sands, the Supreme Bookie; and Memo Paris, Roy's love. The sportswriter, Max Mercy (whose name like that of the Judge has its obvious irony), is their press agent. The Judge has a completely cynical, ruthless attitude toward the game. He is in it to make money and Malamud skillfully contrasts him with his co-owner, Pop Fisher, who manages the team and subscribes wholly to the mythology of the game. Similarly, Gus Sands has no reverence for the game itself. To him it is simply "action" on which to bet. Because of the death of her hero, Bump Baily, Memo Paris has disavowed her belief in the mythology and she now works with the Judge and Gus to destroy the hero.

The hero must meet the challenge to his mythology head-on, and it is one of the central ironies of the novel that Roy Hobbs meets this challenge as he lies bewildered and enfeebled in a hospital bed. The doctor has told Roy that he must quit baseball or risk a heart attack, and Memo, whom Roy covets, has made it clear that she is to be had only for the kind of money which comes to a famous athlete. Thus when Judge Banner appears at the bedside to bribe Roy into throwing the play-off game the hero is at his lowest ebb. Faced with his physical predicament and an uncertain financial future, the hero succumbs. He has at last seen outside the mythology, but in so doing he loses his grip on the mythology itself.

When in the midst of the play-off game Roy attempts to re-attach himself to the mythology he cannot do so. Wonderboy, the magic bat, breaks in two, for once this hero has seen and acted outside the mythology—acted, that is, against it—he can never again act with it; his limited vision will not permit him to. Thus the gates of Roy's Eden are closed forever and there remains for him nothing to do but drag himself up the stairs to the Judge's darkened tower to collect his reward.

This final scene is the novel's best, for in it Malamud makes the reader fully aware of the tragedy of Roy's lost herohood. Divorced forever from the mythology which gave his life meaning, Roy can only beat up Gus Sands and the Judge, tear open the envelope containing the bribe money, and shower it over the Judge's head. The end for this failed hero is to enter the real world and to find it a sordid and bitter place:

> When he hit the street he was exhausted. He had not shaved, and a black beard gripped his face. He felt old and grimy.
> He stared into the faces of people he passed along the street but nobody recognized him.
> "He coulda been a king," a woman remarked to a man. (p. 237)

So with modern man: divorced forever from the mythologies of his past, he finds himself alone, on the street, adrift in a new and mythless world.

And yet, of course, this is not the end for the Malamud hero; it is merely the first installment. Roy Hobbs is the hero of a mythology, but ultimately he fails that mythology by his inability to see and act beyond it without destroying it for himself. The mythology of baseball is what keeps the game alive in the hearts of its fans. Without that mythology the game would disintegrate into a jumble of meaningless statistics and facts. Yet conditions change, and the mythology of baseball must be continually defended on new grounds. What this latest baseball hero *should* have done is to accept Iris Lemon's love, and, sustained by this new and vitalizing outside force, resist temptation and expose the Judge and Gus who represent the greed and corruption which now threaten baseball's mythology. In this way the hero would have remained true to his mythology while at the same time defending it against hostile forces. But Roy Hobbs, as we have seen, is too limited a hero to assume this difficult stance; for him it is impossible to act within a mythology and at the same time see beyond it so as to defend it. For him it must be one thing or the other.

In *The Assistant*, however, we find that Malamud has moved his hero, Frank Alpine, one step further toward the stance finally achieved by Yakov Bok. Frank Alpine begins the novel looking at a myth—Jewishness—from the outside, where we left Roy Hobbs:

"What I like to know is what is a Jew anyway?" [12]

By the time of Morris Bober's funeral Frank Alpine can see part way into the mythology which has sustained the grocer in his long ordeal.

Suffering, he thought, is like a piece of goods. I bet the Jews could make a suit of clothes out of it. [13]

At the conclusion of the novel Frank has entered the mythology completely by virtue of his awareness of the truth of Jewishness. A Jew, says the rabbi at Morris Bober's funeral, is one who wants "for others that which he wants also for himself." So Frank Alpine becomes a Jew. He begins outside a mythology and by learning the truth of it from the outside he comes to enter it. It is clear that this is where Yakov Bok's story begins.

Notes

1. V. S. Pritchett, "A Pariah," *The New York Review of Books* (September 22, 1966), pp. 8-9.
2. George P. Elliott, "Yakov's Ordeal," *The New York Times Book Review* (September 4, 1966), 1, 25-26.
3. Granville Hicks, "One Man to Stand for Six Million," *Saturday Review* (September 10, 1966), pp. 37-39.
4. Hicks, p. 37. Even Leslie Fiedler, whose literary tastes and critical stance might lead us to expect that he would understand *The Natural*, fails to see any connection between this work and later ones. See *Love and Death in the American Novel* (New York, Revised Edition, 1966), pp. 492-493.
5. Interview with Bernard Malamud, *Saturday Review* (September 10, 1966), p. 39.
6. Bernard Malamud, *The Fixer* (New York, 1966), p. 314.
7. See, for example, Norman Podhoretz, "Achilles in Left Field," *Commentary* (March, 1953), pp. 321-326. See also a fuller treatment by Marcus Klein, *After Alienation* (Cleveland, 1965), pp. 255-263. (See Chapter 17 in this collection.)
8. Podhoretz, p. 322.
9. Podhoretz, p. 323.
10. Anyone who doubts the existence and persistence of such a myth is invited to note the careers of such baseball heroes as Babe Ruth, Lou Gehrig, Walter Johnson, Joe Di Maggio, Bob Feller, Mickey Mantle, and Willie Mays as these are given to us in anecdote and "official" biographies. See also the baseball novels of John R. Tunis who draws upon this myth in the creation of his heroes.
11. Bernard Malamud, *The Natural* (New York: The Noonday Press, 1964), p. 32. Subsequent page references in the text are to this edition.
12. Bernard Malamud, *The Assistant* (London: Eyre and Spottiswoode, 1959), p. 114.
13. Malamud, *The Assistant*, p. 209.

Part III
Varied Approaches

Ben Siegel

8.

Victims in Motion: The Sad and Bitter Clowns

Since 1952 Bernard Malamud has published three novels and a collection of short stories. Each is a moral critique, an attempt to explore and reveal the melancholic state of the human condition, its basic—even banal—realities. Having undertaken this Socratic search into the human soul, Malamud's favorite vantage point is the dark prison of the self. From there he looks out upon a somber, cramped, and joyless world in which failure and calamity are daily staples. Thus if such literary compeers as Saul Bellow, Philip Roth, and Herbert Gold create active participants in a prosperous society, Malamud does not. His sad and bitter clowns are outsiders. Most are urban Jews—a few tradition-bound, the majority secularized. But all—Jews and non-Jews alike—are uncertain, unlucky, and unloved.

Malamud does not view modern society as blameless for man's tragic plight, but neither does he consider anyone the mere passive victim of social cruelty or neglect. His people embody their own self-destructive demons. If they are social misfits, it is primarily of their own doing. They are incompetent or unworldly, or both. Like Miller's Willy Loman, they can't stand success; they finally must destroy it.

In *The Natural* (1952), Malamud's only non-Jewish novel, both Roy Hobbs and society contribute to his ultimate tragedy. Roy had emerged from the backlands with a champion's physical co-ordination, a childlike innocence, and the unshakable conviction he would be "the best there ever was" in baseball. Roy pays the price of his humanity. For his *hybris* the gods administer the first blow: they send a tantalizing but demented young temptress who promises him sex but instead fires a silver bullet into his intestines. But much more traumatic than near-death for the young athlete is his glimpse of the chasm between his heroic self-image and actual moral flabbiness.

Seventeen years pass before Roy again reaches the major leagues. Years of wandering and defeat spur him to superhuman feats, but present again is a sexual temptress to hasten his fall; present also are the temptations that have outlasted Rome: bribe money, succulent foods, the crowd's tyrannical adulation. Malamud knows his baseball folklore and makes the diamond exciting, even important, skillfully attributing to Roy some of its most memorable historical moments. But baseball is not Malamud's prime concern. He is interested primarily in the comi-tragic paradoxes of modern existence, particularly as these paradoxes reveal the progressive corruption of a basically honest professional athlete. But to add depth and breadth to his essentially simple narrative, he follows the mythological trail blazed by James Joyce through twentieth-century literature. Malamud's particular guides, however, are Jessie Weston and T. S. Eliot and their handling of the Holy Grail motif in *From Ritual to Romance* and *The Waste Land*. Hence Roy Hobbs becomes not only Shoeless Joe Jackson but Achilles in his tent and Sir Perceval in vain pursuit of the Holy Grail. And his team, the New York Knights, is managed by Pop Fisher, who not only suffers from a skin ailment, but bemoans continually the "dry season" and the woeful state of his "club."

Wielding his lightning-scorched bat, Roy lifts the Knights into pennant contention, but his success and happiness are short lived. To the sin of pride he has added gluttony, and his health fails. Only then does he halfheartedly agree to throw the crucial game—changing his mind when it is too late. As newspaper headlines shout his disgrace, Roy stands in the street and weeps. A newsboy then sobs the immortal words (supposedly leveled at Joe Jackson of the Chicago "Black Sox"): "Say it ain't true, Roy." Suffering has taught him not only "to want the right things" but the difficulty of being a "hero" in a society that demands its knights resist the fruits those of weaker flesh hasten to enjoy.

Overpraised at publication, *The Natural* has since been undeservedly devalued. (Hemingway's *The Old Man and the Sea* offers an obvious parallel.) Actually, its true literary worth falls about midway between past and present critical judgments. For if its symbolism and language are frequently strained, both are handled more effectively than some recent critics (several of whom obviously haven't bothered even to read it) have realized. And if the characters consistently are more metaphor than flesh and blood, they never lose completely their human connections. In any event, Roy Hobbs serves as archetype for all of Malamud's small heroes, who—like their larger Greek and Shakespearean counterparts—fall victim to a tragic flaw aggravated by misfortune.

Malamud's last three books deal primarily with contemporary Jewish life and represent the most consistent—if not the most "realistic"—recent attempt to blend the traditional Yiddish folktale with the modern American scene and its values. Malamud most resembles such Yiddish masters as I. L. Peretz, Mendele Mocher Seforim, and Sholom Aleichem in his concern for morality and ethics rather than aesthetics. Like them, his central subject is ambivalent, unpredictable human nature. And where many contemporary American-Jewish novelists search for the human being in the Jew, Malamud (like his Yiddish predecessors) seeks the Jew in the human being. "All men are Jews," he has declared, and he attempts to raise the alienated Jew's deep personal suffering to the level of universality.

Malamud's second novel, *The Assistant* (1957), is a parable of atonement and conversion reversing the familiar assimilation story: beginning with a sinful act, it traces the painful expiation.

His Jews are not "good" in the traditional sense; few, in fact, reveal any concern for Judaism as a coherent body of doctrine. They share only a communal sensitivity to persecution and suffering. Ritual and custom are for Malamud mere surface trimmings; all that matters is the human heart—that is, man's essential dignity and responsibility to his fellows in a grim, inhuman world.

Roy Hobbs's tragic ineptness and ill-fortune are paralleled by Frank Alpine, a shabby, broken-nosed Italian wanderer from the West who is as uncertain of his identity as the most alienated Jew. With an accomplice Frank robs Morris Bober, an honest but inept grocer whose only "talent" is for poverty. But Frank is a thief haunted by childhood stories of St. Francis of Assisi, whom he resembles in name and appearance. Frank reappears shortly after the robbery seeking to undo his crime, and begs the bewildered grocer to let him work for nothing. When Bober refuses, Frank descends to a living death in the Bober cellar. Only when Bober has a heart attack is Frank able to don the grocer's apron and rejuvenate the dying business.

Frank longs to confess his current past and begin a clean future. But he is afraid of losing what little he now has attained. Nor is he ready for redemption. For despite his sincere repentance, Frank cannot resist stealing from Bober and lusting after the grocer's lovely daughter, Helen. And he is plagued by the certainty that eventually he will cause his own undoing: "Sooner or later everything I think is worth having gets away from me. . . . Just when it looks like I am going to get it I make some kind of a stupid move, and everything . . . blows up in my face."

Nor can Frank shake past prejudices, experiencing self-repugnance for living so close to Jews in such ugly, confined quarters. Only a Jew can imprison himself like this, he thinks. "That's what they live for, to suffer." Yet if the Jews get on his nerves, they also arouse in him a gnawing curiosity. Frank asks Bober why he neither goes to synagogue nor adheres to the dietary laws. Bober replies he is concerned only "to do what is right, to be honest, to be good." But the dissatisfied clerk then inquires why "the Jews suffer so damn much?" and is shaken by Bober's reply: "I suffer for you."

Inevitably, Bober catches Frank stealing and fires him. Hoping to win sympathy, the latter blurts his part in the robbery, but this Bober had guessed. Frank also spoils his chances with Helen —who was beginning to return his love—when he loses self-control and rapes her. Driven from the Bober home, Frank is cut-off from his only means of expiation. But he is able to return when Bober dies of pneumonia. And as a rabbi drones platitudes over her father's body, Helen Bober's thoughts underscore Malamud's recurrent theme: "He made himself a victim. He could, with a little more courage, have been more than he was."

But if dead and a recognized failure, Bober continues to shape the lives he left behind. Frank determines not only to win redemption by taking Bober's place, but to rewin Helen "with discipline and love." He reopens the store and falls into Bober's routine, even to wearing his clothes. Between customers Frank reads the Bible and thinks often of St. Francis. In the spring he has himself circumcized: "The pain enraged and inspired him. After Passover he became a Jew."

Doctrine plays little part in Frank's conversion; Judaism merely provides him with a practical means of enduring the suffering necessary for salvation. As Christian-Jew, Frank Alpine becomes Everyman, exemplifying the fundamental unity of man's spiritual needs. For Malamud, religion's function is to convey the essentials of the "good heart"; he has little sympathy either for the ghetto minded Jew or parochial Christian.

If *The Natural* has been downgraded undeservedly, *The Assistant*'s obvious moral values and rejection of the parochial have caused it consistently to be overrated. Admittedly, Malamud achieves considerable dramatic effect by implication, compression, and suggestion. But in his eagerness to develop his themes of moral indebtedness and responsibility, he describes rather than explains his characters' deeper and darker emotions. His people never are more than ritual figures in a deterministic morality play. Yet *The Assistant* undeniably remains a probing and disturbing study of modern man's social and spiritual confusion.

As much cannot be said, however, for any of Malamud's shorter tales. He is not a major short-story writer. The same impatience to develop idea rather than character is all the more evident in the thirteen wry, ironic vignettes comprising *The Magic Barrel*, which won the 1959 National Book Award for fiction. Despite his award, Malamud is here more entertainer than explorer. However, he does avoid the clichés of the Jewish social-protest and "hot-pastrami" writers, and despite some obvious plot and character indebtedness to the Yiddish storytellers, he does fashion his own vernacular. For example, where Mendele and Sholom Aleichem's prose conveys the slow, deliberate tempo of the European *shtetl*—or small town, Malamud's idiom is terse, rapid, and urban. It is a Hemingwayesque Yiddish-English mannered and highly stylized. Yet the bitterly ironic Yiddish undertone remains.

But if his tales catch eye and ear, they only occasionally arrest heart and mind. Disbelief is seldom suspended, for always there are the ingenious symbols, the picturesque (even grotesque) characters, and the quick, mildly shocking conclusions: two men kissing, two death-chants for the living, several victor-victim reversals, a Negro-Jewish angel, and innumerable flashes of self-revelation. If on occasion these endings actually illuminate the truth behind the masks, more often they leave the reader slightly dazzled and bemused.

Yet even the most disappointing tales remain strangely haunting segments of human experience. "The First Seven Years," moreover, not only recasts the Jacob-Rachel story but reveals the early stirrings of *The Assistant*. Feld, a prosperous shoemaker, is appalled to discover that Sobel, his homely refugee assistant, wants to marry his attractive teenage daughter. Feld is cruel, insulting —and then filled with sudden pity for this sad, bookish man who had missed Hitler's incinerators only to fall in love with an American girl half his age. Sensing the match is inevitable and that his dreams of a better life for his daughter are best forgotten, Feld requests only that his assistant not ask for her hand until she is twenty-one. Sobel is content.

A somewhat similar shock of recognition is experienced by Gruber, the greedy, unfeeling landlord of "The Mourners." Having failed repeatedly to dispossess an elderly tenant from a tenement room, the landlord bursts in to find the old man sitting on the floor moaning. The latter is bewailing his own misdeeds, but the guilt-stricken Gruber interprets the chant as a prayer for the dead. In fact, he decides the old man is mourning for him—for his lost compassion and humanity. Seizing a bedsheet for a prayer-shawl, the abashed Gruber sinks down beside the old man to mourn for himself. The old man's probable surprise at this sudden act of contrition is exceeded only by that of the unprepared reader.

But if one Malamud character wins the right to remain, several others overcome the inner forces imprisoning them in their rooms. Mitka, the unsuccessful novelist of "The Girl of My Dreams," sulks in his room because of repeated failure. But a published short-story by one "Madeline Thorn" fires his interest, and he forces a meeting with the reluctant writer. His resultant disappointment is crushing: "Madeline" is lonely, pathetic, middle-aged. And her name is Olga. His dream girl, like all his dreams, had fragmented, disappeared. He will go back and "entomb himself forever." But Olga feeds and counsels him, assures him "character" is what counts. Mitka pities her, himself, the world. When she leaves, Mitka discovers the crushed, defeated Olga has awakened something in him. Now, whatever his fate, he will meet it in the world.

At that, Mitka's chances for success are better than those of George Stoyonovich, the lost, uneducated youth of "A Summer's Reading." Unable to find a job George, too, hides in his room. To placate his hardworking sister and curious neighbors, George lets slip that he plans a summer reading a library list of one hundred books. He then is able to walk the neighborhood feeling the silent but approving glances. In a few weeks, however, sister and neighbors begin to doubt. George returns to isolation, but admiration and respect have proved heady wines. One fall evening George runs to the library, counts-off a hundred titles and sits down to read. George's failure is inevitable, and the reader is left to ponder its possible ramifications.

But if Malamud returns repeatedly to man's frightened need for success and status, he is no less interested in the mocking irony of human ingratitude. The human animal, as Malamud sees him, neither understands nor appreciates kindness. In "The Prison" that is the candy store bestowed on him by his father-in-law, Tommy Castelli finds life intolerably dull. His one interesting customer is a homely ten-year-old who constantly steals candy. Tommy doesn't know how to help her. When his wife catches the little girl stealing, Tommy defends her. Yet as the frightened child is being led to punishment, she repays Tommy's kindness by sticking out her tongue at him. Obviously, kindness or generosity makes man vulnerable and ashamed.

And in the strangely disembodied tale he calls "Take Pity," Malamud illustrates that selflessness can engender cruelty. Rosen, an ex-coffee salesman, had led a sickly and lonely existence; now he is in a post-mortal state. In life he had attempted to help a friend's widow and two children, asking nothing in return. But the widow, with obvious dislike, had rejected his generous offers. Stubbornly determined to "give" her something, Rosen had willed her his possessions and turned on the gas. Now she stands beneath his window with upraised arms and "haunted, beseeching eyes." However, Rosen, who has given all he has to give, shouts insults at her, orders her home.

Another who misses his chance to pay a debt is tenement janitor Willy Schlegel in "The Bill." Willy runs-up a needless bill of eighty-three dollars at the Panessas' dark little grocery and then switches to the self-service market. Obsessed by guilt, he develops a hatred for the elderly Panessas. When a letter from Mrs. Panessa pleads for ten dollars for her sick husband, Willy hides in the cellar. But the next day he pawns his overcoat and runs back with the money—only to discover the grocer emerging in a coffin. Willy's sinking heart informs him he will never rid himself of his debt. (Only in his later form as Frank Alpine will he achieve expiation.)

Money, of course, need not change hands to scar a friendship or man's inner being. In "The Loan," Lieb the baker and his wife, Bessie, are approached by his estranged friend Kobotsky. He needs money for his sick wife. For Lieb their past friendship is not dead; he is willing. Bessie is not. They, too, she argues, are elderly and sick. A heated debate follows. Kobotsky tells them not to fight: he has lied. His wife has been dead five years; the money is for an overdue headstone. Bessie remains adamant, and Kobotsky is forced to leave empty-handed. Their now-famous parting slices deep into the memory: the two elderly men "embraced and sighed over their lost youth. They pressed mouths together and parted forever." Each again has learned that life's recurrent crises have no "solution"—at least on this earth.

Malamud, however, does hold out the possibility of occasional divine assistance—provided one believes. For much faith is needed to recognize the incongruous shapes of God's possible messengers. In "Angel Levine," for instance, the Job-like Manischevitz is guilty of being man and Jew. A once-prosperous tailor but now a pitiable failure, he is told his dying wife can be saved only by his recognizing a Negro with the unlikely name of Alexander Levine as "a bona-fide angel of God." The tailor's orthodox mind boggles at the seeming irreverence of "a black Jew and angel to boot." But if he rails against God and disavows his previous beliefs, he is forced ultimately to track Levine to a Harlem bar and proclaim him a Jewish emissary from on high. Returning home the tailor finds his wife hale and hearty. Overwhelmed, he blurts the punchline to a score of Yiddish jokes: "A wonderful thing, Fanny. . . . Believe me, there are Jews everywhere." Malamud thus affirms not only the possible presence of God's spirit "in all things" but joins Norman Mailer and Leslie Fiedler in the attempt to say something meaningful about Negro-Jewish relations.

But if Malamud's Jews are not quite "everywhere," a few of them do make it to Italy, that perennial fount of sophistication and self-knowledge for fictional Americans. There Henry Levin, the pretentious hero of "The Lady of the Lake," learns the consequences of moral cowardice and self-denial. When Henry inherits some money, he heads for Europe seeking romance. In the process he changes his name to (what else?) Henry R. Freeman. On an Italian island estate he falls in love with a dark-eyed beauty he believes to be of an aristocratic Italian family. To her pointed question, the unbelievably dense Henry three times denies his Jewishness (strangely enough no cock crows). Only then does she reveal herself as the caretaker's daughter and a Buchenwald survivor. And as she treasures her tragic past, she declares she will marry only a Jew. Henry then quickly admits his Jewishness but embraces "only moonlit stone," for she has fled into the mists. And if Henry Levin-Freeman is a clear Semitic descendent of Henry James's naive pilgrims, his exotic Jewess is obviously out of Shakespeare by way of Scott.

"Behold the Key" presents another American innocent

abroad. Carl Schneider, a young graduate student in Italian studies, is in Rome with wife and children and needs an apartment. He quickly discovers there is much to Italian life not found in books. A shabby rental agent leads him on a picaresque journey through Rome's "apartment" life until the ideal place is found. But the key is held by the owner's discarded lover, who demands a bribe. Carl refuses so un-American a gesture, and is plummeted into a mesh of intrigues and arguments. When entrance to the apartment finally is gained, the weary pilgrims discover the spiteful lover has ruined the interior. As Carl bravely proclaims his undaunted love for Italy, the angry lover appears to hurl the key at his fellow Italian—who adroitly ducks. It strikes Carl on the forehead, leaving "a mark he could not rub out." So if his failure to grasp the Latin character has stirred hatred between brother Italians, Carl now has a key to the enigma marked on his flesh.

A more permanently scarifying experience is Arthur Fidelman's in "The Last Mohican." Having failed as a painter, Fidelman has come to Rome to write a critical study of Giotto. He carries one extra suit and his opening chapter. But his first hello seals his fate. He is spotted as an easy mark by a skeleton in knickers, one Shimon Susskind. The crafty, voracious Susskind—whose single redeeming feature is a compulsion to survive—follows Fidelman everywhere; insisting that he too "knows" Giotto, he demands an equal share of the American's meager money and clothes. When Fidelman gives him four dollars, Susskind asks: "If four, then why not five?" He shrugs-off insults and threats and makes his victim feel guilty at every meal. When the desperate American demands why he should feel "responsible" for him, his tormentor coolly replies: "Because you are a man. Because you are a Jew."

Susskind repays Fidelman's kindness by destroying his manuscript. "I did you a favor," he tells the enraged visitor. "The words were there but the spirit was missing." During the grotesque pursuit that follows, Fidelman has a "triumphant insight." He shouts to the fleeing spectre, "Susskind, come back. . . . All is forgiven." Apparently Susskind's insight is even deeper—he keeps running. But if nothing else, Fidelman, through suffering and loss, has gained wisdom. Heaven's agents come in strange shapes indeed.

Malamud's title story, "The Magic Barrel," underscores again the impossibility of rejecting the demands of the flesh. Nearing graduation Leo Finkle, an ascetic, scholarly rabbinical student, decides to acquire a wife. He calls in a marriage broker, Pinye Salzman, who promises the timid Leo results from the photographs and information cards he keeps in a barrel.

For Leo, looking for a wife proves a soul-shattering experience. One prospect asks how he became "enamored of God," and the future rabbi unconsciously blurts: "I came to God not because I loved Him, but because I did not." But he guiltily consoles himself that he is a Jew and that a Jew suffers—and if he was imperfect, his ideal was not. And he feels this new self-knowledge will help him find a bride.

But his hopes fade; most of Salzman's photographed faces bear the marks of defeat. Yet the final one, a face of sadness, regret, and evil, touches his heart. If Salzman is delighted at the prospect of a commission, he is horrified at Leo's choice. Her picture was a mistake, he protests. The girl is wild, "like an animal. Like a dog. For her to be poor was a sin. This is why to me she is dead now. . . . This is my baby, my Stella, she should burn in hell." Leo is adamant. This girl will understand—perhaps even love—him. Yet when the old man finally agrees, Leo suspects a well-laid trap.

Stella, appropriately enough, awaits him under a street lamp. As Leo rushes toward her, he notes her eyes ". . . are filled with desperate innocence," and he pictures in her "his own redemption." Around the corner the old marriage broker leans against the wall to chant the prayer for the dead. But what has died may be Salzman's honesty, Leo's innocence, or Stella's guilty youth: all merit lamentation. What is clearer is Malamud's reluctance to give up on anyone. Each being is unique, responsible, imperfect, and redeemable. No one is beyond redemption, and in most instances love is the surest means of attaining it.

If in *The Magic Barrel* Malamud fluctuates uncertainly between realism and allegory, he remains essentially a moralist. His persistent theme here is the almost frightening consequences of the human encounter. Those whose lives entangle our own, no matter how lightly, he reiterates, alter irrevocably our and their lives. None is ever the same, and this implies the moral obligation of love, or at least concern, toward one another.

Several critics (most recently Philip Roth, in *Commentary*) have criticized Malamud for his concentration upon the small, innocuous "private life" to the total neglect of controversial public issues. But Malamud's latest novel, *A New Life* (1961), indicates a definite broadening of his social horizon. Not only is it a penetrating satire of the academic life lived at many American colleges, but its hero is Malamud's first to share the social indignation of the angry and misguided proletarian prophets who filled Jewish novels during the Thirties. Seymour Levin, also, is a spiritual wanderer, having severed his Judaic roots and values. He, too, is driven by love and lust, duty and selfishness, and—beneath his waywardness and self-indulgence—by a painfully stern morality. Moreover, Malamud adds to his novel's "realism" by unabashedly settling a series of old and deeply personal scores, for the characters clearly are drawn from his own teaching experiences.

Yet basically *A New Life* repeats Malamud's belief that the human struggle is one of few successes and many failures but that the important thing is to endure. It stresses also that the past is never buried but rises always to poison the present.

Seymour Levin fits easily into the Malamud pattern. For if Frank Alpine, as lonely western Christian, journeyed east to be transfigured and absorbed by the small but unified Jewish world there, Levin merely travels from east to west. There, in the equally isolated Northwest college community of Eastchester, his beard, black fedora, and Yiddish inflection mark him "outsider." But his failure to gain acceptance is due to other reasons. Levin lacks both the Wandering Jew's passive underdog psychosis and Alpine's Christian patience and humility. He cannot remain a spectator to crimes against the liberal spirit. Nor is he the comic *shlemiel* of Yiddish literature, as some critics would have it; rather, he is close to the traditional *shlimazel*: the ill-starred blunderer who can expect the worst return for the best intentions, evil for every kindness, punishment for every misdeed. For him to sin is to get caught. And Levin quickly proceeds to do both.

He has come to Cascadia College in search of integrity, rebirth, continuity, "a new life." He is determined to be a good English instructor, to forget an unhappy childhood, and to live down a series of alcoholic failures. To his pent-up urban spirit the Northwest's vistas present a new world. Like a famous namesake, Tolstoy's Konstantine Levin, he finds the mountains, air, woods, and streams overwhelming. At first he is exultant and hopeful, but his "new life" soon proves little different from what it was. He wanders the streets alone. Reaching out for friendship, he receives only friendliness. He envies the students their youth, good looks, and futures, as well as their sense of belonging. And as had Frank Alpine, he lives in constant fear of not being able to master his inner compulsions.

His work, however, provides his most crushing disappointments. Cascadia College graduates engineers and farmers. The few literature courses are reserved for others; he teaches only composition. The students are interested only in passing grades, while his colleagues—reacting to social pressures and physical setting—long since have lost intellectual curiosity and integrity. Moreover, Levin is compared repeatedly to one Leo Duffy, a "disagreeable radical" who two years earlier had been dismissed for unorthodox behavior. Although he promises himself not to repeat Duffy's errors, he finds himself occupying Duffy's office and reliving his predecessor's ill-fated existence. Excruciatingly lonely, he yields to sexual temptations, becoming involved finally with his department chairman's wife—Duffy's ex-mistress. Yet he can't enjoy his stolen fruits; in addition to his fear of being caught, he is plagued by conscience. For despite having discarded his Judaic heritage, he remains a descendent of Israel's priestly Levites. Hence his shame is intense and spirit-shattering; every sin causes a "pure Levin reaction, for every pleasure, pain."

He shares also the Levitical need to fight misuse of the human spirit and written word. Zealous to impart knowledge to his students, to teach them "what's for sale in a commercial society, and what had better not be," he overdoes it, breeding only incomprehension and dissension among students and faculty. Increasingly frustrated at his failures to establish his ethical standards at the college, he resorts to his opponents' tactics: deceit, connivance, and blackmail.

The final scene is pure Malamud in its symbolism, irony, and pathos. Discharged and beardless, Levin heads south in a second-hand car, crushingly aware his search for integrity and happiness has produced mainly guilt and failure. Not only has he re-lived Leo Duffy's experiences, but he carries with him a woman he no longer loves and her adopted children. She, however, is pregnant, so Levin has, in a sense, found his "new life." If he has mitigated loneliness at some cost to his identity (his child will be but half-Jewish), he actually has gained a partial Malamud victory. In other words, Levin has begun his transformation into Everyman.

A New Life is Malamud's best effort. Plot and background develop more slowly, characters are more fully realized. His sad, eager, little people are neither villains nor paragons; they stand revealed as frightened, love-starved human beings entangled in their own motives, weaknesses, and emotions. But if Malamud here has written his best novel to date, he still could have produced an even better one. He occasionally gives bent to a self-conscious virtuosity which results in lengthy, brittle, and pseudo-poetic ruminations. If dazzled, the reader also is distracted. Also distracting are Malamud's repeated efforts to impose physical nature upon his urban outsider and his essentially urban problems. His Levin is not Tolstoy's, and the pastoral theme so integral to *Anna Karenina* here seems forced and extraneous.

Still, Malamud's technical skills are undeniable. He has an inspired eye and ear for the revealing gesture or word. When under control, as it is during most of *A New Life*, his language is spare, imaginative, and lyrical. If his characters often are left without illusions, they are never completely crushed or dehumanized. If his works are near-achievements rather than major accomplishments, they reveal always an ironic yet compassionate insight into the dark dilemma that is modern life. Surely few of us today can afford to ignore such assistance.

Sam Bluefarb

9.

The Scope of Caricature

Bernard Malamud has often been compared with such great Yiddish writers of the vanished east European ghetto as Sholem Aleichem, Leibush Peretz, and Mendele Sforim. But the most well known of these, the greatest of Yiddish humorists, and the writer Malamud is most often said to resemble, is Sholem Aleichem. Malamud's naturalized—and occasionally assimilated—Jews, however, are not the tightly drawn homogeneous caricatures of Sholem Aleichem's world, those characters we most often think of when we read the work of this American Jewish writer. Caricatures his stories certainly contain, but with a difference. While Sholem Aleichem's characters retain their primary features as children of the ghetto—the self-deprecating irony, the inverted joke, the capacity for suffering, the presence of the *schlemiel* who is both butt and victim of them all—Malamud's people have been diffused into both something more and something less than the Jews of Sholem Aleichem's east European village—the ubiquitous *kleine shtetle*. And while, loosely speaking, they are still Jews, still composed of the small amount of Old World content that went into their creation, they have taken on the New World form. In a word they have become, if not completely assimilated, then—after a fashion—"naturalized." What Malamud's characters have in common, then, with Sholem Aleichem's is the disease of poverty, the capacity for suffering already alluded to, and a vulnerability both of body and soul to the vicissitudes of foul fortune. The knack for ironic self-scrutiny flows from all of these, yet beyond them. Malamud's characters, however, never seem to be endowed with the strength and resilience of their east European forebears —that strength that could counter the pogromist's fist with a wink and a tear-stained laugh, the resilience that catapulted them back into the stream of life after assorted encounters with the angel of death. Nothing short of Hitler's more scientific and efficient methods could extinguish both the wink and the laugh.

If Malamud's characters, like Sholem Aleichem's, are able to sense the irony in their plight, this irony rarely goes beyond the slight grimace, the humorless shrug. His characters are not so much the objects of their own laughter as of ours—and of our commiseration too.

On the other hand, the gentiles in Malamud's stories are quite unlike the gentiles, or peasants, of Sholem Aleichem's tales. In the latter's, they are generally outsiders, hostile forces beyond the perimeter of the ghetto, objects of fear rather than placation. Potentially dangerous in the self-righteousness of their drunken rage, they may kill the Jew as often as curse him. Malamud's gentiles, however, though often portrayed as "different," are as harassed, as vulnerable as his Jews. Indeed, they seem to be mirror-image doubles, "secret sharers," as it were, in the centuries-old trail of blood, guilt, and recrimination. For the many differences between Malamud's gentiles and his Jews are of far less consequence in revealing their common plight—rage and suffering—as is their common humanity. Malamud, like his illustrious east European predecessors, best presents this plight by portraying his characters as caricatures, etched sharply in the dark, gloomy strokes of a Daumier at his most satirical, or a Hogarth at his most mordant. But these caricatures, before Malamud is through with them, ascend to higher altitudes: for the brief moment of insight that is afforded them, they rise from caricature to allegory. One such type is Kessler, in the short story "The Mourners."

The Repentant Reprobate

When we first meet Kessler, he is the lonely Reprobate, the unrepentant betrayer of hearth and home, the man who, years earlier, had abandoned home and family to the cruelties of the world. What we see now, years later, is a lonely bedraggled figure of a man, a former egg candler, who ekes out a bare existence on his post-65 social security. Like so many of Malamud's poor elderly Jews, Kessler lives in a decrepit tenement on New York's lower East Side; here he draws his social security and is haunted by whatever thoughts aged and lonely Reprobates are haunted by. Ignace, the bent-back Polish janitor, who may also be thought of as a caricature—the Polish Janitor has been as much a part of East Side folklore and its milieu as the Prying Parisian Concierge has long been part of the Paris scene—constantly loses at cards to Kessler. In a rage, he latches onto an excuse for getting Kessler out of the tenement: Kessler's flat stinks. The efforts of Ignace, Polish Janitor, and of Gruber, Jewish Landlord, to accomplish that aim are both comic and pathetic. Every ruse and pressure in the book are tried, including both an actual eviction into wintry, snowbound streets and the more benevolent offer to get Kessler a berth in a public home. Nothing suceeds, neither wiles nor threats. Kessler barricades himself in his flat to await his end, so Gruber believes.

One day, overcome by apprehension, Gruber ascends the stairs to Kessler's flat. Gruber has by now threatened Kessler with a forcible dispossession by the marshal. Thus there is no telling just how the old man has reacted to this newer, more formidable pressure. It is then that the idea comes to Gruber to get Kessler into a public home. No one answers Gruber's knock on the door. And so with trepidation the landlord then uses a pass key to gain entrance into Kessler's apartment. With a sigh of relief, Gruber finds the old man very much alive, but far from lively. Instead, he finds Kessler sitting on the floor, shoeless, and in the traditional mourning posture of the religious Jew.

His eyes were downcast, and his body swayed slowly sideways. As the landlord talked on, the old man was thinking of what had whirled through his mind as he sat out on the sidewalk in the falling snow. He had thought through his miserable life, remembering how, as a young man, he had abandoned his family, walking out on his wife and three innocent children, without even in some way attempting to provide for them; without, in all the intervening years—so God help him—once trying to discover if they were dead or alive. How, in so short a life, could a man do so much wrong? This thought smote him to the heart and he recalled the past without end and moaned and tore at his flesh with his fingernails.[1]

From Reprobate as caricature, Kessler has come, through suffering and remorse, to repentance. It is his dissolute past he so repentantly mourns, but in vain now. The final irony, however, is that Gruber, who thinks that Kessler has received bad news, is suddenly jolted into a new, more frightening suspicion: it is he, Gruber himself, whom Kessler is now mourning—Gruber's dead spirit of lost charity. In a sudden fit of contrition for all the pain and suffering which he, Gruber, feels he has caused the old man, and "With a cry of shame he tore the sheet off Kessler's bed, and wrapping it around his bulk, sank heavily to the floor and became a mourner" (p. 26).

In the split second before this impulsive act, Gruber notes that the room no longer lay in its torpor of stench and filth, but "was clean, drenched in daylight and fragrance" (p. 26). The irony of course is that Kessler is not mourning for Gruber—as Gruber mistakenly thinks—but is mourning for the irretrievable past, the irredeemable sins of that past. The mourning here takes on allegoric dimensions, not only for the penitential Kessler the Remorseful Reprobate, but for the repentance of all reprobates—including reprobate landlords. In short, Kessler, who as caricature has been the Sinful Reprobate, rises to become, in his own eyes if not in ours, the throb in the heart of repentance. Man is lost in order that he might be saved—this might well be said of Kessler. And if repentance is the first step on the road to salvation, then Kessler the unsaved, has taken that step.

Other Caricature Types

Mitka—in "The Girl of My Dreams"—is another example of caricature who, by the end of the story, has become something larger. He is of no certain age, but he is probably young—not much beyond his middle or late thirties; with some margin of safety we can probably think of him as the Poor Young Writer; the poverty of course and the lack of visible means of support, though a common plight of Malamud's characters, are especially appropriate here; for this too fits into the form of the overblown caricature. Further, the poverty and the relative youth of Mitka, although generally the boldest strokes in the caricature of a Poor Young Writer, are not the only ones; poverty and youth, under these circumstances, imply certain other elements: obscurity and chronic failure. Mitka has written at least two unpublished novels, the second of which, after a long round of submissions to publishing houses, has just been returned for the last time. At the beginning of the story, Mitka is shown in the remorseless act of burning the thick manuscript of his novel—a kind of self-consciously symbolic act of immolation which Mitka masochistically seems to relish. What we have here are the four classic elements which go into the kind of caricature Mitka is: youth, poverty, obscurity, and self-sacrifice. These elements are of course more universal than the mere caricature suggests. Yet in the combination—as they are presented in Mitka—their effect is unfailing: the character turns into caricature.

One day, Mitka discovers a kindred soul: Madeline Thorne is a poor writer too, who has published a kind of *True Story* confessional in the literary feature column of a newspaper; in this confessional she has revealed within herself the presence of a soul in search of the world's beauty. Her story—the saga of a novel manuscript burnt by mistake (shades of Carlyle!)—becomes so real, so vivid for Mitka that he feels compelled to write to Madeline to tell her how much the story has touched him. Subsequently, they arrange a meeting in—appropriately enough—the reading room of the public library. But instead of the bright girl of his dreams—suggested by the story's title—Mitka meets a lumpy, middle-aged woman whose name isn't Madeline at all but turns out to be—Oh, deceptive world!—Olga. Mitka flees to his ascetic tenement flat, but no longer now the ascetic. No longer will he remain the half starved Writer devoted to a high, but unprofitable, calling. Now he will surrender to the fat, unromantic, silly Mrs. Lutz, his landlady, whose only wishes are that Mitka put on a little weight and be more considerate of her. (To further the first of these wishes, she lavishes on him endless bowls of chicken soup.)

Thus from the caricature of the gaunt, ascetic, half-starved Young Writer, Mitka, through his disillusionment with romance, and his loss of youthful innocence, comes to accept the world of reality. The reality of that world—of the grotesque Madeline and the lustful Mrs. Lutz—has come to replace at last the ruin of Mitka's romantic castle of youth and high hope. Naiveté and innocence—in the person of the Poor Young Writer—has given way to what the world calls adjustment. Mitka may not be much happier, but he is certainly wiser. And though not much happier, he has flung off some of the earlier hardships, starvation, and sexual continence. If, formerly, he has sacrificed the needs of the flesh to those of the spirit, he will now—if sacrifice he must—no longer sacrifice either at the expense of both. He will simply make the best of a second choice. In short, Mitka, in the parlance of the world, has "matured." He has passed from innocence, through experience, to a greater knowledge. He has grown up.

Here, in a sense, as in so many other stories of Malamud, we have both the characters and the milieu of the O. Henry short story, especially as they are represented by the vast impersonality of New York City and its millions. The ingredients are all here —situation (poor starving writer attempts to meet kindred female spirit), plot, suspense, incident, and final twist of ironic ending. Yet while these similarities exist in both authors (and Malamud has perhaps been influenced as much by O. Henry's milieu as by Sholem Aleichem's spirit), the parallel ends not much further beyond them. For while the final "twist" in an O. Henry story usually suggests an optimistic, if not a happy, ending, the final twist in Malamud's stories—when not bathed in the glow of commiserative benevolence—is not so much presented with the flourish of an optimistic pen, but rather with the twist of the ironic knife. O. Henry's caricatures can never escape from the rigid molds prescribed for them by the stringencies of the earlier writer's almost Calvinistically predetermined plots; but Malamud's caricatures became means, not ends in themselves, or ends to satisfy some predesign of plot. His puppets, unlike O. Henry's, draw real blood, surprisingly—not carrot juice —when they are cut by the jagged edges of life. Caricatures, O. Henry's people most certainly are, but they are caricatures who can never rise to allegory; for allegory demands more than the exigency of plot, more than the stock requirements of suspense; it demands nothing less than a view of life which transcends the sentimental to engage reality at both workaday and tragic levels. This Malamud only too effectively achieves in his stories.

The Job Archetype

In the story "Angel Levine," Manischevitz, a middle aged tailor, although he contains elements of caricature, assumes a somewhat larger posture than that of pure caricature—even at the outset. Those elements are there—the Poor Tailor as Suffering Servant—but a larger figure looms, forshadowing both Manischevitz's present (his suffering) and Manischevitz's future (his redemption). For here the figure of the Poor Tailor as Suffering Servant is a re-enactment of the archetypal Job. Although Manischevitz has never quite been the affluent man that Job was supposed to be before *his* disasters were visited on him, Manischevitz has at least been "a man of comfortable means." To this extent the circumstances parallel the biblical story. The fire in which Manischevitz's cleaning store is burnt down, proves to be the initial circumstance in a chain of disastrous circumstances: his son's death in the war, his daughter's elopement with a "lout," his wife's sickness which brings her close to death, the onset of his own nagging backaches, and the downward plunge of the tailor's financial fortunes. Perhaps he might have borne one of these, even two. But coming in "legions" as they have—this is even more than a religious man can stand. Like Job, Manischevitz is a religious man who also finds his faith on trial.

Malamud carries the parallel even further; Manischevitz, like Job who heard God speak out of the whirlwind, is also the recipient of a supernatural visitation . . . except that in "Angel Levine" Malamud, like Henry James before him, never commits himself on the precise nature of the reality he is portraying. Presumably one is asked to accept it on three levels: the real, the supernatural, and the allegoric. For the angel who appears before Manischevitz is none other than a Harlem Negro with the unlikely name of Alexander (Angel) Levine. Levine appears in Manischevitz's small flat one day when the tailor's fortunes have sunk to their lowest ebb, and he is on the verge of denying, or even rebelling against, God. Manischevitz, because of the name, suspects Levine to be a black Jew, a Falasha perhaps—after all he has heard of such people before—who, while there to do him some presumed good, is certainly no angel, not a real, honest-to-goodness angel. But Levine speaks of his being a Jew in the past tense.

" 'You ain't Jewish anymore?' " asks Manischevitz. And Levine's answer is that he has " 'recently been disincarnated into an angel,' " and furthermore an angel who has come to rescue Manischevitz from his sufferings. The test, then, is whether Manischevitz is ready to believe Levine. If one can take the first step, all things, then, will be added. On their first meeting, which takes place in Manischevitz's living room, and which Levine has entered unnoticed, Manischevitz dismisses Levine as a fake. But the Negro is not shaken by this accusation, almost expecting it. Nevertheless, on this occasion, and before he takes his leave of Manischevitz, Levine tells the middle-aged tailor that if he should change his mind, he, Levine, can be found in Harlem.

Although Harlem is a pretty large place in which to search for an "angel"—and a black one to boot!—Manischevitz, the intensity of whose sufferings has risen to an exquisite peak, finally —miraculously?—locates the "angel." When Manischevitz at last runs across him, Levine (implausibly for Manischevitz) is dancing with a mountainous Negress in a neighborhood honky-tonk. But the tailor, still uncertain of Levine's status, returns home—only to be driven back to Harlem by the doctor's announcement that Fanny, his sick wife, cannot last more than another day or two.

On this second occasion Manischevitz braves the sleazy gaudiness of the Harlem joint, the stares, the tauntings of the onlookers, and humbles himself before Levine.

> Tears blinded the tailor's eyes. Was ever a man so tried? Should he say he believed a half-drunken Negro to be an angel?
>
> The silence slowly petrified.
>
> Manischevitz was recalling scenes of his youth as a wheel in his mind whirred: believe, do not, yes, no, yes, no. The pointer pointed to yes, to between yes and no, to no, no it was yes. He sighed. It moved but one had still to make a choice.
>
> "I think you are an angel from God." He said it in a broken voice, thinking, If you said it it was said. If you believed it you must say it. If you believed, you believed (p. 55).

This now is the first step in Manischevitz's redemption. And when, after this trial, he returns, accompanied by Levine this time, to his tenement flat—Hallelujah and Praises!—Fanny is up and about wielding a dust mop under what had almost been her death bed. Manischevitz, overcome with joy, can no longer contain himself and breaks out with, " 'A wonderful thing, Fanny . . . Believe me, there are Jews everywhere.' " Levine is last seen by Manischevitz—or so the tailor believes—taking off from the roof in a whirring noise that suggests the rapid flapping of wings.

In this story, Manischevitz has moved through several levels of experience. From comfortable middleclass owner of a dry cleaning establishment, he has plunged to the depths of grief and suffering, so that he looms large as Suffering Servant embodied in the Job figure. Yet from the moment that Manischevitz affirms his belief in Angel Levine as a genuine angel sent from God—and by so doing, affirming, and even accepting, the very misfortune that sent him to the black angel—Manischevitz is a man reborn. Faith has finally triumphed over suffering and doubt to bring

Manischevitz the redemption that comes of that affirmation. Caricature here is not so pure and undiluted as it was in the case of
Kessler the Reprobate and Mitka the Poor Young Writer. For
here there is also the quality which transcends mere caricature;
it is the quality which casts the *possibility* of Jobian tragedy into
the middle of the twentieth century. And while Manischevitz's
plight is not quite that of Jobian magnitude, there are nevertheless elements in that plight that suggest more than the plight of a
single individual, no matter how small. The presence of a Negro
in the role of angel, and Levine's joyous statement to his wife
that there are "Jews everywhere" suggest also that Manischevitz
is not unaware of the universality of this experience, an experience which has transcended the confines of race, to thrust forth
into the wider unconfined vistas of faith.

Symbolic Images

In "The Magic Barrel," the title story of this collection,[2] the
services of one Pinye Salzman, marriage broker, are enlisted by a
young rabbinical student on the verge of ordination. A friend of
the rabbi suggests that he will find it easier to acquire a congregation if he gets married. Knowing no likely candidates himself,
Leo Finkle, the young rabbi, is forced to turn to the doubtful
services of Pinye Salzman, whom he has discovered advertised in
the back pages of the *Forward*, the Yiddish daily newspaper.

The entire story is an almost stenographic record of the relationship that grows up between Leo and the marriage broker.
Meanwhile, Salzman furnishes the rabbi with seemingly hundreds
of likely—and unlikely—candidates: photographs, descriptions,
specifications, glowing verbal pictures. But no matter how attractive they seem to be, either in personal qualities or in their ability
to fit into the niche of a *rebitzen*, a rabbi's wife, upon further
questioning on Leo's part, something invariably turns up to spoil
the prospect: one candidate is five years older than the twenty-
seven-year-old seminary graduate; another, though young, intelligent, even beautiful, turns out to be "a little lame on her right
foot [as Pinya puts it] . . . but nobody notices on account she is

so brilliant and also so beautiful" (p. 198). Another candidate, who almost turns out to be, perhaps, the most likely—she is only a mere two years older than Leo—has, herself, been completely ensnared by the broker's rapturous, though totally false, picture of the rabbi: Salzman has pictured Leo as a zealous servant of God, a prophet, even a saint. Needless to say, he is anything but. Could the small photograph that one day slips from Salzman's briefcase be another candidate? Leo is interested. But Salzman does his best to discourage him. The picture turns out to be that of Salzman's own daughter ("my baby, my Stella, she should burn in hell!") who, so Salzman tells Leo, is "not a bride for a rabbi." But Leo insists, and Salzman finally, reluctantly, brings them together. What turns into a promise for Leo, becomes disaster for Salzman, who, at the moment of the meeting of the two, stands at a street corner not far from the trysting place, chanting prayers for the dead. Again, the *Kaddish*, the mourner's prayer. Like Kessler, the marriage broker has his own "dead" to remember.

Pinye Salzman, dealer in abortive dreams, has not been able to anticipate such an outcome in his own most ardent dreams. The truth of course is that Pinye as marriage broker, though he deals in dreams—other people's dreams—is altogether too much a cynic, too calloused a character to believe in such dreams himself. In this sense Pinye is both cynic and innocent. That there can be love, Pinye acknowledges, even prates about—with his lips. But it is all he can do to keep from bursting into laughter when Leo talks of love. Of a relationship that goes any deeper than a marriage broker's briefcase, Salzman can have no comprehension, or even sympathy for. The irony of course is that the cynical, calloused marriage broker who deals in dreams isn't able to surmount, or rise above, his own level as a dealer, or better, a trafficker, in dreams. He may talk about the dream of love, the dream of marriage—the sales pitch, as it were, of his cynical view of life—but his course is that he can never really believe in them himself, can never believe in his own products, or believe that these mean any more to others than they mean to himself. And when his own profligate daughter—through an act of God? (there is always the suggestion of this possibility in Malamud's stories) —is drawn to a rabbi, involved in Pinye's own make-believe construct that turns into the real thing, the marriage broker can only begin at last to believe, or perhaps accept, the possibility that marriages may as often be made in hell as in heaven—even a marriage broker's briefcase "heaven." The salesman here, against his will, has been sold his own bill of goods. But with something more than the usual twist.

From Marriage Broker filled with the optimistic myth of hope, love and fulfillment as a sales pitch, Pinye Salzman becomes a creature of his own dark illumination. From Cynical Trader in Dreams, he has himself become the cracked vessel of his own broken dreams.

Other stories of Malamud, in their own way, show caricatures achieving a symbolic image larger than the simple image of the caricature itself: a young New York floor walker, abroad in Italy on a summer vacation, attempts to hide the fact of his Jewish origins from a girl of presumably high-born Italian parentage. He consequently is to learn at last that he has hidden from himself what is most precious about himself. The "high born Italian" girl turns out to be a Jewish survivor of a Nazi death camp. Thus an ungallant Deceiver comes, by way of a counter deception, to learn the price of deceit, and the "innocence" of his prevarication gives way, through experience, to a greater knowledge. Another story, "The Last Mohican," shows Fidelman, an art student on a grant—again the scene is Italy—trailed and plagued through the streets of Rome by Susskind, a *schnorrer,* a cadger. Susskind the poor *schnorrer* proves to be the means by which Fidelman finds his own awakening; from Esthete concerned with the research involved in doing a study of Giotto the Florentine painter, Fidelman finally comes to see in the suffering of a Susskind the Beggar, the root of all suffering, including his own perhaps. As Fidelman comes to stand for more than Esthete, so Susskind comes to stand for more than Beggar. And before the story ends, Fidelman the Esthete, through understanding if not through love, becomes Fidelman the compassionate; and Susskind the *Schnorrer* becomes, through Fidelman's vision, Susskind the hunted, Susskind the outraged human being.

Malamud As Moralist

And so it goes. What seems to contain the ingredient of caricature in Malamud's stories eventually ends as implicit postulate that even in caricature there may be greater truths than the mere caricature itself may suggest. Ben Siegel,* in an incisive and compehensive essay on Malamud which appeared in the spring 1962 issue of *Northern Review*—perhaps one of the best essays on Malamud to date—makes the point that Malamud, if he is nothing else, is "essentially the moralist." Malamud of course is certainly the moralist, but he is the moralist who is capable of stepping out of his immediate role as moralist by objectifying his character into an experience lifted out of the world of allegory. Siegel feels that Malamud fluctuates between realism and allegory. And insofar as Malamud's characters exist in a realistic milieu, they are as "real" as anyone can be: but the reality of a Pinye Salzman, of a Manischevitz, of a Mitka, and a Kessler (not all of Malamud's characters have as much of the caricature in them) depends far more on the act of creation, which extends beyond the reality of "Realism" into the peculiarly distorted reality (in the artistic sense) of the artist. In Malamud's instance this is the art of caricature. The point that Malamud's intent is perhaps highly moralistic—as which significant writing is not?—is perhaps one approach to his place in contemporary American literature.

Certainly a writer who sees the death of six million Jews as the tragedy of our century—and not alone as Jews but as human beings—cannot fail to have his work touched by this signal fact. But beyond Malamud's moral—as distinct from a *moralistic*—scrutiny lies his importance as an artist. Ultimately, Malamud's status as moralist is inextricably bound up with his function as artist—the function which Twain, Shaw, Dickens, and Henry James fulfilled so splendidly as both. We are not suggesting here that Malamud is given to moralizing with a didactic intent, or that those who think of him as a moralist primarily are over-

* See Chapter 8 in this collection.

simplifying the matter either. (One may think of Shaw entirely as a moralist without detracting one wit from Shaw the artist. Indeed, he is the formidable moralist precisely because he was so much the artist!) We cannot say that Twain, Shaw, Dickens, and James were moralists in the narrowly didactic sense either. Yet in no way more than in his ability to view his characters as "viewpoints" which look out on a greater allegorical reality does Malamud resemble his fellow American writers. For the Jews in his stories—while caricatures both as Jews and as human beings—evolve into something larger than either; while they certainly contain within themselves the realism of reality and the distortion of caricature, they also contain elements of the artist's touch which transcend the reality of Realism or the distortion of caricature; in spite of the author's intentions in the matter, they reach larger dimensions. Like the characters of Twain, Shaw, Dickens, and finally Sholem Aleichem himself—who was once called the Jewish Mark Twain and whom Malamud so closely resembles—Malamud's caricatures, though perhaps inspired by his sense of the moral dilemma, in their final effect, end as larger figures than the mere vitality of caricature would indicate; they finally imply a morality which transcends the immediate intentions—whatever they may be—of their creator. Malamud, as creator of these caricatures, has given them a life of their own, and though they are drawn from life itself, the sustenance that sustains these figures has imbued them with these larger dimensions. These dimensions are of course the dimensions of allegory—a result which flows not alone from the artist's moral view of them, but from his deepest insights, his imagination, and ultimately from the control of all these through his art.

Notes

1. Bernard Malamud, *The Magic Barrel* (New York), p. 25 [Random House Vintage paperback edition]. All subsequent references are to this work.
2. This work won the author the National Book Award for fiction in 1959.

Mark Goldman

10.

Comic Vision and the Theme of Identity

In an article entitled "Bernard Malamud and the Jewish Literary Tradition," [1] Earl Rovit * criticizes Malamud for refusing to accept the implications of his own tragic vision. At the crucial moment, it is charged, his characters retreat from tragic self-recognition into Malamud's "Jewish irony—a defensive humor which deflates the portentous moment of his art." They become, for Rovit, "grotesque or ridiculous. . . . And although this deflating common sense approach may be the healthiest way to deal with practical affairs, it falls short of the requirements of the grandest level of art, which demands not common but uncommon sense, not sanity, but poetry." [2]

I would deny that Malamud's seriously drawn characters become "grotesque or ridiculous," whereas other characters move within a complex, ironic world controlled by Malamud's essentially comic view. And I quote these strictures on Malamud's tragic vision, or lack of one, only to suggest that there are really two basic attitudes in Malamud's fiction, tragic and comic (combined in some of his best work), and that to insist that a writer follow the critic's demand for a "poetic consistency" counter to

* See Chapter 1 in this collection.

his own aims, is really to put the critic's cart before the artist's horse.

Malamud's somber mood, with its tragic overtones, permeates many of the stories collected in *The Magic Barrel:* "The First Seven Years," "The Mourners," "Take Pity," "The Loan," etc. These stories take place in a deliberately vague setting of bleak tenement rooms, where characters confront one another and themselves in a Kafkaesque parable of pain and suffering, to emerge in some kind of moral perception. It would be a mistake to think of Malamud as a realistic chronicler of Jewish-American life, though he obviously belongs to an earlier, depression-reared generation than, say, Philip Roth, whose Jews are the heirs of American prosperity, pioneers of the new exodus from the city to Canaans of suburbia. Roth himself has remarked that the Jews of *The Magic Barrel* and Malamud's novel, *The Assistant,* are a kind of "metaphor to stand for certain human possibilities and certain human promises. . . ." And he goes on to say that "Malamud, as a writer of fiction, has not shown specific interest in the anxieties and dilemmas and corruptions of the modern American Jew [Roth's own subject]. . . . ; rather, his people live in a timeless depression and a placeless Lower East Side. . . ." [3] Malamud's rejection of social realism, however, allows him to capture the moment of moral crisis, when his characters transcend their suffering by remembering their common identity as Jews, and recognizing their human stake in the tragic predicament. Readers have been disturbed by Malamud's preoccupation with the suffering Jew. Yet, aside from the fact that Malamud is a Jewish-American writer who uses the material closest to him, he seems to suggest that the Jew's symbolic value is his suffering and what he makes of it. By extension, of course, the moral value of this view extends to all men, and Malamud even satirizes, in a story like "Angel Levine," the Jew as privileged sufferer.

The implications of Malamud's treatment of the Jew and the theme of suffering are summed up in his novel, *The Assistant,* in a crucial dialogue between Morris Bober and the young Gentile, Frank Alpine. Bober is a tragically typical, heroically human Jew whose life has been a long struggle with failure, entombed in the Platonic cave of a grocery store. To this cave comes Frank Alpine (the name suggests his hero, St. Francis, and the outside world). Defeated by life, despairing of his identity in the world, Alpine is employed by the grocer whose store he has helped to rob, befriended by the Jew about whom he still has strange, ambivalent feelings. Though Morris is in no way an orthodox religious Jew, he has a strong ethical sense of the Jewish law, which he tries to explain to the young assistant. Morris Bober's Jewish identity, as he makes clear, is a tragic sense of involvement with life and all human beings. It is a religious pride purged of pride and religiosity. About the Law, Morris Bober says:

> "This means to do what is right, to be honest, to be good. This means to other people. Our life is hard enough. Why should we hurt somebody else? For everybody should be the best, not only for you and me. We ain't animals. This is why we need the Law. This is what a Jew believes."

But this does not satisfy Frank's further suspicion that the Jew enjoys his masochistic role as sufferer.

> "But tell me why it is that the Jews suffer so damn much, Morris? It seems to me that they like to suffer, don't they?"
>
> "Do you like to suffer? They suffer because they are Jews."
>
> "That's what I mean, they suffer more than they have to."
>
> "If you live, you suffer. Some people suffer more, but not because they want. But I think if a Jew don't suffer for the Law, he will suffer for nothing."
>
> "What do you suffer for, Morris?" Frank said.
>
> "I suffer for you," Morris said calmly. . . .
>
> "What do you mean?"
>
> "I mean you suffer for me. . . . If a Jew forgets the Law," Morris ended, "he is not a good Jew, and not a good man." (124)

Morris' answer awakens Frank's guilt over the robbery and

the fact that he still steals from the grocer. More than this, it reveals the assistant's failure to respond to the Jew's humanity and to his own. Only at the end, through love of Bober's daughter Helen (recalling the Jacob-Laban fable of "The First Seven Years") does Frank become Malamud's actual and symbolic Jew.

But as I have suggested, Malamud's art moves through the emotional spectrum, from the serious, tragic temper of *The Assistant* and the stories mentioned earlier, to the serio-comic and purely comic cast of other stories in *The Magic Barrel,* and the novels, *The Natural* and *A New Life.* The comic and tragic views focus on the same material, serve the same thematic ends, though by naturally different fictional means. Malamud's comic fiction is a rich, complex mixture of irony and satire, fantasy and moral fervor. His subject matter is still the Jewish sense of identity and its symbolic, moral meaning. But his characters suffer now from an inverse failure of identity, a comic *hubris* or pride that refuses to see the real self behind the unreal facade. Where tragedy follows man's fate, comedy tries to correct his folly, and Malamud's comic vision returns man to himself and society, though his characters are tested against and apart from their traditional milieu. In their fantasies and frustrations, their defeat and final self-recognition, Malamud's heroes are really modern anti-heroes, like the serio-comic characters of the current "theatre of the absurd." Malamud's humor or satire concentrates on the comic character's flight from himself and reality, but we no longer merely laugh at the foolish or obsessive figure, as in the great comedy of the past. For both writer and reader are no longer clearly on the side of society and its values. We may still laugh at the comic victim, but we are also one with him in his serio-comic search for identity and reality in a world that seems devoid of both.

Though I have referred to Malamud's theme as the Jewish sense of identity—and he has certainly drawn heavily on Jewish material for his subject and style—we should be aware of regarding Malamud as a Jewish-American writer in the older Yiddish or regionalist sense. Malamud has himself insisted on the truism that a writer must create out of the world he knows. And he has been careful to add that he regards himself, Saul Bellow,

Philip Roth and others as essentially American writers (as we must think of Ralph Ellison and James Baldwin in the same way). Actually, the search for identity is not confined to Malamud's so-called Jewish fiction, as I will point out in the discussion of his first novel, *The Natural*. The allusions to Henry James and *The American*, and the deliberate avoidance of specifically Jewish material in his most recent work, *A New Life*, as well as in *The Natural*, should caution us against the easy assignment of Malamud to a purely Jewish literary tradition. Though the sympathetic reader should be aware of the rich Jewish source for Malamud's art, the sophisticated reader should be conscious of the American and universal significance of his moral vision.

As in the more somber tales, Malamud deliberately avoids a realistic social setting for the comic parable or fantasy leading to the moment of self-recognition and reality. Thus, in two stories from *The Magic Barrel*, the title story and "Angel Levine," Malamud uses fantasy as a controlling frame for his mixture of the comic and the serious. The two symbolic characters, Salzman and Levine, matchmaker and Negro-Jewish angel, serve also as comic archetypes or subconscious doubles, those other-selves familiar to readers of Dostoevsky, Conrad, Kafka, and other masters of the modern psyche. This motif of the other- and anti-self is a key to Malamud's comic purpose and the theme of identity. Denial of self, for Malamud, is the demon of unreality, and his heroes suffer the temporary pain and defeat that leads to a comic peripety and recognition of the reality by which they must live. Malamud also creates comic complexity by using the quest motif, where his characters go on a journey in search of experience, romance, or in the words of his latest title, a new life. This is, of course, a classic mode in serious or tragic literature, from *Oedipus* to *Heart of Darkness*, where the spiritual or physical journey begins in innocence and ends in experience or tragic self-knowledge. The comic vision can employ the same device, where the modern anti-hero also moves from blind well-being to self-revelation and reality.

In "The Magic Barrel," Leo Finkle, a young rabbinical student about to be ordained, seeks a wife through the traditional office of a matchmaker. But the matchmaker, Pinye Salzman ("commercial cupid"), is in comic contrast to the proudly shy student. He is full of earthy humor and good sense, smells of smoked fish, has his office "in his socks," and brings the salesman's spirit to the serious question of matrimony. Salzman's hilarious description of his clients reflects Malamud's wonderful use of Yiddish speech rhythms, which he adapts for his own colloquial style.

> "In what else will you be interested," Salzman went on, "if you not interested in this fine girl that she speaks four languages and has personally in the bank ten thousand dollars? Also her father guarantees further twelve thousand. Also she has a new car, wonderful clothes, talks on all subjects, and she will give you a first-class home and children. How near do we come in our life to paradise?"

But all the girls from Salzman's briefcase begin to look alike to Leo Finkle, "all past their prime, all starved behind hard bright smiles. . . . Life, despite their frantic yoo-hooings, had passed them by. . . ." The truth begins to penetrate the academic pride of the young rabbi, as he realizes that his loveless fear of life, and not a pious sense of tradition, has led him to the matchmaker. He sees that he has lived without self-knowledge and that he has not really loved God because he has not loved man. Like Malamud's more purely comic figures, Leo Finkle must finally recognize the truth about himself, and therefore about the world. "The Magic Barrel" ends in fantasy, in a deliberately stagy scene under a lamp-post, where Salzman's own daughter waits for the young rabbi— the fallen woman (in white, with red shoes, smoking a cigarette) finally chosen from the matchmaker's file, out of the depths of the denial of life and demand for penance and salvation that recalls the Biblical prophet Hosea and his God-sent wife and whore. This last scene, like many of Malamud's sudden, summary endings, is a consciously ironic parable and not an escape from tragedy. All the complex meaning is fixed, flashed back upon the story itself in a kind of Joycean epiphany that runs counter to the neatly packaged endings of the naturalistic tale.

"Angel Levine" is a more deliberate fantasy, a serio-comic

folk tale about the tailor Manischevitz (a Jewish Everyman) who, like Job, has lost everything, business, son, daughter; who even now, while his wife lies hopelessly ill, is too sick to work for more than a few hours to maintain their bare existence. But Manischevitz can undercut despair with irony, in the Yiddish tradition of Shalom Aleichem et al., turning the comic cheek only to challenge God's mysterious and perverse ways before man. "Who, after all, was Manischevitz that he had been given so much to suffer? A tailor. Certainly not a man of talent. Upon him suffering was largely wasted. It went nowhere, into nothing. . . ." One evening a Negro suddenly appears in his squalid flat to inform him that he is Alexander Levine, a Jewish angel sent to help Manischevitz. But the astonished old tailor refuses to believe in the Negro Jew —an angel no less—and Levine goes out, saying that he can be found in Harlem when needed. Finally, at the dead end of his suffering, Manischevitz suspends his disbelief and goes on a comic odyssey in search of the angel, wandering through a Harlem where bars become synagogues and praying Negro Jews argue over the "substanceless substance."

Manischevitz finally locates Levine in Bella's bar, much deteriorated (from a lack of belief in him?) into the stereotyped Negro. The tailor reclaims the angel, however, by declaring his faith in him, and Levine goes back to the apartment to perform his deed and depart "on mahogany black wings." The tailor's last words to his restored wife recall the ending of a classic Jewish joke. " 'A wonderful thing, Fanny,' Manischevitz said. 'Believe me, there are Jews everywhere.' " And this is the point of the parable, which throws light on Malamud's cryptic statement, that all men are Jews. In other words, all men suffer, and the need to move beyond narrow religious pride (here the Jew's sense of his unique role as sufferer is parodied) in order to recognize that one's human identity is the real revelation of this comic fantasy.

Malamud's comic approach to the theme of identity can be seen most clearly in two stories from *The Magic Barrel*, "The Lady of the Lake," and "The Last Mohican." In "The Lady of the Lake," the comic hero or anti-hero is Henry Levin, a floor-walker at Macy's who inherits some money and goes abroad "seeking romance." The central character in this story, as in "The Last

Mohican," is a Jamesian innocent traveling to Europe for the experience missed in America. Since Malamud's characters are Jewish, however, their return is an ironic reversal, somewhat comic and unreal, of their escape from the dark oppression of European history. Levin also changes his name for the journey to Henry R. Freeman, another reminder of the Jamesian American (as, in *A New Life*, the hero, newly arrived in the west, stands before his host's bookcase and stares at a novel—James' *The American*). Freeman finally gets to Italy and settles in Stresa on beautiful Lake Maggiore. He visits the islands on the lake and is especially drawn to Isola del Dongo, an enchanted isle that reminds him sadly of his lost years and of what he is still seeking. From this point, the story moves in a mixed atmosphere of romance and ironic realism. With luck and persistence, Freeman finally meets the girl who lives on the island and is immediately awed by her aristocratic, historic beauty. "Her dark, sharp Italian face had the quality of beauty which holds a moment of history, the beauty of a people and civilization." (The full, ironic force of this description is felt at the end of the story.) After so much hunger for love and life, he feels that his fated moment has come at last, but his real comic fate is implicit in their first encounter. "Are you an American?" she inquired, her Italian accent pleasantly touched with an English one. "That's right." The girl studied him for a full minute and then hesitantly asked, "Are you perhaps Jewish?" It is a complex, comic moment; for the crucial question, sudden, incongruous, is the right one at the wrong time. Freeman's reaction is to the near-fatal thrust at his flimsy structure of ambivalent dreams and escapist desires, and he misses the meaning of his temptation. He is stunned into a denial of his identity and pursues his romantic dream, still puzzled by her startling question, "because he absolutely did not look Jewish. But then he figured her question might have been a 'test' of some kind. . . . , quickly to determine eligibility." (In "The Last Mohican," Fidelman, an American art critic just arrived in Rome, is met at the station by a little man in brown knickers, whose first word is the Hebrew greeting, *shalom*. The man, Shimon Susskind, then explains: "I knew you were Jewish. . . . the minute my eyes saw you.") Freeman's lady of the lake tells him what he has hopefully suspected, that she is Isabella del Dongo, the daughter of the famous family who own the island and its historic palazzo. The theme of pretense persists, however, as Isabella shows him through the palace in which Napoleon did not really sleep and the famous paintings and statuary are only copies. Freeman is not so much disappointed by this discovery as by the fact that he could not "tell the fake from the real." Further on, they come to some tapestries depicting scenes from Dante's *Inferno*. Freeman is held by one, of a suffering leper, and wonders what he could have done to deserve such a fate. "He falsely said he could fly," Isabella explains. "For that you go to hell?" exclaims Freeman.

Malamud's moral clues clearly anticipate Freeman's fall. Like St. Peter, he denies his identity three times, unprepared again for his second trial, when Isabella suddenly compares the Alpine peaks to a Menorah, the seven-branched candelabra of the Jewish Hanukkah. For a wild moment, Freeman has a "frightening remembrance of her seeing him naked as he came out of the lake and felt constrained to tell her that circumcision was de rigueur in stateside hospitals, but he didn't dare. She may not have noticed." So he fails the second test, whereupon Isabella confesses that she is not a del Dongo but the daughter of the poor caretaker of the island palace. Though he is disturbed by the lie, Freeman recognizes his equal guilt and decides in any case to declare his love for Isabella. The final scene presents a familiar Malamud composition of romantic moonshine, comic fantasy, and moral truth. To Isabella's goodbye, Henry counters that he has come to marry her. For the last time, like the princess in a fairy tale, she asks the fateful question; to which he replies, deaf to his own damning words: "How many no's make a never?" Isabella then bares her breast, branded at Buchenwald, and tells him that she is Jewish and cannot marry him because he is not. Though Freeman has said that his past is expendable, hers is too meaningful to sacrifice. Crushed by the tragicomic truth of his situation, he cries out: "Oh, God . . . why did you keep this from me, too?" But her answer only probes deeper to the ironic core of his self-deception. "I did not want to tell you something you would not welcome." At the end, Isabella fades into a Walter Scott mist, and Henry R. Levin Freeman is alone, the real victim of his unreal desires. What he hoped to win by escape he loses, and Isabella leaves him groping for her maternal breasts, but embracing now (like John Marcher in James' *The Beast in the Jungle*) "only moonlit stone."

The comic hero of "The Last Mohican" is another innocent Jewish-American, an aspiring art critic named Fidelman who comes to Rome in order to write a book on Giotto. Arriving in Rome, he stands before the railroad station, breathing in the romantic air of the city, bathing blissfully in a sudden moment of complete self (satisfied) knowledge.

> In the midst of his imagining, Fidelman experienced the sensation of suddenly seeing himself as he was, to the pinpoint, outside and in, not without bitter-sweet pleasure; and as the well-known image of his face rose before him he was taken by the depth of pure feeling in his eyes, slightly magnified by glasses, and the sensitivity of his elongated nostrils and often tremulous lips, nose divided from lips by a mustache of recent vintage that looked, Fidelman thought, as if it has been sculptured there, adding to his dignified appearance, although he was on the short side.

Fidelman's self-portrait, distorted by pride or *hubris*, is full of dire, comic portent. Lost in contemplative ego, he is unaware that all the while he is being watched, formulated, by a short stranger in brown knickers, the Shimon Susskind mentioned earlier. If Fidelman is the familiar, innocent American, Susskind is his classic counterpart, the historic European Jew, the exile from those countries whose names are sufficient to evoke the speechless suffering of the past: Germany, Hungary, Poland—"Where not?" Characteristically, he has the spirit and resilience of the wanderer, the *luftmensch* who lives by his wits. Paradoxically, he has even left Israel, unwilling to find a home at last. Refusing to go back, again stateless, he is still jealous of the curious freedom of the alien Jew. In his comic, mysterious way, Susskind also becomes Fidelman's double, the pursuing and pursued something that Fidelman lacks to complete his education as a Jew and scholar. He follows the pedantic art critic through Rome like the shadow of a history Fidelman has forgotten in pursuit of a history he hardly understands. "It was an inspiring business, he, Arthur Fidelman, after all, born a Bronx boy, wallowing around in all this history." Though Fidelman gives Susskind some money, he keeps turning up with propositions to invest in various peddling ventures, persisting in a request for one of the critic's two suits. When Fidelman refuses to give him the suit and recommends that Susskind return to Israel, the little man loudly rejects the suggestion. Exasperated, wishing to be rid of this *schnorrer* (a beggar with style) and to get on with his work, Fidelman finally explodes.

> "Am I responsible for you then, Susskind?"
> "Who else?" Susskind loudly replied.
> "Lower your voice, please, people are sleeping around here," said Fidelman, beginning to perspire. "Why should I be?"
> "You know what responsibility means?"
> "I think so."
> "Then you are responsible. Because you are a man. Because you are a Jew, aren't you?"

After another encounter in a restaurant, where Fidelman again refuses him the suit, the critic returns to his hotel to find his briefcase with the first chapter of his work on Giotto missing. Nothing else has been taken and the crime points to only one person, Susskind; though Fidelman cannot imagine why he should take a briefcase instead of the clothes or money he needed. At this point, the situation is reversed, and Fidelman becomes the pursuer, Susskind the pursued. A methodical scholar, Fidelman is unable to go on without the missing first chapter. But what he is now pursuing is the real missing chapter of his own past, of himself. Now that he is looking for Susskind, he is nowhere to be found, and Fidelman is haunted by his image, dreaming at night of "pursuing the refugee in the Jewish catacombs under the ancient Appian Way, threatening him with a blow on the presumptuous head with a seven-branched candelabra he clutched in his hand." Finally, one Friday night he wanders into a Sephardic synagogue along the Tiber. In the midst of this mysterious past, his own rises up before him. "Where in the world am I?" His inquiry after Susskind then takes him to the Roman ghetto. Slowly, darkly, as if in a dream, he walks the "mazed streets . . . oppressed by history." The quest goes on, as he is directed to the cemetery, Jewish section, where Susskind is sometimes a professional mourner for the dead. And though the ubiquitous ghost of Susskind is nowhere to be found, other spirits haunt Fidelman, as he goes among the Jewish gravestones, with flowers strewn secretly by "renegade sons and daughters," and memorials to those who died in the war, including a cenotaph for a father betrayed by the fascists and exterminated at Auschwitz.

Three months go by before Fidelman finally sees Susskind, selling rosaries in front of St. Peter's (and drawing the obvious parallel between two paradoxes: Fidelman's Giotto and the peddler's rosaries). Though he follows Susskind and later searches his hovel, he does not find the lost briefcase. That night he dreams again, of a cemetery and an empty grave, out of which rises the "long-nosed brown shade, Virgilio Susskind, beckoning."

> Fidelman hurried over.
> "Have you read Tolstoy?"
> "Sparingly."
> "Why is art?" asked the shade, drifting off.

The wonderful Yiddish twist to Tolstoy's title reveals Susskind as the Virgilian guide to Fidelman's descent into himself. The academic, abstract critic has not really understood art and its relation to life. In his last dream, Fidelman sees Giotto's great painting of St. Francis offering his cloak to a poor beggar. The moral of the vision is clear; the Giotto scholar has missed the meaning of Giotto himself. "Fidelman awoke running." He arrives at Susskind's door, carrying the symbolic suit, only half aware of some burning paper being used to light a candle. When Susskind restores the briefcase at last, the chapter is missing, and Fidelman, remembering the flaming paper, cries out:

"You bastard, you burned my chapter."
"Have mercy," cried Susskind, "I did you a favor."
"I'll do you one and cut your throat."
"The words were there but the spirit was missing."

Fidelman chases the flying Susskind but stops suddenly, struck by
a moment of true self-recognition. " 'Susskind, come back,' he
shouted, half sobbing. 'The suit is yours. All is forgiven.' " But the
final glimpse of Susskind is of the disappearing refugee, "still running." He has served as the comic corrective of Fidelman's false
image of himself and has brought him full circle to the final
revelation rooted in the real past.

Malamud by-passed his Jewish subject matter for his first
novel, *The Natural*, and went beyond the familiar world of *The
Magic Barrel* and *The Assistant* for his latest novel, *A New Life*.
The Natural is, curiously enough, a baseball novel; on the surface, a kind of Ring Lardner satire of our national mania, in
which the hero, Roy Hobbs, on the eve of his major league try-
out, is shot by a mad beauty named Harriet Bird, cut down "in
the very flower of his youth." The book really begins years later,
when Roy arrives for a final season with a last place, spiritless
team, the Knights. No longer the corn-fed, bright-eyed hero of
baseball myth; at thirty-four he has lived with chronic defeat but
is still trying to realize the dream that ended long ago in the hotel
room where he met his crazy, unromantic fate. Though the novel
unreels with all the whackiness of a Joe E. Brown film, we begin
to recognize familiar Malamud themes beneath the farcical surface. Like Malamud's other comic heroes, Roy must learn from
his experience in order to break through the circle (like the
baseball sphere itself) of his failures. Ironically, he must learn to
choose the real before he can become the mythic hero he embodies. Yet he continues to suffer because he does not learn, choosing, as he admits, the women who repeatedly "burn" him, types
of the American sexual dream, from Harriet Bird and her silver
bullet (out of Mickey Spillane) to the manager's niece whose
name is its own parody, Memo Paris. The moral tension that tries
so many Malamud heroes is revealed in a dialogue between Roy

and Iris Lemon, the one woman he meets who loves and understands him. She is neither very young nor very beautiful, and she
has also suffered; but unlike Roy she has created life, reality, out
of her experience. Her name is the ironic oxymoron that reflects
Roy's own struggle. At their first meeting, not in love's hothouse,
the hotel room, but in a natural lakeside setting, Roy suddenly
releases all the despair and bitter longing locked for so long
within him.

> He coughed, tore his voice clear and blurted, "My goddam
> life didn't turn out like I wanted it to."
> "Whose does?" she said cruelly. He looked up. Her ex-
> pression was tender.
> The sweat oozed out of him. "I wanted everything."
> His voice boomed out in the silence.
> She waited.
> "I had a lot to give to this game."
> "Life?"
> "Baseball. If I had started out fifteen years ago like I
> tried to, I'da been the king of them all by now."
> "The king of what?"
> "The best in the game," he said impatiently.
> She sighed deeply. "You're so good now."

Roy still does not see what is clear to Iris: his denial of self, the
repeated failure of an unreal quest for false values. She believes
that experience, suffering, can save us if (a persistent Malamud
theme) we will save ourselves. She answers Roy's self-pity out of
her own self-knowledge.

> "Experience makes good people better."
> She was staring at the lake.
> "How does it do that?"
> "Through their suffering."
> "I had enough of that," he said in disgust.
> "We have two lives, Roy, the life we learn with and the
> life we live with after that."

And she concludes about suffering, striking home to the unseeing Roy. "It teaches us to want the right things."

Malamud's fiction suggests certain moral equations. Knowledge of self equals knowledge of the world; to want the right things is to make real choices. In his most recent novel, *A New Life*, the hero, S. Levin, is again the serio-comic innocent, a slow-starter and late-finisher moving from a meaningless, sordid past toward (he hopes) a meaningful future. Unlike the Levin of "The Lady of the Lake," Malamud's hero now goes westward, to the Pacific Northwest for his first job as an English instructor; a Jewish Natty Bumppo (as one reviewer put it) at the other end of the continent from the cave of Morris Bober's grocery store.

The first part of the book is the by-now familiar satire of a petty province of academe, Cascadia College (which Levin mistakes for a liberal arts school), where the English department is dedicated to freshman composition (academic k.p.) and the chairman's text (The Elements of Grammar, 13th ed.); and the head of composition, Gerald Gilley, cuts out old *Life* magazines for a pictorial history of American literature. Early in the novel, Levin is the tenderfoot Easterner, the academic sad sack or *shlimazel* of Yiddish literature, invoking nature like a tenement Rousseau: "Now he took in miles of countryside, a marvelous invention." His first D. H. Lawrence role ("You gave up the Metropolitan Museum of Art and got love in a haystack") ends in comic disaster, however, when his pants are stolen by a Syrian rival, and his waitress partner, after a cold walk home, berates the bearded city boy and would-be lover: "You ain't a man."

. As the book progresses, Levin assumes the ironic moral consciousness that challenges the values around him. He falls in love with Gerald Gilley's wife, Pauline, and their affair is first consummated in the woods, though this flirtation with nature leads to the serious consequence of love (and the heart over the haystack). Like other Malamud heroes, Levin must abandon his romantic notion of a new life as an escape from the old. The move west also becomes a comic critique of the frontier myth in its modern phase; the faith in change of place as a substitute for change of soul, or a kind of moral primitivism. The only escape from the past, as we have seen, is through a new acceptance of it. At the end of the novel, Levin can accept himself in terms of his love for Pauline and the responsibility of marriage to an older woman with two children (and again pregnant). And he must accept an even stranger, more cruel burden, since Gerald has agreed to give up the children if Levin will promise never again to teach in a college. Gerald's weird revenge is part of his bitter attack on Levin the outsider, the bearded city-subversive ("No more New Yorkers, goddamit," Gerald shouts at Levin) who has stolen his wife and challenged his sporting-goods faith in nature with a spiritual faith in ideas. Though the word is mentioned only once in the novel, Levin's Jewishness is clearly implied, and Pauline adds the ironic nail to Levin's comic fate when she admits to having picked his application from a pile discarded by her husband because, she explains:

> "You look as though you needed a friend."
> "Was that the reason?"
> "I needed one. Your picture reminded me of a Jewish boy I knew in college who was kind to me during a trying time in my life."
> "So I was chosen," Levin said.

He leaves Cascadia with Pauline and the children, in a battered car, jobless, on another un-romantic journey. Yet Levin triumphs at last because he has found himself; he can accept what fate and Pauline have willed for him. Gerald has ruthlessly described Pauline's faults as wife and woman in order to reveal to Levin his ridiculous position:

> "An older woman than yourself and not dependable, plus two adopted kids, no choice of yours, no job or promise of one, and assorted headaches. Why take that load on yourself?"

But Levin's answer is fierce with the finality of a new and profound self-knowledge: "Because I can, you son of a bitch." He has found himself beneath the beard, behind the comic mirror. As they drive through the campus for the last time, heading out of town, Levin gives Pauline a pair of earrings he has saved for her. Their concluding words end the search for Levin, happily surrendering S. for Seymour, Sy for sigh, even Pauline's Lev for love, simply to identify with the real past.

> She fastened them on her ears. "God bless you, Lev."
> "Sam, they used to call me at home."
> "God bless you, Sam."

The search for the real is a function of the quest for identity in Malamud's fiction. This notion of identity is especially crucial for the Jewish-American writer, caught between an American ethos, his manifest subject, and a deeper consciousness of his Jewish self and world. Writing about another Jewish-American writer, Saul Bellow, Leslie Fiedler has related the problem to the "need of the Jew in America to make clear his relationship to that country in terms of belonging or protest, and a language and speech enriched by the dialect and joyful intellectual play of Jewish conversation." [4] But this ambivalent role (this duality of the diaspora) applies to the European writer as well, once he has escaped from the Yiddish *shtetl* or village, whose community of values produced a remarkably vital literature despite or because of a self-contained culture surrounded by an alien society. An extraordinary Russian-Jewish writer like Isaac Babel, for example, who was later purged by the Communists, retained a ruthlessly ironic attitude toward his old Jewish identity posed against the new brotherhood of assimilated man proclaimed by the revolution. His *Red Cavalry* stories are brutal, moving accounts of the anomalous Jew as Soviet intellectual in a Cossack world, and Babel's creative force is generated out of this tragicomic union of opposites.

But if Babel's Soviet-Jew and Malamud's American-Jew reflect the conflict of the assimilating hero haunted by the pull of history, what of a younger writer like Philip Roth and his American Jews of the post-war prosperity, safe in suburbia, razed of the dark shadows of the past? Ironically, the Jewish hero of "Goodbye Columbus" is an alien or outsider among his own people. It is as if all the dreams of freedom and safety and comfort have been dazzlingly realized by the Jew in America, only to have the young writer ask, in the midst of the milk and honey, what of the old ways of the mind and spirit? If Malamud's characters are caught between an individual escape and acceptance, Roth's world has escaped *en masse*, as a culture, absorbed like the other immigrant groups into a blurred image of middle-class America, where only the writer's comic pen can trace the outlines of that dissembling portrait. The hero of "Goodbye Columbus" finally abandons his suburban sweetheart, because he cannot accept the new Jewish world of American orthodoxy, the distorted reflection in the middle-class mirror.

The tragicomic dilemma of Roth's suburban Jew is most dramatically explored in the last story from the *Goodbye Columbus* volume, "Eli the Fanatic." Eli Peck is a young lawyer in the town of Woodenton (note the name); a suburb whose comfortable calm is suddenly destroyed by the appearance of a *Yeshivah* or Hebrew school run by a European refugee. Eli is delegated to investigate the strange children who live and study there and the stranger "greenie," an older man who haunts the stores and minds of Woodenton Jews with his dark Talmudic figure and dress. The story moved between the poles of reality in Eli's mind: the comic reaction of the Woodenton Jews to their haunted past, and his own awareness of a secret attraction to that past, to the "greenie" who is, as in Malamud's stories, his double or deeper self. He sends the "greenie" one of his own suits (green tweed) and finds the box returned on his doorstep, with the "greenie's" strange garments inside. Eli puts on the curious clothes, musty, worn with memories he cannot recall, and walks down Coach House Road for the whole town to see his (and their) real identity. But his friends and neighbors are only convinced that he is having a nervous breakdown and he is followed to the hospital where he goes to visit his new-born son. In the hospital, Eli stares through the glass at the boy who is the latest link in the chain of identity, the child to whom he must will the cast-off clothes.

> He'd wear it, if he chose to. He'd make the kid wear it! Sure! Cut it down when the time came. A smelly hand-me-down whether the kid liked it or not!

But his wife's psychiatrist, the town of Woodenton, and the world, lie in wait for Eli. The men in the white coats come for him, calming his screams of protest ("I'm the father!") long enough to administer the modern sedative for the old sickness.

> In a moment they tore off his jacket—it gave so easily, in one yank. Then a needle slid under his skin. The drug calmed his soul, but did not touch it down where the blackness had reached.

Yet the plunge into darkness at the end of "Eli the Fanatic" conflicts with the traditional comic ending and a return to the world with a renewed sense of life. What Roth's ending reveals is his own tragicomic dilemma as a Jewish-American writer, caught between two worlds, conscious of an identity and an ideal no longer subscribed to by a conformist, middle-class society. Malamud appears to resolve or at least escape from this dilemma by avoiding Roth's deliberately social satire. Though Malamud's comic characters deviate from their Jewish identity, their escape is not a social rejection but rather a personal flight from reality.

Malamud is finally the moralist faithful to his comic view of identity. He believes, with T. S. Eliot and "Sam" Levin of *A New Life*, in the pastness of the present and the presentness of the past. Like Levin he also believes that we can go into the world with the old self made new by acceptance, by love. Unlike the tragic idealist, Malamud presents with persuasive force the creed of the comic artist: light over darkness, life over death.

Notes

1. *Critique,* Vol. III, No. 2 (Winter-Spring, 1959), 3-11. (See Chapter 1 in this collection.)
2. *Ibid.,* p. 10.
3. Philip Roth, "Writing American Fiction," *Commentary,* Vol. XXIII (March, 1961), 228-9.
4. Reprinted in *The Modern Critical Spectrum,* edited by Gerald J. and Nancy M. Goldberg (N.J., 1962), p. 156.

Charles Alva Hoyt

11.

The New Romanticism

"Suffering is like a piece of goods," says Frank Alpine, the dogged hero of *The Assistant;* "I bet the Jews could make a suit of clothes out of it." The suffering of the Jews is to Bernard Malamud the stuff and substance of his art; from it he has fashioned works of surpassing beauty and integrity, and a sure place among the best writers of his time.

"The other funny thing," Alpine continues, "is that there are more of them around than anybody knows about." This emphasis upon the universality of the Jew—even the identity of Jew and Gentile, for the two merge in some of Malamud's more interesting characters, including Frank Alpine—and thus, the insistence upon the community of human suffering, lifts Malamud's work from his own period and place and sets it in competition with the best writing of any time. This is as it should be. One hears Malamud referred to as a "Jewish writer." He is a Jewish writer in the same sense that Dickens is a social-protest writer, or Jane Austen a domestic novelist.

Suffering is Malamud's theme, and upon it he works a thousand variations: some comical, some menacing; some austere, some grotesque; some imaginative, others classic. The Jew as symbol for suffering mankind is hardly an original idea. In Malamud there is considerable individuality, however: in his style, for example, which is highly personal yet generous and attentive to the requirements of outsiders, the public; in his characterization, variegated, kaleidoscopic, but in essence shifting combinations of only two or three basic forms. Most of all Malamud reveals his personality in his attitude, which is strikingly and overwhelmingly Romantic.

Because criticism has to stalk its prey from a distance, its dicta sometimes fall to the ground well behind the retreating quarry, the live work of art. In the museum they arrange these things differently. Just at present there is particularly noticeable one of these gaps between the classifier and the classified. The New Critics, sunk into dotage, have bequeathed to their disciples an assortment of missiles which although effective in the nineteen-thirties, have proven totally inadequate when directed at the bounding Romanticism of the sixties. It is becoming increasingly evident that the inevitable has happened; that the athletic fatalism of Hemingway, the closed "realism" of the Naturalistic school, the chipped classicism of Eliot and T. E. Hulme, have engendered their opposites. Romanticism is by now abroad in all its traditional forms, and proliferating: Youth in Revolt (Kerouac and others of the Beat group; England's Angry Young Men), Glorification of Energy, and Passion Unconfined (the Picaresque romps of Saul Bellow and J. P. Donleavy), The Unleashed Imagination (Thomas Pynchon, Joseph Heller), Social Protest (James Baldwin and others above), and of course, the Cult of the Self, which so baffles the classicist critic (J. D. Salinger has certainly out-Wordsworthed Wordsworth here, drawing upon himself new Jeffreys, as has to a lesser degree Norman Mailer). To this exuberant ill-assorted group Malamud stands as philosopher, or deepest thinker, perhaps.

While it cannot be seriously suggested that the writers mentioned above are committed to any sort of concerted program, it is easily demonstrable that many or most of them hold certain principles in common. Instead of taking up these principles at their peripheral positions, I should prefer just at present to move to what I conceive to be their center, their common point of issuance: the fundamental Romantic Rejection of Objectivity. Classicism observes the arrangement of things—very likely records it

—and wisely adapts itself to Order. Romanticism, refusing to accept a mere catalogue, reorders things to suit itself. Naturalism simply despairs.

Take the problem of suffering, for example. Naturalism can offer nothing better than this: "curse God and die." Classicism suggests graceful acquiescence, and an alternate problem, one better adapted to Man's limitations: "Know then thyself, presume not God to scan; / The proper study of Mankind is Man." Romanticism, finally, calls the problem itself into question: "How do you know but ev'ry Bird that cuts the airy way, / Is an immense world of delight clos'd by your senses five?" The tormented characters of Bernard Malamud's fiction, although fated often to despair, curse, submit, and turn aside, still cling to the Romantic's determination to reject old evidence, to present a new solution that will be bigger than the sum of its parts. It is this highly characteristic Romantic drive that supplies the impetus of Malamud's greatness; it can be found, in one form or another, in each of his works to date.

Foremost among these is *The Assistant*, Malamud's second novel, an acknowledged masterpiece. Most of his readers discovered him in the year of its publication, 1958, or in 1959, when his first collection of short stories, *The Magic Barrel*, won the National Book award. These thirteen stories and the novel which crowns them are the products in the main, it would seem, of one intense period of creativity, the nineteen fifties. Early in this period, we have that curious work *The Natural*, published in 1952, Malamud's first novel; after it we have another burst of publication in the early sixties: a third novel, *A New Life*, 1961, and another collection of stories, *Idiots First*, 1963. These later works represent no departure; obviously some of them are partially or wholly products of the fifties. They are closely related in every way to the works published in 1958 and 1959. At least two of the stories in *Idiots First* belong to the early fifties; one, "The Cost of Living," is the source of *The Assistant*, which may explain why it was not published in the earlier collection. Most of the stories in *Idiots First*, however, would seem to date from the early sixties, as does *A New Life*. All of these works represent a continuous flow of ideas in the same direction; and since none of the recent ones has surpassed *The Assistant,* it must be with that novel that we begin our study.

One of Malamud's strongest and best claims to enduring recognition is his instinct for myth. From his first novel, which is at times almost entirely removed from the plane of ordinary reality, to his latest short story, he provides for his characters and their situations a ritual shadow of significance which never seems contrived, and at times is simply astonishing in its effectiveness. It is this quality which has time and again fascinated critics of *The Assistant.* Here Malamud has realized an age-old prophecy: the lion lies down with the kid. Once side by side, they look very much alike.

Frank Alpine, a drifting down-and-outer who has wandered into petty crime, becomes involved in the robbery and beating of Morris Bober, a luck-deserted Jewish grocer. *The Assistant* is the story of Alpine's slow, bitter self-subjection to his former victim; their lives become increasingly entangled until Alpine *becomes* Bober: at the grocer's death he takes his place, an assistant no longer. Out of the dirt and the deprivation of the novel's slum setting there has come, not the Naturalistic cry of pain, but an inescapable sense of mystic union: the identity of the oppressor and the oppressed.

The oppressed is presented as the Jew in this novel; Alpine is Italian—"I am of Italian extraction." But from the start these distinctions are blurred; there is nothing particularly "Italian" about Alpine, except that he understands the preparation of minestrone and pizza; and Bober has his Jewishness called into question at his own funeral. The Rabbi defends him: " 'Yes, Morris Bober was to me a true Jew because he lived in the Jewish experience, which he remembered, and with the Jewish heart. Maybe not to our formal tradition—for this I don't excuse him—but he was true to the spirit of our life—to want for others that which he wants also for himself.' " Thus defined, the Jewish spirit does not differ appreciably from the Christian. As for Alpine, he passes from scorn to wonder at Bober's plight; to sympathy, and finally to identification. Early in the book he stands aloof: "That's what they live for, Frank thought, to suffer. And the one that has got the biggest pain in the gut and can hold onto it the longest without running to the toilet is the best Jew. No wonder they got on his nerves."

But a short time later he is himself called a Jew, with some justice if little delicacy, by his former partner in crime. In some incomprehensible fashion Frank Alpine has taken Bober's fate upon himself, and even a cheap hoodlum like Ward Minogue can see it. Less perceptive and more fearful is Bober's wife, who dreads an entanglement between Alpine and her daughter: " 'But a goy, Helen, an Italyener' "—" 'A man, a human being like us.' " Helen is not always as charitable. Her feeling for Frank suffers a terrible revulsion; at the novel's end they are still estranged, although not hopelessly so. Bober himself frequently discourages his assistant—we are not to understand that any union of Man, even one in misery, is cheaply attained. But Frank Alpine, like most of Malamud's heroes, slogs ahead doggedly, often even in spite of himself. It is at Bober's funeral that he observes that suffering is like a piece of goods from which clothing may be made; shortly afterwards, at the novel's end, he puts it upon himself symbolically as he has already done in actual fact: "One day in April Frank went to the hospital and had himself circumcised . . . The pain enraged and inspired him. After Passover he became a Jew."

The relationship between two men is the heart of the book. They are the grocer and assistant, father and son, aggressor and victim, missionary and convert, even sacrifice and priest—if the idea seems farfetched, it may seem less so upon reconsideration of *The Natural:* the mystic slaughter of the king has apparently occupied Malamud's mind from the start. Quintessentially, both Alpine and Bober are true to one basic type, that which is at once both object and impulse of all Malamud's art: the *schlemiel.* Struggling, striving, always en route, but destined never quite to arrive, the *schlemiel* is both the butt and terror of the Gods. At heart he is decent, but whatever he touches turns to ashes; because he *cares,* he exposes himself continually to rebuffs, absurdities, humiliation. He is well-known to art: as Chaplin's tramp he loves too well, but rarely wisely, so that his love is scarcely ever reciprocated. The *schlemiel's* relationships with women are tragicomic. He intends nothing but good to his fellow

creatures; yet because of his naïveté, his awkwardness, his obtrusiveness, and worst of all, his consistent bad luck, he embroils them
in nothing but heartbreak and confusion. They are not slow to
learn to avoid him, but he will never know why.

In *The Assistant* both the aggressor and his victim are fundamentally *schlemiels*. Consider Frank Alpine:

> "I've been close to some wonderful things—jobs, for instance,
> education, women, but close is as far as I go. Don't ask me
> why, but sooner or later everything I think is worth having
> gets away from me in some way or other. I work like a mule
> for what I want, and just when it looks like I am going to
> get it I make some kind of stupid move, and everything that
> is just about nailed down blows up in my face . . . I want
> the moon so all I get is cheese . . . what I mean to say is
> that when I need it most something is missing in me, in me
> or on account of me. I always have this dream where I want
> to tell somebody something on the telephone so bad it hurts,
> but then when I am in the booth, instead of a phone being
> there, a bunch of bananas is hanging on a hook."

Frank's actions throughout the novel are nothing more than ex-
position of this theme, his introduction of himself in the second
chapter. As for Bober, his is a classic case. Here is his daughter's
evaluation of him:

> The grocer, on the other hand, had never altered his for-
> tune, unless degrees of poverty meant alteration, for luck
> and he were, if not natural enemies, not good friends. He
> labored long hours, was the soul of honesty—he could not
> escape his honesty; it was bedrock; to cheat would cause an
> explosion in him, yet he trusted cheaters—coveted nobody's
> nothing and always got poorer. . . . He was Morris Bober
> and could be nobody more fortunate. With that name you
> had no sure sense of property, as if it were in your blood
> and history not to possess, or if by some miracle to own some-
> thing, to do so on the verge of loss. At the end you were sixty
> and had less than at thirty. It was, she thought, surely a
> talent.

Struck down by his assailant's gun, Bober falls, "without a cry. The end fitted the day. It was his luck, others had better."

The curious thing is that these characters, who dominate Malamud's fiction, are actually dignified, elevated by their plight, or to be exact by their reaction to it. Classicism, when it considers the downtrodden at all, utilizes them for the sake of irony; that is, it is really looking at someone else, someone important. Gay's footpads and whores, and Swift's Clever Tom Clinch, losers all, are not presented on the basis of their own merits. Naturalism, although it deals almost exclusively with such figures, is no more genuinely concerned with them; they are rather pawns, counters in a contest of reproaches with the Deity. Only the Romantic will wish to present them in such a way that they epitomize Man's condition—struggling, stumbling ahead, not winning, but not losing either. The reason the *schlemiel* receives new rebuffs is that he always makes new efforts; and once in a while these efforts are granted success. If none of his triumphs is permanent, neither are his failures.

The *schlemiel* is the proper figure to translate Malamud's theme into action. Anyone with any sense would react differently; anyone with any luck would not have been put in the position of reacting at all. But the Romantic approach to suffering is bold; if logic is no help, then logic must upon occasion be discarded. The brilliant group of short stories surrounding *The Assistant* supports and extends Malamud's findings. One of the most notable among this new collection of *schlemiels* is Arthur Fidelman of "The Last Mohican." Fidelman is a "self-confessed failure as a painter" and a Jew, although again mostly in name (his American background has gone a long way toward Gentilizing him). There is in him something of both Alpine and Bober, but he is in his vulnerable good-will and poverty closer perhaps to Bober. A certain bathetic streak in him reminds us however of Alpine, who slid into the grave during Bober's funeral. Fidelman is pursued relentlessly by Shimon Susskind, a dirty, sponging, obnoxious immigrant who manages to establish a claim upon his victim that both recognize. In despair Fidelman cries, "Am I responsible for you then, Susskind?" "Who else?" comes the answer.

I do not wish to suggest that all these *schlemiels* are identical.

Fidelman is definitely Fidelman; in stressing his essential community with Malamud's other heroes—the critical element in Malamud's theme—I have to neglect such personal characteristics as his humor, which is much more pronounced than that of either Bober or Alpine. Fidelman is so delightful, in fact, that he is brought forward again in *Idiots First*, to general applause. But the *schlemiel*, football of the Gods (and symbol of undignified Man), is constantly in motion; one day up, the next into the mud. Wherever we may find Malamud's characters, we generally leave them on the upswing, usually a modest one, to be sure, but an upward movement nonetheless. Bober dies, but he has lived to see his fat and lucky neighbor offer hard cash for his run-down grocery. Alpine is low at the novel's end, but his new strength of purpose is clear. He has become a Jew and will eventually get the girl. Only rarely do we see a Malamud character on the downward swing. Fidelman is humiliated, robbed, blackmailed and insulted, yet at the story's end, chasing his tormentor (who will of course escape him), he has "a triumphant insight." " 'Susskind, come back,' he shouted, half sobbing. 'The suit is yours. All is forgiven.' " With such an attitude, the *schlemiel* is of necessity irrepressible. Fidelman is treated even worse in *Idiots First*, utterly squashed by a beautiful, hateful, ignorant bitch of a woman; yet at the end of the story he is in bed with her. Most of Malamud's characters must content themselves with successes of a less climactic nature.

The story which gives the collection its title, "The Magic Barrel," obviously a favorite of its author, and of the critics, is not so hilarious. Its hero is a gentle rabbinical student, Leo Finkle, who engages in a series of adventures both ludicrous and touching with a down-at-the-heels marriage broker, one Pinye Salzman. Again the imperative contact between two men—one, like Bober, gentle, lovable; the other a hard-luck hustler, bowed but not quite broken. Again an ending of powerful affirmation: the student, rejecting all of Salzman's goods, fastens upon the broker's own daughter, a girl who is clearly marked as bad luck—her father weeps at the thought of her. (Many such bad-luck women occur in Malamud's fiction.) Yet the student embraces his fate;

the close of the story finds him going to meet her where she waits, her eyes filled with "desperate innocence."

"The Magic Barrel" is one of the most beautiful recreations of Malamud's vision, but it is outdone in some respects at least by the remarkable "Angel Levine." Here the problem of suffering is formally stated, in almost Biblical, or to be more exact, Cabalistic terms. The struggles of its humble hero Manischevitz are those of Job: his business is wiped out, his wealth taken, even the insurance; his health is ruined, but he must work on for his wife, who is on her deathbed:

> "My dear God, sweetheart, did I deserve that this should happen to me?" Then recognizing the worthlessness of it, he put aside the complaint and prayed humbly for assistance: "Give Fanny back her health, and to me for myself that I shouldn't feel pain in every step. Help now or tomorrow is too late. This I don't have to tell you." And Manischevitz wept.

But help does come to him, in this enormously moving story, from a characteristically ludicrous source: a seemingly demented Negro who claims to be an angel sent from Heaven. At first Manischevitz rejects Levine, as the Negro is called, out of hand, but finally he overcomes his logic and his pride and seeks for his own salvation: he goes up to Harlem and publicly confesses his faith in a saloon full of loafers and scorners. Like Job, he finds it is not enough simply to refrain from cursing. At the last his faith has restored his wife and his health to him; looking up, he is granted a vision of dark wings. " 'A wonderful thing, Fanny,' Manischevitz said. 'Believe me, there are Jews everywhere.' " The story ranks with the finest products of the Romantic imagination.

The Magic Barrel has other triumphs, other sufferings, other *schlemiels*. "The First Seven Years" gives us a glimpse of that rare figure, the Malamud villain, in this case a hard-working young man who hopes to be a certified public accountant. He is first cousin both to Helen's suitor in *The Assistant*, the well-

groomed Nat Pearl, and to the sell-out educator Gerald Gilley of
A New Life. Malamud wastes little time with these All-American
Boys; in the story at hand the tension derives, as usual, from a
contest between two more familiar types, a shoemaker and his
refugee assistant, over the shoemaker's daughter. The bemired
graduate student hero of "Behold the Key" is much reminiscent
of Fidelman: he too is a sufferer (but he has a wife and children
to suffer with him); he too is stranded in beautiful, hostile Italy.
This fellow Carl Schneider is one of the few *schlemiels* that we
find on a definite downward course: at the story's end, having
searched in agony for a key, and found it when it is no longer of
any use, he is struck in the face with it. Even worse off is Henry
Levin of "The Lady of the Lake." Because he tries to sell his
Jewish birthright for a glamorous dream, both his past and his
future are taken from him. He sees on a tapestry a figure tormented in Hell: " 'What did he do to deserve his fate?' "—" 'He
falsely said he could fly.' "

The *schlemiel* is permitted to fly, but with his own wings,
no borrowed plumage. Levin, a pathetic figure hoping for a new
life, called himself "Henry R. Freeman." It was not his object that
was wrong, the new life, but the lies he told looking for it. It is
appropriate that we leave this most unhappy of all Malamud
protagonists for a look at a close relation, the S. Levin who is the
hero of the third novel, *A New Life*. Although he has come from
afar, there is little of the escapist about this Levin: he is trailing
visible clouds of glory from a past of the most unmitigated suffering. This is how the book begins: "S. Levin, formerly a drunkard,
after a long and tiring transcontinental journey, got off the train
at Marathon, Cascadia, toward evening of the last Sunday in
August, 1950." He is a Jew, a wanderer—a *schlemiel* too? Well,
he gets his pants wet twice in the first thirteen pages, and from
that point—indeed from the first sentence—the book's import is
predictable. *A New Life* has been called a departure for Malamud,
a venture forth from his familiar ground. No judgment could be
less true. Levin is the archetypal Malamud hero, emerged from
his standard background to fight his eternal good fight for his
place in the sun.

Structural differences are apparent, however. In *A New Life*

Malamud abandons the two-man relationship which forms the basis of most of his best work and returns to the problem of the hero solo, much as he set it up in *The Natural.* In *A New Life,* however, and for the only time in his work, he puts some real effort into a heroine, Pauline Gilley, the married woman with whom Levin falls in love. She is a worthy replacement for the missing male *schlemiel;* she has suffered, she endures, she makes mistakes, she gives somewhat too liberally of her love. Yet she is not developed nearly as fully as is the second man of *The Assistant,* nor even, perhaps, as those of the short stories. To a *schlemiel,* a woman is usually simply bad luck. A female *schlemiel* seems a contradiction in terms. Nevertheless, Malamud explores the new avenues opened by the relationship between Levin and Pauline with insight and affection. The book, however, is fundamentally Levin's; his the principal suffering and his the principal triumph.

I don't know whether it has been much commented upon, but *A New Life* bears a curious resemblance in a number of ways to *Lady Chatterley's Lover.* In both we have a vibrant woman tied to a half-dead man, the intrusion of a virile newcomer (bearded in Levin's case) of a lower order, a powerful but beautiful sex-experience between the wife and the new man in the woods, the establishment of a meaningful relationship between them, and their eventual triumph over the forces of suspicion, guilt, mistrust and calumny. Both books are organized symbolically with the seasons, so that the lovers' awakening into their passion shall coincide with the spring. Both books work effectively in symbols throughout; both have stuffy villains, slightly unbelievable, or at least negligible, because both—and this is the most important of all—both books neglect other considerations to focus upon the necessity of the individual's protest against the forces in the modern world which operate so as to separate man from man and man from woman. Both books celebrate courage —in Lawrence's phrase, "the courage of tenderness," the courage to let down one's defenses. Both thus give utterance to the great Romantic cry against the Machine Age, which was first heard at the appearance of the satanic mills of the late eighteenth century, and has not diminished since.

S. Levin—he achieves the nickname Sam at the end of the book, after sacrificing his protective beard—is one of Malamud's most fortunate characters. Yet we realize, at the end of the book, that he has reached his apogee. Just as we know Frank Alpine must come up, so we know Levin must come down; but he will never again hit bottom. He has done that, and survived. He has his new life at hand, even if it may not be one of wine and song. His defeated adversary taunts him: Levin has now no money and no job, and no prospect of one; a wife of notorious weakness, poor health and inconsistency, and two expensive children not his own. " 'Why take that load on yourself?' " " 'Because I can, you son of a bitch.' " With that remark alone, Levin proves his right to the girl and to whatever suffering and joy may be waiting. We can leave him to fight his future battles without our scrutiny.

The recent short stories continue to investigate the problem of suffering. As usual, it is the problem and not the answer that absorbs Malamud—the answer is as tenuous as each man's sense of responsibility to his fellows, as fleeting as the moments of union among men. Certain of the old strains are sounded boldly in *Idiots First*. There is the return of Fidelman, more foolish than ever, and more indomitable. There are more *schlemiels,* professor Orlando Krantz of "The Maid's Shoes," like Fidelman victimized by the Italians; and most unhappy of the new group, Nat Lime, who wants to marry a Negro. "Black Is My Favorite Color" is an interesting new variation on Malamud's theme, a poignant account of the overwhelming difficulties in the way of honest relationships between different races. Yet at the end of the story Nat Lime, beaten, scorned and rejected by white and black alike for his pains, is trying again. There is "A Choice of Profession," either pilot study for, or overflow from, *A New Life;* and "The Cost of Living," related to *The Assistant.* Perhaps the high point of the collection is the fable called "The Jewbird." A progressive and ambitious Jewish family (the "progress" and ambition derive largely from the father, a seller of frozen foods whose aim is to send his son to the Ivy League) is visited by a ragged, rumpled old bird named Schwartz, who speaks in dialect and smells of herring. The father is embarrassed and wrathful. After much fencing he gets his hands on the bird—but not before it has yanked his nose half off—and wrings its neck. When the little boy asks who is responsible for the murder, the mother tells him "anti-semeets."

It is a strange fact that Malamud's first novel has absolutely nothing to do with the Jew. Strange in particular to those who fancy him as a Jewish writer, for is not the first novel supposed to lay down the bricks and flagstones and cinderblocks for all the edifice that is to come? In fact, that is exactly what *The Natural* does, which is why I have reserved it for last: it provides a valuable test for any theory of Malamud's art, both because it comes first, and because it seems so foreign to him. It is a baseball story, and yet baseball is not the heart of the book; I have it on good authority that Malamud knew little about the game as a young man, and cared less. (There are technical errors in the book, but they do not seem glaring to me.) No, at the center of the novel is nothing less than the myth of sacrifice, the killing of the sacred king. For some reason which will seem important to a biographer, Malamud chose to present his first allegory on suffering in the context of another great symbolic system: baseball, the all-American game. Only after he had stated the problem in these terms did he take up his more congenial image, the wandering, suffering Jew.

The young natural—the almost supernaturally gifted athlete —Roy Hobbs, begins his career by striking out the Whammer, greatest man in the game. This is not only pure American folklore, it is also right out of Frazer: the young God kills the old and takes his place. Roy thus earns the right to be cut down by a crazed woman assassin who wants to kill all the brightest and best men in sports, the heroes of the nation. He is not killed, however; only crippled; his luck turns and he drags on as a *schlemiel*, haunted by bad memories and evil women. After years, he pulls himself to the top again, only to be himself struck out by a new bright-faced boy. He is then plunged into a final scandal and humiliation, because of his own foolish lusts. But as he goes down he crushes the evil that has preyed on him; and there are the usual signs that he will rise again; a good woman waits for him.

Now all of this is open, evident, outspoken. Like many other artists, Malamud begins with the naked statement and spends later years clothing it. Suffering here is as blindingly apparent as the winter sun on a snowy field. The answer, too, falls as swiftly and completely over the scene as a storm front:

> "What beats me," he said with a trembling voice, "is why did it always have to happen to me? What did I do to deserve it?"
> "Being stopped before you started?"
> He nodded.
> "Perhaps it was because you were a good person?"
> "How's that?"
> "Experience makes good people better."
> She was staring at the lake.
> "How does it do that?"
> "Through their suffering."

The later works, though vastly more sophisticated, more complicated, more careful, as the author comes to realize the enormousness of the problem, are essentially reworkings of *The Natural*. Frank Alpine as the tarnished man of good will, Fidelman the silly saint, Sam Levin the *schlemiel* who gets up after his tenth beating: all these are more intelligible, more comprehensible reincarnations of Roy Hobbs, who is even at the end of his book a little larger than real life. But he is of necessity a titan, even if a fallen one, for he establishes the lowly *schlemiel's* divine origin, which is not seen again in Malamud, although constantly alluded to. Within this lowest of characters—Man—there is the God-given fire of decency and determination that enables him to overcome everything arrayed against him.

This is the oldest and finest Romanticism of all, that of Plato and his predecessors, who refused to estimate Man's worth by an objective reckoning of *things*. It is in that tradition, and for that ideal, that Malamud stands. As for the particular background of his sufferers—Jewish grocer, Anglo-Saxon athlete, Italian hobo, German immigrant—that does not matter at all.

Max F. Schulz

12.

Mythic Proletarians

At the end of *The Assistant,* Frank Alpine converts to Judaism. Thus, in his person as well as in his maintenance of the Bober store and family, Frank insures continuation of the dead Morris Bober's richly human ethics. In his essay "Jewish-Americans, Go Home!" Leslie Fiedler exclaims: "This solution of Malamud's already begins to look a little old-fashioned, appearing as it does in a book which seems a belated novel of the thirties, a last expression of the apocalyptic fears and Messianic hopes of those terrible but relatively simple times." [1] In this offhand remark Fiedler inadvertently identifies one of the two grammars which control the form and content of the Malamud novel. As the Depression milieu of *The Assistant* and the pre-Bolshevik context of *The Fixer* insist, these novels are mutations of the proletarian impulse of the Jewish intellectual of the 1930's. As the baseball rites of *The Natural* and the wasteland motifs of *A New Life* [2] slyly (and at times not so slyly) insinuate, the fictional worlds of these novels also accommodate as a second grammar a mythic pattern of vegetation ritual and Grail quest. [3] The Malamud novel conceptualizes this duality of theme and structure in the appropriately disparate language of realism and symbolism. Sidney Richman comments perceptively in reference to *The Natural* that this "deliberately impure yet perfectly organized style" alternates "Passages of idiomatic, terse, and slangy prose . . . with passages of lyrical intensity." [4] The skill with which Malamud combines the colloquial and mundane with the incantatory and religious is paralleled by his capacity to fuse the assumptions of Marx with the patterns of myth. In the Malamud novel the cosmogonies become one. The historical determinism of socialism merges with the cyclical inevitability of mythos; the proletarian hero winning justice for society, with the mythic hero renewing life for the community. That this identification is in some respects inevitable, Frank Kermode has demonstrated in his exploration of *The Sense of an Ending*; for the tendency of any mental structure or "fiction," once it forgets its fictiveness, especially if it has millennial expectations, is to regress into myth.[5]

The Malamud protagonist is a haunting leftover of the Depression years, his sensibility scarred by economic and social inequities. His past life reads like a "Hobo News" true confession of the down-and-outer of the thirties. Sy Levin is an ex-drunkard —son of a thief and a suicidal madwoman—who had drifted sodden with drink in rotting shoes for more years than he could say from "somebody's filthy cellar" to "small dark rooms" in rooming houses "overrun by roaches and bugs" (pp. 186-187). Frank Alpine's early life was similarly "made up of lost chances" until "he gave up and let himself be a bum," sleeping in gutters and cellars, eating "what he scrounged out of garbage cans, . . . bearded, smelly, dragging himself through the seasons without a hope to go by (p. 74)." The Depression "mentality" of a Bottom Dog [6]—with his burning sense of the haves conspiring to maintain the servile status of the have-nots—colors the thinking, as well, of Morris Bober, Roy Hobbs, and Yakov Bok and the tone, particularly, of *The Assistant* and *The Fixer*. Morris bitterly laments the lack of reward for his honesty and industry, while the dishonesty of his ex-partner and the perfidy of his neighbor Karp are allowed to prosper. Roy's request for more salary is sanctimoniously but curtly denied by Judge Goodwill Banner, the penny-pinching majority owner of the New York Knights; while Pop Fisher, the manager of the Knights, is constantly thwarted in his efforts to produce a pennant-winning team by the greed of the front office. And Yakov sees himself as a naked little man, with only his integrity to pit against the impersonal implacability of a monstrous Russian bureaucracy. Malamud's characters have understandably loomed large among the alienated figures of contemporary fiction. Of more significance probably for mastering the vocabulary of his fictional world is to recognize that this alienation assumes the gestures socially of the oppressed victim of an absurd economic system and symbolically of the sick Fisher King.

One of the persistent themes of the radical novels of the thirties and the forties is the conversion of the hero from accommodation with the world of economic power to belief in the worker's cause.[7] This *engagement* is analogous to the commitment of the mythic hero to the redemption of the community.

The Malamud hero is, at first, determined to make his fortune. With Roy Hobbs, it is his Indian Summer career as a rookie home-run king; with Frank Alpine, his aborted effort as a robber Prince; with Sy Levin, his "new life" as a college teacher; and with Yakov Bok, his masquerade as "a sort of Christian overseer" (p. 46). In each instance, however, his selfish search for gain or personal satisfaction metamorphoses into a social and ritualistic quest that ends in at least quasi-revival of spirit in the land. The individual who began as a self-server involuntarily assumes the contrary role of scapegoat and redeemer.

Significantly each Malamud protagonist journeys from his previous abode to a moral and/or economic wasteland, whose regeneration enlists his energies. Roy Hobbs "still in motion" (p. 36) from fifteen years of wandering joins a "last place, dead-to-the-neck ball team" suffering already in early summer from "a blasted dry season" (p. 34). Frank Alpine, newly arrived from the West Coast, assumes the dull routine of assistant grocer in a transitional East Side neighborhood delicatessen. Sy Levin steps off the train from New York City in the Northwest town of Marathon, Cascadia, to join the intellectually moribund English department of Cascadia State College. Yakov Bok leaves his country *shtetl* for Kiev, where he saves the life of an anti-Semite and goes to work as overseer of the man's seedy brickyard.

Inexorably each finds himself championing a struggle against

repressive, annihilative forces. Roy's prowess at the bat revives the
New York Knights. Their game-winning streaks make them a pennant contender and the idols of the aroused fans. Roy's homers
act as a tonic for hospitalized boys and unwed mothers. Against
the ravages of age and the obscene manipulations of the front
office with gambling interests, he battles to keep the hopes of the
team and its fans alive. Frank's back-breaking hours of unremu-
nerated labor prop up both the Bober store and family, and halt
their going under from the attrition of the Depression and a
marginal neighborhood. Sy's energy and idealism as a teacher
make him the leader of a Young Turk's rebellion against the
desiccated policies of the Old Guard. Yakov's endurance of brutal
imprisonment without trial for a crime he did not commit at-
tracts revolutionary support. He refuses a pardon and insists on a
trial to redeem his name and the names of all Jews in the anti-
Semitic eyes of Russion officialdom. This social action of the hero
as proletarian fuses with the regenerative role of the hero as mythic
savior. "A good teacher is a liberator," Sy Levin tells himself
(p. 167). "You suffer for us all," the lawyer Ostrovsky tells Yakov
Bok (p. 305). The political and archetypal nature of the allusions
here underscores the dual regenerative role played by the Malamud protagonist. As a baseball hero—an idol of America's national pastime—Roy Hobbs's fate, especially if one listens to the
roar of the crowd, seems to affect the nation's fate. His home runs
can redeem a people's faith in itself.

One might say with some accuracy that the proletarian sense
that gives these novels their deepest life has a mythic sense in-
truded upon it. Onto the social action of the narrative Malamud
superimposes a framework of vegetation ritual, Grail quest, nature cycle, and wounded Fisher King. Enough has already been
written of the symbolic presence of these elements—and such
others as the Jungian bird, "terrible mother" archetype, wasteland motif, father-son displacement, Christ rebirth, and pastoral
Sehnsucht—in the Malamud novel so that detailed verification
would be gratuitous. Indeed, the mythic trail is so thoroughly
marked by Malamud, that once a few signs are identified one can
follow the trail backward from the contemporary urban scene
to the primordial grove, and forward again, without the need of

a guide. If one is looking for ways to fault the novels, one can easily point to the obtrusiveness and non-structural function of this symbolism. Rarely do the symbols seem to emerge naturally out of the exigencies of plot and character; rather plot and character appear to exist primarily as vehicles for the symbolism. Birds arbitrarily sprout wings on Roy's baseballs, determine Frank's hang-up on St. Francis, elude Sy's bird-watching excursion in the woods, and fly past Yakov's cell window or metamorphose into a bomb thrown at him, to remind us of each one's unhealthy mother fixation and hence psychic wound as Fisher King. Harriet Bird, Memo Paris, and Avis Fliss suffer from sick breasts to identify them as "terrible mother" figures and as victims of the wasteland. Marcus Klein * and Philip Roth [8] have complained that the Malamud novel lacks realistic specificity. Even in such a resolutely realistic novel as *The Assistant,* with its hallucinated aura of the thirties, place and time remain undefined. This vagueness clearly allows the mythic superstructure to assume great thematic importance. Characters and incidents are easily abstracted into symbols and universals. A Roy Hobbs or a Frank Alpine becomes important not for what in himself as a fictional creation he tells us about the human situation, but for what as a symbol he represents in a mythic frame of reference. Such an apparent limitation in Malamud's presentation of human experience, however, can be defended as a strategy of containment, so to speak, to gain a limited but important aesthetic objective.

The overall thematic ends of Malamud's myth-haunted novels are readily evident. Where one may easily go astray is in evaluating the ambiguity of tone which characterizes the fate of the protagonist and the outcome of the action. Roy Hobbs, Frank Alpine, Sy Levin, and Yakov Bok are all symbolically conceived of as maimed kings; their flaw, self-interest. As a great ball player "What will you hope to accomplish?" Harriet Bird asks Roy. His disappointing answer is that he will gain fame and wealth from being the best in the game. "Isn't there something over and above earthly things—some more glorious meaning to one's life and activities?" she responds (p. 27). Her subsequent shooting of him

* See Chapter 17 in this collection.

is thus a mythic enactment of this psychic wound; for it is his narcissistic longing for the luxury-loving Memo Paris and consequent blindness during much of his career to the health of the community that allows him to make a deal with the club owner to throw the play-off game for the pennant. Frank Alpine equally seeks shortcut methods to "live like a prince" (p. 74). Stealing becomes a habit. He pilfers Morris Bober's cash register and ultimately Helen Bober's virtue and self-respect. Sy Levin indulges himself in an adulterous affair with the wife of his colleague and senior member of the English department. Yakov Bok denies his Jewish blood and breaks the Gentile rule against Jews working outside the ghetto. Each transgresses against the moral and legal code, setting his desires above the law and needs of the land. Yet each eventually wins a moral victory over his old self through his conversion to concern for the larger unit of the group. In mythic terms of the regeneration he brings to society, he proves to be a true folk hero. Roy repudiates the syndicate, rejecting Memo Paris's seductive bribe in favor of Iris Lemon's gift of fruitful love. Frank converts to Judaism, keeps the store open and Helen Bober's love alive. Sy regenerates the intellectual life of the English department and arouses love in barren Pauline Gilley, who quickens with his child. And Yakov awakens in the oppressed Russians the power of resistance to tyranny. Each pursues his role of culture hero seemingly to a successful conclusion. New life after a fashion comes to the afflicted land, for the Malamud hero cannot elude entirely the fated outcome of his ritual servitude, but it comes without grace. His flawed character compromises on the realistic level of the story any clear-cut victory posed by such mythic and tragic archetypes.

There is a marked discrepancy between the affirmative claims of the moral, and the negative implications of the social, levels of the action. In the ancient ritual of the vegetation cult, the king's death was a willed sacrifice to ensure continuation of the annual rebirth of nature. The Malamud hero, contrariwise, does not will his fulfillment of the conditions of the archetype. Despite the moral order gained, he remains a victim of what Jason Compson sardonically calls the "rear guards of Circumstance." [9] Furthermore, his mental hesitations and ethical timidities, when measured against the full affirmation of the archetype, seriously qualify the hope that the mythical level of the ending holds out to us. Only after he has wasted three times at bat and beaned Iris with a foul ball does Roy respond to her cry for love and protection: "Win for us, you were meant to" (p. 180). Determined now not to throw the game, Roy ironically strikes out in the ninth inning anyway to retire his team and lose the play-off for the pennant. Suspected of a sellout, he is finished in organized baseball. His is the first of those Pyhrric victories with which Malamud, the severe moralist, burdens his heroes at the end of each novel. Frank's vision of life cannot see beyond his possession of Helen, which he identifies with maintenance of the store. He and Helen will marry in time and repeat, despite Helen's dream of a better existence, the nightmare death-in-life drudgery of her parents, incarcerated day and night in the tomb of the marginal neighborhood store. Sy leaves Cascadia, terrifyingly saddled with another man's children and wife, whom he is not sure he even loves, and with his promise given never to teach again. Even granted the circumstances, his recurrent impulse to flee and his silent reservation about marrying Pauline after her divorce are comically unheroic. Yakov goes before a hostile court for his trial, whose outcome remains decidedly uncertain; but the exploding bomb and hostile crowds that line the street through which his closed carriage passes imply that he will have little to do with the eventual determination of his fate. As he helplessly watches the bomb thrown, he frantically ducks. "If this is my death I've endured for nothing (p. 329)," he pathetically thinks.

The archetypal inevitability of nature's seasonal cycle is analogous in its optimism to a secular faith in the historically determined growth of society toward perfection. Both guarantee the fulfillment of human activity—the triumph over death and the emergence of utopia—that is, if man could consistently observe this blueprint for paradise.

Unfortunately, one cannot arbitrarily propel society toward absolute ends. Man lives in time, not in eternity—in what Frank Kermode defines as *chronos* or passing time, in opposition to *kairos* or moment of crisis, "the season, a point in time . . . charged with a meaning derived from its relation to the end." [10] Both his sense

of self and his sense of his relationship to society, conceived of as
instances of consciousness, can occur only in time. In this existential situation neither moral nor social perfection is obtainable,
for in time man is an incomplete creature of process. The Malamud hero, typically, is bent on finding a new identity, and with
it a new rapport with society. Eternity furnishes man with the
absolute yardstick of his growth and actions. Myth in the Malamud novel functions similarly. It links man in an "ennobling
interchange" [11] with the permanent, while starkly reminding him
of his mortality which alienates him from wholeness of being.
The rebirth of the Malamud hero as a new person is formulated
in the life-death terms of resurrection. As with the womb-tomb-pit
symbolism that figures in D. H. Lawrence's concept of what is
called "a reconstitution of the human personality" by Frederick
J. Hoffman, "Death is in this sense the cessation of a false, a blind,
way, succeeded by the assumption of the skin and soul of a new
personality." [12] Accession to a new being is thus analogous to the
story of Christ's resurrection. Mythically, then, the Malamud hero
is identified with the Christ-Dionysius-Fisher King polarity in the
story. Separated from the archetype, however, like Christ separated
from his divinity, the Malamud hero becomes merely a scapegoat.
Socially and psychically, not release to a new life but imprisonment by the old Adam marks his efforts to transform himself. One
thinks of the pitch black office of the Judge (not to mention the
dark pools of water) through which the new Roy gropes to face
and recognize himself with hatred, the tomblike store that claims
the new Frank Alpine, the dreams of death by water that torment
Sy Levin, and the prison cell that possibly still awaits Yakov Bok.

The mythic and social levels of the Malamud novel face each
other in a perfect stand-off. The incompleteness of human nature,
Malamud seems to say, precludes any final design. So he gives us
Roy Hobbs, a Paul Bunyan of the baseball diamond with a flawed
bat; Frank Alpine, a drifter and thief, who inhabits obstinately
the airless confinement of a Jewish delicatessen in a Gentile
neighborhood, out of mixed motives of guilt, lust, and *caritas;*
Sy Levin, a New Yorker, who quixotically seeks fresh air in the
sterile vacuum of a cow-college in the Northwest, out of a naive
faith in Horace Greeley's slogan about the West; and Yakov Bok,

scapegoat of society as the pun on the German meaning of his name suggests, who trades the claustrophobia of the *shtetl* for the spiritual expansion of a Russian prison cell. Each aspires (as the puns on Alpine's and Levin's names suggest) to renewed kinship with man; but each is hobbled (implicit as morpheme in Hobbs's name) by the limitations of a past and by the shortsightedness of self. The feeling of being trapped haunts all Malamud's protagonists.

The most difficult problem for the proletarian novelist in the first half of this century, according to Walter B. Rideout, has been the conclusion to his book. Revolutionary optimism and Marxist reasoning dictate that his story end in a vision of the classless society. In this sense Marxism is as relentlessly apocalyptic as myth. The conventions of realism which govern the form require that the internal logic of the story prefigure the affirmative note at the end. Since capitalism and a class-structured society stubbornly persist in America, and most of the radical novelists of the thirties especially "were not really novelists at all but Tractarians," they were forced to "sloganize" their endings, "flatly asserting a doctrinal message in their own persons or through inadequately concealed mouthpieces." A few of the best—James T. Farrell, Henry Roth, Robert Cantwell, and Nelson Algren— refused either to "consider the possibility of overt moralizing" or of "forced optimism." They persisted in letting the "logic of their design" come honestly to its bitter, negative end. Surprisingly, Rideout remarks, almost none of these novels "turned fully to symbolism as a solution to the problem of the ending; for the symbolic conclusion can be either a thrusting toward intensified vision or an easy retreat from it into verbal wish-fulfillment." [13]

Malamud in a bravura extension of form has utilized the solution of symbolism, while maintaining the integral thematic development of his story. In the symbolism of the Grail and vegetation myths, he has a human drama as inexorable in its insistence on the renewal of life as that of socialist dialectics. In the quest hero he has as committed a national redeemer as the proletarian revolutionary. And in the moral victory of this protagonist over material corruption and fleshly temptation, which ironically limits the full achievement of his earthly dreams, Malamud retains the psychological and structural consistency of the story.

It should be clear by now that the mythic superstructure of the Malamud story satisfies the affirmative demands of the proletarian novel; and that the antithetical requirements of the symbolic and realistic strata of the story dictate the ambiguity of the Malamud conclusion.

One additional point as regards this dichotomy may be worth mentioning. Systems of dialectical contraries such as Hegel's, Blake's, and the Neoplatonists' presuppose an ultimate synthesis, or in the case of Blake at least a persistent balance, of contraries. The Marxist viewpoint, working ostensibly within the same framework of thought, similarly anticipates a final solution. Yet underlying the Marxist formula, and intrinsic to most nineteenth-century designs of progress toward perfection, is the Darwinian notion of conflict and never completed process. The Marxist belief in the inevitability of class warfare betrays its Darwinian genes. This contradictory note of continual becoming, which precludes of course any final form of being, is ironically inimical to an archetypal vision of human nature. Hence, a mythic affirmation necessarily defines perfection in a frame of reference distinct from that characterizing a social *promise* of completeness. The special ambience of the Malamud novel derives essentially from this tension between the ideal and the actual.

The Malamud protagonist functions simultaneously as mythic savior and as social scapegoat. His growth in conscience represents symbolically a victory for society and the forces of life. His personal transgressions (bribery, theft, adultery, rape, perjury), which eventually cause him to fall short of his human goals, provide society with a vicarious castigation of its recurrent failure to realize utopia. In the refusal of the novels to resolve these rhetorical equivocations, Malamud opts firmly and unambiguously for a radically sophisticated comprehension of the human predicament.

Notes

1. Leslie Fiedler, *Waiting for the End* (New York: Stein and Day, 1964), p. 92.
2. Bernard Malamud, *The Natural* (New York: Farrar, Straus and Cudahy, 1952), *The Assistant* (New York: Farrar, Straus and Giroux, 1957), *A New Life* (New York: Farrar, Straus and Giroux, 1961), and *The Fixer* (New York: Farrar, Straus and Giroux, 1966). All references are to these editions.
3. Passing critical allusion to the mythic elements in Malamud's novels has become *de rigueur*. Only a few critics, however, have addressed themselves directly to this problem. They include Norman Podhoretz, "Achilles in Left Field," *Commentary*, XV (1953), 321–326; Earl R. Wasserman, "*The Natural:* Malamud's World Ceres," *Centennial Review*, IX 1965), 438–460; James M. Mellard, "Malamud's Novels: Four Versions of Pastoral," *Critique,* IX 1967), 5–19; Sidney Richman, *Bernard Malamud* (New York: Twayne Publishers, Inc., 1966); and Jonathan Baumbach, "The Economy of Love: The Novels of Bernard Malamud," *Kenyon Review*, XXV (1963), 438–457; and also his *The Landscape of Nightmare* (New York: New York University Press, 1965). (See Chapters 4 and 5 in this collection.)
4. Sidney Richman, *Bernard Malamud* (New York: Twayne Publishers, Inc., 1966), p. 46.
5. Frank Kermode, *The Sense of an Ending: Studies in the Theory of Fiction* (New York: Oxford University Press, 1967), pp. 35–43.
6. From the title of Edward Dahlberg's novel *Bottom Dogs* (New York: Simon and Schuster, 1930).
7. Walter B. Rideout, *The Radical Novel in the United States 1900-1954* (Cambridge, Mass.: Harvard University Press, 1956), p. 73 and *passim*.
8. Marcus Klein, "Bernard Malamud: The Sadness of Goodness," *After Alienation: American Novels in Mid-Century* (Cleveland: World Publishing Company, 1964), pp. 247–293; Philip Roth, "Writing American Fiction," *Commentary*, XXIII (1961), 228–229. (See Chapter 17 in this collection for Klein's essay.)
9. In the Dilsey section of William Faulkner's *The Sound and the Fury.*
10. Frank Kermode, *The Sense of an Ending* (New York: Oxford University Press, 1967), p. 47.
11. William Wordsworth, *The Prelude*, XII, 376 (1805); XIII, 375 (1850).
12. Frederick J. Hoffman, *The Mortal No: Death and the Modern Imagination* (Princeton, N.J.: Princeton University Press, 1964), p. 411.
13. Walter B. Rideout, *The Radical Novel in the United States* (Cambridge, Mass.: Harvard University Press, 1956), pp. 222–224 and 228.

Part IV
Specific Novels and Stories

Ihab Hassan

13.

The Qualified Encounter

In Bernard Malamud we find further testimony that the urban Jewish writer, like the Southern novelist, has emerged from the tragic underground of culture as a true spokesman of mid-century America. It may be difficult to classify Malamud in the scheme which Fiedler devised for Jewish authors of the last two decades: Bellow (highbrow), Salinger (upper middlebrow), Shaw (middle middlebrow), and Wouk (low middlebrow).[1] If Malamud does not possess the intellectual vitality of Bellow, his finest work shows an order of excellence no critic—however beetling or elevated his brow—can justly deny. The first and most obvious quality of his fiction is its "goodness." This is a complex quality, compounded of irony, trust, and craft—a touch of Dostoyevsky and Chagall, someone observed. It is the product of a sensitive yet enduring heart, vulnerable where it counts, and deeply responsible to its feeling of what transforms a man into *mensch*. Behind it is a wry vision of pain, and also of hope. We are not surprised, therefore, to hear Malamud say that "Jews are absolutely the very *stuff* of drama," or that the purpose of the writer is "to keep civilization from destroying itself"; or that much of current fiction is "underselling Man." [2] But these pronouncements, which may express the natural bent of a man reared virtuously among immigrants in Brooklyn, do not explain the subtleties of his craft. Malamud's vision is preeminently moral, yet his form is sly. It owes something to the wile of Yiddish folklore, the ambiguous irony of the Jewish joke. Pain twisted into humor twists humor back into pain. The starkness of suffering, the leaden weight of ignorance or poverty, the alienation of the Jew in a land of jostling Gentiles—all these become transmuted, in luminous metaphors and strange rhythms, into forms a little quaint or ludicrous, a bittersweet irony of life, into something, finally, elusive.

His first novel, *The Natural*, 1952, is a bizarre, authentic, troubled work about a thirty-three-year-old baseball player who suddenly emerges from painful oblivion into the crazy light of fame and big league corruption. The snappy slang of sport and gloomy language of the soul are fused in an allegorical tale which probes deep into the meaning of personal integrity but fails ultimately to make itself comprehensible. His collection of short stories, *The Magic Barrel*, 1958, includes some of his worst and best fiction. The poorer pieces are usually set abroad; the best deal with native Jewish material and have in common with his second novel, *The Assistant*, 1957, a blazing poetic insight into the daily aches and indignities of man which add up, somehow, to a kind of nobility, a form of aspiration.

The Assistant, presumably, is a love story, a domestic romance, a grocery store idyll of unwarranted poverty and harsh spiritual deprivation. It is a tale of loneliness, of lifelong frustrations and delicate, budding hopes. It is a "human" story albeit deeply ironic. For irony is indeed the key to Malamud's attitude toward man, to his estimate of him. The irony is not "dry," not scathing; it is best described by Earl Rovit * when he says, "The affectionate insult and the wry self-deprecation are parts of the same ironic vision which values one's self and mankind as both less and more than they seem to be worth, at one and the same time." [3] This is the ambivalence of vision which qualifies, sometimes even undercuts, the affirmative power of Malamud's fiction.

* See Chapter 1 in this collection.

The world revealed by *The Assistant* is, materially speaking, bleak; morally, it glows with a faint, constant light. Morris Bober and his wife, Ida, toil sixteen hours a day in a grocery store, barely eking out a living. They are well past middle age, and have given up their lives, their illusions, even the promise of a richer future which comes with education for their single daughter, Helen. The store, as we are told many times, is an open tomb. Twenty-one years are spent in it, and in the end Bober dies of double pneumonia, leaving his family penniless; he has to be buried in one of those huge anonymous cemeteries in Queens. America! "He had hoped for much in America and got little. And because of him Helen and Ida had less. He had defrauded them, he and the blood-sucking store." [4] This is what Bober thinks as one of two men who hold up his store slugs him on the head, because he is a Jew, and Bober falls to the ground without a cry. An appropriate ending to his weary, profitless day. Others may have luck, like the affluent Karp who owns a liquor store across the street, or the Pearls whose son, Nat, attends law school—and takes Helen's virginity. But the Bobers live on stolidly, honestly, in squalor and sickening destitution. They are, like the grocery "assistant," Frank Alpine, victims of circumstance. What, then, gives these characters the measure of spiritual freedom they still possess?

The nature of the characters themselves holds the answer. Morris Bober, to be sure, is another example of the *eiron*, the humble man. He is more. He has endurance, the power to accept suffering without yielding to the hebetude which years of pain induce. He is acquainted with the tragic qualities of life—"The world suffers. *He* felt every schmerz"—and he defines the Jew as a suffering man with a good heart, one who reconciles himself to agony, not because he wants to be agonized, as Frank suggests, but for the sake of the Law—the Hebraic ideal of virtue.[5] Yet this is only one source of Bober's strength. His other source is charity, which in his case becomes nearly quixotic. Bober, though close to starvation himself, extends credit to his poor customers. He wakes up every day before dawn so that he may sell a three-cent roll to a Polish woman on her way to work. He takes in Frank Alpine, feeds him, and gives him an opportunity to redeem himself, though Frank begins by stealing the grocer's bread and milk. Nor can he bring himself, in the extremity of despair, to burn down his property in order to collect insurance. Inured to failure, Bober still strives to give suffering the dignity of men who may trust one another in their common woe. But Karp calls him a "schlimozel."

The central action of the novel, however, develops from Bober's relation to Frank Alpine, and from the latter's relation to Helen. Frank, as the title suggests, is probably the hero of the book. He, too, is an *eiron*, a collector of injustices—with a difference. The regeneration of Frank—his literal and symbolic conversion to the Jewish faith—is the true theme of the book. His regeneration, at best, is a strange and mixed thing. When Frank first appears, he is a wanderer, an anti-Semite, even a thief. Yet one of his idols is St. Francis, and his hardened face conceals a hungry soul. "With me one wrong thing leads to another and it ends in a trap. I want the moon so all I get is cheese," he tells Bober.[6] The grocery store, which is Bober's grave, becomes a cave or haven for Alpine. It also becomes the dreary locus of his painful rebirth. Impelled by his gratitude to the grocer, and motivated by his guilt at having robbed him, with the aid of tough Ward Minogue, Frank puts all his energies into the store and ends by pumping some of his own obstinate life into the dying business. Meanwhile, he falls in love with Helen Bober.

From here on, ambiguities prevail. The racial prejudices of Frank are matched by those of Ida Bober, and to some extent, of her daughter Helen, against Gentiles. (The store improves, it is suggested, precisely because Frank is not a Jew.) Frank's gratitude to Morris does not prevent him from continuing to steal petty cash from the register—which he keeps account of and intends to return. Yet when Bober is incapacitated by sickness, Frank takes a night job, in addition to his grocery chores, and secretly puts his pay in the cash box. And his gnawing love for Helen, which she is slow to return, finally ends, ironically, with an act of near-rape as he rescues her from the clutches of Ward Minogue, only to force her himself, right there and then in the park, at the very moment in their relationship when she is at last ready to surrender herself freely to him. "Dog," she cries "—uncircumcised dog!" [7] Guilt, gratitude, love—perhaps even the hope of a life he could glimpse but never attain—combine to sustain Frank Alpine, Bober's strange, saintly, pilfering assistant, in his impossible struggle against poverty, against hopelessness itself.

He wanted her but the facts made a terrible construction. They were Jews and he was not. If he started going out with Helen her mother would throw a double fit and Morris another. And Helen made him feel, from the way she carried herself, even when she seemed most lonely, that she had plans for something big in her life—nobody like F. Alpine. He had nothing, a backbreaking past, had committed a crime against her old man, and in spite of his touchy conscience, was stealing from him too. How complicated could impossible get?

He saw only one way of squeezing through the stone knot; start by shoveling out the load he was carrying around in his mind. . . .

So the confession had to come first. . . . He felt he had known this, in some frightful way, a long time before he went into the store, before he had met Minogue, or even come east; that he had really known all his life he would sometime, through throat blistered with shame, his eyes in the dirt, have to tell some poor son of a bitch that he was the one who had hurt or betrayed him. This thought had lived in him with claws; or like a thirst he could never spit out, a repulsive need to get out of his system all that had happened —for whatever had happened had happened wrong; to clean it out of his self and bring in a little peace, a little order; to change the beginning, beginning with the past that always stupendously stank up the now—to change his life before the smell of it suffocated him.[8]

Purgation in humility, rebirth through love—this is Frank's inchoate purpose, the reason for his willing acceptance of a backbreaking burden others—Minogue, Karp—find easy to reject. Yet it is in consonance with the character of the novel that purgation and rebirth both should appear ironic, awkward, and inconclusive. Frank tells Bober about his complicity in the robbery only to discover that the latter already knows. Bober catches his assistant rifling his till just when Frank had resolved never to steal again. And Frank's attempt to make a clean breast of it all to Helen merely serves to confirm her revulsion. His dogged and desperate love expresses itself in the form of a physical outrage. The savior of the Bobers is, in a sense, their archenemy. (The symbolic inversion of this relation may be discovered in the burial scene in which Frank topples accidentally into Bober's open grave.) But enemies suffer too, according to their conscience. Frank Alpine, it seems, can only expend the last vestige of his money, energy, or hope in agonized silence, a prey to the ironies which rip and twist his purpose. In the end, the value of confession is to the soul that makes it. And even love is a kind of realized solitude. Like Frank, Helen goes her lonely way, carrying the broken dreams of the Bobers to some distant and uncompromising end.

It is obvious that if the world of *The Assistant* is not drained of values, it is nevertheless saturated with pain, flooded with contradictions. Its two major characters find their identity in humiliation, an extreme and quixotic sense of obligation. They are not tragic heroes but merely heroes of irony. They retreat before the ultimate tragic ordeal: the fullness of tragic awareness itself. This is a fact the form of the novel supports.

Time, we know, leaves the characters suspended in the void which their failures create; the hints of regeneration are barely audible. Morris Bober dies in bankruptcy; Helen continues at her dreary job, dreaming of a better life; Frank slaves at the store, trying to provide for the Bobers, send Helen to college, and win back her love. The fate of each remains less than what it could be in heroic tragedy, less even than what it usually amounts to in realistic fiction. Thus, for instance, does Helen evaluate the life of her father: "People liked him, but who can admire a man passing his life in such a store? He buried himself in it; he didn't have the imagination to know what he was missing. He made himself a victim. He could, with a little more courage, have been more than he was." [9] And thus does Frank reflect upon his incessant labors: " 'Jesus,' he said 'why am I killing myself so?' He gave himself many unhappy answers, the best being that while he was doing this he was doing nothing worse." [10] Whatever awareness time brings to the characters, whatever qualified dignity it confers upon their failures, every act in the novel is whittled by irony, every motive is mixed with its opposite.

Because time cannot unravel the knotted relations of the characters—what could be more gnarled than the relation of Gentile to Jew, of savior, seducer, and thief to those upon whom he preys, those from whom he gains an identity—the point of view of *The Assistant* dissociates itself from the protagonists, veering toward one then the other in friendly detachment. The characters are simply there, and they criticize each other's behavior; the point of view encourages us to perceive how ludicrous pain can be, and how unhappy virtue. The subtle, incredible twists of the plot, the reversals and accidents which affect the fortunes of the Bobers, are finally envisioned in a moral as well as dramatic perspective which acknowledges no certainties except the fact of suffering. (It is appropriate that Morris Bober should be an unorthodox Jew, and that at his funeral the rabbi should say, "Yes, Morris Bober was to me a true Jew because he lived in the Jewish experience, and with the Jewish heart. . . . He suffered, he endured, but with hope.") [11]

The achievement of Malamud's style, which survives his ironic play, lies in the author's capacity to convey both hope and agony in the rhythms of Yiddish speech.

> "I think I will shovel the snow," he told Ida at lunchtime.
> "Go better to sleep."
> "It ain't nice for the customers."
> "What customers—who needs them?"
> "People can't walk in such high snow," he argued.
> "Wait, tomorrow it will be melted."
> "It's Sunday, it don't look so nice for the goyim that they go to church."
> Her voice had an edge in it. "You want to catch pneumonia, Morris?"
> "It's spring," he murmured.[12]

There is a Hemingway cleanness in this dialogue, a kind of humility and courage, but also a softness Hemingway never strove to communicate.

Morris, however, does catch pneumonia and die. Nor can the poetry of the style persuade us to forget that the search of Frank Alpine for an identity ends, in the last, brief paragraph of the novel, with the ritual of circumcision. The act is one of self-purification, of initiation too, in Frank's case, but it is also an act of self-repudiation, if not, as some may be tempted to say, of symbolic castration.

Notes

1. Leslie Fiedler, "Saul Bellow," *Prairie Schooner* (Summer 1957), p. 107.
2. *Current Biography Yearbook*, 1958, ed. Margaret Dent Candee (New York, 1958), p. 272.
3. Earl H. Rovit, "Bernard Malamud and the Jewish Literary Tradition," *Critique* (Winter-Spring 1960), p. 5. (See Chapter 1 in this collection.)
4. Bernard Malamud, *The Assistant* (New York, 1958), p. 25.
5. *Ibid.*, p. 10.
6. *Ibid.*, p. 32.
7. *Ibid.*, p. 133.
8. *Ibid.*, p. 72f.
9. *Ibid.*, p. 181.
10. *Ibid.*, p. 189.
11. *Ibid.*, p. 180.
12. *Ibid.*, p. 173.

Walter Shear

14.

Culture Conflict

Although the novel as form is not always restricted to a concern with social milieu, certainly it is a type of literature that is often associated with social awareness. In a given society the writer has available classifications and stratifications which can provide some elements of a literary order and can give an indication, at least, of kinds and qualities of relationships between individuals. Culture, perhaps because of the ambiguity of the term itself, presents materials of a different order, even though it may, in appearance, seem spooned from the same pot. Pervaded with invisible, collective motivations, the novel of culture, as contrasted with the novel of manners, examines more minutely the ambiguities in the relationship between the individual and his values —and thus is both closer to its characters and at the same time attentive to an area beyond them.

Because of the diffused and dynamic society confronting it, the American novel has been inclined toward the broad area of culture rather than toward the national amalgam of behaviors available in its society. This tendency in American literature, a favorite of Eliot-inspired mythseekers, has not only achieved academic respectability but has inevitably been subject to more and more analysis, one result of which has been to make contemporary novelists increasingly aware of their material, its limitations and possibilities. This is not to say that a critical trend has imposed literary methods on current novelists, but by constant reminder of what kind of novel has been written and will probably be written, literary analysis has contributed to the more sophisticated attitude the current novelist has toward his fictional forms.

Perhaps no one better illustrates this kind of sophistication than Bernard Malamud, whose knowledge and manipulation of cultural and literary archetypes has frequently been commented on. Avoiding the analytical preoccupations of other American novelists, Malamud's treatment of his characters is flavored with sympathy, frustration, and exasperation. Knowing that he, as creator, is also contributor to their troubles, he cannot take their situations as seriously as they do. Often he seems to play with his role as "artist" by deliberately blurring the disinction between the archetype, which has universal significance, and the literary cliché, a mode which has exhausted its significance. The result of his peculiar relationship to the characters is that he becomes manipulator of the values they crucify themselves on and in order to remain true to both himself and his characters, two fictional modes—realistic and symbolic—so interact in his fiction as to comment upon each other simultaneously.

In *The Assistant* two cultures, the Jewish tradition and the American heritage (representing the wisdom of the old world and the practical knowledge of the new), collide and to some degree synthesize to provide a texture of social documentation which is manifested in a realistic aesthetic. However, the dichotomy is preserved and in fact given emphasis through an entirely different aesthetic presentation, one which tends to project the characters as types and treats their motivations, environments, and ideas as symbolic threads which link the narrative to the deeper level of personal significance from which the elements of human strength and weakness manage to emerge in the actions which both define and dramatize culture as a phenomenon.

Despite its more overt concern with a Jewish way of life, *The Assistant* deals basically with an implicit conflict between a heritage of ancient wisdom and traditional values and the American atmosphere of practicality and success, a conflict which not merely envelops the characters but—since they are not fully aware of its influence—exists as a constant source of confusion and bewilderment. For the characters these two systems of values become burdens, handicaps, imposers of demands which they cannot meet, most frequently because these demands pull them in opposite directions. Both these value worlds are embodied in all the characters, but the characters also exist in an ironic relationship to the worlds: all are in America, and all are basically secular, thus effectively removed from the traditional religious and social environment in which the old values flourished; in addition all of the major characters are the "have-nots" and blunderers in a country which sanctifies success and efficiency. Thus the characters in a most peculiar way are in the world but not completely in contact with it, a situation Malamud further emphasizes by omitting specific references to time.

On the other hand, the book presents the theme of alienation pushed to the point of an unphilosophic absurdity, and this situation is reiterated in the relationship of the characters, most of whom regard each other with almost premeditated misunderstandings. There is, however, a common meeting ground on the personal level that becomes an important part of the theme: as Solotaroff states, "Malamud's Jews (and his Gentiles) are connected to each other not by religious and social ties but a common fate of error and ill luck and sorrow, of having lost much by their mistakes and recovered little by their virtues."

With montage-like effects, Malamud dramatizes American culture with casual, almost comic allusions, ranging from the popular to the more aesthetic conceptions of American life. Occasionally he even moves beyond national boundaries to treat America as a symbolic pattern for the direction of Western civilization, but for the most part, his social focus is confined to the American dream as nightmare, in particular terms to a poor neighborhood in New York where success, instead of being a goal or source of hope, serves to mock and eventually to envelop everyone like a shroud. Within the realistic bounds of the neighborhood, however, the characters tend, at times, to embody what might be called archetypal images from the level of popular middle-class American culture. The assistant himself, Frank Alpine, is the young man, unencumbered by a past filled with family obligations, who is poor but ambitious, ready to start climbing to the top. In this respect he suggests the typical Horatio Alger hero, but Malamud complements and complicates this portrait with a related stereotype and, with some allusions to *Crime and Punishment* and Raskolnikov's great man theory, pushes Frank toward the journalistic and Hollywood underworld, toward the success dream of the gangster who may become a popular hero by gaining his own kind of fame and fortune.

In presenting such pieces of popular culture Malamud allows the characters to formulate their self-conceptions and speculate on their destinies as those destinies are popularly articulated. For example, Frank's vision of his criminal career is from a pseudo-romantic, sensational point of view with equal parts of the tabloids and Hollywood: "At crime he would change his luck, make adventure, live like a prince. He shivered with pleasure as he conceived robberies, assaults—murders if it had to be— each violent act helping to satisfy a craving that somebody suffer as his own fortune improved" (see p. 74; all references are to *The Assistant,* New York: Signet, 1957). Eventually, through the combination of misfortune, conscience, and the influence of a "good" woman, Frank is able to adjust his dreams to a more socially acceptable goal, that of a college education, and he proudly tells his girl, Helen, that he is going to make something of himself.

By juxtaposing such participations in national reveries with Frank's more real experiences, which reveal both incompetence and a deeper moral awareness, Malamud is able to criticize the more romantic tendencies in American culture and the willingness (frequently desperate) of many to prefer an imagined future to a personally unacceptable present.

This willingness to postpone life by a preoccupation with abstract goals is made even more explicit in Malamud's treatment of Helen, a girl who is at once more practical and more idealistic than the confused Frank Alpine whose dreams are big but always dreams. Helen is the person who knows what she wants; she is very much aware of the importance of status and she reads—thereby coming in contact with the "higher things in life" and being intellectually cognizant of other levels of experience than the practical and materialistic.

But with her knowledge and experience (her loss of virginity and innocence is both a realistic and symbolic key to some of her practicality), she still remains determinedly a feminine Jay Gatsby, only slightly more mature. Certainly it is not an accident that some of her comments seem to be heavily colored by the Fitzgerald style: "When a person is young he's privileged with all kinds of possibilities. Wonderful things might happen, and when you get up in the morning you feel they will. That's what youth means, and that's what I've lost. I want a larger and better life. I want the return of my possibilities" (p. 37). "Her constant fear," Malamud informs us, "was that her life would not turn out as she had hoped. . . . she could not part with the substance of her dreams" (p. 107). Dreams, of course, have no substance. Eventually, with the assist of peculiar circumstances, she projects her fantasy into the man least able to bear the kind of ideals associated with success, Frank Alpine; and the dream-world turns to one version of a "practical" outlook, a woman's scorn; "She was filled with loathing at the fantasy she had created, of making him into what he couldn't be—educable, promising, kind and good, when he was no more than a bum" (p. 139). Thus one form of the American dream disintegrates again into the psychological tensions which Malamud seems to prefer, and the cultural tendencies of the characters are reduced to the level of personal relationships.

If we look at Morris Bober as a figure in the American success myth, we find a poor businessman, one who lacks the "get up and go" necessary "to reach the top." The business has not changed with the times—the sign which fell down ten years ago has never been replaced, and the customers are not an occasion for social amenities. Morris does not use the hard sell or the soft sell; he is simply there to serve the customers. (And in this regard Morris contrasts with Frank Alpine's later success as a salesman.) Yet Morris, who can be condemned by his family for failing to be at least the good provider and secure the better things in life for his daughter, strangely echoes an old legend about Abraham Lincoln; the rabbi in his funeral oration mentions that he ran two blocks to give back a nickel. Certainly Morris Bober *is* a part of American history, actually almost a stereotype of those many immigrants seeking to escape tyranny, famine, or persecution, who arrived in the New World with some hopes, some ambitions (at one time *he* had planned to be a pharmacist). To some degree he has not done badly; others have faced worse circumstances and have lived with more misery, but the images and dreams of success—even in his little neighborhood—are continual reminders that something has gone wrong, that Morris Bober, immigrant, has not lived or moved in harmony with the cultural dream. One might say that Morris does not move with the times (the new world constantly becoming newer); this, in fact, occurs to him: "America had become too complicated. One man counted for nothing. . . . What had he escaped to here?" (p. 162). However, his thoughts also accuse him: "He had the will of victim, no will to speak of" (*ibid.*). At this point he seems to be close to one of those truthful lies Malamud seems to relish— to live faithfully in the aura of the success dream one must believe; a defeatist attitude is fatal. At the end of a day of defeat Morris' unuttered words touch the heart of what sociologists might call the relationship between a man and his environment: "He went downstairs and had coffee at a dish-laden table in the Automat. America" (p. 163). As a final ironic twist of this half truth, Morris in his last thoughts accepts the American verdict upon him, "I gave away my life for nothing."

This is one version of *The Assistant,* but not the final word, for the old world has also figured deeply in the lives and actions of the characters, and in Malamud's treatment of its values, expressed chiefly in more traditional symbols and associations, tells us much more what matters about these people because it alone can explain these values in religious and ethical forms. Since the cultural backgrounds are not exclusive, since they do interact, the old not only explains the lives more fully than the immediate environment; it completes them.

While the characters spend much time thinking of the future and its more promising possibilities, they also at times examine themselves (never with complete insight), and they do want to *be* and *do* good. Thus they are capable of responding, if not morally at least with sympathy, to those around them. This tendency towards introspection and self-analysis is, in fact, what gives much comic and pathetic quality to the characterizations and what brings them closer to Malamud's own ethical perception; they know and think better than they are or can be for long. Malamud widens this discrepancy with what seem superficially to be ridiculous symbolic devices. Frank Alpine, the bungling petty criminal, is almost too heavy handedly associated with St. Francis. When he first appears, he just happens to open a magazine in Sam Pearl's counter and immediately recognizes St. Francis preaching to the birds; it is like a vision out of his childhood. St. Francis, Frank tells Sam, said "poverty was a queen and he loved her like she was a beautiful woman" (p. 28). In his comments here Frank expresses the major motives of his character: Like St. Francis he wants "a new view of things," to slough off the old life and put on garments of true worth. He will, in a stumbling way he has never dreamed, pursue both poverty and a woman; and poverty, love, and the woman will be completely intertwined. At first Frank's character, especially his past, seems to resemble the flitting birds more than St. Francis, but he comes very close to complete embodiment at times, most overtly in a scene in the park where Helen sees him feeding the birds and finally rising from the bench, "the pigeons fluttered up with him, a few landing on his arms and shoulders, one perched on his fingers, pecking peanuts from his cupped palm" (p. 94). Yet this brief identification is shattered in the next sentence: "Another fat bird sat on his hat," and we return to reality.

Because he is almost a composite of fleshly weaknesses, Frank Alpine can never really be Francis of Assisi, but he can struggle under the awareness of the image, approach it at times, turn from it and back again. His Catholic heritage, which for the most part is far in the background, seems to be at least indirectly a source of his pangs of conscience and his compulsion to confess everything to Morris. It is, however, this other compulsion, stealing—also the fruits of his childhood—that first involves Frank with Morris Bober, and this wrong becomes the thin but inseverable cord linking them simply as human beings. These ties of evil which Frank establishes with all the major characters are the strongest bonds Frank has with the human race, and it is only his conscience which forces him to live in terms of such simple elemental obligations and to attempt to correct what he cannot correct, what is already past. For all the unthinking harm he brings to others, he remains somewhat absurdly, "a man of stern morality," whose major problem is "to do good if he wanted." He thereby demonstrates the gap, which for Malamud seems permanent, between the will and the way.

Not simply an incompetent criminal and aspiring saint, Frank is also in love with Helen, the symbol and the person—a role which permits Malamud to explore the mixture and madness in traditional views of love. Frank is a lover with a vast range— from the sensuality of the peeping-tom and the sexual enthusiast to the idealism of a clumsy meeter of minds and unselfish giver of gifts and of himself. Throughout his relationship with Helen he attempts to formulate the proper kind of love, some com- bination of attitude and action that will be acceptable to both himself and his beloved, but the time and situation are never right. On the physical level his love suffers constant frustration by Helen's "ideals in sex"; from spying on her in the bathroom he progresses to an unsatisfactory meeting in his room and finally to a physical fulfillment in the rape-seduction scene in the park, a culmination on the physical level which is disastrous to the love itself. As the bearer of gifts and the intellectual companion, he also fails. Gifts, which for Helen seem tinged with responsibilities and involvement, are returned or thrown away; and his literary background and appreciation are too limited for the amorphous atmosphere of the intellect. Love in Frank's case is a matter of both receiving—on the physical level—and giving—in an ideal- istic sense; both difficulties seem to be reflected in a basically literary methodology, the search for an adequate correlative in actual terms which might allow the love relationship to flourish. As a key symbol for the entire relationship, Malamud uses the traditional rose, a token of his love which Frank carves out of wood, thus giving a form of beauty to natural material. As an emotionally charged object, however, "the flower reminded Helen of her unhappiness," and she drops it into the garbage can. But in Frank's day-dream at the end of the novel it reappears and changes into a real flower, specifically identified here with Helen and presented not by Frank Alpine, but by his idealized vision of himself, St. Francis.

Helen, as her name suggests, comes to represent the beauty and love all the major characters seek, but she herself is too practical to accept this as an accurate description of what she is at the moment. She is a Helen whose better judgment warns her away from the confusion between unrealized potentials and things as they are. Not wanting to exist merely as an object of love, she shies away from involvement even though she feels most acutely the loneliness which may be her fate. For her, love with Frank becomes a resignation to fate, an accepting of the present with all its disappointments as a permanent condition, and therefore love turns to hatred—as she realizes, to divert hatred from herself. Ironically, the more she refuses to acquiesce to circumstances, the more abstract and symbolic she becomes to the others who feel they must be deeply immersed in ordinary life.

Both Morris and Ida seem to think of Helen more in terms of her future, and perhaps inevitably in terms of their future as well, than as an individual. As a man of deeper understanding who is aware of a past involving more than simply his own disappointments and of a future which goes beyond his personal goals, Morris sees other people as having a value in themselves but also as a part of a broader fabric of life which incorporates, rather than transcends, the personal psychology of all individuals. Thus, while he is aware of the importance of success to his family obligation, his orientation is not toward the remedying of his failure but toward a form of duty and the acting out of a role, the basis for which he is only dimly aware of. His generosity is evidenced early in such acts as the giving of credit to the little girl whose mother is a drunk and who, Morris knows, will never pay.

He does this not with the conscious pride of doing a good deed—indeed, his conscious thoughts are that this is foolish, bad business—but with the half-awareness that he has done what, for his character, is the easiest course. Morris is the fool of goodness; he does good and helps others because it is his nature, an integral part of the worldview he can only vaguely formulate. Basically,

Morris is a product of Jewish thought, perhaps closely connected with the man whose name he echoes, Martin Buber, and this aspect of his character is so insisted upon that the reader is immediately aware of the importance of his comments on the Jew and the funeral message of the Rabbi which claims, perhaps on slim evidence, that Morris "was . . . a true Jew because he lived in the Jewish experience" (p. 180). In the discussions between Morris and Frank on the Jewish experience—and this must be interpreted as both historical and current experience—the characters shift from the contemporary roles of storekeeper and assistant to their purer religious selves, teacher and novitiate. The Jewish Law, Morris explains, "means to do what is right, to be honest, to be good. This means to other people" (p. 99). As Frank points out, these ideas are embodied in other religions, but he gets closer to the particular emphasis of Morris' view by asking about suffering. Do Jews merely suffer because they want to? "If you live, you suffer," Morris says, thereby giving voice to a point of view which sets him apart from the faith in success displayed by most of the people around him. Enlarging the proposition, Morris states that everyone suffers for everyone else. Thematically, such a statement can be illustrated by the lives of all the major characters, who sacrifice themselves for others—with much resentment in most cases, since they do not possess Morris' vision. The statement is, however, hardly as convincing out of context as it is an insight into the way Morris' actions make religious sense and a vision of the lost path in which he walks.

As an outsider, rootless and moving, Frank Alpine is at first attracted by the stability of the store, unaware at the beginning that the Bober family regards it as a tomb from which they wish to escape into the American life. Once he starts to realize what it can really be, he struggles to make it a part of the thriving business community of America, gradually succumbing to its necessity to be what it is. In time he succeeds his teacher and accepts the philosophy of suffering and acquiescence, symbolically represented by his conversion to Judaism and his circumcision, the pain of which both "enraged and inspired him." In Malamud's manipulation of another old story, the wanderer has at last become a Jew.

On the other hand, the ideas about suffering and the willing-

ness of Frank and Morris to accept such ideas can be accounted
for by admitting that only in such a scheme of things could their
lives make sense and have purpose. There is, however, imbedded
in the novel an ultimate religious perspective that carries the ideas
even further than mere apprehensions of roles and duties. Just as
Morris is entombed in the store, so all the souls of all the characters are imprisoned in external circumstance, in their culture,
and in the very limitations of their senses and the physical demands of their bodies. Norman Leer mentions the social barrier
as a symbol of alienation in this novel, but actually all the limitations of the characters serve to set them apart and contradict their
best intentions toward one another. Malamud's conception of
character is heavily influenced by the naturalistic view of human
nature, but his idea of an escape from circumstances in love, and
the awareness of the meaning of suffering goes back to an older
tradition. The final meaning of such lives, if fiction can ever be
final, is in the past, buried in old wisdom of which the characters
have only a sketchy knowledge. Perhaps this tendency of Malamud to both give and withdraw his message is also reflected in
Marcus Klein's view of his fiction: "The world does not come
easily to Malamud, everything is on the verge of not being, and
the process of his own holding on, rather than any moralizing
he does, is indeed the excitement of his fiction, and its tension."

Oddly enough, a minor character named Breitbart seems to
summarize many of the cultural tensions in the novel. As a sufferer, both comic and grotesque, he is the typical victim appearing in sensational tabloid stories—his wife runs away with his
brother, leaving him with "a drawerful of bills . . . and a not
too bright five-year-old boy." On his back he lugs around a burden
of light bulbs, suggesting many frames of reference from the spark
of humanity or conscience to the modern world of progress. Perhaps all these meanings work in the same confused, half-comic,
intermittent light which pervades the entire novel. At any rate
he appears in the final scene still trapped in his economic journeys,
stops briefly for a cup of tea, and gives Frank a last word which
may be both advice and description, "Schwer." Moving between
existence and nonexistence he has no definite role within either
context of meaning and yet a possible place in each. His routine,

like those of the other characters, is invested at different times with differing values.

Marcus Klein, paraphrasing some comments by Saul Bellow, writes, "The fat gods of the new materialism are all about us demanding our energies." One might say that in *The Assistant* the same situations exist in regard to meaning, and man, caught between the conflicting claims of cultural values, suffers not only because of his circumstances but because a fragmented abundance of world-views produces uncertainty about intentions, actions, and roles. If Malamud here seems to be on the side of older values, he refuses his characters willed preferences or convictions. They have faith enough to persevere but doubt enough to suspect themselves.

Select Bibliography

Bellman, Samuel, "Women, Children, and Idiots First," *Critique,* VII (Winter, 1964-65), 123-139. (See Chapter 2 in this collection.)

Goldman, Mark, "Bernard Malamud's Comic Vision and the Theme of Identity," *Critique,* VII (Winter, 1964-65), 92-109. (See Chapter 10 in this collection.)

Hicks, Granville, "Generations of the Fifties: Malamud, Gold, and Updike," *The Creative Present* (Garden City, New York: Doubleday, 1963), pp. 217-237.

Klein, Marcus, *After Alienation* (Cleveland: World, 1964), pp. 247-294. (See Chapter 17 in this collection.)

Leer, Norman, "Three American Novels and Contemporary Society: A Search for Commitment," *Wisconsin Studies in Contemporary Literature,* III (Fall, 1962), iii, 67-86.

Solotaroff, Theodore, "Bernard Malamud's Fiction: The Old Life and the New," *Commentary,* XXXIII (March, 1962), 197-204. (See Chapter 16 in this collection.)

Peter L. Hays

15.

The Complex Pattern of Redemption

I. The Novel

Bernard Malamud's use of the medieval myth of the Grail Quest to inform *The Natural* is by now a critical commonplace,[1] and a broad mythic pattern of rebirth has also been seen by these same critics in both *The Assistant* and *A New Life.* Malamud's protagonists (*schlemiels*, "football[s] of the Gods," Charles A. Hoyt * calls them) struggle against a bleak, unfavorable world and their own bad luck and ineptitude; usually the world strips them of material goods and any sense of real accomplishment, but their author endows them with, and communicates to us, their courage, their compassion, their humanity: from hellish depths of human misery they come forth, reborn as secular saints. What is remarkable in *The Assistant*, in addition to the vigor of the individual characters, is the complexity with which this realistically presented redemptive pattern is reinforced with myth, symbol and a philosophy remarkably like that of Martin Buber.

The protagonist in *The Assistant* is Frank Alpine, a wanderer without home and without values, except for some basic human compassion tempered by prejudice. Desperately poor and hungry

* See Chapter 11 in this collection.

and without direction to his life, he helps Ward Minogue, an acquaintance, rob Jewish grocer Morris Bober one November day. Frank is more willing to participate in the robbery because his victim is a Jew, someone for whom he need not feel sympathy. Yet when Ward impatiently pistol whips the old man, Frank gives Bober a cup of water. Alpine is twenty-five and looks much older; of Italian extraction, he was raised in an orphanage as a Catholic, but he no longer believes in that religion or much of anything. He has never known love, success or satisfaction; he is a born loser, a *schlemiel*. As he says:

> "I've been close to some wonderful things—jobs, for instance, education, women, but close is as far as I go. . . . Sooner or later everything I think is worth having gets away from me in some way or other. I work like a mule for what I want, and just when it looks like I am going to get it I make some kind of stupid move, and everything that is nailed down tight blows up in my face.
> . . . With me one wrong thing leads to another and it ends in a trap." [2]

In this case, the trap is Morris' grocery. Frank, ashamed of his part in the robbery and sorry for Bober, returns to help the old man—to become Bober's assistant in work as he was Ward Minogue's in theft. Like Fitzgerald about the rich, Alpine has conflicting feeling about goodness. In the orphanage where he was raised, Alpine had been taught about St. Francis, of whom he says:

> "He said poverty was a queen and he loved her like she was a beautiful woman. . . . Everytime I read about somebody like him I get a feeling inside of me which I have to fight to keep from crying. He was born good, which is a talent if you have it." (p. 31)

But Alpine lacks this talent and neither comprehends St. Francis nor his own feelings about the saint. Yet he sees that Bober's life, like St. Francis', is one of both poverty and goodness, and in his longing for a code to live by, an end to his own aimlessness, he is attracted by Bober's endurance in the face of calamity, by his acceptance of life with all its hardships, by his compassion and by his religion. At the same time, Alpine is repelled by the pain, the suffering and the lack of comfort which Morris' code brings the grocer. He asks Morris what it is to be a Jew. The grocer replies:

> ". . . The important thing is the Torah. This is the Law—a Jew must believe in the Law. . . . This means to do what is right, to be honest, to be good. This means to other people. Our life is hard enough. Why should we hurt somebody else? . . . We ain't animals. . . . This is what a Jew believes."
> (p. 124)

Frank is also attracted to Bober's daughter Helen and gradually wins the friendship of father and daughter—only to lose both. Unable to do right, even when he wants to, Frank continuously steals meager sums from the small amounts in the grocery store cash register, causing Morris, when the grocer can finally prove theft, to fire him. The same night Frank goes to the park to meet Helen, who is falling in love with him and has been meeting him in spite of her mother's objections; he arrives at their rendezvous and finds Ward Minogue attempting to rape Helen. But after he drives off Ward, Frank takes her by force himself.

Later when Bober becomes ill, Frank sneaks back into the store, operating it while Morris recuperates. When the grocer is better, he forces Frank to leave. At the end of March, however, Morris catches pneumonia while shoveling snow and dies three days later. At his funeral on a warm, spring-like April day, Frank slips and falls into Morris' grave, landing on the grocer's coffin. Afterwards Frank goes back to the store that had been Bober's tomb-in-life for twenty-two years, assuming the support of Mrs. Bober and Helen, and working at an additional night job as well so that Helen can attend night school. Frank also assumes Morris' values, his honesty and his compassion: his descent into Bober's grave marks Frank's death as an uncommitted wanderer and his rebirth as Bober's spiritual son—one who lives by the Law. The last paragraph in the novel relates the events of the spring a year after Bober's death:

> One day in April Frank went to the hospital and had himself circumcised. For a couple of days he dragged himself around with a pain between his legs. The pain enraged and inspired him. After Passover he became a Jew. (p. 246)

II. Myth and Symbol

That Frank should have himself circumcised and formally convert to Judaism at Passover-Easter time is highly significant: it is the season of Nature's renewal of life in the spring and coincides with the resurrections of Christ, Attis and Adonis. It is also the time of the redemption (resurrection) of the Jewish nation from Egyptian bondage. And that Frank should drag himself around during these holy days is also significant, for *pesach*, the Hebrew word for Passover, is etymologically related not only to *pasahu*, an Assyrian word meaning to propitiate, but also to several Hebrew words meaning lame or hobbling. Thus Malamud has used, consciously or not, religious and mythic allusions, as well as obviously purposeful seasonal changes—the novel moves twice from wintry fall to warm spring—to mark the pattern of death and rebirth. Frank undergoes a rite of initiation, begun at Morris' side in the living death of the grocery store, marked by his descent to the grocer's grave and by his circumcision, and expressed by his conversion from a spiritually empty life: he experiences resurrection, which prepares him for (to borrow from Malamud) a new life, based on the role of the grocer and endowed with Bober's responsibilities, beliefs and values. Frank's material gains are negligible, or nonexistent, but he does grow in heroic stature and in our admiration. And we can measure Frank's conversion away from his sterile, self-centered life in terms of his relationship with Helen, who is also endowed with mythic characteristics.

Although critics disagree about their relationship at the

novel's conclusion,[3] I feel that they probably will marry. At the end of the novel, Helen confesses to herself her feelings for Frank.

> Although she detested the memory of her experience in the park, lately it had come back to her how she had desired that night to give herself to Frank. . . . She had wanted him. . . . If he had made his starved leap in bed she would have returned passion. She had hated him, she thought, to divert hatred from herself. (p. 239)

She learns how hard Frank is working and thinks:

> He had kept them alive. Because of him she had enough to go to school at night. . . . It came to her that he had changed. It's true, he's not the same man, she said to herself. I should have known by now. She had despised him for the evil he had done, without understanding the way or aftermath, or admitting there could be an end to the bad and a beginning of good. . . . He had been one thing, low, dirty, but because of something in himself—something she couldn't define, a memory perhaps, an ideal he might have forgotten and then remembered—he had changed into somebody else, no longer what he had been. She should have recognized it before. What he did to me he did wrong, she thought, but since he has changed in his heart, he owes me nothing. (p. 243)

The next week she enters the store and speaks to Frank—only the second time in almost a year since her father's death, and the first time of her own volition—to thank him for all his trouble. She tells him that she will consider his offer to take more money from him so that she can go to college during the day, blushing as she does so, and also tells him that she is still using a volume of Shakespeare he had given her as a present long before. And that night Frank hears her fight with and leave—perhaps permanently—her one boyfriend.

Perhaps Frank and she never become completely reconciled,

but most of the barriers that had existed between them have been removed. After Frank's assault on Helen, the one comment from her which Malamud gives us, the one that closes the chapter, is, "Dog—uncircumcised dog!" (p. 168). The adjective, at least, is no longer valid.

As Baumbach has noted, "Frank's attraction to Helen is an uneasy fusion of the sensual and the spiritual . . ." (p. 117); also, Frank's "redemption is made possible by his uncompromising love for Helen—which provides the impetus for his commitment to the store." [4] It is undoubtedly part of the impetus for his commitment to Judaism, too. Frank was strongly attracted to Judaism and to Helen, and wished to "belong" to both; and he has taken what steps he can, accomplishing the first goal, doing as much as he could to achieve the second. The first brings him a form of rebirth and spiritual peace; the second would bring him sexual fulfillment, a satisfaction of his social needs and probably children, too. The Spartan Moon-goddess was called "Helen," and marriage to her made Menelaus a king. Her name is etymologically related to Helle, bright goddess of death and resurrection. So that to the extent to which Helen has redeemed Frank and brought him to his goals, and could bring him to the others, she is a fertility goddess.

To emphasize this role of hers, Malamud frequently has her described in terms of obvious symbols of fertility: flowers (harbingers of spring's renewal) and birds (roosters; the doves of Noah, Aphrodite and Christian symbolism; the Thanksgiving turkey). Morris thinks Helen "looks like a little bird" (p. 20), and when Frank spies on her in the bathroom he thinks of her "breasts like small birds in flight, her ass like a flower" (p. 75). And like Aphrodite, Helen leaves a floral fragrance about her in the air (p. 184).

The bird and flower symbols, especially the former, are also significant because of Frank's symbolic relationship to St. Francis of Assisi. There are, of course, their analoguous names; there is also the fact that Frank spent most of his early life in the city of St. Francis, San Francisco (p. 81). Moreover, Malamud frequently associates the two. There is the initial reference when, in Sam Pearl's candy shop, Frank sees a picture of the saint surrounded by a flock of birds, with a grove of leafy trees in the background

(p. 30). At one point in the novel, Helen goes for a walk in a nearby park; as she approaches it, she sees "a man squatting by one of the benches, feeding the birds. . . . When the man rose, the pigeons fluttered up with him, a few landing on his arms and shoulders, one perched on his fingers, pecking peanuts from his cupped palm. Another fat bird sat on his hat" (p. 118). The man, of course, is Frank. At another time, Frank, in his loneliness and desire for Helen, tells her a story he remembers of St. Francis, who, wondering one snowy evening what his life would have been if he had married and had a family, went outside and made a snow wife and several children (p. 95). At the end of the chapter, Helen associates the saint with the thieving assistant: "Who was he making into a wife out of snowy moonlight?" (p. 102). Helen and the moon, again.

The snow that barefoot St. Francis trod upon occurs again in the novel, in a dream of Frank's. After his assault of Helen, he tries again and again to apologize. Then, one night

> he dreamed he was standing in snow outside her window. His feet were bare yet not cold. He had waited a long time in the falling snow, and some of it lay on his head and had all but frozen his face; but he waited longer until, moved by pity, she opened the window and flung something out. It floated down; he thought it was a piece of paper with writing on it but saw that it was a white flower, surprising to see in wintertime. Frank caught it in his hand. As she had tossed the flower out through the partly opened window he had glimpsed her fingers only, yet he saw the light of her room and even felt the warmth of it. Then when he looked again the window was shut tight, sealed with ice. Even as he dreamed, he knew it had never been open. There was no such window. He gazed down at his hand for the flower and before he could see it wasn't there, felt himself wake. (p. 185)

Obviously, the rose, the flower Frank desires to receive from Helen, is her love and Helen herself. At her father's funeral, it is a rose which Helen throws onto the coffin and which Frank, intent on observing, follows so blindly that he stumbles into the open grave. But besides these allusions, there are others equally explicit. To pass the time one day, Frank begins to carve a board "into something. To his surprise it turned into a bird. . . . He thought of offering it to Helen but it seemed too rough a thing" (p. 192). Here, the bird may carry its more conventional symbolic weight, the soul, Frank's, which he desires to offer Helen and then refuses in recognition of his unworthiness, of his being "too rough a thing." Next he carves for her, appropriately, "a flower . . . a rose starting to bloom" (p. 192). He gives it to her, to atone in part for his forcing of her, and she, still indignant, throws it in the garbage.

In the penultimate paragraph of the novel, these elements come together for emphasis:

> As he [Frank] was reading [the Bible] he had this pleasant thought. He saw St. Francis come dancing out of the woods in his brown rags, a couple of scrawny birds flying around over his head. St. F. [*sic*] stopped in front of the grocery, and reaching into the garbage can, plucked the wooden rose out of it. He tossed it into the air and it turned into a real flower that he caught in his hand. With a bow he gave it to Helen, who had just come out of the house. "Little sister, here is your little sister the rose." From him she took it, although it was with the love and best wishes of Frank Alpine. (pp. 245-246)

By associating Helen with flowers, especially the rose, symbol of love and femininity, and by making her the motive and inspiration for Frank's recurrent redemptive acts and the possible means for his greater personal fulfillment, Malamud has endowed her with characteristics of mythic fertility goddesses. The bird imagery serves the same purposes, and also, through Frank's identification with St. Francis, reinforces my contention that we are meant to believe that Frank and Helen will come together after the novel's close.

There is still another sign which attests to the special nature of Helen's role. In *Symbolic Wounds* (New York, 1962) Bruno Bettelheim discusses the relationship of circumcision to ritual forms of emasculation. Speaking of the self-mutilation of the priests of Cybele, he says, "This example of ritual castration, and many others not mentioned here, indicates that it was exacted by maternal figures as a sign of devotion and submission on the part of their male followers. . . ." (p. 92) If Mrs. Bober objects to Helen's consorting with a non-Jew, if Helen herself loathes Frank because he is "an uncircumcised dog," then Frank is willing to have himself circumcised as a sign of "devotion and submission"—to the Law of Judaism, as Morris Bober spoke of it, and to Helen. Bettelheim also says, "Loeb is convinced that circumcision was originally performed as a sacrifice to a female goddess. . . . He follows Barton who holds that originally all circumcision was a sacrifice to the goddess of fertility." [5] And Frank's circumcision for love and religion during the Paschal season, the time of propitiation, coincides not only with the death and resurrection of Christ at the time of hobbling, but also with the castration of Attis and Adonis (and their priests) on behalf of their respective lovers and fertility goddesses, Cybele and Aphrodite. To call Helen a fertility figure, though, to compare her, however removed, to Cybele and Aphrodite, is not to say that Malamud has written modern Greek myth, as John Updike has in *The Centaur*. The source of the power which Helen may dispense, the nature of her *mana*, is the same with which the priestess of Isis heals Lawrence's Man Who Died; as Baumbach and Richman have noted, redemption comes to Malamud's protagonists through their ability to give of themselves unselfishly, to love.

III. Philosophy

. . . In a receptive hour of my life a man meets me about whom there is something, which I cannot grasp in any objective way at all, that 'says something' to me . . . speaks something that enters my own life. It can be something about this man, for instance that he needs me. But it can also be something about myself.

. . . Perhaps I have to accomplish something about him; but perhaps I have only to learn something, and it is only a matter of my 'accepting'.[6]

The foregoing could well serve as a commentary on the essential relationship in the novel between Frank and Morris, but it was not written for that purpose; instead, it is part of the philosophical canon of Martin Buber. Many readers have stumbled over the similarity in names—Martin Buber, Morris Bober—and there is also a distinct similarity, not only in the beliefs expressed and acted upon by these two men, but in the philosophy one can infer from the novel as a whole.

Bober is not an orthodox Jew, for he does not obey Mosaic dietary laws, nor does he regularly attend religious services. Similarly, ". . . Buber does not regard the Jewish law as essential to the Jewish tradition. . . . He contrasts the false desire for security of the dogmatists of the law with the 'holy insecurity' of the truly religious man who does not divorce his action from his intention." [7] As Buber himself has said in *Between Man and Man*, "I have given up the religious" for "the everyday. . . . I know no fulness but each mortal hour's fulness of claim and responsibility. Though far from being equal to it, yet I know that in claim I am claimed and may respond in responsibility. . . ." And for the grocer, too, the key to a moral existence is personal responsibility for others: "A Jew must believe in the Law. . . . This means to do what is right, to be honest, to be good. This means to other people. Our life is hard enough. Why should we hurt somebody else?" (p. 124)

That life is indeed hard, that it is replete with suffering, is part of the view of life expressed by Martin Buber and in *The Assistant*. In the latter, Morris says to Frank, "If you live, you suffer," and Frank asks, "What do you suffer for, Morris?" " 'I suffer for you,' Morris said calmly" (p. 125). In fact, at one point, Malamud says, "The world suffers" (p. 7). Buber also thinks that suffering is an essential part of man's life and is, in fact, what redeems him and gives him stature. Defining a moral man, Buber says he is one "with responsibility for the action of those who act, since he is wholly defined by the tension between being and 'ought to be,' and in grotesque and hopeless courage casts his heart piece by piece into the insatiable gulf that lies between them" [8]—a comment which could well describe either Morris or Frank. For Morris' suffering is simply a measure of his endurance and humanity. For Frank, suffering because of what he has done against Morris and then, through relation with Morris, taking over the grocer's very suffering is a path to personal redemption. Frank is indeed defined throughout the course of the novel by the gap he is aware of between what he is and what he ought to be, and so he casts his energy, his endurance, his pride and his heart in "grotesque and hopeless courage"—an apt description of all of Malamud's protagonists from Roy Hobbs to Yakov Bok—into the gap between them. Frank does not become what he thinks he ought to be—rich, powerful, "a big shot"—but his efforts do allow him to become what Buber and Bober would say he ought to be —a man, moral and responsible.

Perhaps the greatest common bond, however, between the philosopher and the grocer's creator, the novelist, is their treatment of "relation" and "dialogue." As I have noted, Baumbach and Richman state that love redeems Frank Alpine. Richman, quoting *I and Thou,* even uses Buber's "Love is responsibility of an *I* for *a Thou"* as epigraph for his chapter on *The Assistant,* but uses Buber primarily in discussing Malamud's writing that shows the influence of Hasidism (or Chasidism), which Buber invigorated in modern Jewish theology.[9] More important, I feel, is the way in which Malamud has exemplified Buber's precept of the I-Thou relationship, what denying it causes, and what allowing it to exist achieves.

According to Buber, there are two forms of existence: the I-It, which is a subject and object, person and thing, organizing, arranging, advantage-taking relationship; and the I-Thou, which is an interpersonal, mutually addressing, mutual exchanging one. Further, Buber states that a man defines himself in his relation with others. And wholeness, integration of personality, depends on eschewing the I-It impersonal for the I-Thou: "Entering into relation is an act of the whole being—it is in fact *the* act by which we constitute ourselves as human . . ." (Friedman, p. 83).

And so it is with Frank, who develops morally in proportion as he sees Helen less as a sexual object, and more as a person to love and be loved by; as he sees Morris less as a Jew, a type of victim for his or anyone's greed, and more as a fellow man, eventually, as a spiritual father. Everyone else in the novel but

Bober—Julius Karp, Ward Minogue, Frank (at first), even Helen and Morris' wife Ida—seek to use others, to manipulate them for personal benefit. Only Morris tries constantly to establish I-Thou relationships, even with those who have stolen from him, like his former partner Charlie Sobeloff, or like Frank Alpine. This faith in humanity is what makes Morris the *schlemiel* that he is, like the cartoon character Charlie Brown in "Peanuts," but it is also that which makes him admirable and nearly heroic.

Ultimately, Frank, too, achieves these qualities. Through dialogue—both his conversations with Morris about the Law and with Helen about life and literature, and his turning to the Bobers in his silent observation of the code by which they live—Frank achieves I-Thou instead of I-It, and because of that relation he becomes an assistant for the third time in the novel; first to Ward Minogue, then to Morris, and finally to Helen and her mother. Moreover, Buber defines every approach to another's Thou as an approach to God, the Eternal Thou; for him relation is essentially triadic, involving self, other and God (*I and Thou,* p. 75). Therefore, Frank's entering into relation with the Bobers is, by Buber's definition, an approach to God, a religious act, and thus prepares for Frank's conversion to Judaism.

In the early part of the novel, Frank fits Buber's definition of evil, for the philosopher considers evil as absence of relation and lack of direction generally—specifically, "lack of direction toward God." [10] Moreover, Buber insists that "man repeatedly experiences the dimension of evil as indecision. . . . These moments merge into a course of indecision, as it were into a fixation in it" (p. 134). Certainly this describes Frank, as does the remedy: "To the extent to which the soul achieves unification it becomes aware of direction. . . . It comes into the service of good or into service for good" (p. 127). At the beginning of the novel, Frank is aimless, without direction. His only desire is generalized materialistic success. But in its place, Morris tells him of the Torah, the Law; as Buber explains: "The intention behind that collection [of psalms] may have been to complete the 'Torah' or 'direction' . . . by means of hymns and songs of a 'directing' kind. Here 'to direct' means to show the way which man should 'choose' (Ps. 25, 12), and that means to teach man to distinguish this way, the right way, from the other, wrong ways" (p. 51). By his own life, Morris provides Frank with the example of different, better values; and hope of attaining Helen gives Frank a distinct purpose, a definite direction.

> "The man with the divided, complicated, contradictory soul is not helpless: the core of his soul, the divine force in its depths, is capable of . . . binding the conflicting forces together. . . ." Again and again temptation overcomes the soul, and "again and again innate grace arises from out of its depths and promises the utterly incredible: you can become whole and one." (Friedman, p. 91)

IV. Conclusion

I have not meant to imply in the preceding section that Malamud immersed himself in the philosophy of Martin Buber and then set about embodying it in fiction,[11] but the striking parallels remain. That love redeems is not an idea original to either Buber or Malamud; neither is the concept that one defines oneself and finds oneself through his relation to others. Maurice Friedman defines Jung's concept of myth, which manifests itself through expressions of archetypes and the collective unconscious, as "an embodiment in different forms and cultures of a perennial reality . . ." (p. 231). The collective unconscious is a difficult concept for many to accept. But perhaps the "perennial reality" is not some Platonic ideal existing independently of man; rather, it might simply be that intelligent, feeling men, especially two with similar religious backgrounds and sharing elements of a common tradition, living in the same difficult world and experiencing generally the same crises of despair, misfortune, loss of identity and pain see the problem and answers in roughly the same form: man inevitably suffers; to endure that suffering with as much dignity as possible is a virtue; to continue to strive to do right and to suffer for others is a mark of humanity. When Frank Alpine learns these lessons from Morris Bober, which would have been the same had Martin Buber been his teacher, he redeems himself and approaches a state of secular sainthood where he is indeed worthy of identification with St. Francis of Assisi.

Throughout the novel, Malamud has characterized Alpine by his relation to others, by the extent to which he establishes dialogue. Ward Minogue and he curse at each other and use each other to gain private goals; Frank spies on Helen, possesses her, and is cursed by her. But eventually he speaks, not just of Helen and Morris, but with them. For more than two years he shares their lives, making their needs his responsibilities; by controlling his own impatient, undirected desires he learns to love others, and finds direction, and himself.

Thus Bernard Malamud, with religious allusion, Mediterranean mythology, sacrificial rites and fertility imagery infusing a philosophy of existence very much like Martin Buber's, has created a modern parable in the form of a naturalistic novel, a story of redemption which expresses perennial realities of psychological and philosophical truth.

Notes

1. Leslie Fiedler seems to have been the first to recognize the myth in *The Natural* in his *No! in Thunder* (Boston, 1960), p. 105; among others who refer to or discuss its presence are Jonathan Baumbach, *The Landscape of Nightmare* (New York, 1965), pp. 107-111; Charles Alva Hoyt, "Bernard Malamud and the New Romanticism," *Contemporary American Novelists,* ed. Harry T. Moore (Carbondale, 1964), p. 78; Sidney Richman, *Bernard Malamud* (New York, 1966), pp. 28-49; and Robert Shulman, "Myth, Mr. Eliot, and the Comic Novel," *Modern Fiction Studies,* XII (Winter 1966-1967), 400-403. (See Chapter 11 in this collection for Hoyt essay.)

2. Bernard Malamud, *The Assistant* (New York, 1959), p. 36. All subsequent quotations from the novel or its author wil refer to this edition and will be paginated in my text.

3. Granville Hicks feels that Frank and Helen may marry ("Portraits of the Authors as Men," *Saturday Review,* July 10, 1965, p. 29), but Baumbach (p. 119) and Theodore Solotaroff ("Bernard Malamud's Fiction," *Commentary,* March 1962, p. 198) do not—Baumbach explicitly, Solotaroff implicitly. Nor does Ihab Hassan hold out hope for them in *Radical Innocence* (Princeton, 1961), p. 116. (See Chapter 16 in this collection for Solotaroff essay.)

4. Jonathan Baumbach, "The Economy of Love," *Kenyon Review,* XXV

(1963), 456. This article was the basis of Baumbach's chapter on Malamud in *The Landscape of Nightmare*.

5. *Symbolic Wounds*, p. 95; B. M. Loeb, "The Blood Sacrifice Complex," *Memories of the American Anthropological Association*, No. 30 (1933), p. 18. George A. Barton, "Semitic Circumcision," *Encyclopedia of Religion and Ethics* (New York, 1911), p. 680. Cf. Ihab Hassan: "The act is one of self-purification, of initiation too, . . . if not of symbolic castration" (*op cit.*, p. 168). (See Chapter 13 in this collection for Hassan essay.)

6. Martin Buber, *Between Man and Man*, trans. Ronald Gregor Smith (London, 1947), pp. 9, 10.

7. Maurice S. Friedman, *Martin Buber: The Life of Dialogue* (London, 1955), p. 261.

8. Martin Buber, *I and Thou*, trans. Ronald Gregor Smith (New York, 1957), p. 108.

9. Richman says that in *The Assistant*, "as in Martin Buber's famous depiction of the holy men of Chasidism, [there is] the 'hallowing of the everyday,'" *Ibid.*, p. 70, citing Malcolm Diamond, *Martin Buber: Jewish Existentialist* (New York, 1960), pp. 110-137. "Hallowing the everyday" is a basic tenet of Buber. Cf. Smith's introduction to *I and Thou*: Buber asserts "the present moment as the real time for faith. . . . His thought is rooted in the concrete situation. . . . The concrete reality . . . is the situation where responsible persons confront one another in living mutual relation" (pp. x-xi).

10. Friedman, p. 103; Martin Buber, *Good and Evil*, trans. by Ronald Gregor Smith and Michael Bullock (1952, 1953), pp. 87 and 97. The following three quotations, identified only with page references in the text, are also from *Good and Evil*.

11. Mr. Malamud was kind enough to reply to a letter and said that he had only a very general acquaintance with Buber's work when he wrote *The Assistant* and did not intend to identify Morris Bober with the renowned philosopher.

Theodore Solotaroff

16.

The Old Life and the New

I would say that Bernard Malamud has been a writer almost unique in our time. He has found the objects and idiom and viewpoint that allow him to see the will directly and portray its commitment to moral struggle. While the work of the other contemporary novelists has been seriously affected by the forces of fragmentation and cynicism that demoralize our lives and efforts, the best of Malamud's has stood against these forces by resolutely ignoring them. Most often, and in his most characteristic fiction, he has created a type of half-legendary world in the middle of New York City—the Malamud province of moral comedy and affirmation. In this spectral province, with its familiar streets and strange interiors, live a few lost souls with Jewish names, their figures deeply etched by their creator's fantasy. But their needs are so simple and so complete that fundamental human feelings and values can be insistently expressed and defined. This original folk poetry has been obviously inspired by the Jewish immigrant experience and the ghetto sensibility. Yet its main significance has not been in its Jewishness. Malamud's creation has signified, as Norman Podhoretz so well said when he reviewed *The Magic Barrel,* "an act of spiritual autonomy perfect enough to persuade us that the possibility of freedom from the determinings of history and sociology still exists."

The province in which Malamud's characters live is not a simple place. Morris Bober, the moral exemplar in *The Assistant*, goes to his death with the realization that "I gave my life away for nothing. It was the thunderous truth." Nor is there anything very reassuring about the fate of the two characters in "Take Pity" who both are eventually driven to suicide by the difficulties of extending and accepting charity. And in "The Magic Barrel," love finally comes to the careful Rabbi Finkle in the person of a whore. Malamud's figures have, or gain, an expert knowledge of suffering, whether in the flesh from poverty and illness, or in the mind from frustration and remorse. Character is almost invariably formed by hunger, and at twenty-three a pretty girl already fights "a sense of mourning to a practiced draw." Malamud's Jews (and his Gentiles) are connected to each other not by religious and social ties but by a common fate of error and ill luck and sorrow, of having lost much by their mistakes and recovered little by their virtues. The back streets of life become a kind of timeless depressed area, where dying men go begging for money to send idiot sons to California and bakers weep in their bread; when their children manage to escape to the modern world, they carry the ghetto's aches with them.

It is an implacably comic world of absurd reversals and last straws and of uncertain stairs that lead seemingly nowhere. But this antic world is shaped by a tough and subtle intelligence in the service of an embattled ethic. Its people are not charming or vigorous; they are usually too impoverished to represent any real range of contemporary human possibilities. But their lives are suffused with a directing earnestness that we miss in ours and are formed from assurances that ours are increasingly without— the assurance that principles matter, that the "soft" facts of life are more important than the "hard," that there are ways men can change themselves and become free, if not rich.

From where do these assurances come? Most of the figures who contain them are unassimilated Jews, which is less to the point than one sometimes likes to think. The truth is that Malamud's Jews are creatures of a particular moral vision which is as accessible to Christians as to Jews. To be sure, one can make (as Malamud himself sometimes explicitly does) a correlation between the nature of their lives and of Jewish experience and values, particularly of the East European Pale where history preserved the extremities of deprivation, irony, and idealism in a virtually pure and congruous form. Yet Jewishness is a source of Malamud's sensibility rather than the object: just as his characters are almost entirely detached from any real Jewish community— of the past or of the present—so are the causes and purposes of their suffering. There are times when Malamud's feelings for the immigrant Jewish melancholy and ethos, and for its idiom and wit, produce an objectification such as the story of "The Magic Barrel." But, in general, the sense of the ghetto experience is abstracted from the communal life in which its social and religious meanings were embedded. Malamud's Jewishness is a type of metaphor—for anyone's life—both for the tragic dimension of anyone's life and for a code of personal morality and salvation that is more psychological than religious. To the extent that the Jew and his problems become a way of envisaging the human condition, he becomes more symbol than fact, fashioned to the service of an abstraction. Hence, when, at the end of *The Assistant*, Frank Alpine gets circumcised and becomes a Jew, the whole point is not that he will now *daven* or move into a neighborhood that has a synagogue but that he has confirmed his investiture of a set of moral attitudes. In effect, the Malamud Jew is partly Jew and partly construct—a way of viewing the relation of the conscience to deprivation and love, of exploring the resources and process by which, as Ihab Hassan phrases it, "a man can become a *mensch*."

Which is to say that for all the homely trappings and Yiddishisms of his fiction, Malamud is nevertheless a modern American writer—detached, introspective, preoccupied with the problems of contactlessness and self-integration, for which each man's experience is his own gospel. *"Each in his prison/Turning the key"*: the lines from Eliot suggest the burden of Malamud's vision, the consistency with which his chief figures are confronted less by the world than by themselves. I want to explore some of Malamud's work in this connection, before taking up his most recent novel, *A New Life*, which though it seems like an obvious departure, is very close in theme to his earlier work. By doing so, it seems to me that some of the problems raised for the reviewers by Malamud's latest book can be clarified.

His first novel, *The Natural*, opens with this bit of imagery:

Roy Hobbs pawed at the glass before thinking to prick a match with his thumbnail and hold the spurting flame in his cupped palm close to the lower berth window, but by then he had figured it was a tunnel they were passing through and was no longer surprised at the bright sight of himself holding a yellow light over his head, peering back in.

The image is central. It foreshadows the fate of Roy Hobbs —whose fabulous and brief baseball career is to be but another stage in an endless train ride through life, marked by obscure awakenings and illuminations which reveal only himself. But more, this single sentence introduces the centering point of Malamud's vision. As in the romances of another moralist, Nathaniel Hawthorne, there are a good many mirror and light images in Malamud's tales, and they signify much the same preoccupation with those moments when the distinction between the objective and the imaginary is suspended and the spirit sees either itself or, in Hawthorne's term, its "emblems." Around this core of revelation the other elements are laid, the action moving toward and away from self-confrontation, the tone either controlled by or within easy reach of the introspective and hallucinatory. However, the psychology is in the service of a moral construct: the Malamud hero who sees himself sees his chief adversary, and what he learns from the experience determines his life.

Spelled out in the terms of his most characteristic fiction, this preoccupation creates the story of the man who emerges from the past of deprivation, isolation, or failure and who struggles for fuller and better connections with life against the drag of the old hungers and habitual errors. Thus Malamud's fiction is often set in the crucial period when the disabilities of the past contend with the future's possibilities, the old defeats with the new aspirations. In *The Natural*—which is usually read as a wacky mock-heroic satire on baseball but bears deep parallels with Malamud's other work—the heroine, Iris, tells Hobbs, "We have two lives . . . the life we learn with and the life we live with after that. Suffering is what brings us to happiness. It teaches us to want the right things." Roy Hobbs suffers for fifteen years for one mistake before he gets his chance to play in the major leagues and become a great star. Frank Alpine, an orphan and another drifter, has his chance to learn through his relations with the honest, impoverished Bober and Helen. These are Malamud's loose men (usually Gentiles) who, lacking self-control, go on making the same mistakes. There are also the tight men (usually Jews) such as Rabbi Finkle and Fidelman (the art scholar in "The Last Mohican") whose lives are overly regulated and narrow, who are armored heavily against the dangers of sympathy and desire. Each of these two is anxious to change his life—Finkle to marry, Fidelman to redeem his failures as a painter by producing a work on Giotto. They have "principles" but the wrong ones, and they are torn apart, no less than Alpine, by the fantastic figure who in each case enters to teach them about misery and passion. Alpine finds his own way to the pit: with the stricken Bober lying unconscious on the floor, the air filled with the wails and screams of his wife and daughter, the young Italian puts on the Jewish grocer's apron: "I need the experience," he says.

Suffering can kill feeling—as with Hobbs—or educate it— as with Alpine, who emerges from his ordeal capable of relationships, of respecting the human bonds of sorrow, sympathy, and consideration. "Our life is hard enough," Alpine learns from Morris Bober and his situation. "Why should we hurt somebody else? . . . We ain't animals." With tenderness for others comes Alpine's insight and aspiration and, finally, his wisdom and self-control—the freedom to see and do the right thing. Without this freedom conferred by connection and self-integration, life dribbles away; the will struggles but remains attached to habits of lust or defensiveness and each man lives out his mistakes and awaits the end. However, morality, in Malamud's view, is a slow and bloody business and has little noticeable effect on fortune. He has been too intelligent a moralist to freeze his vision of failure into a formula and too saturnine to exaggerate the benefits of regeneration.

Roy Hobbs suffers but doesn't learn; cut down in his youth by a sexy psychopath, he makes the same hungry mistake fifteen years later with the corrupt Memo and destroys himself by throwing the last game of the World Series for her sake. However, there is also the better Iris, who pays for her adolescent error with a stranger in the park, sacrifices her life to raising her daughter and hence to learning about the right things, only to be left at the end almost exactly where she started—seduced by another stranger in the park, made pregnant, and probably abandoned. What makes Malamud so cogent in his treatment of these matters is the complication he can give to character, and to morality, by focusing on the chain of habits which tie a man to his mistakes and frustrations and make his face stare back at him even as he awakens to new possibilities. He convinces us of the gravity of a single act of moral decision (or, as Alpine puts it, "how easy it was for a man to wreck his whole life in a single wrong act"), for he makes us aware of the determinisms of guilt and self-deprecation, of the ease with which circumstances overcome the weakened will, to lead a man away from resolutions back into chains.

Even one who, like Alpine, does make the break is left with little else beside his new wholeness and freedom. Along with Bober's humaneness, Alpine has received the grocer's way of life and the grocery store on a dead street, the Jew's justice and charity but accompanied by the rut of his days. The store is still a "fate." Such a conclusion seems both pat and in excess of the facts, weighting the scales in a way that becomes a defect in Malamud's otherwise clear moral intelligence. Yet it is, indeed, the defect of Malamud's very particular virtue. Whatever Malamud's beliefs may be, the source of power in his works is in the struggle toward affirmation—his faith in the resources of the human spirit contending against a deep-seated sense of complication, so that in the end change may only be measured in inches of progress, shades of gray. It is Malamud's pessimism that has allowed him to make convincing the main idea that a man is not necessarily bound within his limits.

Most modern literature has conditioned us to accept the idea that a man's limitations are the main truth about him. The technique of modern fiction, stemming from Flaubert and Joyce, has been designed to discover these limitations. If *The Assistant* came as a revelation, as it did for me, partly the reason was that it restored a sense of the dynamics of character and of the older intention of fiction to show the ways men change. Despite its small compass and thinness of social reference, *The Assistant* could thus take on some of the power and clarity of the great 19th-century novels by the graphic depiction of Alpine's development from a bum to a man of principle.

That Malamud's fiction has been able to support its heavy moral interests is due to other resources as well. He has a particular gift for portraying the obsessive kinds of relationship that lead his characters into themselves or otherwise dramatize the ambiguities of their hearts. The resonance of such brief tales as "The Loan," "The Bill," and "Take Pity" result mainly from Malamud's uncanny sense of what types of people belong in the same story, of the subtle and unexpected ways in which relations bind and influence. His sense of character, like his sense of episode and place, is rooted in a strong feeling for the bizarre—the kind of spiritual inventiveness and wit that creates a Negro *shul* and a debauched Negro angel named Levine. His imagination, in fact, seems most highly charged before the extremes of personal confrontation and crisis, which he succeeds in authenticating by macabre comedy. Out of these situations come his semi-hallucinatory demons such as the *macher* in *The Assistant* or Susskind in "The Last Mohican" or Salzman in "The Magic Barrel," who provide the electrifying quality of the Malamudian vision and allow the tone to fill out to the dimensions of the theme. Similarly the moments to which one assents in *The Natural* are usually those in which Malamud gives up the horseplay about baseball and produces the tortured and truly wacky images of Hobbs's inner life.

In general, the special achievement of Malamud's technique has been the movement back and forth between the grimly plain and the fantastic, the joining of the natural to the supernatural, the endowing of his abstracted version of the commonplace with the entanglements of a dream. His most impressive prose has been a similar mixture of a hard common speech, twisted by Yiddishisms or by his own syntax so that it vibrates, and lit here and there by a sudden lyrical image. The solidity of his best work has come from an obsessive mood and vision which from moment to moment seems to take the place of the realist's eye for physical detail. The slow, grueling development of Frank Alpine unfolds against the mood of the vacuous, mean neighborhood and of the mixed atmosphere of suffering and aspiration, discipline and defeat within the Bobers' milieu. Similarly, in his religious stories Malamud manages—as much by abstraction as by detail—to create a vividly spiritualized reality. A dying man in search of money for his idiot son, the *malach-ha-moves* who pursues and frustrates him, the bitter city streets, and the iron gates of Pennsylvania Station all come to belong, through the sustained unity of the writing, to the same order of things.

Bypassing contemporary reality, then, and the techniques of realism, Malamud has relied instead mainly upon his memories of ghetto life and his idiosyncratic imagination to create situations of sufficient density—and intensity—for his moral concerns. His excursions beyond the old ghetto life have been noticeably less sure and distinguished, except in some of the later Italian stories such as "The Last Mohican" and "The Maid's Shoes," which are both really extensions rather than departures. Thus when the word got out that he was doing a novel about a college teacher in the Northwest, there was a great deal of interest in what he would make of the subject.

As the title of the novel suggests, *A New Life* is again mainly a study in the difficulties of undoing the hold of a deprived and wasted past, of breaking "through the hardened cement of self-frustration" to freedom and control. The hero is S. Levin, an ex-drunkard and depressive from Malamud's New York, who has managed to pull himself out of the gutter by means of certain mystical revelations about life and an M.A. from New York University. Part Hobbs and Alpine in his melancholy impulsiveness and grossness of desire, part Finkle and Fidelman in being constantly on guard against his old habits, Levin has come to teach in the new world of Cascadia, whose mountains and forests and seasons are as stunning to him as its social and academic life is flat, frivolous, and intellectually inert. As a liberal and humanist as well as the Malamud *shlimazel* "who creates his own peril," Levin soon sees that he has more to worry about than the secret of his past. The time is 1950 and Levin's predecessor—another exotic from the "East"—has been fired for his radical views and for disturbing the peace of a school which is quite content—without any liberal arts curriculum—to train engineering and forestry students and good football players. The leading question indicated in the early chapters is whether Levin will follow in the steps of the disgraced Leo Duffy. "I can't fail again," Levin grimly warns himself, but the question of what failure will and will not mean in Cascadia is portentous from the start.

However, the events that follow take a course not very different from Malamud's first two novels. There is the period of mixed achievements and satisfactions as the new possibilities of teaching, using his hands, taking hold in a new and promising environment fail to lay the old ghosts of dissatisfaction and guilt. "The past hides but is present," as Levin keeps finding out. "The new life hangs on an old soul." Behind the formidable beard he has grown and inside the solemn English composition teacher lurks the mournful, clumsy clown, out of step with the opportunities but thirsty with desire. After two near-misses, Levin finally comes to grief in much the same way that Hobbs and Alpine lunged past their resolutions, in order to take an easy sexual advantage. After a weekend by the sea with a willing enough coed, Levin caves in, and in a scene strongly reminiscent of the self-confrontations in *The Natural* and *The Assistant,* S. Levin lies alone in his room and writhes:

> His escape to the West had thus far come to nothing, space corrupted by time, the past-contaminated self. Mold memories, bad habit, worse luck. He recalled in dirty detail each disgusting defeat from boyhood, his weaknesses, impoverishment, undiscipline—the limp self entangled in the fabric of a

ᴠ ill-less life. A white-eyed hound bayed at him from the window—his classic fear, failure after grimy years to master himself. . . . More than once he experienced crawling self-hatred. It left him frightened because he thought he had outdistanced it by three thousand miles. . . .

As is also the case with several other Malamud heroes who pass through these crises, Levin's emotional life then begins to soften and run more clearly; charmed by the tender winter landscape and its connections to his own feelings, he gradually grows more in touch with himself. Still buttoned up in his raincoat but looking for a "triumph over nature," he is drawn into a love affair that begins in the woods with the wife of the man who hired him. A daughter of the modern American hinterlands—much as Memo embodies the neurotic and corrupting success offered by the baseball world of *The Natural* and Helen Bober the hungry but earnest world of *The Assistant*—Pauline Gilley is at first an "object of experience" for Levin, "not necessarily of commitment." But eventually love and its problems come to overwhelm Levin, and he goes through the Malamudian fire of passion and frustration, sacrifice and insight. In the end he emerges deeply disciplined enough to choose the encumbrances of marriage to Pauline and the destruction of his former conception of a new life of personal satisfactions and freedom, in return for the possibility of love—"the short freedom you had in the world, the little of life to be alive in." Unlike the failure of Hobbs who spurns Iris, the honest woman, to chase after the meretricious Memo, Levin suceeds in having himself through Pauline; but it is a success, like Alpine's, that is qualified to the bone. Just as we leave the newly circumcised grocer limping about in Bober's "tomb," so we last see Levin going down the highway with a pregnant woman he has already fallen out of love with, and her two children, and bearing the promise he has had to make to get them that he will never again teach in a college.

The point of this summary is that the dramatic and moral core of *A New Life* is less related to the specific social and ethical issues of teaching and living in Cascadia, America, than it is to the themes of Malamud's other work. To be sure, Levin comes a cropper in Cascadia because he not only takes Pauline away from her husband, the departmental whip, but also eventually takes a stand against the department's illiberalism and inanity. However, the novel is only slightly more convincingly in touch with this subject by the end than *The Natural* was with major league baseball. The book's failure to make good on its early promise of contemporary actuality could be attributed to the possibility that Malamud is out of his proper element, as he was in major league baseball in *The Natural*, where he used various literary and subliterary sources (from Homer to *Dime Sports*) to do much of the work of detail and definition. However, the descriptions both of the Northwest and, up to a point, of the community, are among the finest features of *A New Life*. Levin is perhaps most comic and moving, certainly most of a piece, in those passages that register with unmistakable authority his reactions to the huge, fertile beauty of the country and the modifications it produces on the spirit of a city man whose life had all but dwindled away in city parks and seasons. Similarly, the early scenes in which Levin is introduced to Cascadia College are very nearly perfect in their evocation of that special mixture of blandness, intimacy, and pomposity common to third-rate colleges and of the eager-beaver compulsiveness of a highly organized English composition program. Some of the narrative interludes are equally brilliant, such as Levin's frantic trip over the mountains to get to his coed. All of which is to say, though, that the writing is most solid when it is least concerned with the major problem that Malamud set for himself—to transpose his themes and treatment of deprivation, suffering, and regeneration to the green and pleasant doldrums of Cascadia College.

Beneath the highly inventive but unsteady language of most of the book, one senses Malamud's struggle to bring the two elements together and at the same time preserve their given qualities. But the attempt to align Levin—the taciturn desperate man who enters the novel—with Cascadia—dull, contented, moderately corrupt—soon creates another Levin and another Cascadia. The ex-drunk with a miserable past to overcome begins to fade into and out of another image—that of the academic innocent from N.Y.U. with stars in his eyes about the liberal arts and the humanistic tradition—eager to know the score, to get involved, to take a position. The college, on the other hand, begins to double as a chamber of intrigue and polite horrors in order to function in the unwieldy and elaborate plot and remain commensurate with the old moral and the new social preoccupations. So that after a time each new disclosure of English Department policies and politics becomes either another turn of the screw on which Levin is being wracked or another betrayal of the goals of higher education. The technique of self-confrontation soon starts to be worked to death—often not because anything very critical is happening but because S. Levin is constantly being confronted with the question of whether he is "Sy"—the solemn faculty screwball and radical *naif*—or "Sam"—the hard case with his "last chance," who emerges hamstrung but healed at the end. Meanwhile, Malamud wrestles for an attitude and tone that will hold the two types in the same characterization, but finally relies upon a gifted literary clowning which simply doesn't fill the gap between satire and seriousness that the split in Levin opens in the novel. "The sorrows of Levin: his mouth thickened with thirst." Similarly, compare the passage quoted earlier on Levin's crisis with these reflections from the other Levin:

> . . . But Levin had long ago warned himself when he arrived at this intensity of feeling—better stop, whoa. Beware of the forms of fantasy. He had been, as a youth, a *luftmensch,* sop of feeling, too easy to hurt because after treading on air he hit the pavement head first. Afterwards, pain-blinded, he groped for pieces of reality. "I've got to keep control of myself. I must always know who I am." He had times without number warned himself, to harden, toughen, put on armor against love.

And so it goes through most of the key passages in the novel. Without a steady, coherent grasp of Levin and Cascadia, reality and feeling keep running out almost as soon as they are re-created, and in the end Malamud can only again pile burdens on his hero which he has implausibly arranged and send him on his way. In the process the powerful themes of *The Assistant* are reduced to a series of stated platitudes about the responsibilities of love and the holiness of life and the moving aesthetic of morality, along with some pronouncements about liberalism and the humanities. And there is also a kind of malice toward Levin as there is eventually toward everyone and everything else in Cascadia, except the landscape and the character who loves Sterne, that makes the novel finally inscrutable.

However, I am less interested in making out a case against *A New Life* than of pointing to the problem that Malamud like most writers today is now up against. In a number of ways, the novel illustrates the points Philip Roth recently made . . . about the difficulties of the present-day American scene for the novelist, and the tactics he has been put to in order to get around them. Clearly in *A New Life* Malamud has had difficulty in presenting Cascadia College to stand from beginning to end as a contemporary institution rather than a vague collection of academic types and stock grotesqueries. But further, *A New Life* also suggests that to write about Cascadia today one must be prepared to receive its life directly rather than try and plug it in to another set of preoccupations and values. This last is what Malamud has done. "The past hides but is present"—in the end the statement defines Malamud's difficulties in writing of a new life more than it does Levin's rather arbitrary difficulties in trying to live one. Venturing into a new setting and new problems, Malamud spends much of his novel unpacking and examining the luggage he has brought from his other world, as well as using it to arrange and order the moral scene. As a result, the book struggles from beginning to end to discover what it is really about and what its proper tone and treatment should be. Now strikingly comical and touching, now turgid and arbitrary, now opening out resourcefully to grasp new areas of life, now withdrawing into pat attitudes and narrative habits, *A New Life* finally seems to me to fail because its writer is unable to give himself up to a much more indeterminate and ambiguous experience than he has dealt with before. Which is only to say that Malamud is in the same soup with the rest of us. The surfaces of life still look stable enough, but underneath, massive and fearful changes are obviously at work that undermine our bearings. What attitude to take, what orientation to adapt to? Between the cautious concern for factuality and the felt need for apocalyptic judgments, the sense of reality runs out and the will struggling for purchase grasps at its own platitudes. Meanwhile the ties that hold a man to a place and confer a steadiness of purpose and perception—even in places like Cascadia—are lost in the telling. The sense of contactlessness makes us exaggerate.

In *A New Life* constructs take over. I don't believe after the first chapter that S. Levin was once a drunk—not only because he doesn't behave like one but because he doesn't need to. His hunger and frustration are cogent enough simply in terms of the ambiguities of his making his way out of the ghetto by means of an education and then finding in the world only a mixed and possibly corrupting vocation as a teacher of English. The real point of the novel—all but buried under the moral theme—is the collision, not infrequent today, of the post-ghetto sensibility and the culture of the hinterlands. The word "Jew" is never mentioned in the novel, but Levin is the only Jewish name in the book and when Gilley tells him to go back to New York, he has something else in mind than its "stinking subways." Conceived more freely, *A New Life* might very well have been a deeply moving or a really comic novel about the situation of a determined Jewish instructor in Cascadia. As is, it is neither. Bernard Malamud in search of a new life never quite gets beyond the old. But a writer like Malamud grows through each venture, and it will be particularly interesting to see where he goes next.

Marcus Klein

17.

The Sadness of Goodness

A New Life, an academic picaresque composed directly, so Malamud has said, according to the influence of Stendhal,[1] is certainly a discipline, strenuous but comic, in real things. The "new life" his hero, S. Levin, seeks, is, it turns out, an alternative not merely to his past life. Levin sighs much in the novel about the encumbering presentness of his past, but that past, as he deals with it directly and briefly just once, is a vague history of drunkenness and a fairy tale of family horrors, in effect a non-life. The new life is life itself. And it is to be life with possibilities much more extensive than those provided by Malamud's claustral grocery store.[2] Levin is set down in a place where, for one thing, nature is present—nature, Morris Bober had reflected, "gave nothing to a Jew." Moreover, this place will contain a community, a variety of private histories and domestic troubles, jobs, politics, a presence of American history, and, because the place is an academic community, it will provide as well for a clear encounter with large social forces and ideals. *A New Life* is oddly enough one of the few novels not journalism, of the mid-century, that contains specific speculations on Korea, the cold war, McCarthyism, Hiss and Chambers, loyalty oaths, the plight of liberalism, the definition and the duties of radicalism. Levin's speculations on these matters are not indeed analyses, but the materials are there as materials for his adventures, and it is the point of his adventures that he is to engage them, along with all the other present realities.

Near the beginning of the novel, Levin knows and he chooses to avoid the events and the meanings of current history. "America was," he says, "in the best sense of a bad term, un-American," and he is "content to be hidden amid forests and mountains in an unknown town in the Far West," and then, "Teaching was itself sanctuary—to be enclosed in a warm four-walled classroom." Toward the end of the novel, he commits himself to social leadership. In the same way, the novel moves Levin to a close engagement with nature, from New York City and an abstract, distant love of it. Levin's new life is a matter, indeed, as he repeatedly expresses his ambition, of coming out from his privacy, and virtually every pattern of events in the novel is designed to illustrate his coming out. Levin wears a beard, and at a certain point in the novel he shaves it off. He wears a hat and a raincoat and carries an umbrella, when none of the rugged Westerners do, and the progress of his consciousness, like Lear's, urges him to stripping in the wilderness. Levin learns to carry golf clubs, to rake leaves, to fire a furnace, to drive a car. He learns to distinguish friends and enemies. And he falls in love and learns how to have a family.

Levin is a young man from the capital, it happens, who in order to secure his initiation moves to the provinces. That would be the way of a contemporary American Julien Sorel. It is specifically to the Pacific Northwest that Levin goes, a place called Eastchester in the state of Cascadia,[3] where it might be expected that the American civilization could be discovered pure. Quite by the spirit of Stendhal, he is introduced there to manners and morals, passions, intrigues, hypocrisies, the workings of power, and the things of civilization, all of such a civilization as this is. The spirit is Stendhal's, as Malamud has said, but the facts are different ones. Quite like Julien Sorel's Paris, of the Bourbon Restoration, Eastchester is fallen into betrayal of the ideals of its own recent past, but the ideals are, or were, radical democracy, progress, and enlightenment, not empire and glory. And the circumstances of its past are different. In the spirit of Stendhal,

Levin is introduced not to a surviving aristocracy, but to nature—
nature, as Levin says on an occasion, is Eastchester's true history.
And the social facts which this young-man-from-the-capital is in
his new life to engage are those of a civilization no longer creative, but not sophisticated, either, and this is a civilization that
has gone stale but that is without the certainties either of institu-
tions or of social nuance upon which a Stendhal could depend.

The spirit is Stendhal's, but neither the problem nor the
manner nor the voice could be. Remarkably, Malamud does discover a great deal and he does get it down on the page. For the
first time in Malamud's fiction, the real things have a real and,
more to the point, a continuous specificity. The physical descriptions are frequent, detailed, and exact. The place in which Levin
finds himself makes demands. And there is a felt social organization available to him, re-created by a scrupulous, and a consistently
ironic, attention to its manners. A New Life is indeed, one half
of it at least, vivid social satire. But it is social satire in the
manner and the voice—astonishingly, considering Malamud's
dedication to a European literary tradition—not of Stendhal but
Sinclair Lewis. But then inevitably. These are fallen democrats
to whom Levin is to be given, whose society is not an institution
complicated and refined by the ages but a relatively simple process of enthusiasm generated by loneliness. Their salience is their
protective heartiness, and the literary apprehension which as a
society they demand is caricature, just enough so that the hollowness may be heard. "People aren't too formal out this way," Levin
is told as he arrives. "One of the things you'll notice about the
West is its democracy," and his answer, tart and Yiddish, is "Very
nice." And that, the hollowness of the democratic gesture, is just
the demonstration to be made. Eastchester is not Gopher Prairie,
of course. For one thing it contains Levin. But it would seem not
to be far from Gopher Prairie, and in any event Malamud's pro-
cedures and perceptions are those of a somewhat harsher Sinclair
Lewis.

So it is a completely amiable society that is to be seen, a
society under an iron discipline of amiability. It is a society whose
members nevertheless are in hot, fussy pursuit of petty ambitions.
The imagination, the ideals, the sap have gone out of it. Its tone

is a broad charade of its worthy past. The satire serves the purposes, since this is an academic novel, of an academic exposé,
another exposé of the English Department, but the locale has
larger uses. Because culture is this community's business, the past
will be the more uncomfortably and the more tauntingly present.
And this is a society whose members are all good guys, just a little
on edge, open, sincerely devoted to harmlessness, pietistic about
certain things, and, it will turn out by function of their organized
effort toward triviality, altogether vicious. The basic materials are
those of Gopher Prairie. Given them, the voice and the very
inventions of specific character must be echoes of Sinclair Lewis.
Levin's immediate superior and principal antagonist, Gerald
Gilley, in their first talk talks boosterism:

> You're our twenty-first man, most we've ever had full-
> time in the department. . . . Professor Fairchild will meet
> you tomorrow afternoon at two. He's a fine gentleman and
> awfully considerate head of department, I'm sure you'll like
> him, Sy. He kept us going at full complement for years
> under tough budgetary conditions. Probably you've heard
> of his grammar text, *The Elements of Grammar?* God knows
> how many editions it's been through. The department's been
> growing again following the drop we took after the peak load
> of veterans, though we've still got plenty of them around.
> We put on three men last year and we plan another two or
> three, next. College registration is around forty-two hundred
> now, but we figure we'll double that before ten years. . . .
>
> We've been hearing from people from every state in the
> Union. For next year I already have a pile of applications
> half a foot high.

And in the next moment he talks cautionary self-exculpating
Babbittry: "I like your enthusiasm, Sy, but I think you'll under-
stand the situation better after you've been here a year or two.
Frankly . . . Cascadia is a conservative state. . . ." And then,
Gopher Prairie *redivivus,* the Department is "service-oriented."
Professor Fairchild, the community exemplar, resonates one-hun-
dred per cent American clichés.[4] The community spirit has its

opportunity in the college's football and basketball teams, and therefore they are a serious concern. The underground, as one should expect, consists of a couple of village atheists, one old and one young, both of whom confine themselves to cautious ironies. And even Malamud's heroine, Pauline Gilley, the wife whom Levin will steal from Gerald Gilley, emerges in the image of Carol Kennicott—she is a rangy girl vaguely dissatisfied with the narrowness and the restriction of the community, willing to take a chance, vaguely ambitious for something not very clear.

A New Life, Malamud predicted,[5] would be something new for his readers, and it is. The half of it that is social satire is, much of it, broadly funny. The fun is sometimes very good fun— Professor Fairchild, who will expire with the words "The mys-mystery—of the in-fin—in-fin—in-fin—In-fin-i-tive," in the beginning tells Levin an endless moralizing tale of his drunkard father who on his way to Moscow, Idaho, succumbed to drink and never got there, a tale that sounds like a biography by Tolstoy of W. C. Fields. And then the fun is sometimes corny—Levin meets on the road an old hayseed of a farmer who hands him a pair of pliers and asks Levin to pull his tooth: "Got an achin' tooth here at the back of my mouth. Could you give it a pull with these pliers?" And Levin declines. But fresh or corny, the fun is fabricated from perceptions not usual to Malamud. The perceptions are social and they are directed toward manners and they have breadth. It is here an American humor that, apparently, Malamud is after, to be discovered in a folk, in some Americans as they are in the first place typical, as they typically constitute a certain society, and then as they have just in back of them a certain folk tradition. This humor is far removed from the desperate uncertainties of the *shtetl.*

Levin's new life, then, is to be a serial engagement with the West, with nature, with a community, with some facts, current and traditional, of American history, with social forces, with American civilization and the American folk, all credibly realized. But then the fact is that though the real things are, at least in instances enough, really there, Levin never does come to the point of participating in them. More than that, Levin's adventures consist really of lengthy and private speculations leading to a series of fumbling and abortive attempts at engagement, followed by long retreats, culminating in a plunge into a situation which is meant to represent for Levin and for us a fullness of real life because it is unpleasant. The novel was to be written according to Stendhal, so Malamud said before he had written it, and it was to be, so Malamud also said, "a romantic love story, with warmth and richness." [6] The two intentions are not dissimilar. They meet in an intention toward engagement. And at the end of *A New Life* Levin does get the girl, all right, but in the end he no longer wants her, and at the end his love is neither romantic nor warm nor rich, but sternly dutiful. The story that Malamud tells in *A New Life* is at the end the old story: the real things propose not themselves but a moral imperative, and the hero plunges uncertainly after the things for lack of anything else. And what then is demonstrated is the extremity of the hero's attempt.

One half of *A New Life* is social satire and the other half is Levin, and the verve of the one is made uneasy by the melancholy of the other. Malamud does not accomplish for Levin the forward movement that will bring him progressively into the world, and that will, incidentally, bring the novel together. Levin's desire for a new life is in the first place merely desperate, an urge forced from the impossible dreamy loneliness of his past, a matter of discipline, and his true history is, so the evidence will come to suggest, his inevitable frustration. One of the items of his desperation is his need not for lovers but simply for a friend or two, and some good part of his early adventuring in the novel is his searching for some casual friendship. Levin as he knocks on the doors of his various colleagues is in one instance after another rebuffed, but then more significant than his defeat is the fact that he is never in his search brought to any climactic confrontation. The matter simply tires itself out and is dropped, and what is dramatized, no matter what is intended, is a great weariness in Levin's searching and an inevitability of defeat.

What is dramatized in every other instance is a conviction of the inevitability of frustration, the consequence of which is inertia, against which by main force Levin stumbles and fumbles for engagement and discovery. Nature is a large part of the reality which Levin is to engage, and he does learn to perform some chores of gardening and such. Indeed he is moved to lyrical appreciation of natural beauties in such a way as perhaps only a boy from Manhattan might be. But the intimate connection, the real engagement, despite Malamud's forcing of a couple of moments, just never takes place.

The test is in those moments. Levin would seem to be derived in part from his namesake in *Anna Karenina*.[7] Like that Levin, he is provided in a set scene in an open clearing in a woods with opportunity for a redemptive insight. The scene in *Anna Karenina* apparently contains a special suggestiveness for Malamud. Frank Alpine was made to happen upon it in his reading and to be "moved at the deep change that came over Levin in the woods just after he had thought of hanging himself," and Frank had reflected that unlike Anna, at least Levin wanted to live. Malamud's Levin, on a spring day miraculously burst in the middle of January, in the middle of the novel, with some temerity enters a local woods to do some bird-watching. Bird-watching has consequences in Malamud's fiction, and here Levin meets and for the first time makes love to Pauline Gilley. This is an important scene, an anagnorisis. Levin has fumbled unhappily after other girls, but this is love. This forest, it happens, is a place where foresters are trained. And the moment, so Levin reflects, is marvelous. He has become at once a lover and Natty Bumppo. "In the open forest," he says to himself, "nothing less, what triumph!" He has discovered the promise of life.

Or that should be and would be the case except that the moment, brief as it is, is so qualified by ironies as to be contradicted. This time in nature is, first of all, a time out of nature—midwinter spring is its own season. The unusual weather for January indeed prompts Levin, as he sets out for the out-of-doors, to speculate with "a touch of habitual sadness" on "the relentless rhythm of nature," the eternal sameness which prevents human freedom. And whatever insight this day will offer, it will not offer nature as it is. Nature-as-it-is hovers nearby to cancel the illumination. Moreover, then, the promise of life, as it should be certified by Levin's love-making with Pauline, reneges on itself. Pauline, as her husband will much later tell Levin, is no bed of roses. And Levin finds out now that she is unfortunately flat-chested, a fact which, were Levin permitted to know Malamud's iconography, he would recognize as a symptom of failure at love.[8] In his passion clutching at her breasts, which is to say clutching after engagement with her, Levin seizes nothing. And then finally such joy and freedom as there is in this love-making is qualified by the secretive messiness of adultery it looks forward to. The sun shines brightly as he and Pauline leave the forest, but Levin opens an umbrella over their heads. And in the quick course of things the forest will shrink to a double bed in Levin's bachelor room.

The episode is forced—what Malamud asserts, he takes back. And then it is in its achievement the more suspicious because it should be redundant. The episode follows shortly upon another in which Levin, having suffered from a cold and from a long bout of dreary loneliness and from a recidivous thirst for alcohol, walks abroad to discover a magnificent Western sunset. He felt, so it is said, "like a man entering a new life and entered." But that is the abrupt end of that episode. In fact Levin's harmony in the woods is followed shortly by still another greeting from nature, occurring when he admits what he thinks he knows, that he is in love with Pauline Gilley.

> Above the tops of budding trees he watched the flaring, setting sun, wanting to abolish thought, afraid to probe the complexion of the next minute lest it erupt in his face a fact that would alter his existence. But nature—was it?—a bull aiming at a red flag (Levin's vulnerability, the old self's hunger) charged from behind and the Manhattan matador, rarely in control of any contest, felt himself lifted high and plummeted over violet hills toward an unmapped abyss. Through fields of stars he fell in love.

The experience does not, however, alter his existence. In the next moment, in the very paragraph, he will retreat back into his habits of anxious speculation, the moment of his full engagement still before him, the reiteration necessary because the moment refuses finally to occur.

Levin reflects in the beginning, after some preliminary attempts at gardening, that "he had come too late to nature," and in fact all his efforts are conducted against a sense of something— whether or not his particular past—dragging him back. The Levin presented is a lonely, bearded Jew, locked in himself, desperate to get out, after great effort coming too late to everything. The best of an external reality that Malamud will allow him is one at second hand. So Levin buys a secondhand car, observing that "he had come too late to mechanics," as later he observes more largely, in the middle of his woodland adventure, that "he had come too late to the right place." He will reflect still later that he is no Chingachgook; wherever he had been, someone had been before. This new life after which he will finally plunge is forced from a sense of its opposite, and then if it isn't just the old life again to which Levin falls, it doesn't either contain anything entirely new. At the very end of the novel, Levin will drive off in his secondhand car with his secondhand wife and with the children she had in the first instance adopted. Pauline is pregnant with Levin's child, and that might be something new, but the child is only another possibility of the future, for which Malamud does not make himself responsible.

There is something secondhand and stale even in the objects of Levin's purely social commitment. There is no doubting the sincerity or the urgency of his idealism. "I worry," he says to one of his teaching colleagues, "I'm not teaching how to keep civilization from destroying itself," and if the statement is faintly pretentious, as Levin admits it is, it is also so blunt as to prove conviction.[9] And Levin's idealism should be of special usefulness to Cascadia College, which is "service-oriented," which (like, it is to be said, America) lost the liberal arts shortly after the First World War, which has lapsed into a viciously self-protective narrowness of political reaction, and which is on its way toward destroying the civilization by which it was nurtured. But Levin's passionate idealism accomplishes no revolution and it is impossible that it might, despite the fact that Levin actually does urge himself to the point of running for the position of head of the English Department, despite the fact that he actually does enter himself into such politics as there is. His idealism is a matter of his subscribing himself passionately to ideals—democracy, humanism, liberalism (and the liberal arts), radicalism, freedom, art, and intellect. The words are ever and easily at his lips. And splendid, and necessary, as his ideals are, they exist pure and at a tremendous distance from the social facts. Levin becomes aware of that distance, as apparently Malamud became aware at a certain point in the novel. Malamud presents Levin with, indeed, some particulars of social action. As Levin is a reform candidate, he urges upon the English Department: elimination of the Department's grammar text and also the examination in grammar, elimination of "censorship of responsibly selected texts," recommendation that every instructor teach a course in literature, and some other similar matters, all to an effect comparable to Trotsky lecturing at the local P.T.A.

Between Levin's ideals and the social facts there is tremendous distance and a total absence of social analysis. His ideals are not tested in the large social complication they require, and certainly they are not forged from social experience. Levin's ideals are the convenient instruments of his idealism, and what his idealism accomplishes, aside from elimination of the grammar text, is its own integrity. His idealism is not what it seems to be and should be, the way of his engagement with the new life out there. Confronted in his idealism by the facts, Levin is in fact apt to be foolish. So when he is told of a photograph of a man and woman swimming together naked, he refuses, quite with Malamud's assent, to believe that they were lovers, on high juridical grounds of reasonable doubt. There is in such idealism something not merely naive but also forced. It has no sensible commerce with the world, and what about Levin's idealism is effectively dramatized is its uncertain relevance to the real world.

But of course Levin will be a man who believes that ideals, as he says, "give a man his value if he stands for them," just as he will be a man for whom love is finally neither a joy nor an enrichment nor an emotional fulfillment, but a stern moral imperative. The world doesn't beckon to Levin. He and Malamud invent disciplines by which to secure an accommodation to what is only uncertainly there. So Levin's final plunge after Pauline is, as it must be, entirely dutiful, and merely desperate. After adventures in adultery, he no longer wants her. Moreover he has discovered reason to believe that she does not love him, but, instead, a previous lover whom he resembles. Then, in a final interview, her husband rubs Levin's nose, as it were, in Pauline, a woman who, as Gerald points out, was born dissatisfied, who is thrown off balance by almost anything, who is not a good housekeeper, who is unpunctual, who is afraid of growing old, and who suffers chronically from constipation and menstrual troubles. And the children Levin will inherit are not easy to live with either. He will love Pauline nevertheless because he can discover, so he tells her, no reason not to. He will love her without feeling, and on principle, and because, so he says to Gerald, he can. And off he then goes, with a car full of luggage, two children, one crying for its real daddy, the other, suffering eczema, covered with ointment, and his bride in a white dress.

Stendhal would have written a different ending, with irony less excruciating and a resolution more secure. At the end of *A New Life* nothing, no experience, has yet really happened, and the end is just a more extreme attempt by which Levin is to be got into life, under the rule of a stern discipline, and out of himself. But the record of Levin's failure is Malamud's startling strength. Malamud is not a Stendhal or a Balzac and—it is exactly his informing trouble—the world does not tumble in upon him, and so he is forced to extremes to discover it. The strenuosity of such a hero as Levin is of the mood of Malamud's taut balance, elsewhere, on the edge of supernaturalism, and it is created in an apprehension of a world in which nothing certainly exists.

Notes

1. Bernard Malamud in an interview by Joseph Wershba, "Closeup," *New York Post Magazine*, September 14, 1958.
2. Levin's ambitions obviously parallel Frank Alpine's. Indeed, it was Frank Alpine who first discovered for his ambitions the phrase "a new life."
3. Levin's locale has some relation, presumably, to Oregon State College in Corvallis, Oregon, where Malamud was a member of the faculty from 1949 until 1961.
4. The monger of pious clichés is a constant character in Malamud's fiction. Professor Fairchild's forebears are to be seen in the owner of the baseball team, Goodwill Banner, in *The Natural*, and in Julius Karp in *The Assistant*.

5. *New York Post Magazine* interview.
6. *Ibid.*
7. For a briefly extended comparison with *Anna Karenina* see Eugene Goodheart, "Fantasy and Reality," *Midstream*, VII (Autumn 1961), 102-105.
8. In a preceding episode Levin himself affirms, if he does not recognize, Malamud's pectoral iconography. A sexual encounter with a lady named Avis Fliss is frustrated because the lady, having suffered a fibroma, is sensitive in her breasts.
9. There is no doubting Levin's sincerity furthermore because he echoes Malamud's statement of his own purpose as a writer: "The purpose of the writer . . . is to keep civilization from destroying itself." *New York Post Magazine* interview.

Ruth B. Mandel

18.

Ironic Affirmation

Bernard Malamud's *The Assistant* and *A New Life* are novels of ironic affirmation. Both novels offer a similar affirmation for the possibility of human salvation and identity through a consciously constructed personal ethic. The central character in each book discovers this personal ethic and is redeemed, but redeemed only after he has suffered, only after purgatorial fires have refined him during his search for self-discipline and a new, meaningful life directed by humanistic values. Malamud's vision, in effect, offers the possibility for living a moral life. The redeemed hero of *A New Life,* Seymour Levin, tells us that morality is necessary in order to "protect the human, the good, the innocent." [1] The best kind of morality has two positive consequences—one for the world as a whole, and one for the individual moral man. The sum of evil in the world is reduced each time one acts morally; and the value of one's own life is increased each time one values other human beings. Although Malamud is interested in this double consequence, his major concern as an artist is with dramatizing the process involved in creating the moral man. The man who can at last act to produce the double consequence is one who suffers and learns to renounce, consciously and consistently, the temptation to make any choice but the moral one. "To be good,

then evil, then good was no moral way of life, but to be good after
being evil was a possibility of life." ² This possibility for living is
Seymour Levin's salvation just as it is Frank Alpine's. And it is
Morris Bober's way of life, his Law: " 'If a Jew forgets the Law,'
Morris ended, 'he is not a good Jew, and not a good man.' " ³

The affirmation itself is ironic in that the state of grace is
unaccompanied by paradise. Redemption is at once hopeful and
hopeless, a redemption realistically conceived for a world where
a personal set of humanistic values does not effect a change in
society and does not offer material comfort for the ethical man.
Rather, it offers personal grace accompanied by continual suffering and a constant challenge daring the redeemed man to maintain his spiritual freedom and integrity in the face of a world
made up of grocery-tombs and Cascadian vacuums. A moral man
is an ironic hero simply because he does live by the Law. When
Frank suggests that Morris try a couple of tricks to increase his
pitiful income, Morris replies, " 'Why should I steal from my
customers? Do they steal from me?' " ⁴ Yes, they sometimes do
steal from Morris, but this is not the law to live by. Yet the irony
is that the law one should live by makes one an isolated victim
of the world.

Morris's Jewish Law is synonymous with Malamud's secular
moral code. The Jew himself is not used in a religious or ethnic
sense: he is a symbol of modern man, a symbol of hopefulness,
humility, and self-identity in the face of suffering and isolation.
Becoming a Jew always refers to a secular, personal, inner struggle; and the best Jews are those who become moral men while
continuing to suffer because the nature of their moral code demands self-abnegation. If a Malamud hero denies his Jewishness,
his humanity, he is lost.

The process of redemption—of becoming a moral man or a
good Jew—is a process of learning how to love. Malamud's concept of love is central to his affirmation and is identical in these
two novels. Both major characters find love—a selfless love which
represents the set of values or moral code one must attain, and
which, for Malamud, is only attained when suffering accompanies
love. Redemption does not come through mystical vision. It comes
through a private struggle to discipline the will—a fight to con-

quer old and bad habits, to overcome the dark past, and to control oneself so that primitive impulse is overpowered by principle.

Frank Alpine must completely control his desire to peep in the bathroom window for a glimpse of naked Helen Bober. Seymour Levin must get rid of a "fiery pain in the butt" and discover that "Love ungiven had caused Levin's pain. To be unpained he must give what he unwillingly withheld." [5] Levin's bedroom activities with Pauline Gilley, the woman he eventually comes to love, had been loveless. For Malamud's affirmation carnal love alone is not acceptable. Levin must free himself for a more complete love; then he must be able to control himself and deny his love in order to protect Pauline (this is the necessary suffering); and finally in spite of the fact that he has effectively killed his love for Pauline, he must willingly sacrifice everything for her or for the ideal of love:

> that he, S. Levin, the self again betrayed by the senses . . . did not presently desire her, in no way diminished her as one worthy of love (his), and what is worth loving is worth love, or the other way around. What I had from first to last frustration was worth having—I respect what it was. If I could have it again, I would. I have no cause now not to love her, granted I love; I grant. I loved her; we loved. She loves me still, I have never been so loved. That was the premise, and the premise you chose was the one you must live with; if you chose the wrong one you were done to begin with, your whole life in jail. . . . No matter what he had suffered or renounced, to what degree misused or failed feeling, if Pauline loving him loves; Levin with no known cause not to will love her. He would without or despite feeling. He would hold on when he wanted terribly to let go.[6]

Levin, devoid of feeling at the moment, comes to the logical conclusion that his possibilities for life must come through a commitment to love. He has moved from sex and a waitress, sex and his colleague Avis, sex and his student Nadalee, sex and Pauline Gilley, to Pauline minus sex, to self-sacrifice for the idea of love. Similarly, Frank Alpine although still desirous of Helen, will not lose his head and rape her again; instead, at the end of *The As-sistant,* he wants to work so that she can go to school.

In these two novels salvation through love is presented in the form of male-female romance. And here we find a peculiarly Ren-aissance form of male worship for the ideal of love. However, in neither case is the woman presented as a goddess. Pauline Gilley is a flat-chested, frustrated housewife with big feet; and we believe her husband's account of her when he warns Levin about marry-ing Pauline. Helen Bober is a lonely New Yorker, somewhat soph-omoric, but sensitive enough to want a fuller love than the carnal kind that her old boy friend Nat Pearl offers, dissatisfied enough to yearn for the return of possibilities (those of a college educa-tion and an educated, sensitive husband) which her home in the Bober grocery-tomb cannot provide. Both Seymour and Frank find salvation in a dependence upon their love for these women and in their willingness to suffer and sacrifice everything selfish for that love. We realize that it is not so much these particular women that Malamud is interested in presenting as worthy of so much sacrifice.[7] Yet they represent possible objects for the love that Frank and Levin come to believe in—an unselfish love which is directed at two other lonely, unhappy human beings.

Although in both novels the object of love is a woman, Mala-mud does not confine himself to male-female relationships. Morris Bober is a pure soul because he is by nature a man of heart, charit-able, tolerant and human to all men—to Breitbart the peddler as well as Karp the moneyman, to the customers who must buy on credit as well as to Frank Alpine the thief. In the short story "The Mourners" Kessler and Gruber, two men devoid of human sym-pathy, are redeemed at the end of the story when they acknowl-edge their sins and through suffering, sympathy, and repentance mourn for their loss of humanity. Fidelman, the central character in "The Last Mohican," must make the realization that when the impecunious Jew, Susskind, asks for a suit of clothes, Fidelman is obligated, as a Jew, to give away his gabardine suit.

Malamud's creed of personal relationships, of human sym-pathy and love, is a fairly familiar theme which finds expression in some modern writers like E. M. Forster but which reaches back to the Ten Commandments and to Christian doctrine. Not, however, in the same form. Mr. Malamud's uniqueness lies in his mode of presenting suffering and a moral vision.

It is extremely difficult to make a simple statement about this aspect of the works. One must resort to terms like fantasy, comedy, and bizarreness when describing short stories like "Angel Levine," "Take Pity," "The Last Mohican," and "The Jew Bird." Yet these terms alone do not satisfy until we emphasize the overwhelming ironic qualities in Malamud's fiction. Undeniably, irony is an important—a crucial—part of the theme and vision. One need only recall the conclusion in *The Assistant* and see that the redeemed man, living "in the future to be forgiven," is imprisoned in a broken-down grocery shop hoping for the good life which will never come. This is the fate of the world's Franks and Morrises. "At first he waited patiently. What else was there to do? He had waited and was still waiting. He had been born waiting." [8] Frank had traveled all over the country and had found no answers. The Brooklyn grocery store had no answers either—except the ethic represented by Morris. Since there are no possibilities outside, the only alternative is found within. Frank will wait forever for any outside change.

But this is certainly not the only irony in the novel. Morris Bober's whole life is an ironic nightmare perhaps best explained when he reflects on his failures and thinks, "The years had passed without profit or pity. Who could he blame? What fate didn't do to him he had done to himself. The right thing was to make the right choice but he made the wrong. Even when it was right it was wrong." [9] "Even when it was right it was wrong" exactly describes Frank's position at the end of the novel, Levin's position at the end of *A New Life*, and Morris's whole existence. Morris had come from Russia to America for a better life, and he ended up in his grocery shop. At one point in the novel the future looks hopeful—Karp offers to buy the store, and Morris agrees to sell—so Morris dies. (And a few pages later we learn that Karp could not have bought the store anyway.) Why does Morris die? Because for once he broke out of the tomb for a moment of freedom. He dies because " 'It's spring' " and " 'Tomorrow is April,' " the time of rebirth. And when Morris tells Frank about his experience in night school, what is it that he remembers but a poem he had learned, " ' "Come," said the wind to the leaves one day, "come over the meadow with me and play." ' " [10] Yet Morris "as a man, in America . . . rarely saw the sky." [11]

Malamud piles irony upon irony to achieve the tremendously oppressive and suffocating atmosphere of *The Assistant*. It is the disparity between the hopes, dreams, and aspirations of the characters in the novel and the horrible reality that is insisted upon over and over again as it denies the fulfillment of their dreams that produces the overwhelming pathos. This shocking and repeated juxtaposition of hope and reality is an essential part of the ironic technique in *The Assistant*.

There is another significant juxtaposition in many of *The Magic Barrel* stories and in *The Assistant* which explains part of the artistic achievement. This is found in the idiom in which the Yiddish characters think and in the dialogue; it refers to the antithesis between the *way* that characters like Morris and Ida Bober speak and *what* they say. Here Malamud treads a precarious line between humor and desperation in order, again, to produce overwhelming pathos. Taken out of context, the immigrants' distortion of the English language into Yiddish-American sometimes sounds comic. Remarks such as " 'A buyer will come next Purim,' " and " 'Also helps a little the new apartment house that it opened in December,' " if inserted into the script of a Molly Goldberg television program would provoke laughter. The mixture of Yiddish and English, the distorted syntax, characteristic figures of speech, ellipsis, and the intonation of Yiddish-American tend to be comic. Yet in Bernard Malamud's work the breath is sucked out of the laugh. As it is used in *The Assistant*, this seemingly humorous language cannot be funny in the right sense of that word. The whole weight of the novel crushes laughter. It is unlaughable comedy about the funny little man who is not funny at all.

This is the artistic achievement—the grotesque mixture of high seriousness with what seems funny and yet is not. All of which heightens the pathos. During the most somber moments in *The Assistant* this technique is applied. Just before two thieves enter the grocery shop, Karp and Morris are referring to them as "holdupniks," a term which, because of the diminutive's effect, makes these public menaces seem like children playing cops and robbers. But of course they are not playing. And when Morris has exposed himself to the pneumonia which will kill him, he describes, in broken English, his need for a moment of freedom: " 'For twenty-two years stinks in my nose this store. I wanted to smell in my lungs some fresh air.' " There is pathos and desperation here— not humor.

The rabbi who delivers the eulogy at Morris's funeral is depicted as a semi-ludicrous figure in his manner of speaking. Again Malamud treads a fine line between the ludicrous and the serious, and again it results in a heightening of pathos. The rabbi makes a futile attempt to describe Morris, a man he never knew. That he never knew Morris is clear when we examine his speech, for in his remarks is an implicit denial of all the ironies Malamud has so devastatingly presented in *The Assistant:*

> "Who runs in winter time without hat or coat, without rubbers to protect his feet, two blocks in the snow to give back five cents that a customer forgot? Couldn't he wait till she comes in tomorrow? Not Morris Bober. . . . This is why the grocer had so many friends who admired him. . . . He was also a very hard worker, a man that never stopped working. . . . And for this reason that he worked so hard and bitter, in his house, on his table, was always something to eat. So besides honest he was a good provider." [12]

Here the rabbi draws two conclusions about Morris Bober: because he was an honest man everyone admired him; and because he worked so hard, he was a good provider. Who admired Morris? Karp called him a *schlimozel* and betrayed him; Soboleff embezzled from him; his wife disapproved of everything he did; and the customers to whom he was kind left him and patronized the new supermarket. Was he a good provider? His store was almost bankrupt; he could not find a job when he visited the agencies; Helen had to get a job with a ladies undergarment manufacturer so that Morris could continue making payments on the house; and he could not provide for Helen what she wanted most—a college education. Obviously, then, the rabbi's conclusions are all wrong and Morris has been misrepresented. For the rabbi believes what we would all like to believe and what Malamud will not allow us to even hope in *The Assistant:* that honest, selfless men are rewarded with people's admiration, and that hard work is rewarded with material success. Just as Frank Alpine cannot recognize the real Morris when he looks at the body in the coffin, so the Jewish clergyman cannot recreate Malamud's Jew—Morris Bober.

Malamud's treatment of Ida Bober, Morris's wife, once more denies the possibility of real laughter. Ida has all the stereotyped characteristics of a perpetually worried, nagging Yiddish wife. She has the typical fears and aspirations. She wants to move into a Jewish neighborhood, be blessed with a Jewish son-in-law (a professional of course), and she warns her husband about being too kind to penniless customers and stray *goyim* in search of a job. Given these characteristics, one could imagine a satirical portrait of the woman who pounds on the floorboards every time her husband smokes a cigarette and who follows her daughter to see if she is dating a non-Jewish man. But Ida slaves in a worthless store despite her sick legs. Within a period of months her husband is wounded by robbers, almost dies in a gas-filled apartment, roams the streets searching for a counterman's job, suffers from lung ailments, gets pneumonia, and finally dies just when things look good for a moment. She has one hope: a buyer will come and purchase the store. This is the one event in the book for which she dresses up. The buyer does not come, and when he finally appears, he leaves without buying the store. She fears everything; yet this cannot be a humorous caricature of the woman who is unnecessarily perpetually worried and afraid, for all Ida's fears are realized. Her life is miserable, her suffering unalleviated.

Thus, in *The Assistant* Malamud offers moral affirmation while, at the same time, employing an ironic technique and laughless humor which function thematically to dramatize his world of hopeless hope.

We do not have to read far in *A New Life* before we find comedy. In this novel the humor demands real laughs and is used for satiric, farcical and even slap-stick effects. The interview scene between the new English instructor, Levin, and the chairman of

Cascadia College's English Department, Fairchild, is very funny in its characterization of Professor Fairchild. The renowned author of *The Elements* (Fairchild's grammar text for Freshman English) is ludicrous as he runs through that crucial list of items to which every new Cascadian instructor must be subjected, and as he narrates the paper-marking habits of one Leo Duffy, the ex-English instructor who brought radical ideas to Cascadia: " 'I subsequently learned that he threw away, ungraded and unrecorded, more than one set of themes, because his dachshund, which had been trained to react on paper, wet on them. He apparently did his grading on the floor . . . Where do you grade your papers, Mr. Levin?' " [13] Finally Professor Fairchild unintentionally reduces himself to absurdity as he describes an afternoon tea party when his wife hysterically flings hot tea at his nudity, and Mrs. Freeny of the Anti-Liquor League faints—Duffy all the while consumed with maniacal laughter.

The comedy connected with Cascadia College's English Department is employed satirically. Here is a stereotyped, mediocre, service-oriented English Department. The instructors are organization men of the worst kind, men who should know better, men educated in the humanities. The school is a Cascadian Madison Avenue, a school where the emphasis is on practical learning, prestige, school-board approval, and the well-rounded, shallow man who must be an athlete instead of a scholar if he wishes to be accepted. And this wasteland of insensitivity is found in the middle of a lush, inspiring land of natural beauty. The attack is devastating; Malamud's intentions are clear.

However, there is a problem here. The novel seems to have divided intentions. Obviously Malamud is concerned with social comment, with satirizing the state of Cascadia and especially its College. Obvious also is Malamud's intention to write a novel about a man in search of love, identity, a set of values. There is nothing inherently wrong in conceiving of a novel in which these two elements work together. But this does not seem to happen in *A New Life*. The comic and satiric elements do not function thematically in relation to the novel's serious theme. Levin's ultimate sacrifice and affirmation really have nothing to do with his experiences as English instructor at the College. The whole controversy over the new chairman simply fizzles out when Malamud again picks up the Levin-Pauline plot. Even the impact of Levin's sacrifice, his promise not to teach in college, is diminished in view of the almost hopeless possibilities for a man like Levin to effect liberal reform in the academic world Malamud has presented. And I do not know how to take the last page when I want to be serious about Levin's departure and am confronted with Gilley's " 'Got your picture!' "

Mr. Malamud has stated that this line, the last one in *A New Life*, is to be taken as a sign of hope for Gilley's development; that is, as a sign that Gilley will perhaps have been affected enough by Levin's and Pauline's commitments (he will have their picture imprinted on his memory) to learn something significant from the experience.[14] That would be fine indeed! But it is not possible for the reader to perceive this from the novel itself. The whole weight of Gilley's characterization in *A New Life* prevents the reader from arriving at Mr. Malamud's intention in the last line. Gilley has been portrayed as narrow-minded, shallow, insensitive, and even unscrupulous. His hobby has always been photography. And among his collection of photographs were those he took of Pauline and Duffy naked together, those which he intended to use against his wife. So that when he takes this last picture at the end of the novel there is no way of knowing that he will come to any realization about himself or his life. Recall that after he took those first blackmail photographs of Pauline and Duffy he did not learn anything about himself, for he resorts to similar methods during Pauline's affair with Levin when he (without her knowing it) tape records Pauline's confession. Consequently, one short remark at the end of the novel—a remark in itself ludicrous and incomprehensible in view of Gilley's situation, a remark which makes Gilley a ridiculous figure when he cries " 'Got your picture!' " as he watches his wife drive off with her lover—cannot succeed in conveying the possibility of a character change in a person so consistently portrayed as incapable of sensitivity. It can only result in puzzlement.

The major problem in the novel stems from divided intentions and, consequently, a rather baffling hero. Is Seymour Levin himself a character strong enough to inspire the reader's confi-

dence and admiration? Is he strong enough to make his final
choice credible and profound? Levin, the outsider, appears in
Cascadia sporting a beard which immediately produces its effect
on the citizens who equate bearded men with untouchables. He
has a dark past, a challenging present, and we expect him to behave the man. But more often than not he is simply an amusing,
somewhat naive fellow who entertains us as we follow him through
a series of comic adventures. The whole episode with the waitress
is much funnier than it should be if the real concern is with
Levin's inability merely to relieve himself once the intruder has
broken in and spoilt the romance of the situation.[15]

Levin hops from adventure to adventure taking himself very
seriously, always losing the game. The comedy which we associate
with his adventures serves to prevent the serious response which
Malamud seems to be ultimately interested in evoking. Even
though we are told in sentence one that Levin is a former drunkard from New York, his antics during most of the book tend to
make us forget his dark past or at least decide that it is unimpor-
tant since the Levin who arrives in Cascadia does not spend most
of his time struggling with an ugly past and bad habits in a way
comparable to Frank Alpine's real conflicts.

During the novel's first few scenes, Levin is shadowy and does
not emerge as a personality. Granted, he is the stranger in Cascadia and is feeling his way around; thus, his more or less pat
remarks and his unresponsiveness to the Gilleys can be accounted
for. But for a long time after this we do not really know what
sort of person he is. He appears as the innocent who arrives in
the West and visits department members, makes frank, disarming
inquiries and is cooly greeted; and he gets himself involved in
comic adventures with girls and cars. After all is said and done
he is more the victim of circumstance and the actions of other people than a vigorous, active character. He is only in Cascadia because Pauline picked him out of a pile of applications. Yet it is
important that we believe in him if we are to respect the significance of his choice at the end of the novel.

We always expect Levin to bloom into a forceful personality,
a personality like Leo Duffy. Duffy is used as a myth—the myth of
the liberal radical who can make no significant dent in a Cascadian

world which shields itself with a protective, impenetrable padding
of insipidity and self-righteousness. The myth allows us quickly to
understand almost everything about Cascadia College. Duffy also
functions as a comic device in the interview scene between Levin
and Fairchild, as a way of revealing Pauline Gilley, and as a momentary complication in the Levin-Pauline love plot. But, most
important, he functions as a parallel and sometimes a contrast for
Levin: they are both radical in terms of Cascadia College; they
both have an affair with the same woman; they are both dismissed
from school on the same moral charge. But Duffy commits suicide
because he cannot live in the world as it is, while Levin finally
accepts the world and the suffering that becomes a necessary part
of living in a flat world. Duffy's principles and his eventual suicide
are related to social problems, to Duffy battling a conservative,
conformist, inane society. Levin's final affirmation resolves the
problem of Levin against Levin and not Levin *against* society.
His moral affirmation is purely personal. Which is fine. The problem is, how does it grow from or relate to the elaborate Cascadia
College plot and Levin's involvement in English Department
politics?

There is the possibility of a different reading. It is striking
that Levin, the hero, is such a shadowy character. The others (men
like Gilley, Fairchild, and Bullock) are predictable, public men—
exaggerations of real men. They have all the recognizable external
characteristics: conformity to the system, "proper" moral attitudes,
appropriate leisure-time activities like football and fishing. Levin,
on the other hand, is the shadow of one man—Leo Duffy—at the
same time that he is many men. At the beginning of the novel he
introduces himself as S. Levin; Gilley immediately nicknames him
Sy; others call him Seymour; Pauline calls him Lev. And on the
last page, as he and Pauline are driving off, Levin says " 'Sam, they
used to call me back home,' " and Pauline answers, " 'God bless
you, Sam.' " The obvious question is, who is Levin. He is not sure
himself. There is the old self, the "New Levin, man of purpose"
—the man who grew the beard "in a time of doubt . . . when [he]
. . . couldn't look [himself] . . . in the face." And there is the man
who cut off the beard just at the point when, in love with Pauline,
he was about to give her up in order to protect her.

Levin came to Cascadia for a new life and tried to forge himself into a New Levin; but the new life, he finds, is as full of doubts as the old life. And the American West betrays his naive expectations of liberal arts idealism. When he leaves Cascadia, beardless and once more Sam Levin, he knows (as he did not know when he arrived in Cascadia) what he is getting involved in; he knows that he is again committed to a new life, but this time he is not naive, for he does not love Pauline; he has again lost his ability to feel, and he is aware that the near future will not necessarily be blissful.

Perhaps Levin is supposed to be the only really real man in the story—the man who is a complex of a dark past and a lonely present. He takes himself very seriously, and the reader must often take him seriously; but he is also often a burlesque or farcical character. It is this confusion between Levin's understanding of himself, and the reader's various conceptions of the man—our inability to formulate and cling to an understanding of him as he moves around from S. Levin to Sy to Seymour to Lev to Sam—that makes the hero of *A New Life* a shadowy and inscrutable character. If it was Mr. Malamud's intention to form an elusive anti-hero hero, it may be that a hero treated so ironically, a hero undercut so much, a hero who is so many people at once, cannot quite come off in a novel even in the twentieth-century world where absurdity is a common enough concept.

Notes

1. *A New Life* (New York: Dell, 1963), p. 237.
2. *Ibid.*
3. *The Assistant* (New York: Signet, 1958), p. 100.
4. *Ibid.*, p. 69.
5. *A New Life*, pp. 199-200.
6. *Ibid.*, pp. 310-311.
7. It is true that both women are unhappy people who yearn for an escape to a new life which would be more meaningful to them than their present existence. Both are willing to take risks in order to find fulfillment. But these women cannot offer Frank and Seymour external comforts—money or status—*or* a life of happiness.
8. *The Assistant*, p. 107.

9. *Ibid.*, p. 162.
10. *Ibid.*, p. 68.
11. *Ibid.*, p. 9.
12. *Ibid.*, pp. 179-180.
13. *A New Life*, p. 44.
14. Mr. Malamud made this statement during a University of Connecticut seminar in contemporary American literature, May 8, 1963.
15. The novel's fragmentary nature is obvious here too, when we realize that the Syrian student is going to disappear from the story after he has performed what seems to be his only function: stealing the couple's clothes.

Maurice Friedberg

19.

History and Imagination—Two Views of the Beiliss Case

Slightly over a half a century ago, in September of 1913, a chilling, weird trial took place in a Kiev courtroom. An ordinary, unassuming Jewish employee of a local brick factory was charged with the murder of a Christian boy whose blood was then to be used for ritual purposes allegedly prescribed by the Jewish religion. Mendel Beiliss' case ended in an impasse. While he was eventually declared innocent of the crime, the court expressed no opinion on the possibility that such murder could, indeed, be committed by a professing Jew *pro ecclesia Dei,* nor was anything done to punish those who had unleashed a hysterical campaign against Beiliss prior to his formal trial and, by the sadly inevitable extension, against the Jews in general. The World War and the Revolution and then, some years later, the Nazi massacre of European Jewry, have all contributed to the oblivion of the *affaire Beiliss.* Now, however, the story was resurrected by two distinguished American Jewish authors, the novelist Bernard Malamud and the veteran historian, journalist and lecturer Maurice Samuel.

To be sure, Mr. Malamud's publishers enter the usual dis-

claimer to the effect that the story of Yakov Bok, "the fixer" or
"handyman," is universal in its implications and that "any innocent victim of a miscarriage of justice, whether his name is
Vanzetti or Dreyfus or Mendel Beiliss or Timothy Evans, would
illustrate the theme equally well." Yet one finds it difficult to take
this claim seriously—and not only because the settings or the details of the story are so transparently modeled after those of the
Beiliss case. Unlike Vanzetti and unlike Evans—and even, to a
lesser extent, unlike Dreyfus—Beiliss was not being tried as an
individual, and it was not an ordinary miscarriage of justice, tragic
though it may have been, that was at stake. Mendel Beiliss was a
mere pawn, personally so insignificant and colorless as to be of
no value whatever to his jailers and tormentors except as a symbol
of Russia's Jewry which was, in effect, placed on trial as a community—thus magnifying, in the final analysis, the eventual ir-
resolution of the case.

Mr. Malamud's distillation of history into a product of artistic imagination demonstrates the firm hand of a skilled craftsman.
Whenever advisable, the actual events are remolded to fit the inner logic of the narrative, and the novel itself deals only with
events preceding the trial itself. And when the trial is about to
begin on the last page of the novel, the reader is left convinced
that it would not be Mendel Beiliss (or Yakov Bok) who would
be judged, but rather his oppressors.

Malamud wisely built his novel around those happenings in
the life of his protagonist which are least subject to the limitations that historical record imposes on fiction. His concern is
mainly with the pitifully modest aspirations of Yakov Bok, with
his efforts to merely survive which cause him to break the law,
and with his one real transgression—living in a *Judenrein* district
of the city—that resulted in the fact that it was he and none other
who was accused of the macabre crime. The pictures of life in the
stifling and famished *shtetl* in which the timid pursuit of much
less than total happiness is severely punished are drawn both spar-
ingly and effectively. Yakov Bok, a Jew who had lost his ancestral
faith, has now for his spiritual sustenance only anguish spiced,
as it were, with crumbs of half-understood Spinoza ("it is not easy

to be a free-thinker in this terrible cell," Bok confesses to his
father-in-law when the latter visits him in jail). Bok's wife, barren
and miserable for many years, finally begets a son from an adulterous relationship—who needless to say, brings her no joy. But then,
the lot of those who have submitted to fate in the old *shtetl* is
hardly more enviable. The humble and the meek suffer no less
than the rebels, except that their travail is less spectacular and for
that reason, perhaps, more bleak and hopeless. Malamud's can-
vases of old Russian jails bear, not surprisingly, a strong imprint
of Dostoyevsky—after all, these are known to most Westerners
from *Crime and Punishment, Memoirs from the House of the
Dead* and *The Brothers Karamazov*—resulting, in some striking
borrowings (I have, incidentally, often wondered about the apt-
ness of this term which, by definition, presupposes an eventual
return of a borrowed idea). Thus, we will readily recognize not
only the different types of jailers and prisoners and the reading
of the New Testament, but even the scene of the cruel beating
of a horse. On the other hand, Mr. Malamud's pages in which
Yakov Bok tries to recapture some of his forgotten Judaism, while
not wholly original in concept, are beautifully executed. Thus,
languishing in his cell, Yakov Bok

> . . . recalled things from the Scriptures, in particular, frag-
> ments of Psalms he had read in Hebrew on old parchment.
> He could, in a sense, smell the Psalms as well as hear them.
> They were sung weekly in the synagogue to glorify God and
> protect the shtetl from harm, which they never did. Yakov
> had chanted them, or heard them chanted, many times, and
> now in a period of remembrance he uttered verses, stanzas
> that he did not think he knew. He could not recall a whole
> Psalm, but from fragments he put together one that he re-
> cited aloud in the cell in order not to forget it, so that he
> could have it to say. In the morning he said it in Hebrew,
> and in the dark as he lay on his mattress, he tried to translate
> the verses into Russian. He knew [the warden] Kogin lis-
> tened when he said them aloud at night. . . . He thought of
> himself pursuing his enemies with God at his side, but when
> he looked at God all he saw or heard was a loud Ha Ha. It
> was his own imprisoned laughter. (p. 207-09.)

And again, on pages 239-40:

> Yakov read the Old Testament through the stained and muddied pages, chapter by fragmentary chapter. He read each squat letter with care, although often the words were incomprehensible to him. He had forgotten many he once knew, but in the reading and rereading some came back; some were lost forever. . . . At first he read only a few minutes at a time. The light was bad. His eyes watered and head swam. Then he read longer and faster, gripped by the narrative of the joyous and frenzied Hebrews, doing business, fighting wars, sinning and worshipping—whatever they were doing always engaged in talk with the huffing-puffing God who tried to sound, maybe out of envy, like a human being.
>
> God talks. He has chosen, he says, the Hebrews to preserve him. He covenants, therefore he is. He offers and Israel accepts, or when will history begin? Abraham, Moses, Noah, Jeremiah, Hosea, Ezra, even Job, make their personal covenants with the talking God. But Israel accepts the covenant in order to break it. That's the mysterious purpose: they need the experience. So they worship false Gods; and this brings Yahweh up out of his golden throne with a flaming sword in both hands. When he talks loud history boils. Assyria, Babylonia, Greece, Rome, become the rod of his anger, the rod that breaks the heads of the Chosen People. Having betrayed the covenant with God they have to pay: war, destruction, death, exile—and they take what goes with it. Suffering, they say, awakens repentance, at least in those who can repent. Thus the people of the covenant wear out their sins against the Lord. He then forgives them and offers a new covenant. Why not? This is his nature, everything must begin again, don't ask him why. . . . God is after all God; What he is is what he is: God.

Still, later in the narrative, there is a powerful display of rebellion against God whom only recently Yakov appeared about to accept. In an outburst obviously modeled on the dialogue between Alyosha and Ivan in *The Brothers Karamazov*, we see Yakov Bok mocking Him and charging Him with the murder of "all the servants and innocent children of Job" for a ridiculously selfish reason, merely "to win a lousy bet with the devil" (p. 258). And, like Ivan Karamazov, Yakov Bok expresses his readiness to resign from God's Kingdom, "to return the ticket."

While the portrayal of Yakov Bok is eminently successful, the secondary characters in *The Fixer* are less satisfactory and on occasion tend to degenerate into schematic caricatures, thus weakening the inner logic of the narrative (e.g., the anti-Semitic owner of the brick factory, policemen, priests, and several others are each endowed with a single dominant trait, like the heroes and villains of neoclassical drama). Still, *The Fixer* is, beyond question, a *serious* novel, probably Malamud's most impressive work to date, and while this reviewer is not inclined to accept the extravagant claim of its publishers that it "will last as long as books are read," there can be no doubt of its artistic merit. It certainly deserves to be read for many years to come.

The implications of the old adage that truth is stranger than fiction and that some events are just too pathetic or tragic to lend themselves to literary treatment—at least, in the modern sense of the word—were understood by some of the great masters of the written word. We know, for example, that Tolstoy would, on occasion, tone down overly melodramatic *factual* material on which his works were based in order not to strain the credulity and taste of his readers. It is perhaps also not altogether accidental that, unlike in the aftermath of World War I, no entirely satisfactory literary treatment of World War II has appeared so far—a quarter of a century after the outbreak of hostilities. Similarly, many a memoir or even journalistic account of the last three decades of Jewish history is more likely to stir the imaginations of readers than the bulk of fiction attempting to deal with the subject. The real events, it seems, overshadow in their grandeur and horror anything that artistic imagination might contrive.

One has a strong suspicion that in his *Blood Accusation*—a book based on years of painstaking research in published materials and conversations with some of the surviving participants and eyewitnesses of the Beiliss trial—Maurice Samuel made a conscious effort to understate his findings and to remain as calm and dispassionate and matter-of-fact as is humanly possible in relating a nightmare of man's inhumanity to man. By combining seemingly inexhaustible patience in working with dust-covered archives with his writing talent, Samuel, although no academic specialist in Russian history, has succeeded in producing that rare kind of book that will hopefully be read by intelligent laymen throughout the English-speaking world and that simultaneously constitutes a major contribution to the history of twentieth-century Russia.

The tone of the book is highly informal, and the narrative is occasionally interrupted by personal asides—as indeed befits an author who has vivid personal recollections of the period that most of his readers know only from textbooks. The whodunit plot— easily one of the most breathtaking in the annals of courtroom literature—is never allowed to obscure the tragic significance of the trial. While Samuel's sympathies with Beiliss are inevitable, his feelings of outrage are kept under control. Not only is he not blinded to the efforts of such liberal Russians as V. G. Korolenko, V. A. Maklakov and Vladimir Nabokov (father of the novelist) as well as to the steadfastness of some bureaucrats and policemen who would not go along with the prosecution for reasons of professional integrity, but even tries his best to highlight the activities of such moderates within the Imperial Government as Witte, and makes a valiant attempt to defend the thesis that Tsar Nicholas II, far from being a sadistic villain, was merely a weak, confused and passive monarch whose ineptitude, rather than ill-will, was exploited by the extreme reactionaries.

Samuel's book opens with a section entitled *dramatis personae* —a very appropriate title for the list of participants in the absurd courtroom drama. We are introduced to the victims, the bigots, the defenders and the bystanders—all of them catapulted to front pages of European newspapers when some viciously anti-Semitic groups in Russia decided to exploit for their nefarious purposes the murder of the teen-age boy Andrei Yushchinsky by a gang of Kiev hoodlums. To accuse a simple Russian Jew of the murder would have served their cause well enough. Yet, with the encouragement of some highly-placed protectors, the Kiev anti-Semites decided to increase the stakes. Beiliss would not be accused of

ordinary murder, but of one with religious motives. The prosecution would strive to demonstrate that the Jew Beiliss needed the
blood of the murdered Christian boy for the preparation of Passover matzos. His guilt, once proven, would therefore automatically
be extended to all of his coreligionists, to all consumers of matzos.
That Beiliss was not particularly observant, did not seem to matter. Neither was it considered important that similar accusations
had never been proven in the past. Writes Mr. Samuel:

The Blood Accusation, as it is called, the accusation that the
Jewish religion calls for the periodic ritualistic consumption
of the blood of a Christian, was born in the Middle Ages at
about the time of the First Crusade; it was a revival, with
certain changes, of the accusation leveled at the early Christians by the Romans. Young William of Norwich (d. 1144)
was the first victim to be claimed by the legend; after him,
like a pestilence that had lain dormant for a thousand years,
it kept on reappearing here and there across the centuries. It
was denounced by four popes [Innocent IV in 1247; Gregory
X in 1272, Martin V in 1422 and Paul III in 1457] as a
sinful slander; not one pope, even among those whose attitude toward the Jews was the harshest, ever endorsed it.
Nevertheless the Blood Accusation persisted down into modern times, and nearly every recurrence was attended by the
threat or perpetration of massacre and pillage. The nineteenth century was particularly rich in such episodes, the
most famous among them being those of Damascus (1860),
Saratov, Russia (1857), and Tisza-Eszlar, Hungary (1882). In
the twentieth century, before the Beiliss case, there occurred,
among others, the case of Blondes, the Jewish barber of
Vilna (p. 4).

How, then, could the Black Hundred chieftains expect to obtain a conviction? Their hopes were pinned not on the merits of
the transparently flimsy evidence, but rather on the poisonously
anti-Semitic atmosphere in the country. There was the wave of
pogroms that had swept Russia recently, the most shocking being
that of Kishinev—the one recorded in the famous poem of Chaim
Nachman Bialik. Then there was the veritable flood of anti-Se-

mitic literature, among which the forgery known as *The Protocols of the Elders of Zion* was but the most notorious. But above all, there was the silence of most of the country's spiritual leaders, a silence which was, needless to say, interpreted as acquiescence to, if not outright support of, those who had organized the massacres of the Jews and who were now preparing the crucifixion of Beiliss. Subservient to the government and long dominated by extreme reactionaries (the enlightened Solovyovs had been sorely outnumbered by the obscurantist Pobedonostsevs) the Russian Orthodox Church, as a body, failed to raise its voice in opposition to the conspiracy behind the blood libel trial. One wishes Mr. Samuel had devoted more attention to an examination of the latter problem, particularly in view of his admirable handling of the pronouncements by those outside Russia who had adopted a "neutral" attitude toward the issue of Beiliss' guilt. To quote Mr. Samuel:

> The reactions of the world press may be divided into three groups: (a) condemning the conspiracy—the vast majority, (b) approving or condoning it—a small minority and (c) neutrals—a somewhat larger minority. If we think of (a) as liberal and (b) as reactionary, we must label (c) as super-reactionary, for there are certain cases, of which this is one, in which the pose of neutrality is the most effective moral support of reaction (p. 233).

A splendid specimen of such "neutrality" is found in Mr. Samuel's quotation from *The Oxford and Cambridge Review*, then considered a spokesman for high-church England:

> . . . it is absolutely certain that Orthodox Judaism—nay, Judaism as a whole—stands free from even the slightest suspicion of blood-guiltiness; but to say that is not to say that no Jewish sect exists which practices ritual murder. . . . We do not know where the truth lies, and we are sure that widely-signed protests are not a good way of eliciting the truth.

Mr. Samuel comments:

> It is of course impossible to disprove the existence of a
> Jewish sect that practices ritual murder; it is also impossible
> to disprove that ritual murder has never been practiced
> secretly by the Kiwanians or the Daughters of the American
> Revolution. And it is true that popular protests are not the
> best way of eliciting the truth about anything, including the
> intellectual trickery of *The Oxford and Cambridge Review*.
> However, if the truth about ritual murder was still unknown,
> it was surely not improper to protest publicly against the
> claim of Russian officialdom to have discovered it—and this
> is to say nothing about the uses to which the 'discovery' was
> being put (p. 239).

It was this passage that appears to have irked some of Samuel's
reviewers as being overly "partisan." Yet one cannot help agreeing
with Mr. Samuel that on certain moral issues abstentions may be
more reprehensible than taking any stand. And there is no evidence to be found in *Blood Accusation* which would for an instant suggest that Mr. Samuel's opinions have in any way inter-
fered with his functions of an impartial observer and truthful re-
porter of an infamous episode in Russian history.

While the Nazi experience of the recent past inevitably di-
minishes the impact that the story of Mendel Beiliss is likely to
have on a modern reader, one cannot say that, with the vindica-
tion of Beiliss, blood libel was finally and irrevocably discredited
as an effective anti-Semitic canard. Not unlike *The Protocols of
the Elders of Zion*, it continues to reappear periodically in various
parts of the globe, but always serving the same cause. Thus, some
twenty years ago, shortly *after* the destruction of the Nazi empire,
a group of Jewish survivors of concentration camps was massacred
in the Polish city of Kielce—with blood accusation serving as a
pretext for the blood-bath. At approximately the same time a
similar tragedy was narrowly averted in Cracow. And only quite
recently there was another sinister echo of the blood libel—this
time, from the Soviet Caucasus. As Mr. Samuel somberly warns
in the closing lines of his book, we cannot afford to "believe this

or that noxious force to be worsted beyond the possibility of a resurgence in our midst."

Mr. Malamud's and Mr. Samuel's are vastly different books; and yet there are points of convergence. Both concede that, as an individual, any victim of the most horrendous injustice may be a mediocrity or even quite unattractive. Yet both insist that the quality of the victim's suffering is not affected by his stature as an individual; it should—unlike in the status-conscious Greek tragedy—instill us with the same terror and pity as the pain and death of heroes and kings, for all men are equals in martyrdom. Both writers shun the sophistry of some modern authors who begin with the assumption that evil is banal, then proceed to observe that there is a mystic cooperation between victims and murderers, and ultimately deny the very foundations of the concept of justice itself. Both authors have written moral books, and both books are the better for it.

Alan Warren Friedman

20.

The Hero as Schnook

From the small crossed window of his room above the stable in the brickyard, Yakov Bok saw people in their long overcoats running somewhere early that morning, everybody in the same direction. Vey iz mir, he thought uneasily, something bad has happened.

This passage, the opening sentences of Bernard Malamud's latest and finest novel, *The Fixer*, contains the essential Malamudian note: simultaneous passivity and seemingly senseless action, intimations of bitterness and defeat, a vague but certain sense of impending doom.

Malamud's writings are not all of a piece, for only half (two novels and about a dozen short stories) are what I would call uniquely Malamudian, portraying a way of life, an essence, which we recognize as definitely Jewish almost to the point of stereotype. Not fundamentally a realist, Malamud often deploys Gothic elements of fantasy, grotesquerie, surrealism; but in *The Natural* and *A New Life*, his two weaker novels, these elements often seem unearned—too easy or abstract. In *The Natural*, Roy Hobbs, the title character, is almost killed when shot with a silver bullet by a near-naked seductress; he associates his baseball prowess with

Wonderboy, his charmed bat; in a dismal slump, he is restored by making love to a thirty-three-year-old unmarried grandmother who comes to him as the fulfillment of a fortune teller's prophecy; and so on. Ultimately, and for all his inherent prowess, the protagonist, a mythical country hick, falls victim to the world's essential shoddiness and his own continuing inability to cope with it. Clearly enough, in fact all too clearly, the novel is a reworking of Homeric, Waste Land, and Holy Grail legends, but the baseball formula is too frail to bear the weight of imposed meaning; and the inevitable drive from last place to first, resulting in the playoff loss as Roy's role shifts from superstar to Casey at the Bat, is so predictable it is gratuitous. The novel lacks artistic or "historical inevitability" because Roy Hobbs—swinging wildly from titanic heroism to abject failure and never staying still long enough to become human—exists more as his author's instrument than the world's victim.

A New Life is less surrealistic but more grotesque: Seymour Levin, an ex-drunkard ex-New Yorker, becomes an instructor of English at a small inbred Western college. He carries on an affair with, among others, the breastless wife of the seedless heir apparent to the departmental chairmanship; Levin himself tries for the chairmanship and fails primarily because his double rival announces the affair on election eve; and he finally goes off with the now pregnant wife and her two small adopted children—having obtained the husband's permission to take them in exchange for, of all things, a promise never again to teach at a college. And as if to underscore the absurdity of it all, Malamud concludes *A New Life* with the husband, alone and ensconced as chairman, triumphantly snapping a picture of the new-lifers as they drive past the campus, out of his life, and out of the book.

It is obvious that Malamud plays, or rather works, at allegory throughout these two novels—as well as many of his lesser stories —but allegory cannot be earned by sacrificing coherence or perspective. Realism and surrealism must not serve antithetical ends if our sense of incredulity is to be suspended. As one of Malamud's Jewish characters might say, "Allegory is not a novel. A novel is not allegory."

In the writings I take to be predicated on Malamud's essential and unique note, fantasy and grotesquerie are functions of realism. If the Matter of England is Arthur and his nobly chivalric entourage and the Matter of ancient Greece is the Homeric vision of epic confrontation between and among gods and would-be gods, then the Matter of Malamud is the poor schnook who runs a hole-in-the-wall pisher grocery; who has little to begin with and usually loses his little before long; who suffers and endures, suffers and endures, while profits become an ever receding dream and hope an obscenity. Yet he knows that suffering is the Jew's lot and so, having in a sense foresuffered all, he carries on grimly but comically. All Malamud asks of us here is that we accept as given an existentially absurd universe which manifests itself as the Brooklyn world of permanent Depression or as virulently anti-Semitic Czarist Russia. From these worlds, fundamentally and irreconcilably at odds with the beauty and dignity of the human spirit, all the grotesqueness of *The Assistant* and *The Fixer* follow. Here, the assumptions may be impossibly ludicrous, but God knows they are quite real.

The terminology with which we speak of the contemporary novel is, I think, familiar enough. The protagonist, an antihero, is the victim of a universe beyond his control; he is in anguish to the point of despair because his life, which he deems of value, evokes only indifference or hostility; his interminable misery implies, in fact, his insignificance, even his irrelevance, the sheer gratuitousness of what he is and what he endures. Here, for instance, is Manischevitz, a true Malamudian sufferer cast in the form of Job:

Day by day, hour by hour, minute after minute, he lived in pain, pain his only memory, questioning the necessity of it, inveighing against it, also, though with affection, against God. Why *so much*, Gottenyu? If He wanted to teach His servant a lesson for some reason . . . why then any of the tragedies that had happened to him, any *one* would have sufficed to chasten him. But *all together*—the loss of both his children, his means of livelihood, Fanny's health and his —that was too much to ask one frail-boned man to endure. Who, after all, was Manischevitz that he had been given so much to suffer? A tailor. Certainly not a man of talent. Upon him suffering was largely wasted. It went nowhere, into nothing: into more suffering.[1]

The antihero is predicated as beaten from the first: he is either will-less or too feeble to translate his will, his personality, into a viable pattern of action. Despite the fixer's quest for a better world, such a protagonist does not meaningfully proclaim himself an adventurer seeking to make the world yield up its fortunes and its answers to him. Modern man is so very much smaller than his environment that such a quest is foredoomed to ludicrous and dismal failure; instead, something like the reverse occurs. The world thrusts itself against him, eroding his physical and spiritual resources until, stripped and shivering, he is reduced to a Cartesian minimum: "I suffer, therefore I am."

But Malamud's characteristic writings not only define themselves by the force of existential anguish, they derive their special quality from the ancient Jewish teachings and spirit embodied in the Torah (the first five books of the Old Testament) and the Talmud (the collection of writing constituting the civil and religious law). Fundamental to the faith—and to the people stubbornly maintaining and embodying it long after, by any ordinary historical reckoning, they have become an anachronism—is the notion that God's ways are righteous and inscrutable, and that man must walk humbly and a little warily to survive from day to day. The vision is dual—simultaneously experiencing the harsh realities of limited mortality and affirming an abiding faith (perhaps a little condescendingly) that God really *is* in control of things and does indeed know what He is doing. Perhaps Shmuel, the father-in-law of *The Fixer's* title character, best expresses the Jew's paradoxical acceptance of the world's inadequacies and God's continuing presence when he warns his son-in-law against anti-Semitism and atheism: " 'Be careful,' Shmuel said, agitated, 'we live in the middle of our enemies. The best way to take care is to stay under God's protection. Remember, if He's not perfect, neither are we.' "[2] Like Job, the Jew is awed by the magnificence and power of his God, yet he knows too much about unjust suffering and his own relative innocence to blot out the experience of the world: "Though he slay me, yet will I trust in him:/but I will maintain mine own ways before him" (*Job*, 13:15).

Unlike both the theater of the absurd and the experimental novel of forty or so years ago, the contemporary novel of the antihero is not noticeably marked by distinctive style; its writers are more "realists" than are such technical innovators as Joyce and Virginia Woolf, even Conrad and Faulkner. But Malamud is of special interest for at least two reasons. First, his Jewish victims are not simply realistic, they are naturalistic almost to the point of predetermined misery. *The Fixer* is the *reductio ad absurdum* Naturalistic novel; Yakov Bok, the title character, is a Naturalistic victim-hero with a vengeance, and he not only inhabits but becomes a symbol for the lowest of "lower depths." Macbeth says, "I dare do all that may become a man; who dares do more is none." At the other end of the spectrum, Yakov Bok is stripped seemingly of all that separates man from the beasts below him: in his case, "who dares do less is none."

In addition, Malamud's superb understanding of the endlessly enduring Jewish spirit—simultaneously despairing and comic—best reveals itself in a masterful stylistic and thematic device I call "Talmudic tautology." It is a term easier to illustrate than to define. For example, in one of the short stories, a recent suicide named Rosen, in limbo awaiting judgment, is being questioned by Davidov the census taker about the death of a poor refugee grocer, the husband of the woman Rosen secretly loved:

> "How did he die?" Davidov spoke impatiently. "Say in one word."
> "From what he died?—he died that's all."
> "Answer, please this question."
> "Broke in him something. That's how."
> "Broke what?"
> "Broke what breaks. He was talking to me how bitter was his life . . . but the next minute his face got small and he fell down dead. . . . I am myself a sick man and when I saw him laying on the floor, I said to myself, 'Rosen, say goodbye, this guy is finished.' So I said it." [3]

Talmudic tautology, then, has the wit of a pun, the quiet bitterness of stoic resignation, the force of sudden truth; it accepts and expresses both the transcendence of God's ways and the essential crumminess of this world. " 'What happened then?' [Davidov] asked. 'What happened?' mocked Rosen. 'Happened what happens.' "

Both *The Assistant* and *The Fixer* are founded on this note, this attitude; the universe, the given, is impossibly antithetical to human dignity and worth, and its impoverished creatures struggle gamely to make a go of things. And usually, as a consequence, out of the dungheap seemingly conducive only to despair, glimmers of values begin to assert and affirm themselves. The short story "Idiots First," for example, is a successful allegory of man's feeble, hopeless existence and the irrelevance of his death. Mendel, who knows he is to die this night, spends his last few hours scrounging for money to get his thirty-nine-year-old idiot son, Isaac, a train ticket to California—where eighty-one-year-old Uncle Leo, drinking tea with lemon under a warm sky, presumably waits to care for him. Mendel's steps are dogged by death in the person of Ginzburg, "a bulky, bearded man with hairy nostrils and a fishy smell," who turns out to be the ticket collector at the station and who refuses them access to the still-waiting train because it is after midnight —after, that is, the time when the train was *supposed* to leave and Mendel was *supposed* to be dead. As he has throughout the evening, Mendel, in anguish, once again cries out for compassion, for human relevance—and again receives rules for an answer. The millionaire he had earlier appealed to had told him, "I never give to unorganized charity," and now Ginzburg disclaims any responsibility for Isaac's helplessness.

> "What then is your responsibility?" [Mendel asks.]
> "To create conditions. To make happen what happens. I ain't in the anthropomorphic business."

But Mendel persists:

> "Whatever business you in, where is your pity?"
> "This ain't my commodity. The law is the law."

"Which law is this?"

"The cosmic universal law, goddamit, the one I got to follow myself." [4]

But Mendel goes Job one better, for after having laid bare the essence of his misery, he refuses to accept inscrutability and power as a valid response. In desperation, he "lunged at Ginzburg's throat and began to choke. 'You bastard, don't you understand what it means human?' " And Ginzburg, though he laughs at Mendel at first, is as astounded as Mendel himself at the dying man's "awful wrath," and he accedes, allowing Mendel to put Isaac on the train and see the train depart. Only afterwards, "when the train was gone, [did] Mendel ascend . . . the stairs to see what had become of Ginzburg."

Scratch a naturalist then and you find a humanist. For Malamud, man has nothing but the misery and intensity of his suffering—but the point is that it *is* intense; he is committed to it because it defines his uniqueness, his humanness. As a consequence, he can—at least at odd moments—impose meaning where God has not. He can make the universe take notice of him and pay some attention to his claims.

The contemporary American Jewish novelist—and writers like Henry Miller who mourn their not being Jewish—no longer feel the need to maintain defensively that "To be Jewish is to be human." Instead their work increasingly demonstrates that "To be human is to be Jewish," for the Jew suffers for us all. Frankie Alpine, the dark-bearded, prematurely old title character of *The Assistant,* is an Italian who comes on like a long-suffering Jew: " 'The week after I was born my mother was dead and buried. I never saw her face, not even a picture. When I was five years old, one day my old man . . . takes off and that was the last I ever saw of him. . . . I was raised in an orphans' home and when I was eight they farmed me out to a tough family. I ran away ten times, also from the next people I lived with. . . . I say to myself, "What do you expect to happen after all of that?" . . . All my life I wanted to accomplish something worthwhile—a thing people will say took a little doing, but I don't. . . . The result is I move into a place with nothing, and I move out with nothing.' " [5]

A goyish embodiment of "Talmudic tautology," Frankie Alpine first does great injury to the long-suffering, hapless Jewish grocer who

> had never altered his fortune, unless degrees of poverty meant alteration, for luck and he were, if not natural enemies, not good friends. He labored long hours, was the soul of honesty . . . coveted nobody's nothing and always got poorer. The harder he worked—his toil was a form of time devouring time—the less he seemed to have. He was Morris Bober and he could be nobody more fortunate. With that name you had no sure sense of property, as if it were in your blood and history not to possess, or if by some miracle to own something, to do so on the verge of loss. At the end you were sixty and had less than at thirty. It was, [his wife] thought, surely a talent (p. 17).

Yet having made an imposisble situation still worse, Frankie gives up everything to identify with the Jew and his suffering, and the book ends on this note: "One day in April Frank went to the hospital and had himself circumcised. For a couple of days he dragged himself around with a pain between his legs. The pain enraged and inspired him. After Passover he became a Jew" (p. 192). Thus Frankie, who had complained of moving into a place with nothing and moving out with nothing, leaves a little piece of himself in *this* place—and the little which symbolizes the all of commitment contains, as it were, the seeds of possibility for "the new life" offered in Malamud's next novel.

In *The Fixer*, Malamud has pulled out all the stops and written a searingly brilliant novel. His mastery of dialect achieves new heights of artistry in order to express new depths of misery. Like Morris Bober, Yakov Bok thinks he keeps hitting new bottoms until he learns there are none. He is an archetypal victim with nothing going for him—except the rather dubious advantage of knowing that there is always worse than the worst and that he'd better get ready for it. Yet where Morris Bober, at last too worn out to endure, finally dies, Yakov Bok, though he dies a little on every page, gains kinship with the Mendel of "Idiots First." Out of his nothingness—not despite but *because* he suffers—he asserts and he affirms. He is not a classical tragic hero whose suffering is magnificent because of grandeur of character and the height from which he falls; on the contrary he is a poor schnook distinguished only by misery and his sense of victimization. But because he embraces these, and because, in rejecting a God seemingly obsessed with the perpetuation of injustice, he finds something in himself and in his life to affirm, he becomes a paradigm of a new kind of hero—one who, given the context of his meaningless, arbitrary world and his own feebleness, even irrelevance, when confronting it, triumphs because he endures.

The traditional Jewish attitude expresses itself in an old Yiddish proverb: "God will provide; but if only He would till He does." The characteristic reactions are resignation and complaint. "That's what they live for [thinks Frank Alpine in one of his more cynical yet incisive moments], to suffer. And the one that has got the biggest pain in the gut and can hold onto it the longest without running to the toilet is the best Jew" (p. 71). Malamud's Jews, with the major exception of Yakov Bok, the fixer, are living Talmudic tautologies: they know they are of "the chosen people"; it's just that they wish God would choose someone else occasionally. But it is for Yakov to learn that, like Job, he *too* has been chosen—chosen despite his desires, despite his forlorn plea that he wants only to be left alone. When Shmuel warns him not to forget his God, Bok responds angrily, " 'Who forgets who?' " He maintains that God has rendered Himself irrelevant: " 'He's with us till the Cossacks come galloping, then he's elsewhere. He's in the outhouse, that's where he is.' " But he also begins by rejecting the possibility for reform in *this* world: " 'Where I ought to go is to the Socialist Bund meetings. . . . But the truth of it is I dislike politics. . . . What good is it if you're not an activist? I guess it's my nature. I incline toward the philosophical although I don't know much about anything.' " So Yakov must learn, and by the end he begins to understand both what it means to be a Jew and that there's no such thing as an unpolitical man, especially a Jew.

Yakov starts out then by rejecting both God and his Jewishness. Setting the book in motion, he flees the Jewish town, the shtetl, "an island surrounded by Russia." He leaves because "the shtetl is a prison. . . . It moulders and the Jews moulder in it. Here we're all prisoners . . . so it's time to try elsewhere I've finally decided." A reluctant Jewish Don Quixote, a mock-epic hero once removed, he journeys to Kiev to wrestle with and slay the dragon-windmill—that is, to find what the world has for him to find. His even more reluctant horse, one of the great beasts of literature, is a broken-down, flatulent nag with eroded teeth, whose haphazard motion constantly rouses Yakov's intense but feeble wrath: " 'I'm a bitter man, you bastard horse. Come to your senses or you'll suffer' " (p. 24). For the fixer, who drinks his bitter tea unsweetened and blames existence, the horse, a semitic Rosinante, becomes a symbol of all the "trials, worries, circumstances" he associates with the shtetl world he is fleeing: "Like an old Jew he looks, thought the fixer," who trades the horse and what he embodies for a surrealistic, equivocal journey across the Dnieper River into Kiev and "a new life."

The virulently anti-Semitic boatman, to whom Yakov gives over his horse and entrusts his own life, embodies and fore-shadows the doom which awaits him.

> ". . . God save us all from the bloody Jews," the boatman said as he rowed, "those long-nosed, pock-marked, cheating, bloodsucking parasites. . . . They foul up earth and air with their body stink and garlic breaths, and Russia will be done to death by the diseases they spread unless we make an end to it. A Jew's a devil—it's a known fact—and if you ever watch one peel off his stinking boot you'll see a split hoof. . . . Day after day they crap up the Motherland, . . . and the only way to save ourselves is to wipe them out. I don't mean kill a Zhid now and then with a blow of the fist or kick in the head, but wipe them all out. . . ." (p. 27)

It is no wonder that, as Yakov later attempts desperately to retain his sanity under insane conditions, the Jewish horse he has given in trade should reappear in a nightmare vision: " 'Murderer!' the horse neighed. 'Horsekiller! Childkiller! You deserve what you get!' " (p. 249).

In Kiev Bok seeks meaning and possibility. "Among the goyim his luck might be better," he thinks, "it couldn't be worse." He thinks: " 'To have luck you need it. I've had little luck.' . . . So the fixer went looking for luck." And what he finds is a drunken "man lying with his face in the trodden snow . . . a fattish, bald-headed Russian . . . ," a member of the violently anti-Semitic Black Hundreds. And Yakov saves him. As a consequence, Yakov's position becomes increasingly ambiguous: he rescues a persecutor of his people and he receives money, respect, even the sexual advances of the daughter; he conceals the fact of his Jewishness, and he receives a well-paying job and a place to live.

But this is the high point of Yakov's rise and already inherent is the nightmare obverse world which follows, for he has succeeded in isolating himself as much as Oedipus in the blindness of his self-righteous purpose. He has laid himself doubly bare and vulnerable. Symbolically, he has denied his people, his inherited scheme of values: rejecting his wife, fleeing the shtetl and the God who dwells there, bartering the horse, concealing his Jewishness. On the literal level, not only has he aroused the enmity of the boss's daughter, but his job forces him both to live in an area forbidden to Jews and, as a kind of overseer-policeman, to antagonize all his coworkers. Thus, when the catalytic event occurs —the murder of a Christian boy and the discovery of his mutilated body—all the forces of potential destruction descend on Yakov's wavering, vulnerable head. As a consequence of all he has done and been, he is where he should not be, and he thus becomes a handy scapegoat for those whose ends are served by the cry of ritual blood murder. And while the circumstantial incriminating evidence mounts and his youth dribbles away, he spends almost all the rest of the book (270 pages and two and a half agonizing years) in solitary confinement: brutalized, dehumanized, intimate with pain and misery of every form—beatings, hunger, poison, vermin, numbing cold, insanity—the list is almost exhaustless, and there is worse:

> twice a day . . . there were inspections of the fixer's body; "searches" they were called. . . . Yakov had to remove his clothes . . . raise his arms and spread his legs. The Deputy

Warden probed with his four fingers in Yakov's armpits and
around his testicles. The fixer then had to open his mouth
and raise his tongue; he stretched both cheeks with his
fingers as Zhitnyak peered into his mouth. At the end he had
to bend over and pull apart his buttocks. . . . After his
clothes were searched he was permitted to dress. It was the
worst thing that happened to him and it happened twice a
day (pp. 194-195).

And soon it happens six times a day, with the time in between
spent in chains.

For all that it is possible to detail the causes of Yakov Bok's
sufferings, the sins of commission and omission that bring him in
fateful conflict with his environment, such "causes" ultimately
bulk no larger than, say, Iago's realistic motivations for destroying Othello. Yakov is kin to Job, that archetypal suffering Jew,
who suffers because he exists—and because he is innocent. But
unlike Job he suffers also because he denies his place in Jewishness (a quality word here, the sense in which all good men are
Jewish), and his place therefore in mankind. Refusing to accept
the role, he dismisses both Job and Job's God:

"To win a lousy bet with the devil [he tells Shmuel, who has
accused him of pride in his bitterness], he killed off all the
servants and innocent children of Job. For that alone I hate
him, not to mention ten thousand pogroms. Ach, why do you
make me talk fairy tales? Job is an invention and so is God.
Let's let it go at that . . . take my word for it, it's not easy to
be a freethinker in this terrible cell. . . . Still, whatever reason
a man has, he's got to depend on" (p. 258).

Job, for all the misery he endures and all his cryings out, has always his God to depend on. Despite the clichés about "patient
Job," he refuses to submit to his suffering, to accept it as valid;
rather he asserts his righteousness, demands answers to his questions, and awaits with certainty the definitive response he knows
must come. The answer Job gets at the end may not be the one
he sought, but it satisfies him. God himself speaks, and he awes

Job with the sheer fact of Creation, of order out of Chaos. And Job, properly chastened, bows down and repents. Again, we may feel that God is cheating, that Job asks legitimate questions concerning good and evil, the morality of unjust suffering, and instead of answers receives Power out of the Whirlwind and the bribe of new children and new possessions. Nonetheless, there is no doubt that Job's universe is not absurd; God is, after all, in His Heaven and, whether or not we morally approve of Him any more than we do of the Greek gods, we are convinced that He is indeed in control. Consequently, Job's losses and anguish are predicated as meaningful, for Divinity implies pattern, a larger scheme of things within which even innocent suffering can achieve validity.

Yakov's plight, in contrast with Job's, *is* existentially absurd, for his world offers no possibility of a perspective in which his plight will partake of a controlling context. Job's situation is never hopeless because it is framed by our knowledge of God's participation, His ability to call a halt at the psychologically appropriate moment. Yakov Bok's world contains no *deus ex machina,* in fact no *deus* at all; and with God dead or feeble, Yakov's situation becomes ludicrous, for against this poor schnook, this apparently will-less excuse for rational, heroic man, are arrayed all the forces of organized despotic society, with its prejudices and power, its bland indifference to the individual and its degrading and abusive violence. The contest is so utterly uneven that we are appalled, and ever more appalled as the odds against Yakov become ever more impossible, and as he curses loud and long, and curses still more when he receives in response neither freedom nor damnation, but nothing, nothing, nothing at all— and then still more injustice and meaningless suffering. And we feel ourselves desperately clinging to our own cherished verities— as Yakov Bok on the ferry clung with wavering certitude to his knowledge that his feet were *not* cloven—in order to avoid sharing the fate of a human life being crushed like an egg beneath a tank.

In contrast to his son-in-law, Shmuel is a more common Jewish stereotype; he endures all, complains stoically, and remains firmly committed to his faith because, as he would put it, after all what else has he got? Like the long-suffering father in *Fiddler on the Roof,* he asks in effect, "Would it spoil some vast eternal plan if I were a wealthy man?" But neither really expects an answer. Yakov, on the other hand, knows the answer—or thinks he does—that, yes, it *would* spoil some vast eternal plan, for Jews by the fact of their being Jews and alive in this world of shtetls and pogroms and Black Hundreds are designed to suffer, and to survive tenaciously to suffer still more. Yakov, even before his suffering had begun in earnest, had asked *his* key question, "Who invented my life?"—and now he begins to realize that he has got to invent it himself.

And so Yakov both pities himself and maintains his own ways in the face of all he is forced to endure alone. He is pressed to confess the crime, pressed by promises of freedom if he does and strident threats of pogroms if he refuses. He has miseries to confess but nothing more; "A confession, he knew, would doom him forever. He was already doomed" (p. 224). His tautological resignation, his refusal to sign a confession, seems as much a negative act as a positive one; with good reason, he refuses to trust either the promises or the threats, believing he would give all and gain nothing. But later he is offered freedom *without* conditions—he need sign nothing, he need confess to no crime: "He was to be pardoned and permitted to return to his village" (p. 294). And Yakov Bok, long victimized by a horror and degradation that would make the strongest of men despair, and long after we who have identified with him—and to read the book *is* to identify with him—long after we have stopped hoping for a way out, have in fact asked ourselves again and again why the poor schnook doesn't simply give up this farce, this absurd parody of human life, then Yakov Bok is offered this way out— and he refuses, refuses because he is to be pardoned as a criminal rather than freed as the innocent man he is. And our shock at his absurdly magnificent refusal is intense, and it endures long after we have finished the book, and it remains with us as perhaps its supreme affirmation. No one, we feel, no one—and certainly not us—could have made such a grand refusal under such circumstances. But Yakov Bok, the littlest of little men, who began with nothing and has been going downhill ever since, he refuses—and

his refusal shames us: for with our surpassing comfort and adequate faith we have complacently and condescendingly pitied
"poor" Yakov whose fate, thank God, is not our own. At this
climactic refusal everything changes: we learn that to the degree
that our fate is not Yakov's, it is not because we are especially
favored, but because we are not worthy—and because Yakov's
suffering earns *him* worthiness.

What changes now is not that Yakov Bok no longer despairs;
he does, over and over again, every day of his life, on every page
of the book. But despair, like his cursings, no longer controls and
defines him. Instead Yakov learns, he learns about people—
slowly, painfully, one at a time. For example, his initial action
contained among other things a rejection of Shmuel and all that
that good man embodies, and later, after Shmuel at great cost
and personal risk had come to see him to bring what little comfort he could, Yakov had cursed him for additional torments he
received when the fact of a secret visitor was discovered. But
then, after a nightmare vision of Shmuel's death, grief and guilt
overwhelm him: "Live, Shmuel," he sighs, "live. Let me die for
you."

Yakov—chained, allowed to do nothing for himself, bound
utterly in a life he called death because it lacked all freedom, all
choice—had finally opted for suicide as the only possible escape.
But now "he thinks in the dark, how can I die for [Shmuel] if
I take my life? . . . He may even die for my death if they work
up a pogrom in celebration of it. If so what do I get by dying,
outside of release from pain? What have I earned if a single Jew
dies because I did? Suffering I can gladly live without, I hate the
taste of it, but if I must suffer let it be for something. Let it be
for Shmuel" (pp. 272-273). And when, from the lawyer he is permitted at last, he finally learns that Shmuel is indeed dead, his
new knowledge, like everything he learns, is both bitter and
essential:

> Poor Shmuel, the fixer thought, now I'll never see him
> again. That's what happens when you say goodbye to a friend
> and ride out into the world.
> He covered his face with his hands and wept.

"He was a good man, he tried to educate me."

"The thing about life is how fast it goes," Ostrovsky [the lawyer] said.

"Faster than that" [Yakov answered] (pp. 304-305).

And now Raisl his wife comes. When she had cuckolded and deserted him, he recalls, "at first I cursed her like somebody in the Bible curses his whorish wife. 'May she keep her miscarrying womb and dry breasts.' But now I look at it like this: She had tied herself to the wrong future" (p. 213). For the moment they are together again; they review the bitterness of the life they had had, and he berates her with tautology: " 'So we got married,' he said bitterly. 'Still, we had a chance. Once we were married you should have been faithful. A contract is a contract. A wife is a wife. Married. Married is married' " (p. 285). Now he looks at her: "This is where we left off, thought Yakov. The last time I saw her she was crying like this, and here she is still crying. In the meantime I've been two years in prison without cause, in solitary confinement, and chains. I've suffered freezing cold, filth, lice, the degradation of those searches, and she's still crying. 'What are you crying for?' he asked. 'For you, for me, for the world.' "

And her tears cleanse and redeem a multitude, and Yakov tells her he's sorry, he blames himself, he has learned: " 'I was out to stab myself, so I stabbed you. . . . What more can I say, Raisl? If I had my life to live over, you'd have less to cry about, so stop crying.' " And she does, and because he has spoken this way she is able to confess what she has come to reveal—that with someone else she has had the child they always prayed for. "There's no bottom to my bitterness," thinks Yakov, who now must add sexual potency to the unending list of all he lacks. But he agrees to what she asks, he acknowledges that the child is his, so that it may have a name, so that Raisl may be accepted back among her people. And this superb affirmation, this suffering for and restoring of the wife who had betrayed him, earns him much—including one of the quietest, richest, most beautiful lines in the entire book. The czar, a visionary antagonist throughout his imprisonment, appears one final time to defend himself, to say that he too suffers, to blame the fate that gave him a haemophiliac heir. He says, " 'Permit me to ask, Yakov Shepsovitch, are you a father?' " And Yakov answers the answer he has earned: " 'With all my heart' " (p. 332).

First for only himself, then for Shmuel, and now for Raisl as well—Yakov, for all his initial alienation and continuing agnosticism, has at last earned the right to suffer for others, and he begins to recognize that he is responsible for all his people, that long-suffering nation without a country, alienated by birth and history, whose trials and traditions Yakov had mocked by his rejection. He realizes that "there is no way of keeping the consequences of his death to himself. To the goyim what one Jew is is what they all are. If the fixer stands accused of murdering one of their children, so does the rest of the tribe." And he now pities not himself, but all the Jews. "So what can Yakov Bok do about it?" he asks himself. "All he can do is not make things worse. . . . He will protect them to the extent that he can. This is his covenant with himself. If God's not a man he has to be. Therefore he must endure to the trial and let them confirm his innocence by their lies. He has no future but to hold on, wait it out. . . . 'I'll live,' he shouts in his cell, 'I'll wait, I'll come to my trial' " (pp. 273-275).

And finally his suffering gains perspective, a self-validating context. " 'Why me?' he asked himself for the ten thousandth time. Why did it have to happen to a poor, half-ignorant fixer? Who needed this kind of education? Education he would have been satisfied to get from books" (p. 313). But the education of existential man can be learned only through encountering the absurdity of experience: "Why?" he asks again,

because no Jew was innocent in a corrupt state, the most visible sign of its corruption its fear and hatred of those it persecuted. . . . It had happened . . . because he was Yakov Bok and had an extraordinary amount to learn. He had learned, it wasn't easy; the experience was his; it was worse than that, it was he. . . . So I learned a little, he thought, I learned this but what good will it do me? Will it open the prison doors? Will it allow me to go out and take up my poor life again? Will it free me a little once I am free? Or have I only learned to know what my condition is—that the ocean is salty as you are drowning, and though you knew it you are drowned? Still, it was better than not knowing. A man had to learn, it was his nature (pp. 315-316).

Yakov, who now fears less and hates more, realizes too that commitment is a concomitant of existence: "One thing I've learned, he thought, there's no such thing as an unpolitical man, especially a Jew. . . . You can't sit still and see yourself destroyed" (p. 335).

Yakov suffers then, man suffers, as a scapegoat, so that others will suffer less; he suffers too so that he may learn, so that he may be purged, so that his innocence may be renewed; and he suffers finally because man is a creature who *can* suffer. But because he is man he can also choose, as Yakov increasingly does, to validate his suffering to make it meaningful. What kind of chance does Yakov ultimately have? Well, what kind of chance has any man? His lawyer tells him: " 'You have a chance. What kind of chance? A chance. A chance is a chance, it's better than no chance . . . an opposition exists, which is good and it's bad. Where there's opposition to reaction there's also repression; but better repression than public sanction of injustice. So a chance you've got.' " Should he hope? " 'If it doesn't hurt, hope' " (pp. 310-311).

It hurts, it hurts mightily, but Yakov hopes; what else can he do? Besides, who has less cause and more right? As a poor schnook, a fixer whose own fix seemed irredeemably beyond repair, he had clung to his life and suddenly discovered it had value—as if anything desired with such tenacious and stupid stubbornness must indeed be desirable. And the miracle which is Yakov's affirmation of his existence has taken its toll of his enemies; for all that they do they cannot break him and they exhaust themselves in the process—until, in the end, two of his guards sacrifice themselves for him, so that he may live, so that he may go to trial and confront whatever awaits him there, so that he will not have endured for nothing.

At the end, heading defiantly for the trial he has so long demanded, Yakov clearly has achieved the searing recognition and acceptance of self and world which is modern man's equivalent for the anagnorisis of the traditional tragic hero. As a consequence, he has already come through the trial of greatest significance, of rock-fundamental testing—and perhaps we too have come through a little, we who have created a world which denies its heroes and renders them impotent, who select as champion and scapegoat a poor schnook who, in prison, can look back on his earlier misery and ask, "How bad was bad if you were free?" and who, later still, can look back with nostalgia at his early months in prison because he did not yet have chains to bear along with all his other torments. Perhaps we too have come through a little because Yakov Bok—his past a horror, his present still worse, and his future the worst yet because unknown—can blow on the coals of the heart and discern a responding warmth that validates his suffering for him and for all. Perhaps we too may ultimately partake of his redeeming sacrifice and affirmation. As Yakov might say with a weary shrug and ironic pride, "Suffering I know intimately; I do it well. What's one or two more to suffer for?" And in such a response from such a man may lie our own last best hope. Certainly Yakov Bok and Bernard Malamud, who create magnificently and enduringly out of negation and despair, give us cause to believe and to maintain that man who disposes may at last propose.

Notes

1. Bernard Malamud, "Angel Levine," in *The Magic Barrel* (New York, 1966), pp. 48-49.
2. Bernard Malamud, *The Fixer* (New York, 1966), pp. 17-18. All subsequent references to this book will be cited in the text.
3. Bernard Malamud, "Take Pity," in *The Magic Barrel*, pp. 87-88.
4. Bernard Malamud, "Idiots First," in *Idiots First* (New York, 1966), pp. 10, 15.
5. Bernard Malamud, *The Assistant* (New York, 1957), pp. 32-33. All subsequent references to this book will be cited in the text.

Sidney Richman

21.

The Stories

One of Bernard Malamud's early short stories, "The First Seven Years," has an opening sentence so arrestingly simple and clumsy that it demands repeating: "Feld, the shoemaker, was annoyed that his helper, Sobel, was so insensitive to his reverie that he wouldn't for a minute cease his fanatic pounding at the other bench." [1] A good many of Malamud's other stories, both later and earlier than "The First Seven Years," begin in a similarly rough-and-ready fashion. Here, for instance, is the opening of "The Mourners": "Kessler, formerly an egg candler, lived alone on social security" (p. 17)—and here the start of "Take Pity": "Davidov, the census-taker, opened the door without knocking, limped into the room and sat wearily down" (p. 85). The beginning of another story, "The Loan," varies the formula only by the position of the name but enlarges the clumsiness with the intrusion of a rhyme: "The sweet, the heady smell of Lieb's white bread drew customers in droves long before the loaves were baked" (p. 183).

Whatever is apparent in these beginnings, drawn from the first collection of Malamud's short stories, *The Magic Barrel*, it is assuredly not their grace. If anything, they seem, for their matter-of-factness as well as for their suggestion of a rough and untutored speaking voice, to belong to a tradition so old that its reappearance is slightly unnerving. The last thing to expect from the modern author is the author himself. But Malamud never seems to fear his own voice, even if it means sounding like an immigrant out of night school translating the prophets, as in the opening of "Angel Levine," the story of an East Side Job:

> Manischevitz, a tailor, in his fifty-first year suffered many reverses and indignities. Previously a man of comfortable means, he overnight lost all he had, when his establishment caught fire and, after a metal container of cleaning fluid exploded, burned to the ground. Although Manischevitz was insured against fire, damage suits by two customers who had been hurt in the flames deprived him of every penny he had collected. At almost the same time, his son, of much promise, was killed in the war, and his daughter, without so much as a word of warning, married a lout and disappeared with him as off the face of the earth. Thereafter Manischevitz was victimized by excruciating backaches and found himself unable to work even as a presser—the only kind of work available to him—for more than an hour or two daily, because beyond that the pain from standing became maddening. His Fanny, a good wife and mother, who had taken in washing and sewing, began before his eyes to waste away (p. 43).

Needless to say, it has been a long time since an author could pass off a line like "His Fanny, a good wife and mother," and make it work. It has been an even longer time since an author's own compassion could convince one of the reality of pains so directly evoked. If one of the tests of a successful author is his ability to make convincing what should *not* be convincing, then Malamud has surely passed the test. In reading his better stories, one has the strange sensation of entering a world in which the most complex of realities masquerade with ease in a motley of folk-wisdom and genuine naïveté. Although the subjects are, as in the novels, the thorny ones of spiritual growth and decay, the terrors of alienation and salvation, there is about many of them an echo of a long dead voice intoning directly, "I will tell you now of dragons."

It goes without saying, of course, that the only thing that can sustain such artlessness is art of a very difficult kind; and so it is that, as a writer of short fiction, Malamud seems to have emerged full-grown and mature with his first collection. Published in 1958, the year after his second novel, *The Magic Barrel* not only received the National Book Award, but more importantly it represents, along with *The Assistant*, his major achievement. If assuredly uneven, the thirteen stories in the work contribute to a triumph rarely granted a writer so early in his career. With them he achieved what many writers, and even better ones, must struggle for years to attain: a voice which is distinctively his own.

I. Literary Traditions

For this very reason, however, it is also difficult to assess the stories. Norman Podhoretz wrote that the tales possess a quality which "very nearly beggars description." [2] And the general critical response to *The Magic Barrel* bears him out. Blending in some indeterminate way both the resources of naturalism and symbolism, a vernacular steeped at one and the same time in the rhythms of European Yiddish storytelling, and a laconic irony reminiscent of Hemingway, the stories have inspired oddly divergent searches after influences. As a short-story writer Malamud has been called a disciple of I. L. Peretz, a Sherwood Anderson and a Chekhov of the East Side, and frequently an amalgamation of all these things. Nor is the obverse side of the coin slow to rise: one often learns that the Jewish elements in the stories are neither essential nor even particularly significant—even from those critics who readily agree that the "Jewish" stories are precisely the best.

But there is no reason to deny the efficacy of the comparative approach. That Malamud has mastered his craft with the aid of "models" is as true of the stories as of the novels. A good many of the pieces, especially the shorter ones, are approximately if not precisely in the tradition of Yiddish folk-realism; and there is about them, in their pained but rarely bitter evocation of suffering and inhumanity, a narrative echo, as Earl Rovit * beautifully put it, "of the eternal chant."

* See Chapter 1 in this collection.

But if the intonations are reminiscent of the literature of the Pale, Malamud's handling of form reveals a sensibility "keenly aware," as Rovit adds, of the "formal demands of the short story." [3] Not only do many of the tales, and even the most "Jewish" of them, rely heavily on the technique of epiphany, but they reveal a formal concentration as spare and as devoted to symbolic design as the stories of Chekhov or Joyce. Moreover, there are times when the stories, both in their fusion of poetry and outright horror, as well as the reiterated images of alienation and psychic crippling, sound curiously like Sherwood Anderson's tales of the grotesque.

II. The Stories and the Novels

But comparison with other authors, by virtue of the extensiveness of the possibilities, is misleading. For Malamud, borrowed technique seems only the means of shoring up and extending a vision that is essentially his own. That is why, perhaps, the novels themselves offer the readiest and the most illuminating approach to the stories. For not only do the shorter pieces recapitulate the central themes of the novels, but they also reflect in their variety and in their unequal value all the pressures that went into the creation of the three longer works. Variously, and sometimes at once, the stories move from the extremes of symbolism to realism; from a deft and conscious use of myth and ritual to a seeming artlessness; from fantasy to naturalism. In each case, the reader finds also the same interrelationship of fictional modes and successives-and-failures which undercut *The Natural, The Assistant,* and *A New Life.*

In the light of the previous chapters, it might be expected that the finest achievement in the collection would belong to those stories which share most closely the techniques and the vision of *The Assistant.* Such, in fact, is the case. The half-dozen best stories, and preeminently the title story, though reminiscent of the ethical folk tales of Aleichem and Peretz, unfold in a remarkably tough-minded and spare crucible. In each case the major ingredients are the same. The Jewish heroes, most of them elderly,

sit behind closed doors (the essential setting) in a twilight tenement world. With their hungers stripped to fundamentals and
their bodies shaken by memories of ancient lore, they manage to
translate misery into a bemused humanity. In each case, the dramatic conflict, to which all else is subordinant, is between man
and assistant, man and enemy, the pursued and the pursuer. The
conflict is so intense at times that it breeds angels and *luftmensch,*
doppelgangers and ghosts; but finally it breeds a miracle, a moment of painful unmasking which resolves the conflict and often
transforms the hero into something more than he was originally.

III. The Tales of New York Jews

The initial tale in the collection, "The First Seven Years,"
might illustrate them all; for the opposition and final integration
of Feld, the shoemaker, and Sobel, his assistant, is pure Malamud.
The aged Feld is the real center of the story by virtue of the
special moral demands imposed upon him. Like most of the protagonists in the stories, Feld must choose between alternate values;
and the choice, made in terror and suffering, distinguishes finally
the shoemaker from the *mensch.*

Like Morris Bober, Feld is in part the victim of his own goodness. Spinning daydreams out of the February snow, and agonizing
over memories of his youth in a Polish *shtetl,* the shoemaker has
sworn to create for his daughter Miriam a better life than he has
known. But the dream, with true Malamud irony, redounds not
to Feld's glory but feeds the guilt which tortures his relationship
to Sobel, a spectral young-old refugee who five years before had
saved Feld from ruin by becoming his assistant. Aware without
full consciousness that Sobel labored only for love of Miriam, Feld
arranges a date for his daughter with a young accounting student
who is the harbinger of a better life. For this action, Feld immediately loses his infuriated assistant and, for his guilt, his own
sense of well-being.

A single date convinces Miriam, who had already been won
by Sobel, that the budding accountant is an inveterate materialist;
and when a new assistant proves a thief, Feld in despair takes to

his bed with a damaged heart. Later, driven by a complex of needs, the old man pushes himself to Sobel's cluttered rooming-house and the kind of confrontation which is Malamud's special province: a meeting in which the denied self begins, in pity, to leak past one's guard and for a decisive moment pours forth in a sanctified stream. Listening to Sobel's tearful declaration of his love, Feld shuttles from exasperation to a compassion that proves his undoing:

> Watching him, the shoemaker's anger diminished. His teeth were on edge with pity for the man, and his eyes grew moist. How strange and sad that a refugee, a grown man, bald and old with his miseries, who had by the skin of his teeth escaped Hitler's incinerators, should fall in love, when he had got to America, with a girl less than half his age. Day after day, for five years he had sat at his bench, cutting and hammering away, waiting for the girl to become a woman, unable to ease his heart with speech, knowing no protest but desperate (p. 15).

Though Feld feels a gripping sorrow for his daughter's future, he submits to the relationship and the return of the assistant. But Feld exacts from the now young-looking Sobel the promise that he wait two years before the marriage (and so invokes the mythic cycle of fertility). That is all of the story; but for Feld there is an instant of real though muted triumph, a gesture which, despite the winter night and the continuous poverty for himself and his daughter, stamps the story with a spectral promise of salvation through love. His success is no more perhaps than the ability to walk the whitened street "with a stronger stride," or to hear, without anxiety, the consecrated labor of his assistant, who, him-self now the father and provider, sits at his work desk "pounding leather for his love" (pp. 15-16).

Despite the brevity of the form, Malamud's ability to evoke a sense of full experience with an odd verbal twist, as in the last line, or to intimate the Biblical parallels of the story, seems to raise behind the actual story a canvas far larger than the described one. But what sustains "The First Seven Years" most effectively is what sustains *The Assistant,* an alteration of techniques which continually shifts the character into a strange borderland world which becomes the emblem of the author's belief in the possibility of a leap beyond determinism. The intensity of Feld's emotion, the fragments of myth, the grotesque beauty of Sobel, and most particularly Malamud's own beautifully clumsy and compassionate voice charge the story not only with the suggestion of human mysteries but human miracles. Here, for example, is the description of Max, the poor accounting student: "He was tall and grotesquely thin, with sharply cut features, particularly a beak-like nose. He was wearing a loose, long slushy overcoat that hung down to his ankles, looking like a rug draped over his bony shoulders, and a soggy, old brown hat, as battered as the shoes he had brought in" (p. 5).

That Max might pluck a magic flute from the folds of his monstrous coat seems only the result of the faith of the teller himself: that weirdly ironic, poetic voice which reminds the reader —by an occasional clumsiness, a halting rhythm, or the folk tale form itself—that what he is relating is more than just art. What finally makes the miracle most believable, however, is that it does not occur. Malamud's tongue is "forked"; for, though it rings at times with the visionary simplicity of a child, it is nonetheless thick with the sour disaffection of a cynic which enforces upon the whole, despite the clear drift toward sentimentality, a drama of pained possibility.

Techniques so delicately balanced, however, can easily become uncoupled and spill over either into outright fantasy or the grotesque. While it is true that Malamud rarely loses control of his Jewish tales, he does occasionally slip. Stories like "The Mourners" or "Angel Levine" illustrate this tendency.

"The Mourners," the second of the tales, recounts an incident in the life of a sixty-five-year-old retired egg candler who seeks to end his days closeted in a wretched little flat at the top of an East Side tenement. But unlike Morris Bober or Feld, the protagonist, Kessler, is frankly a Jewish grotesque: an aged isolato who had long before forsaken wife and children and now, in filthy old age, devours himself in loneliness, speaking to no man and, for his contempt, being shunned by all. For this reason "The Mourners" is assuredly one of the most dismal stories in the collection, over-burdened with a sense of futility that is enlarged by Kessler's fanatic resistance to the landlord's efforts to evict him. The weight of despair is so intense, in fact, that the resolution, despite numerous anticipatory clues, offers less relief than a weird shock.

Climbing to Kessler's flat, Gruber, the landlord, agonizes over his guilty conscience even while intent on reaping the financial rewards that Kessler's eviction promises. Once in the room he finds the old man in a state of mourning, "rocking back and forth, his beard dwindled to a shade of itself." Although Kessler is mourning for himself, for his past misdeeds and for his abandoned wife and children, Gruber, "sweating brutally," decides that Kessler is mourning for *him*. In a gesture that plunges him out of the role of landlord and back into Jewish history, Gruber wraps himself in a sheet and drops to the floor as a fellow mourner (pp. 25-26). While spectacular and even haunting, the epiphany of ".The Mourners" is simply too abrupt and too meaningful to be supported by the two-dimensional characters and the unrelieved weight of horror. It is, finally, *only* the conclusion which remains in the mind, a sudden frozen tableau.

However, it is quite otherwise with "Angel Levine," the fourth fable in the collection and one which, while drenched in fantasy, exercises a bold, unmistakable magic. By virtue of its very extremes, the story also serves as a map for the implicit fantasy of the other tales. Manischevitz, whose tribulations remind one of a latter-day Job, is offered salvation if only he will recognize in the form of a mysterious visitor—a large bonily built Negro named Alexander Levine—a heaven-sent Jewish messenger. But in outrage against what he believes to be the pretensions of the Negro, and, wonderfully, his own naïve inclination to believe, Manischevitz denies Levine. Moreover, he persists in his denial despite the evidence that Levine's mere presence relieves both the former tailor and his wife Fanny of some of their pains. For his disbelief, however, the pains return in greater fury; and Fanny sinks quickly toward death.

And so Manischevitz, with unwilling willingness, sets out in search of the black angel through the streets of Harlem. His feet carry him to such unlikely spots as a Negro synagogue where a Talmudic disquisition is occurring, then to a satanic honky-tonk where Levine, denied the salvation of Manischevitz's trust, is succumbing to Bella, the Circe of the establishment. In the end, Manischevitz does credit Levine as a Jewish divinity; and for this act he experiences a moment of vision in which he sees the Negro mount heavenward on a pair of magnificent wings. Rushing home to the magically recovered Fanny, the tailor whispers the tag-line to a millennium of Jewish encounters with the unexpected forces of humanity: "A wonderful thing, Fanny," he breathes. "Believe me, there are Jews everywhere" (p. 56).

Because of the supporting fantasy, "Angel Levine" is the only one of Malamud's stories to deal explicitly with the religious implications that offer subtle support to many of the other stories, as well as to *The Assistant*. But the difference is only a question of degree, and the story relies on the same kind of formal tension and resolution that directs the drama in most of the author's fiction. Like Feld, Manischevitz is required to acknowledge the divine essence in another, an act which redeems both the truster and the trustee. Because Manischevitz must extend his trust beyond the confines of differing skins, he has only a more difficult burden than most. What Manischevitz must learn, in fact, is the author's theme that Jews are indeed "everywhere"—in Protestants, in Catholics, in Negroes who can intone Chassidic wisdom in synagogues (p. 54). As Norman Podhoretz has suggested of Malamud's characters, "The Jew is humanity seen under the twin aspects of suffering and moral aspiration. Therefore any man who suffers greatly and who longs to be better than he is can be called a Jew." [4]

But if Jewishness generalized into metaphor and construct is Malamud's subject, the Jew particularized is his triumph. This particularization is certainly true of Manischevitz, whose every gesture or intonation reveals not only superficial Jewish aspects —superbly rendered—but the deeper attitudes and postures which have developed through ages of accommodating ethical vision to historical necessity. The Jobian parallel, in other words, is funny; but it is no joke. In Manischevitz's relationship to God, which runs from mild despair to the sense of abandonment, there is only loving reproof, never disbelief. His prayers, in fact, reveal an elemental closeness to God: " 'My dear God, sweetheart, did I deserve that this should happen to me? . . . Give Fanny back her health, and to me for myself I shouldn't feel pain in every step. Help now or tomorrow is too late. This I don't have to tell you' " (p. 44).

That Malamud loves his old Jews, and particularly those in whom misery has only induced more kindliness and gentleness, is unquestionable. Moreover, through them he has managed, as Dan Jacobson has suggested, to achieve "What has baffled and defeated greater writers: the capacity to make goodness of the most humble and long suffering kind real, immediate, and attractive." [5]

"Angel Levine" is, however, only one of the better stories of its kind in the collection. It is certainly not the best, and the trouble seems to be that the fantasy is so enlarged in the service of victory that the story lacks the second property which cinches conviction in Malamud's best work. It lacks failure, the sense of continuing despair. However, in two other of the fables, "The Bill" and "The Loan," the blend of the real and the fantastic, of horror and triumph, borders on the miraculous.

"The Bill," structurally the more complex of the two stories, sounds again the problems of trust, of Jewish-Gentile relations, and of imprisonment in a grocery store which marked *The Assistant;* but it does so with an economy and directness that is remarkable. The opening paragraph is a weird blend of cameo realism and symbology that is sharply angular and impressionistic at the same time:

> Though the street was somewhere near a river, it was landlocked and narrow, a crooked row of aged brick tenement buildings. A child throwing a ball straight up saw a bit of pale sky. On the corner, opposite the blackened tenement where Willy Schlegel worked as janitor, stood another like it except that this included the only store on the street—going down five stone steps into the basement, a small, dark delicatessen owned by Mr. and Mrs. F. Panessa, really a hole in the wall (p. 145).

Though the relationship of the Schlegels and Panessas supplies the tale with its dramatic center, the story proper belongs to Willy; for he observes the progress of the store and broods upon the disconsolate weariness of his life in an East Side wasteland that promises neither escape nor relief. Wandering into the Panessa store one day, Willy finds himself relating to the attentive Panessas the horrors of his barren life; and, as he speaks, he buys item after item. When he cannot pay, Mr. Panessa offers credit, ennobling the act with the thought ". . . because after all what was credit but the fact that people were human beings, and if you were really a human being you gave credit to somebody else and he gave credit to you" (pp. 146-47).

But the tale is not about goodness alone, nor in this case even about particular forms of Jewish goodness. Instead, the subject is the depressing one of how, in a world ruled by the ineluctable demands of economics and accidents, even good can turn rank. Or better, it is a story which depicts the manner in which the soul descends into an embittering nightmare when the need to extend goodness is denied. And Willy Schlegel encounters such a nightmare when, after weeks of frantic buying on credit, the Panessas are forced to ask him for payment. Unable to pay, he retreats from the store, nursing an obscure grievance. As the season turns toward winter, Willy spends the nights dreaming of repaying and the days lamenting his inability to do so. In time, the pain of his guilt transforms his sympathy for the aged couple to hatred. In the spring, there is a momentary turning, a flash of redemption that hovers for a moment over the stony streets. Rising from a dream-filled sleep, Willy dashes to a pawnshop, receives ten dollars for his overcoat, and rushes to the Panessas' store.

When he arrives, a hearse is standing before the grocery and two men are carrying a coffin from the house. Told it is the grocer who lies within, Willy plunges into inarticulate despair in which only the author's words can find a grotesque glory: "He tried to say something but his tongue hung in his mouth like a dead fruit on a tree, and his heart was a black-painted window." The following paragraph, the last, belongs only to the narrator, who is now in full retreat; and it closes out the story with granitic objectivity: "Mrs. Panessa moved away to live first with one stone-

faced daughter, then with the other. And the bill was never paid"
(p. 153).

Though only eight pages long, the impact of "The Bill" is
unaccountably powerful. One senses in it the impersonal weight
of a naturalistic universe that balances precariously on the moral
give-and-take of a few struggling nonentities—and then quickly
crushes them. And in the second of the two stories, "The Loan,"
the method and the intent are similar—a swift fragment of action
that freezes despair into permanent ice and yet leaves within, like
Willy's "black-painted window" of a heart, a forlorn and foolish
flicker of hope.

Fantasy supports "The Loan," but only as an undercurrent;
for the aptly named baker, Lieb, blinded by cataracts and gray
with sorrows, is also the dispenser of a strange communion.
Though his pastries do not sell, his bread, after thirty years of
failure, now "brought customers in from everywhere." The yeast
was tears, the misery he wept into the dough. Successful but ill,
Lieb tends the ovens while his second wife Bessie serves customers
and worries over finances. It is Bessie who first notices the arrival
of Lieb's skeletal friend Kobotsky entering the store with a face
that "glittered with misery" to greet Lieb after a separation of
fifteen years (p. 181).

Overjoyed by the reunion, Lieb seats the grim Kobotsky on a
tall stool in the back room, and forgetting the misunderstanding
over a debt that had long ago ended their friendship, they recall
their early days in America. But Kobotsky, it is soon revealed, has
not come for memories but for money; and this fact fills Lieb
with apprehension and Bessie with horror. In fury, as she swirls
about the room, she recalls to the anguished Lieb the deceptive-
ness of their prosperity, the bills, the impending operation on his
eyes. Kobotsky, rising like a ghost, prepares to leave; but he stops
long enough to pour out a tale of woe. The money would have
been used, he tells them, to purchase a stone for the grave of his
wife, dead more than five years.

As Kobotsky catalogues his misery, it is not only Lieb who
cries but Bessie as well. For a moment, the baker is reassured:
"She would now say yes, give the money, and they would all sit

down at the table and eat together." But the last word is not Lieb's nor Kobotsky's. The finale belongs to Bessie, and it is her tale which transforms the incipient sentimentality into a dreadful glance at demonic frustrations:

> But Bessie, though weeping, shook her head, and before they could guess what, had blurted out the story of her afflictions: how the Bolsheviki came when she was a little girl and dragged her beloved father into the snowy fields without his shoes; the shots scattered the blackbirds in the trees and the snow oozed blood; how, when she was married a year, her husband, a sweet and gentle man, an educated accountant—rare in those days and that place—died of typhus in Warsaw; and how she, abandoned in her grief, years later found sanctuary in the home of an older brother in Germany, who sacrificed his own chances to send her, before the war, to America, and himself ended, with wife and daughter, in one of Hitler's incinerators (p. 190).

Against Bessie's past and her wretched dream of the future, Kobotsky's woe expends itself. Woe and woe, fused together in opposition, deny them the expression of anything but compassion. As the loaves in Lieb's ovens turn into "charred corpses," Kobotsky and the baker embraced ". . . and pressed mouths together and parted forever" (p. 191).

"The Bill" and "The Loan" thus share alike the terrible consequences of morality and poverty in collision; and both gain their power from the nature of the theme itself: the horror attendant on the frustration of man's need to give. Another fable in the collection also sounds the same message, but it does so with such unmitigated directness that, like "The Mourners," it is more dismal than affecting. Entitled "Take Pity," the story is narrated in a sustained and brilliant Yiddish idiom, and tells how Rosen sought to give all to the widow Eva and her children; and, because of her repeated rejections, he finally assigns his possessions to her and commits suicide. But now in limbo, and narrating the story to Davidov, the census taker, Rosen and the widow suffer a weird turnabout. Having nothing left to give, Rosen inveighs against Eva who pleads for him with upraised arms: "Whore, bastard, bitch," he shouts at her. "Go 'way from here" (p. 95).

That "Take Pity" falls short of the other two stories stems in part from the discrepancy between the abrupt conclusion and the supporting structure. Most of all, however, it fails because the author's own voice is missing. In the better fables, it is primarily his voice which lends the ambience of religious sensibility— enough at any rate to convince us that, as in "The Loan" and in "The Bill," the world may pervert the overt act but not the re- sources of communion. But in "Take Pity" Malamud employs, for the first time in his career, extended first person narration. With his own voice gone, the story slips quickly into an almost Gothic evocation.

IV. The New York Tales Without Jews

What is most revealing about Malamud's difficulties in manip- ulating the fable form, however, stems from his attempts to apply it to an investigation of similar themes without Jewish characters, as in "The Prison" and in "A Summer's Reading." The first, the better of the two, is again concerned with the accidents which despoil communion. Trapped in a candy store (the prison of the piece) by his criminal past and by an arranged marriage, Tommy Castelli seems in many ways a prototype of Frankie Alpine—a young man yearning for release from the blight of possibilities. Unable himself to escape, Tommy in part discovers the means of salvation through a surrogate, a ten-year-old girl who steals candy from the shop, and who Tommy dreams of rescuing from the mis- takes which had forced him into his time-rotting corner of the world. Though he prepares for the moment of confrontation with calculation, his wife discovers the girl's thievery: When Tommy interferes in the child's behalf, he finds himself refuted not only by his wife but by the girl herself.

In the same fashion as Tommy, George Stoyonovich, the young man of "A Summer's Reading," seeks unavailingly to es- cape the prison of self and a jobless East Side existence by telling his friends that he is spending the summer reading a hundred books. For the lie, George reaps the respect of his neighbors and a bemusing sense of personal worth. But the lie quickly turns rank when George realizes that Mr. Cattanzara, an early father image, suspects his dishonesty. George flees the recognition, but Mr. Cattanzara proves to be a giver of trust, one of those elderly saints whose goodness forces its way into the heart of its "victims." In the final paragraph George appears closeted in the public library, ticking off a hundred titles and settling down to a season of protracted reading.

While deft and compelling, both these stories are curiously unlike "The Loan" or "The Bill"; and the difference, of course, is the absence of a central Jewish character. Far from being a small difference, however, it accounts precisely for what the stories lack: the sense of the pertinacity of spirit, an indefinable aura of "goodness" which, through the agency of the Bobers and the Felds, transforms the most extreme of failures into a sad redemption. "The Prison" and "A Summer's Reading" are in fact naturalistic tales which reveal more of Malamud's virtuosity than his fundamental skills.

The same losses and gains are also apparent in the five remaining stories in *The Magic Barrel*—all of which either depart from the folk tale or seek to extend it into more elaborate and significant forms. Among them are Malamud's best and his worst stories, but even the worst possess power. The first, "The Girl of My Dreams," swings irresolutely between realism and symbolism; but it resolves itself ultimately into a farcical, ebullient account of the breakthrough into communalism of a shattered young Jewish novelist, Mitka by name, whose literary failure, curiously enough, has to do with an inability to record experience directly. Locked in his tiny room, Mitka tortures himself with the sense of failure and agonizes over his landlady, Mrs. Lutz, who unavailingly bears love and chicken soup to his door. To all her entreaties, however, Mitka presents closed ears with a tenacity humorously reminiscent of Raskolnikov's masochistic misanthropy. But Mitka, for all his self-incarceration, is one of Malamud's fractured young men who find their need for love and communion welling up in a strangling ooze; and, while resisting it, they are ripe for success. Success comes, moreover, through the appearance of a mysterious female writer whose newspaper stories had deeply affected Mitka and with whom, half in love, he had arranged a meeting. But "the girl of my dreams" turns out to be no girl at all; instead, she is a "lone middle-aged female . . . Hefty . . . Eyeglassed, and marvelously plain" (p. 36).

Mitka, however, is a man of character; and Olga, the "girl" of the story is also a cosmic mother. Steeling himself to her ordinary face, Mitka indulges in a lengthy colloquium, is fed, admired, and advised; and, under the influence of her faith, he opens like a spring flower. Returning home from the encounter with this new version of Iris Lemon, a woman who had suffered her way into humanity, Mitka vows to go on with his writing; and, more importantly, he decides to fling wide his door to Mrs. Lutz with whom he imagines a new relationship: "They would jounce together up the stairs, then (strictly a one-marriage man) he would swing her across the threshold, holding her where the fat overflowed her corset as they waltzed around his writing chamber" (p. 41).

Despite the humor, and the fact that "The Girl of My Dreams" is the first and only story in the collection to deal with sexual communion (one of Malamud's favorite novel subjects), the story remains, at best, only interesting. It lacks not only the concentrated effect of "The Loan" or "The Bill," but also the tangible persuasiveness that Malamud seems always to derive from his ancient Jews. The primary difference is of course Mitka himself, who, like S. Levin, is a young ostensible intellectual and so resists the kind of reduction to bedrock properties upon which Malamud's stories depend. To render Mitka viable to his theme, the author must rely too exclusively on satire and farcical symbolism—as, in fact, he does with almost all of his stories which deal with second-generation American Jews.

V. The Italian Stories

This same problem, moreover, comes to the fore in two of the three stories in the collection which deal with young Americans in Italy, a setting which Malamud seems to delight in almost as much as in New York's East Side—and for similar reasons. At once real and fabled, Italy (and particularly Rome) surrounds the *angst*-ridden Malamud protagonist with the smell and detritus of ancient lore at the same time that it benumbs moral hunger with fanciful romance. In some ways, in fact, Italy serves Malamud in much the same way it served Henry James in his depiction of the naïve American in an international world: a fairyland supported by the thinnest of ice that, upon breaking, precipitates a plunge into depths of feeling hitherto overlooked, denied, or transmuted.

The first of these stories, "Behold the Key," is the most enigmatical. The protagonist, Carl Schneider, a student and a lover of things Italian, comes to Rome with his wife and children and spends his time, not with books, but in apartment hunting. Guided by an inexplicable Virgil, one of those shabby ministers of grace who frequently appear in Malamud's stories, Schneider encounters all manner of deceptions and intrigues, criminal landlords and outright knaveries until, at the end of his patience, a "perfect" apartment is found which can be his if he will tender a bribe. Carl refuses and not only loses the apartment but bears on his forehead the mark of the key thrown by the outraged former tenant, the individual who had insisted on the bribe.

If deceptive, there is at the heart of the story a grim, telling theme. What is being tested is not only Carl Schneider's patience but his humanity: his ability to understand the behavior of a people who, because of war and poverty, bear little resemblance to the literary curiosities that had nourished his dream of an ideal Italy. Because he fails to comprehend, he bears the mark of his failure—a failure of brotherhood—upon his brow.

The second of the Italian stories, which also deals with the failure of a young American in Europe, is perhaps closer to the center of the author's real interests in that it imports into the ancient setting a New York Jew: a thirty-year-old former book clerk who, "tired of the past—tired of the limitations imposed upon him," has come to Europe in search of adventure, romance, and, though he hardly dare name it, love" (p. 105). Entitled "The Lady of the Lake," the story is, like all the Italian pieces, longer, less concentrated, and more indebted to symbolist techniques than are the New York tales. Indeed, these stories which deal exclusively with young men in Europe clearly evoke in the author a technique closer to that of *The Natural* than to *The Assistant.*

However, the themes are the writer's in any setting. In "The Lady of the Lake" Henry Levin, who calls himself Henry R. Freeman, is precisely the kind of out-of-touch, past-denying, and self-denying specimen of incompletion thāt Malamud can stick wriggling to the wall with telling effect. Rushing through Europe, his heart bubbling with need, Levin finally finds romance and love (in a perfumed garden on the Isolo del Dongo) in the person of a hungry-eyed goddess, transparent with mystery, whom he takes to be Isabella del Dongo, last of a mighty lineage. To her unexpected question: "Are you, perhaps, Jewish?," Levin, cocking ear and eye to the future, replies that he is not (p. 113). With romance flaming and wallowing through her further questions as to his Jewishness and his further denials, Levin pursues Isabella in a cloud of frustration and guilt. Needless to say, the guilt is ironic to the core, for what grieves Levin about his lie is his own Jewishness; and it is Jewishness finally which ends his happiness. In a penultimate meeting, Isabella tells Levin that she is not a del Dongo but a della Setta, child of poor people. Romance crucified, Levin retreats, his dreams shredded like confetti.

But with romance gone, love bounds to the fore, and Levin rushes back to the island to find Isabella waiting for him in a white dress. When he tells her he has come to offer marriage, she asks again if he is Jewish. Levin, his life trembling, flounders and denies it. The denial is catastrophe. Isabella suddenly unbuttons her bodice to reveal the marks of Buchenwald; and, as Levin stares, she tells him: "I can't marry you. We are Jews. My past is meaningful to me. I treasure what I suffered for." Though Levin-Freeman cries "I—I am," it is too late, for Isabella disappears into the mists which have risen from the lake. Levin, for his denial of self, embraces "only moonlit stone" (pp. 132-33).

Intensely funny and marked by a brilliantly controlled metaphorical style, "The Lady of the Lake" hovers of course directly and illuminatingly over Malamud's chief preoccupations. But neither the comedy nor the richness of theme obviates the fact that it is, like "Behold the Key," far from his best work. Slick in its manipulation of symbol and sparse in its "felt" experience, the story is another case of the resultant weakness when Malamud attempts to extend his themes into non-Jewish areas or into a contemplation of the young and divided or intellectual Jew. In the former case, the stories persist in dissolving into bitter realism. In the latter, Malamud inevitably loses the tone and perspective that clings to his contemplation of elderly Jews who seek to expiate their "other." Toward Mitka and toward Levin, as well as toward the Levin of *A New Life*, the author must find, in lieu of the aged Jews of the better stories, some new vehicle to supply conviction. And he finds it not in the resources of character but in satire, irony, and a metaphorical style that more often than not is strained and obvious.

VI. "The Last Mochican" and "The Magic Barrell"

But what is lacking in "The Lady of the Lake" is assuredly not absent from the concluding Italian story, "The Last Mohican," nor from the final story in the collection, "The Magic Barrel," which reverts to the New York setting but which also concentrates on a youthful Jewish protagonist. For in both these stories Malamud has found a new character to further the redemptive cycle: an aged Jew in place of an Iris Lemon, one who fastens to the tormented heroes like a spiritual cannibal and does not release his hold until the younger man submits to the terrors of rebirth.

The first of the two stories details the old-world adventures of Arthur Fidelman, a "self-confessed failure as a painter" (p. 156) who arrives in Italy clutching the pigskin brief case which contains the first chapter of a projected study of Giotto and wearing the tweed suit and oxblood shoes which are the uniform of his new identity as an art critic. As Fidelman stands on a street corner staring at his reflection with an exalted sense of the future, the image becomes compounded by the appearance of Shimon Susskind—a knickered skeleton in "small porous, pointed shoes" who

flight, Susskind, "light as the wind in his marvelous knickers," shouts back the final, and who can doubt it, true verdict upon Fidelman's earlier identity: "Have mercy, I did you a favor. . . . The words were there but the spirit was missing." For a moment Fidelman continues the chase, but the spirit he had lacked is no longer missing. With a "triumphant insight," he calls, "Susskind, come back. The suit is yours. All is forgiven." But the refugee, when last seen, was still running." (pp. 181-82).

By and large, "The Last Mohican" has the neat advantage, like Fidelman himself, of unifying the elements in "Behold the Key" and "The Lady of the Lake," and yet reasserting them in a more successful manner. In a sense, the work cuts across both the two earlier Italian stories, for Fidelman's task is to find, as Carl Schneider could not, the sources of compassion and humanity; and like Henry Levin-Freeman, Fidelman finds them in a descent into his true self. Moreover, that Malamud has himself discovered the literary means for unifying these elements, and in the process makes of the Italian setting a more capable frame for his themes, is clearly the result of opening the form to the Jewish parable that he always handles with consummate skill. "The Last Mohican" indicates not only the full range of Malamud's concerns but, equally important, it illustrates the direction he must take to accommodate and enlarge them in more convincing literary structures.

Yet it must be said before leaving the first collection that even without "The Last Mohican," or for that matter even without "The Bill" or "The Loan"—the work would still contain sufficient evidence of the reach of Malamud's art. The title story, which is also the last story in the collection, would alone serve; for it is not only the finest piece in the collection, uniting all that is best in the other stories, but is perhaps one of the finest stories of recent years.

The impact of "The Magic Barrel" is, however, inexplicable —certainly as inexplicable, and for much the same reasons, as *The Assistant*. The story of the love and maturation of a young rabbinical student, it conspires like the author's second novel in a boundary world which pulsates now with the bright energy of a fairy tale, now with something of the somber tones of a depression tract. Both qualities are immediately apparent in the opening: "Not long ago there lived in uptown New York, in a small, almost meager room, though crowded with books, Leo Finkle, a rabbinical student in the Yeshivah University" (p. 193).

The key to Leo Finkle's rebirth, however, lies not alone in the protagonist, a poor and lonely student hurrying after six years of study toward his June ordination. A Frankie Alpine in a black fedora, Leo unites myth and anti-myth in his own person. Passionately interested in Jewish law since childhood, Leo is nonetheless Godless. Bound in his deceit, he throbs through the torment that washes over Malamud's love-hungry and God-hungry young Jews. Like Fidelman on Giotto, Finkle knows the word but not the spirit; and he makes it clear in every gesture that in a secret part of his heart he knows it.

But Leo Finkle's heart is too secretive, and his salvation depends upon another who can test all there is of humanity in the student. The "other" does not arrive, however, until the last page; in her place there comes a marriage broker whom Leo has summoned when he learns that a wife will help him win a congregation. But from the moment Pinye Salzman materializes, the student is on the way. For, reeking of fish and business, the broker seems only another Susskind. Half criminal, half messenger of God, Salzman whips from his battered portfolio a select group of feminine portraits, for "is every girl good for a new rabbi?"

As Pinye exalts his merchandise, however, Leo persists in positing reservations; and they are not alone a matter of distrusting Salzman's grossness (indeed, he seems *too* gross to be believed). When Pinye plays his trump card: "Ruth K., Nineteen years, Honor student. Father offers thirteen thousand cash to the right bridegroom," Leo, sick of the whole business, gives himself away: "But don't you think this young girl believes in love?" (pp. 197-98).

Dismissing Pinye, Leo slides into misery; but the misery is only the signal of breaking ice. Trying to analyze his reactions, he wonders if perhaps "he did not, in essence, care for the matchmaking institution?" (p. 199). From this thought, slightly heretical, he flees throughout the day; and it is only at nightfall, when he draws out his books, that he finds any peace. But Pinye, like a haggard ghost—and he grows more desperate-looking with each meeting—is soon at the door, his presence thrusting Leo out of his books and threadbare composure. Bearing the vitae of Lily Hirschorn, high-school teacher and linguist, young (twenty-nine instead of the thirty-two of the night before), Pinye dispels Leo's lack of interest with a mournful imprecation: "Yiddishe kinder, what can I say to somebody that he is not interested in high school teachers?" (p. 201).

Despite the retiring young scholar's hesitancy, a meeting is arranged; and one Saturday afternoon he strides along Riverside Drive with Lily Hirschorn, oldish but pretty, hanging to his arm. From the beginning, however, Leo senses the presence of Pinye, somewhere in the background, perhaps "flashing the lady signals with a pocket mirror; or perhaps a cloven-hoofed Pan, piping nuptial ditties."

But if Pinye is directing the proceedings, he is after more than a quick profit; for about the walk there is strong suggestion of ritual indoctrination, a testing by question and answer that suddenly exposes Leo. Lily, having been primed by Salzman into the belief that Leo Finkle is the true anointed of God (or is Lily another Iris?) addresses herself as if to a holy image: "How was it that you came to your calling?" When Leo, after some trepidation, replies, "I was always interested in the Law," Lily's questions soar: "When did you become enamored of God?" In mingled rage at Pinye and himself, Leo finds himself speaking with shattering honesty: "I am not a talented religious person. I think that I came to God not because I loved Him, but because I did not" (pp. 202-4).

After the smoke-screen of hatred for Pinye dissipates, there is a long week of "unaccountable despair" in which Leo's beard grows ragged and his books meaningless. Feeding on his confession to Lily, which had revealed "to himself more than her—the true nature of his relationship to God," Leo bounds to further revelations. He realized that, "apart from his parents, he had never loved anyone." Then, with a quick jolt, the two ragged ends of his lovelessness fuse: "Or perhaps it went the other way, that he did not love God so well as he might, because he had not loved man" (p. 205).

Made desperate by the unexpected image of himself, Leo contemplates leaving Yeshivah. "He had lived without knowledge of himself, and never in the Five Books and all the Commentaries —mea culpa—had the truth been revealed to him." The knowledge sends Leo scurrying into near hysteria, a state disagreeable and pleasurable at the same time, and then into a long swoon, a kind of moral way-station from which he "drew the consolation that he was a Jew and that a Jew suffered." The revelation, needless to say, represents a turning; and when Salzman returns—at precisely this moment—he must listen to a new Leo: "I want to be in love with the one I marry. . . . I find it necessary to establish the level of my need and fulfill it." Discharged, Salzman disappears "as if on the wings of the wind"; but he leaves behind a manila packet (pp. 205-7).

The pattern of pursuit which dominates the first half of "The Magic Barrel" parallels also the early sections of "The Last Mohican"; moreover, like Fidelman's in the Italian story, Leo Finkle's redemption involves the reversal of the pattern, the quest of the once despised. Coincident with the arrival of March and the turning toward spring, Finkle remains closeted in his room, gloomy over the frustrations of his hopes for a better life; and so, finally, he is drawn to open the manila packet which had all the while been gathering dust. Within he finds more photographs, but all seem versions of Lily Hirschorn. But, as the scholar puts them back, he discovers another snapshot, small and cheap, which without preliminaries evokes a shout of love. Staring back at him is a composite of every heroine Malamud has yet written about, from Iris Lemon and Harriet Bird through Pauline Gilley and Helen Bober. In shreds of images, some mythic, some terrifyingly real, the face closes, like fate itself, over Leo's heart:

> . . . spring flowers, yet age—a sense of having been used to the bone, wasted; this came from the eyes, which were hauntingly familiar, yet absolutely strange. He had a vivid impression that he had met her before, but try as he might he could not place her although he could almost recall her name, as if he had read it in her own handwriting. . . . *something* about her moved him . . . she leaped forth to

his heart—had *lived,* or wanted to—more than just wanted, perhaps regretted how she had lived—had somehow deeply suffered. . . . Her he desired . . . he experienced fear of her and was aware that he had received an impression, somehow, of evil. (pp. 208-9)

Dashing into the streets, Leo rushes off in pursuit of Pinye Salzman, only to discover from his wife (and "He could have sworn he had seen her, too, before but knew it was an illusion"), that the matchmaker was nowhere about, that he "lived in the air." "Go home," she suggests, "he will find you." When the student returns to his flat, Salzman, standing at the door, asks, "You found somebody you like?" Without hesitation, Finkle extends the snapshot. But for his eager love the student must submit to the final horror. With a groan, Pinye tells him "this is not a bride for a rabbi . . . She is a wild one—wild, without shame." When Finkle presses Salzman for a clearer answer, the old man dissolves in tears: "This is my baby, my Stella, she should burn in hell" (pp. 210-12).

Under the covers of his bed, a makeshift chapel perilous, Leo, beating his breast, undergoes the climactic test. "Through days of torment he endlessly struggled not to love her; fearing success he escaped it. He then concluded to convert her to goodness, himself to God. The idea alternately nauseated and exalted him." Though brief, the ordeal finally draws Leo from bed with a long "pointed beard" and "eyes weighted with wisdom." A mixture now of lover and father, he meets Salzman again (and the marriage broker seems unaccountably young) and, despite Salzman's pleas to desist, a meeting is arranged.

The rendezvous, held on a spring night, is Malamud at his ambiguous best. With flowers in hand, Leo finds Stella standing in the age-old posture of the prostitute, under a lamp post smoking: "She waited uneasily and shyly. From afar he saw that her eyes—clearly her father's—were filled with desperate innocence. He pictured, in her, his own redemption. Violins and lit candles revolved in the sky. Leo ran forward with flowers outstretched."

This paragraph, however, is the penultimate one: as if the mixture of goddess and prostitute, the promise of hope through a future of willfully chosen agony, were not sufficiently confusing, Malamud allows the final paragraph to focus on Pinye, who, leaning upon a wall around the corner, "chanted prayers for the dead." It is impossible to tell for whom Pinye chants—for himself and his guilt (for even Leo had finally suspected "that Salzman had planned it all to happen this way"), for Finkle's past or Finkle's future, or for all these reasons. In some ways, the last alternative —that Salzman chants for everything—seems only proper; for if Leo has graduated into saint and rabbi, it is only by succumbing to the terrors which the role prescribes. What better reason to chant when to win means to lose?

But such confusions, as demonstrated in *The Assistant*, are the only possible vehicles for Malamud's faith. If the ironies undercutting the story preserve it from a kind of mythic schmaltz, the myth preserves the story from the irony. The same strange tension is surely in the characters—in the infested goddesses, like Stella, who can only be redeemed by the hero as victim, and in those unstable ministers of God, now devils and now angels, the Pinye Salzmans and the Shimon Susskinds. In that inexplicable and indeterminate character, they signal, as Alfred Kazin has said, "the unforeseen possibilities of the human—when everything seems dead set against it." [6] One finishes "The Magic Barrel" as one finishes *The Assistant*—not with the exaltation of witnessing miracles, but with the more durable satisfaction of witnessing possibilities.

Notes

1. *The Magic Barrel* (New York, 1958), p. 3. All subsequent page references are to this edition.
2. Norman Podhoretz, "The New Nihilism in the American Novel," *Partisan Review*, XXV (Fall, 1958), 589.
3. Earl Rovit, "Bernard Malamud and the Jewish Literary Tradition," *Critique*, III (Winter-Spring, 1960), 5. (See Chapter 1 in this collection.)
4. Podhoretz, *op. cit.*
5. Dan Jacobson, "Magic and Morality," *Commentary*, XXVI (October, 1958), 360.
6. Alfred Kazin, "The Alone Generation," reprinted in *Recent American Fiction: Some Critical Views*, ed. Joseph J. Waldmeir (Boston, 1963), p. 10.

Selected Bibliography

This bibliography consists of an alphabetical list of the more important biographical, critical, and scholarly studies of Bernard Malamud. Where more than one essay appears by the same author, the entries are listed in chronological order. We have omitted foreign criticism, unpublished theses or dissertations, transient reviews, and routine discussions in encyclopedias, handbooks, and histories of literature. Our bibliography covers materials through the summer of 1969. Essays and excerpts of books which appear in this present collection are noted by an asterisk.

Alley, Alvin D. and Hugh Agee. "Existential Heroes: Frank Alpine and Rabbit Angstrom," *Ball State University Forum*, 9:1 (Winter 1968), 3-5.

* Alter, Robert. "Bernard Malamud: Jewishness as Metaphor," in his *After the Tradition: Essays on Modern Jewish Writing* (New York: E. P. Dutton & Co., Inc., 1969) pp. 116-130. Appeared earlier as "Malamud as Jewish Writer" in *Commentary*, 42 (Sept. 1966), 71-76.

Bailey, Anthony. "Insidious Patience," *Commonweal*, 66 (June 21, 1957), 307-308.

Baumbach, Jonathan. "The Economy of Love: The Novels of Bernard Malamud," *Kenyon Review,* 25 (Summer 1963), 438-457.

————. "All Men are Jews: *The Assistant* by Bernard Malamud," in his *The Landscape of Nightmare: Studies in the Contemporary American Novel* (New York: New York University Press, 1965) pp. 101-122.

————. "Malamud's Heroes," *Commonweal,* 85 (Oct. 1966), 97-98.

* Bellman, Samuel I. "Women, Children, and Idiots First: The Transformation Psychology of Bernard Malamud," *Critique,* 7:2 (Winter 1964-65), 123-138.

————. "Henry James' 'The Madonna of the Future' and Two Modern Parallels," *California English Journal,* 1:3 (1965), 47-53.

————. "Fathers and Sons in Jewish Fiction," *Congress Bi-Weekly,* 34:10 (May 22, 1967), 18-20.

* Bluefarb, Sam. "Bernard Malamud: The Scope of Caricature," *English Journal,* 53:5 (May 1964), 319-326, 335.

* Eigner, Edwin M. "Malamud's Use of the Quest Romance," *Genre,* 1:1 (Jan. 1968), 55-74.

Elman, Richard J. "Malamud on Campus," *Commonweal,* 75:5 (Oct. 27, 1961), 114-115.

Featherstone, Joseph. "Bernard Malamud," *Atlantic Monthly,* 219 (March 1967), 95-98.

Fiedler, Leslie A. "Malamud: The Commonplace as Absurd," in his *No! in Thunder* (Boston: Beacon Press, 1960) pp. 101-110.

————. *Love and Death in the American Novel* (New York: Dell Publishing Co., 1966) pp. 492-493.

Francis, H. E. "Bernard Malamud's Everyman," *Midstream,* 7:1 (Winter 1961), 93-97.

Frankel, Haskel. Interview with Bernard Malamud, *Saturday Review,* 49:37 (Sept. 10, 1966), 39-40.

* Friedberg, Maurice. "History and Imagination: Two Views of the Beiliss Case," *Midstream,* 12:9 (Nov. 1966), 72-76.

* Friedman, Alan Warren. "Bernard Malamud: The Hero as Schnook," *Southern Review,* 4:4 (Oct. 1968), 927-944.

* Goldman, Mark. "Bernard Malamud's Comic Vision and the Theme of Identity," *Critique,* 7:2 (Winter 1964-65), 92-109.

Goodheart, Eugene. "Fantasy and Reality," *Midstream,* 7:4 (Autumn 1961), 102-105.

Graber, Ralph S. "Baseball in American Fiction," *English Journal,* 56:8 (Nov. 1967), 1107-1114.

Greenfield, Josh. "Innocence and Punishment," *Book Week* (Sept. 11, 1966), pp. 1, 10.

Greiff, Louis K. "Quest and Defeat in *The Natural*," *Thoth*, 8 (Winter 1967), 23-34.

Gunn, Giles B. "Bernard Malamud and the High Cost of Living," in Nathan A. Scott, ed., *Adversity and Grace: Studies in Recent American Literature* (Chicago: University of Chicago Press, 1968) pp. 59-85.

* Hassan, Ihab. "The Qualified Encounter: Three Novels by Buechner, Malamud, and Ellison" in his *Radical Innocence: Studies in the Contemporary American Novel* (Princeton, N.J.: Princeton University Press, 1961) pp. 161-168. (Reissued by Harper & Row, 1966.)

* Hays, Peter L. "The Complex Pattern of Redemption in *The Assistant*," *Centennial Review*, 13:2 (Spring 1969), 200-214.

Hicks, Granville. "Generation of the Fifties: Malamud, Gold and Updike," in Nona Balakian and Charles Simmons, eds., *The Creative Present: Notes on Contemporary American Fiction* (New York: Doubleday & Co., 1963) pp. 217-237.

————. "One Man to Stand for Six Million," *Saturday Review*, 49:37 (Sept. 10, 1966), 37-39.

Hollander, John. "To Find the Westward Path," *Partisan Review*, 29:1 (Winter 1962), 137-139.

* Hoyt, Charles Alva. "Bernard Malamud and the New Romanticism," in Harry T. Moore, ed., *Contemporary American Novelists* (Carbondale, Ill.: Southern Illinois University Press, 1964) pp. 65-79.

Hyman, Stanley E. "A New Life for a Good Man," *The New Leader*, 44:34 (Oct. 2, 1961), 24-25. Reprinted in Richard Kostelanetz, ed., *On Contemporary Literature* (New York: Avon Books, 1964), pp. 442-446.

Kazin, Alfred. "Fantasist of the Ordinary," *Commentary*, 24:1 (July 1957), 89-92.

————. "Bernard Malamud: The Magic and the Dread," in his *Contemporaries* (Boston: Atlantic-Little, Brown & Co., 1962) pp. 202-207.

Kermode, Frank. "Bernard Malamud," *New Statesman*, 63 (March 30, 1962), 452-453.

* Klein, Marcus. "Bernard Malamud: The Sadness of Goodness," in his *After Alienation: American Novels in Mid-Century* (Cleveland: World Publishing Co., 1962) pp. 247-293.

Leer, Norman. "Three American Novels and Contemporary Society: A Search for Commitment," *Wisconsin Studies in Contemporary Literature,* 3:3 (Fall 1962), 67-85.

Leibowitz, Herbert. "Malamud and the Anthropomorphic Business," *The New Republic,* 149:25 (Dec. 21, 1963), 21-23.

Ludwig, Jack. *Recent American Novelists.* University of Minnesota Pamphlets on American Writers, No. 22 (Minneapolis: University of Minnesota Press, 1962) pp. 39-41.

* Mandel, Ruth B. "Bernard Malamud's *The Assistant* and *A New Life*: Ironic Affirmation," *Critique,* 7:2 (Winter 1964-65), 110-121.

Marcus, Steven. "The Novel Again," *Partisan Review,* 29:2 (Spring 1962), 171-195.

Meeter, Glenn. *Bernard Malamud and Philip Roth: A Critical Essay* (Grand Rapids, Mich.: William B. Eerdmans Publishing Co., 1968).

* Mellard, James M. "Malamud's Novels: Four Versions of Pastoral," *Critique,* 9:2 (1967), 5-19.

————. "Malamud's *The Assistant:* The City Novel as Pastoral," *Studies in Short Fiction,* 5:1 (Fall 1967), 1-11.

Mudrick, Marvin. "Who Killed Herzog? Or, Three American Novelists," *University of Denver Quarterly,* 1:1 (1966), 61-97.

Perrine, Laurence. "Malamud's 'Take Pity,'" *Studies in Short Fiction,* 2:1 (Fall 1964), 84-86.

Podhoretz, Norman. "Achilles in Left Field," *Commentary,* 15:3 (March 1953), 321-326.

————. "The New Nihilism in the American Novel," *Partisan Review,* 25:4 (Fall 1958), 589-90. Reprinted in Norman Podhoretz, *Doings and Undoings: The Fifties and After in America* (New York: Farrar, Straus & Giroux, Inc., 1964), pp. 176-178.

Popkin, Henry, "Jewish Stories," *Kenyon Review,* 20:4 (Autumn 1958), 637-641.

Pritchett, V. S. "A Pariah," *New York Review of Books,* 7:4 (Sept. 22, 1966), 8, 10.

Rahv, Philip. "Introduction," *A Malamud Reader* (New York: Farrar, Straus & Giroux, 1967), pp. vii-xiv.

Ratner, Marc L. "Style and Humanity in Malamud's Fiction," *Massachusetts Review,* 5:4 (1964), 663-683.

————. "The Humanism of Malamud's *The Fixer,*" *Critique,* 9:2 (1967), 81-84.

Notes on Contributors

Robert Alter, Professor of Hebrew and Comparative Literature at the University of California at Berkeley, is a regular contributor to *Commentary* and the author of *Rogue's Progress: Studies in the Picaresque Novel, Fielding and the Nature of the Novel,* and *After the Tradition.*

Samuel Irving Bellman is Professor of English at California State Polytechnic College, Pomona. He has published in *California English Journal, Western Humanities Review,* and *Critique.*

Sam Bluefarb is Assistant Professor of English at Los Angeles Harbor College. His articles have appeared in a variety of journals, including *College English, Texas Quarterly, Studies in Short Fiction,* and *Journal of Popular Culture.*

Edwin M. Eigner, Professor of English at the University of California at Riverside, has published articles on Melville, Bulwer-Lytton, and Faulkner and a book, *Robert Louis Stevenson and Romantic Tradition.*

Maurice Friedberg is Professor of Slavic Languages and Literature and Director of the Russian and East European Institute at Indiana University. He is the author of *Russian Classics in Soviet Jackets, The Party and the Poet in the USSR,* and editor of *A Bilingual Collection of Russian Short Stories.*

Alan Warren Friedman is Associate Professor of English at the University of Texas at Austin. He is the author of *Lawrence*

Durrell and "The Alexandria Quartet": Art for Love's Sake
and articles on Lawrence Durrell, Thomas Hardy, Christopher
Marlowe, and Henry Miller.

Mark Goldman, Associate Professor of English at the University
of Rhode Island, has published articles on Virginia Woolf as
well as poetry in various magazines, and is writing a book on
Virginia Woolf as a literary critic.

Ihab Hassan is now Viles Professor of English at the University
of Wisconsin, Milwaukee. He is the author of *Literature of
Silence: Henry Miller and Samuel Beckett; Crise du Héros
Americain, Lettres Modernes;* and *Radical Innocence;* and he
has contributed regularly to *Western Review* and other journals.

Peter L. Hays, Assistant Professor of English at the University of
California at Davis, has published in *Critique, Studies in Short
Fiction, Western Humanities Review,* and *Modern Drama.*
He is completing a book on lameness as a literary archetype.

Charles Alva Hoyt is Chairman of the Department of English at
Bennett College, Millbrook, N.Y. He is the editor of *Minor
British Novelists* and *Minor American Novelists.* His articles
have appeared in *Contemporary English Novelists* and *Tough
Guy Writers.*

Marcus Klein is Chairman of the Department of English at the
State University of New York at Buffalo. He is the author of
After Alienation, co-author of *Innocence and Experience* and
Short Stories: Classic, Modern, Contemporary, and editor of
The American Novel Since World War II.

Ruth B. Mandel is currently teaching at the University of Pitts-
burgh, School of General Studies. Her Ph.D. dissertation was
on Melville and Gothicism.

James M. Mellard, Associate Professor of English at Northern
Illinois University, has written many articles on Faulkner and
has published in a variety of journals, including *PMLA, Bucknell Review, Studies in Short Fiction,* and *Critique.*

Sidney Richman, Associate Professor of English at California State
College at Los Angeles, has published poetry and articles on
I. A. Richards, Hart Crane, and Theodore Dreiser, and is com-
pleting a book on the modern American novel.

Earl H. Rovit, Assistant Professor of English at City College,
CUNY, is the author of *Herald to Chaos* and has written on
Ernest Hemingway and Saul Bellow.

Max F. Schulz, Chairman of the Department of English at the

University of Southern California, has published widely on Coleridge, Wordsworth, and contemporary American authors. He is the author of *The Poetic Voices of Coleridge* and *Radical Sophistication.*

Walter Shear is Professor of English at Kansas State College at Pittsburg. He has written on Benjamin Franklin and Flannery O'Connor and is currently at work on the fiction of Edgar Allan Poe.

Ben Siegel is Professor of English at California State Polytechnic College, Pomona. His books include *The Puritan Heritage: America's Roots in the Bible* and *Isaac Bashevis Singer.* He has published extensively in a large variety of journals.

Theodore Solotaroff, editor of *New American Review,* was formerly associate editor of *Commentary* and editor of *Book Week.* His essays and reviews have appeared in *Commentary, Book Week, New Republic,* and *Atlantic Monthly.*

Frederick W. Turner, III, is Assistant Professor of English at the University of Massachusetts. His articles have appeared in *Serif, Centennial Review,* and *Novel.*

Earl R. Wasserman is Professor of English at Johns Hopkins University. His books include *Elizabethan Poetry in the 18th Century; The Finer Tone, Keats' Major Poems; Pope's Epistle to Bathurst;* and *Shelley's Prometheus Unbound, A Critical Reading.*

Notes on the Editors

Leslie A. Field is an assistant professor in the Department of English at Purdue University. Born in Montreal, he was educated at Wayne State and Indiana Universities. In 1969-70 he was a Senior Fellow and Lecturer at Bar-Ilan University in Israel. His published work has appeared in *Bucknell Review, Modern Fiction Studies, South Atlantic Quarterly,* and other journals. He is co-editor of *Thomas Wolfe's Purdue Speech: "Writing and Living"* and *All the King's Men: A Critical Handbook,* and editor of *Thomas Wolfe: Three Decades of Criticism* in the Gotham Series.

Joyce W. Field is an instructor in the School of Industrial Management at Purdue University. Born in New York City, she was educated at Wayne State, Indiana, and Purdue Universities. Her previous publications have been in *Modern Fiction Studies, The Journal of Popular Culture,* and the *Journal of Reading.* She was formerly an assistant editor of the *Journal of Reading.*

Index